CHANGE AND CHALLENGE IN
THE WORLD ECONOMY

CHANGE AND CHALLENGE IN THE WORLD ECONOMY

Bela Balassa

Professor of Political Economy
The Johns Hopkins University
and
Consultant, The World Bank

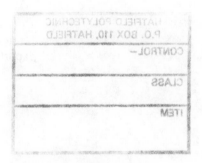

MACMILLAN PRESS

First edition 1985
Reprinted 1987

Published by
THE MACMILLAN PRESS LTD
Houndmills, Basingstoke, Hampshire RG21 2XS
and London
Companies and representatives
throughout the world

Printed in Great Britain by
Antony Rowe Ltd
Chippenham

British Library Cataloguing in Publication Data
Balassa, Bela
Change and challenge in the world economy.
1. Economic policy
I. Title
330.9   HD87
ISBN 0-333-39197-7

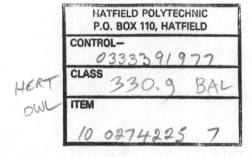

To Mara and Gabor

Contents

List of Tables

Preface

The decade following the 1971–3 worldwide boom saw important changes in the world economy. Oil prices quadrupled in the years 1973–4 and increased two-and-a-half times in 1979–80. The anti-inflationary policies adopted by the developed countries deepened the ensuing recessions and, after 1980, increases in real interest rates further aggravated the world economic situation.

The changes that occurred constituted challenges to economic policy-makers in the individual countries. The essays of this volume examine the different ways in which policy-makers responded to these challenges. They also consider possible future policy changes that may be desirable to meet the challenges which lie ahead in the future.

Following a review of incentive policies and their economic effects in developed, developing, and socialist countries in Part I of the volume, the essays of Part II examine policy responses to external shocks in the developing countries and the implications of these policies for their external debt. In turn, the essays of Parts III to V, respectively, analyze the policies applied by several developing countries, Mexico, Chile, Portugal, Turkey, and Korea; review the reform efforts made in two socialist countries, Hungary and China; and evaluate recent policy changes in a developed country, France. Finally, the essays of Part VI of the volume investigate recent developments in trade in manufactured goods between the industrial and the developing countries and make recommendations for future changes in their trade policies, with a view to promoting structural transformation and economic growth.

The country essays of Parts III to V have been prepared as policy advisory reports for the governments concerned or written for international conferences and seminars. These essays, as well as the general essays of Parts I, II, and VI, have been published in professional journals or collective volumes. Permission for publication to all concerned is acknowledged in the Reader's Guide to the volume. Essays 1, 2, 4 to 14, 18, and 19 have been prepared in the framework of a consultant arrangement with the World Bank.

I am indebted to Kenneth Meyers, Eric Manes, and Shigeru Akiyama for research assistance beyond the call of duty. Special thanks are due to Norma Campbell, who patiently bore the burden of typing the text and tables, with innumerable revisions. Keith Povey has done an excellent job as editor.

I wish to express my appreciation to government officials, economists, and businessmen in the individual countries for useful discussions. However, I am alone responsible for the opinions expressed in the essays that should not be interpreted to reflect the views of particular governments or those of the World Bank.

Washington, D.C.   BELA BALASSA

A Reader's Guide

The volume begins with a review of incentive policies and their economic implications in developed, developing, and socialist countries. The introductory essay examines the effects of government directives and interventions that create distortions in the system of incentives.[1] The broad conclusion is that reductions in policy-imposed distortions in product, labor, and capital markets would permit reaching higher levels of efficiency and raising the rate of economic growth in the countries concerned.

Essay 2 examines in greater detail policy-imposed distortions in developing economies, and it reports available estimates of the impact of these distortions on the allocation of existing resources, savings, investment efficiency, and economic growth.[2] The findings show the high economic cost of policy-imposed distortions in product and factor markets in terms of foregone incomes and point to the gains that may be obtained by removing or alleviating these distortions.

In turn, Essay 3 analyzes the economic consequences of the social policies applied by the industrial countries.[3] It is shown that, in reducing the demand for, and the supply of, labor, social policies have adversely affected employment and economic growth in Western Europe. These distortions are of lesser importance in the United States, which fact has contributed to the superior performance of the American economy in recent years. In the essay, recommendations are made for reforming social policies in European countries, with a view to promoting structural change and reducing the burden of social legislation on the working population.

The three essays of Part I on incentive policies and their economic effects are followed by the essays of Part II that examine the policies applied by developing countries following increases in oil prices in 1973–4 and 1979–80 and the world recessions of 1974–5 and 1980–2. Essays 4 and 5 evaluate policy responses to these external shocks by developing countries pursuing outward-oriented and inward-oriented policies while Essay 6 considers the implications of policy differences for the debt problem in developing countries.

Following a brief discussion of the policy experience of twenty-eight developing countries in the 1973–8 period, Essay 4 considers the principal elements of a policy package that may be applied in developing countries to respond to external shocks while undertaking policy reforms.[4] Such a package would include improvements in production incentives, in incentives to save and to invest, in the allocation of public investment, in sectoral policies, as well as in budgetary and monetary policies.

Essay 5 examines the policies applied in developing countries in response to the external shocks of the 1974–6 and 1979–81 periods.[5] It is shown that while outward-oriented economies pursued output-increasing policies of export promotion and import substitution, inward-oriented economies relied largely on foreign borrowing to finance the adverse balance-of-payments effects of external shocks.

The policies applied led to economic growth rates substantially higher in outward-oriented than in inward-oriented economies. Also, the foreign indebtedness of the latter group of countries increased to a considerable extent, leading to repayment problems. In turn, exports rose *pari passu* with foreign borrowing in the former group of countries that maintained their creditworthiness. These consequences of alternative policies are considered in Essay 6 of the volume that also makes policy recommendations aimed at improving the debt situation in inward-oriented economies.[6]

The comparative studies of Part II are followed by essays devoted to individual countries in Part III of the volume. These essays analyze the policies applied, and the economic consequences of these policies, in Mexico, Chile, Portugal, Turkey, and Korea during recent periods of external shocks. The essays deal with incentives and macroeconomic policies and make recommendations for future policy changes.

Essay 7 on Mexico indicates the similarities observed in the policy cycles of the 1972–6 and 1977–81 periods.[7] It is shown that, under fixed exchange rates, expansionary fiscal policies repeatedly led to the overvaluation of the peso, triggering the application of protectionist measures. The overvaluation of the currency was supported by borrowing abroad but, in the absence of the efficient use of borrowed funds, the accumulation of external debt eventually gave rise to a foreign exchange crisis. The essay makes recommendations for remedying macroeconomic disequilibria, reducing price distortions, and liberalizing trade in Mexico, so that the deflationary effects of the stabilization policies applied after December 1982 can give place to rapid economic growth under increased outward-orientation.

In Chile, an outward-oriented development strategy was adopted after the military takeover in September 1973, involving the establishment of realistic exchange rates, the elimination of import licensing, reductions in import tariffs to 10 percent, the freeing of interest rates, and the liberalization of prices.[8] However, in June 1969, the exchange rate was fixed in terms of the US dollar, leading to the increasing overvaluation of the currency as official wage adjustments continued and wages doubled over a period of less than three years. At the same time, with a virtual exchange rate guarantee, Chile experienced an excessive capital inflow, eventually giving rise to a financial crisis. The reversal of policies applied, entailing increased price distortions, then, undermined the beneficial effects of the reform measures of 1973–8.

Following a successful stabilization program in 1978–9, growing government deficits and the poor performance of public enterprises contributed to a rising balance-of-payments deficit in Portugal. Improvements occurred following the measures applied in June 1983, but they entailed a substantial cutback in private investment. Yet, new investments are necessary to improve the competitiveness of the Portuguese economy on entering the European Common Market. Essay 9 makes recommendations for policies that may be applied in the pursuit of this objective, involving reductions in the financial requirements of the public sector, improvements in the operation of public enterprises, and the provision of appropriate incentives to the private sector.[9]

Turkey had long pursued a policy of inward orientation, accompanied by considerable government intervention. The January 1980 measures, including a substantial devaluation, export incentives, import liberalization, and the freeing of prices and interest rates, represented important steps towards outward orientation and increased reliance on market forces. These measures led to rapid export growth that, in turn, permitted increasing output and improving the balance of payments. However, private investment remained low and difficulties were experienced in the financial sector. Essay 10 makes recommendations to remedy these shortcomings and to attain the objective of stable economic growth in Turkey by further increasing the outward orientation of the economy and the scope of operation of market forces.[10] Steps in these directions have been taken after the installation of the new Ozal Government in December 1983; the postscript to the essay reviews these developments and makes recommendations for further changes.

Korea has been considered as one of the success stories among developing countries. Following the application of an outward-oriented development strategy, it achieved high rates of economic growth and successfully surmounted the external shocks of the 1973–5 period. Essay 11 describes the unfavorable economic effects of the policy reversal that occurred in 1978–9 and evaluates the measures taken to remedy these adverse consequences in 1980. It also makes recommendations for policies to re-establish and further advance Korea's outward-oriented development strategy.[11] The postscript to the essay describes the measures that have since been taken in the pursuit of this objective.

The essays of Part IV evaluate the policy reforms applied in two socialist countries, Hungary and China, and make recommendations for further reform measures. Essay 12 reviews the new economic mechanism introduced in Hungary in January 1968. This reform represented an important departure for a socialist economy in replacing centralized planning by decentralized decision-making and involving the use of prices linked to world market price relations in the allocation process.[12] The essay examines the favorable impact of the original reform measures, the adverse economic consequences of the partial recentralization of decision-making after 1972, and the introduction of new measures in 1980–1 that carried forward the original reform effort.

In turn, Essay 13 examines the measures applied in 1980–1 in greater detail and makes recommendations for further changes to pursue the objectives of the reform.[13] The recommendations concern strengthening the link of domestic to world market prices, adopting a realistic exchange rate, giving a greater role to firms in decisions on investment, and decentralizing economic decision-making in general.

As in Hungary, economic reform in China would have to involve the decentralization of decision-making, the use of prices as signals for resource allocation, appropriate incentives on the firm level, and competition among producing units. At the same time, in view of differences in the size of their national economies, there is scope for domestic competition in China while Hungary needs to rely to a considerable extent on import competition. Correspondingly, apart from standardized products that enter international trade, a system of price determination in the framework of domestic markets would be appropriate in China whereas links to world market prices need to be strengthened in Hungary. Essay 14 reports on progress made in reforming Chinese agriculture and suggests further reform measures for the future.[14] The reforms announced in October 1984 represent important steps in the reform effort.

Among developed countries, France provides a particularly interesting case of successive policy reversals. The policy of stability under Raymond Barre was followed by efforts aimed at economic expansion via social measures under the socialist government, subsequently leading to policy changes as the balance of payments deteriorated and inflation accelerated. The essays of Part V examine the policies applied and their economic effects, with further attention given to possible future changes.

Essay 15 evaluates the policies followed by the government of Raymond Barre, aiming at economic growth with stability while increasingly liberalizing the economy.[15] It is noted that, following improvements in economic performance, adverse developments in the world economy contributed to increased unemployment in France. In the essay, recommendations were made for remedying the situation by increasing the rate of investment.

In the event, high unemployment contributed to the socialist economic victory in the Spring of 1981. Essay 16 examines the economic policies adopted by the new socialist government. Following a discussion of the structural policies of nationalization, decentralization, and planning, attention is given to the expansionary measures applied that led to wage inflation and the deterioration of the balance of payments.[16] While policy was reversed after March 1983, in Essay 17 it is shown that adverse consequences in the form of low profit margins and high external indebtedness remain.[17] The essay makes recommendations for measures that may be taken to improve the situation, including reductions in the budget deficit, the rationalization of public enterprises, price liberalization, decreases in the share of wages and salaries, and reductions in social charges for enterprises.

Finally, the essays of Part VI investigate the changing division of labor in manufactured goods between the industrial and the developing countries and provide an appraisal of the measures of protection applied by the industrial countries in recent years. Proposals are further made for trade liberalization by the industrial countries and the NICs, with a view to promoting structural transformation and economic growth.

Essay 18 examines recent trends in manufactured trade between the industrial and the developing countries that assumed increased importance as markets for each other's manufactured products.[18] This has occurred, notwithstanding the imposition of protectionist measures in some areas by the industrial countries. These measures are described in

Essay 19 that argues the need for a new round of multilateral trade
negotiations to reverse recent protectionist tendencies and to avoid
further backsliding.[19] It is further noted that involving the developing
countries in the negotiations would not only allow the more industrialized of these countries to adopt rational trade policies but would
strengthen the argument for trade liberalization in the developed
countries.

Essay 20 further develops the arguments for a new round of
multilateral trade negotiations.[20] The essay examines the interests of
industrial and developing countries in the mutual liberalization of their
trade. It also considers the steps that may be taken to prepare the
negotiations, the modalities of the negotiations themselves, and the
need for taking adjustment measures to accompany the trade liberalization effort in both the industrial and the developing countries.

NOTES

1. The essay was prepared as an invited paper for the conference on
   Economic Incentives, organized by the International Economic Association
   and held in Kiel, Germany, in June 1984. It appeared in *Weltwirtschaftliches Archiv* CXX (1984) and will be included in the Conference proceedings to be published by Macmillan, London.
2. Essay 2 was presented as an invited paper at the December 1981 meetings
   of the American Economic Association held in Washington, DC; it first
   appeared in *World Development*, a publication of Pergamon Press Ltd,
   Oxford X (December 1982) pp. 1027–38.
3. Essay 3 was presented at the Institute of World Economics, University of
   Kiel, upon receiving the Bernhard Harms Prize on 23 June, 1984. It
   appeared as No. 11 in the Bernhard-Harms-Vorlesungen series (1984) and
   in *Weltwirtschaftliches Archiv* CXX (1984) pp. 213–27. It will be published
   in French translation in *Commentaire*.
4. This essay, prepared for the World Bank, originally appeared in *World
   Development* X (January 1982) pp. 23–38.
5. Essay 5 was presented as an invited paper at the December 1983 meetings
   of the American Economic Association held in San Francisco. It was
   published in *World Development* XII (December 1984) pp. 1027–38.
6. This essay was presented at the Conference on The International Monetary
   System and Economic Recovery, organized by the Istituto Bancario San
   Paolo di Torino and held in Turin, Italy in March 1984 and, in a revised
   form, at the 40th Congress of the International Institute of Public Finance,
   held in Innsbruck, Austria in August 1984. It will be published in the
   Proceedings of the Conference by the Istituto Bancario San Paolo di
   Torino and in the Proceedings of the Congress by the Wayne State
   University Press.
7. Essay 7 was prepared for the Conference on Industrialización y Comercio
   Exterior, organized by the Colegio Nacional de Economistas and held in

Mexico City in January 1983. It was published in *World Development* XI (September 1983) pp. 795–812 and, in Spanish translation, in *Comercio Exterior* XXX (March 1983) pp. 210–22.

8. The essay was prepared as an advisory report for the Government of Chile. It was published in Gary M. Walton (ed.), *The National Economic Policies of Chile* (Greenwich, Conn.: JAI Press, 1985). Spanish translation in *Estudios Públicos* No. 14 (Otoño, 1984) pp. 49–90.

9. Essay 9 was prepared as an advisory report for the Government of Portugal. It was published in *Economia* (October 1984).

10. This essay was presented as an invited paper at the Third Conference in the Role of Exchange Rate Policy in Achieving the Outward Orientation of the Economy, organized by Meban Securities and held in Istanbul in August 1982. It appeared in *The Middle East Journal* (Summer 1983) pp. 429–47. The postscript to the essay was excerpted from a presentation made by the author at the Council on Foreign Relations in June 1984.

11. Essay 10 was prepared as an advisory report for the Government of Korea and published in 1981 as No. 10 in the *Consultant Paper Series* of the Korea Development Institute.

12. This essay was presented as an invited paper at the US–China Conference on Alternative Development Strategies, organized by the Committee on Scholarly Communication with the People's Republic of China and held in Racine, Wisconsin in November 1980. It first appeared in the *Banca Nazionale del Lavoro, Quarterly Review* No. 145 (June 1983) pp. 163–84.

13. The essay was presented as an invited paper at a joint session of the American Economic Association and the Association for Comparative Economic Studies, held in Washington, DC, in December 1981 and at the Conference on Hungarian Economy and East–West Relations held at Indiana University, Bloomington, Ind., in March 1982. It was published in the *Journal of Comparative Economics* VII (September 1983) pp. 253–76.

14. Essay 14 was presented as an invited lecture at the Economic Institute of the Chinese Academy of Social Sciences in May 1982. It appeared in *Banca Nazionale del Lavoro Quarterly Review* No. 142 (September 1982) pp. 307–33.

15. This essay was prepared as an invited paper for the Conference on The Political Economy of France: Current Developments and Prospects, organized by the American Enterprise Institute for Public Policy and held in Washington, DC, in May 1980, and appeared as Johns Hopkins Working Paper in Economics, No. 62. It was published in French translation in *Commentaire* III (Autumn 1980) pp. 437–51.

16. This essay was presented as an invited paper at a seminar held at the American Enterprise Institute for Public Policy in Washington, DC, in September 1982. It was published in the Institute's series *Studies in Economic Policy* (1982), in *Tocqueville Review* IV (Fall–Winter 1982) pp. 337–58, in *Quadrant* (July 1983) pp. 54–62 and, in French translation, in *Commentaire* V (Autumn 1982) pp. 415–28.

17. Essay 17 was presented as an invited paper at a seminar held at the American Enterprise Institute for Public Policy in Washington, DC, in March 1984 and appeared in the Institute's series *AEI Occasional Papers*, Studies in Economic Policy (April 1984). It was published in *Tocqueville*

Review VI (Spring–Summer 1984) pp. 183–98 and, in the French original, in *Commentaire* VII (Printemps 1984) pp. 13–22.

18. This essay was presented as an invited paper at the Seventh World Congress of the International Economic Association, held in Madrid 1983. It appeared as World Bank Staff Working Paper No. 611 and will be published in the Proceedings of the Congress. Spanish translation in *Información Comercial Española* No. 605 (January 1984) pp. 58–68 and in *Industrialización y Desarrollo* (January–June 1984) pp. 85–100.

19. Essay 19, written jointly with Carol Balassa, was published in *The World Economy*, the quarterly journal of the Trade Policy Research Centre, London, VII (June 1984) pp. 179–96.

20. This essay was prepared for the Secretariat of the Organization for Economic Co-operation and Development and published in *OECD Economic Studies* No. 3 (Fall 1984) pp. 7–25.

Part I
Incentives and Economic Performance

Essay 1   Prices, Incentives and Economic Growth

INTRODUCTION

The period since the depression of the nineteen-thirties has seen a multiplication of government interventions in economic life – although in some respects a reversal has occurred in recent years. Government interventions take a variety of forms, depending on the system of economic decision-making applied. The present essay will examine the economic effects of these interventions in developed, developing, and socialist economies.

A brief survey of changing views on the role of prices and incentives (Section I) will provide an introduction to the discussion. This will be followed by an analysis of government interventions in product markets (Section II), labor markets (Section III), and capital markets (Section IV), and by a review of the effects of these interventions on the relative prices of capital and labor (Section V). Finally, the impact of taxes on economic growth will be examined (Section VI).

I THE ROLE OF RELATIVE PRICES

Relative prices were at the center of economics during the one-and-a-half centuries following the publication of the *Wealth of Nations*. Classical economists never doubted that economic activities respond to price incentives, generating economic growth in the process. The choice between work and leisure was seen to be affected by the relative prices of goods and labor; the choice between present and future consumption by the rate of interest; and the choice among goods by their relative prices. The interactions of these choices, in turn, were seen to determine the allocation of resources among industries and the pace of economic growth, with full employment being maintained over time.

There were few dissenting voices. The existence of a reserve army of labor keeping wages at the subsistence level and periodic over-production resulting from lack of effective demand underlied Marx's theory of capitalist crises, but he and his disciples remained outside the mainstream of economics. And, while Marshall recognized the existence of market failures in the form of external economies and diseconomies, these were considered rather unimportant exceptions.

The classical consensus was shattered with the emergence of effective demand as the principal factor affecting the level of employment in the *General Theory*. This was followed by the Harrod-Domar model, in which economic growth was determined by technical relationships, leading to a knife-edge situation that was not remedied by changes in relative prices. Prices were also banished from structuralist explanations of economic development and the reserve army of labor re-emerged in theories of unlimited labor supply.

There further came a fascination with central planning. In an earlier period, Lange and Lerner attempted to reproduce the workings of a private market model in the framework of a decentralized socialist system. After the Second World War, Soviet-type central planning, eschewing the role of prices in resource allocation, attracted the interest of economists particularly in developing, but also in developed, countries.

Mathematical economists established the conditions under which the centralization of economic decisions was superior to decentralization. While explicit or implicit use was made of prices in these models, economic agents were assumed to respond to orders from above rather than to economic incentives. Furthermore, general equilibrium theorists gave increasing emphasis to market failures that would not permit reaching Paretian competitive equilibrium, thus legitimizing public interventions in market processes. At the same time, estimates were put forward purporting to show that the economic costs of governmental actions, creating distortions in resource allocation, were rather small.

These developments did not fail to influence economic policy-making. In developed countries, Keynesian policies held sway, with little attention given to their possible adverse consequences for the longer term. In several Western European countries, attempts were made to introduce some form of planning. Also, social legislation proliferated, neglecting its effects on economic incentives.

In the newly-established socialist countries after World War II, the

Soviet system of central planning was copied, notwithstanding differences in economic conditions in the countries concerned. In particular, attempts were made at self-sufficiency in industrial products in the framework of small national markets that lacked the balanced natural resource endowment of the Soviet Union. At the same time, agriculture was neglected and the lack of scarcity prices obstructed rationality in foreign trade.

The neglect of agriculture was also characteristic of developing countries that followed a pattern of inward-oriented industrialization. The governments of these countries failed to consider the adverse effects on agricultural output of the disincentives inherent in high industrial protection. Also, they largely disregarded the rising cost of import substitution as the imports of capital-intensive manufactured goods subject to economies of scale came to be replaced by domestic production.

While this thumbnail sketch can do no more than indicate some general tendencies without any pretension to accuracy, the main features of the story are reasonably clear. Policy-makers followed economists in de-emphasizing prices and incentives, with government directives and interventions distorting the price mechanism in developed and, in particular, in developing countries and supplanting it in socialist countries.

The importance of prices and incentives has re-emerged in the more recent period. In the developed countries, the efficacy of Keynesian remedies has come to be questioned; planning has fallen into disuse; and the adverse economic consequences of social leglislation have been given attention. In turn, economic decision-making has been decentralized in Hungary; attempts at decentralization have been made in some other socialist countries; and a reform effort is under way in China. Finally, the example of Far Eastern economies has been followed by several developing countries in adopting an outward-oriented strategy and giving an increased role to the market mechanism.

This essay will examine in the following the economic effects of government directives and interventions applied in developed, developing, and socialist countries that create distortions in the system of incentives. In Bhagwati's terminology,[1] the discussion will concern policy-imposed distortions rather than endogenous distortions, which find their origin in market imperfections; government measures designed to correct market imperfections will not be considered in the essay.

In the course of the discussion, consideration will be given to policy-imposed distortions in product and in factor markets, and the effects of these distortions on the efficiency of resource allocation and economic growth that have been often neglected in the past. In so doing, use will be made of empirical evidence that has accumulated in recent years.[2]

II POLICY-IMPOSED DISTORTIONS IN PRODUCT MARKETS

In developed countries, distortions in product markets may result from government interventions in the form of price control and limitations on competition. In the case of non-traded goods, governments may set the price of the particular service and/or restrict entry by new firms; in the case of traded goods, protection is an important device limiting competition, thereby raising costs to the user and to the national economy as a whole.

Among services, one may single out transportation that is subject to regulations in most developed countries. In turn, while conclusive results are not yet available, deregulation in the United States appears to have importantly reduced the cost of air and surface transportation. This has occurred as competition has led to the streamlining of operations and to reductions in featherbedding practices.

Estimates of the cost of protection in developed countries are generally low, hardly reaching one percent of the gross national product. These estimates, however, fail to consider the losses involved in foregoing the exploitation of economies of scale in protected markets. Taking account of economies of scale, it has recently been estimated that protection has reduced potential output by about 10 percent in Canada.[3]

Protection rates are much higher, and vary to a considerable extent among industries, in inward-oriented developing economies. Partial equilibrium estimates show the cost of protection to range between 4 and 10 percent of GNP in these countries even without adjusting for economies of scale.[4] At the same time, the estimates understate the cost of protection by excluding substitution among products (traded and non-traded) and factors, that is taken into account in a general equilibrium framework. In fact, higher cost estimates have been obtained in a general equilibrium model for Colombia, even though Colombia has lower levels of protection than the countries referred to above.[5]

All these estimates concern the static effects of protection on the efficiency of resource allocation. Economic growth will nevertheless be affected as the efficiency of investment declines and the loss of incomes reduces the availability of domestic savings. Furthermore, as Johnson[6] first showed, under certain conditions capital accumulation may lead to a decline in GNP if the protected sector is capital-intensive. Finally, protection may foster a 'live and let live' attitude while technological change is stimulated by the carrot and the stick of foreign competition.

Evidence on the effects of protection on economic growth in the developing countries is provided by the experience of the 1973–79 period of external shocks. During this period, outward-oriented economies that gave similar incentives to sales in domestic and in foreign markets reached higher rates of economic growth than inward-oriented economies, even though they suffered larger external shocks owing to their greater exposure to international trade. While this result was originally obtained for newly-industrializing developing economies, it has subsequently been shown to apply to less developed economies and even to the low-income countries of Western Africa.[7] The latter conclusion is of special interest, given the often expressed view that price incentives have limited effects in low-income countries.

Data for the three groups of countries have been combined in an econometric study of 43 developing economies, in which initial trade orientation and policy responses to external shocks have been separately introduced. The extent of outward-orientation has been estimated as deviations of actual from hypothetical values of *per capita* exports, the latter having been derived in a regression equation that includes *per capita* incomes, population, and the ratio of mineral exports to the gross national product as explanatory variables. In turn, alternative policy responses have been represented by relating the balance-of-payments effects of export promotion, import substitution, and additional net external financing to the balance-of-payments effects of external shocks.[8]

Including further the extent of external shocks, *per capita* incomes, and the share of manufactured exports in total exports among the explanatory variables, it has been shown that initial trade orientation as well as the character of policy responses to external shocks importantly affected rates of economic growth in the 1973–79 period. GNP growth rates differ by 1.0 percentage point between countries in the upper and the lower quartiles of the distribution in terms of trade orientation in 1973; also, there is a difference of 1.2 percentage points in growth rates between countries in the upper and the lower quartiles of the distribution in terms of export orientation.

The results are cumulative, indicating that initial trade orientation and reliance on export promotion in response to external shocks explain much of the inter-country variation in GNP growth rates that were 6.5 and 3.3 percent, respectively, for countries in the upper and the lower quartiles of the distribution. The results are not materially affected if data on increases in capital and labor are introduced in the estimation.

Among socialist countries, its natural resources endowment was an important factor contributing to the introduction of the 1968 economic reform in Hungary. The reform aimed at replacing plan directives by market relations among firms; limiting the scope of central price determination; linking the domestic prices of exports and imports to prices in the world market; and decentralizing a major part of investment decisions.

The reform was intended to reverse the decline in the rate of economic growth that occurred in the first half of the sixties, when it became increasingly difficult to make production decisions centrally in an economy that became more sophisticated and to ensure that foreign trade conformed to the interests of the national economy without reliance on scarcity prices. In fact, economic growth accelerated after 1968 as Hungary gained export market shares in capitalist as well as in socialist countries.

A reversal occurred after 1973, when economic decision-making was partially recentralized and prices were increasingly divorced from world market price relations in an effort to isolate Hungary from the vagaries of the world economy. But, as the adverse effects of these actions on economic growth came to be recognized, reform measures were again taken from 1980 onwards. The break-up of monopolistic firms, the increased role given to the 'second economy', and the actions envisaged for the 1985–8 period to liberalize prices and wages go well beyond the original 1968 reforms.

III POLICY-IMPOSED DISTORTIONS IN LABOR MARKETS

Distortions in labor markets due to governmental actions may take a variety of forms. Some of these distortions affect the supply of labor, others the demand for labor. Among government interventions affecting the supply of labor, unemployment compensation and regulations aimed at ensuring job security tend to increase the rate of unemployment, while the provision of certain social benefits and the taxation of labor incomes lower labor force participation rates. In turn, the demand for labor is affected by minimum wage legislation and by social security schemes. Apart from their effect on employment, these regulations also influence the efficiency of resource allocation and economic growth.

Unemployment compensation is provided in developed but generally not in socialist or in developing countries. The rate of compensation and its duration was increased to a considerable extent after 1973, with the value of unemployment benefits reaching 75 percent of after-tax incomes in the major European countries. While some reductions have occurred since, there is evidence that the high rate and the long period of unemployment compensation have raised the level of unemployment and lengthened its duration.[9]

In Western Europe, dismissing workers 'for cause' is a difficult and time-consuming process as is reducing the firm's labor force for economic reasons. In cases when labor can be discharged for economic reasons, those with seniority have to be retained and often high payments have to be made to those who have become redundant.

While these regulations aim at limiting unemployment, their impact appears to have been the opposite as firms are reluctant to hire labor that has become a quasi-fixed cost. Also, the mobility of labor is hindered and firms that have to retain labor turn to the government for compensation, thereby perpetuating the life of inefficient establishments. Finally, there is less incentive on the part of workers to improve productivity, and absenteeism tends to rise. The liberal treatment of sickness leave has further contributed to absenteeism.

Regulations limiting the dismissal of labor and high redundancy payments for those discharged have also been introduced in some developing countries, with consequences similar to those observed in Western Europe. The dismissal of labor was prohibited for several years in Turkey and redundancy payments may amount to one year's salary in Latin America.

Labor regulations have rather pronounced effects in the socialist countries. On the one hand, the existing regulations have given rise to overmanning in some factories while other firms cannot obtain the necessary labor. On the other hand, the development of a 'second economy' in several of these countries has occurred in part at the expense of production in state-owned firms as workers reorient their efforts.

In Western Europe, attempts have been made to lower unemployment through reductions in working hours. Such measures will have the desired effect in the short run, provided that there are no compensating wage increases. However, in reducing the workweek from 40 to 39 hours in January 1982, the French Government decided on full compensation, and the German metal workers' union made similar demands to accompany a cut in the workweek from 40 to 35 hours in early 1984. While the demands of the union have been only partially met, the conclusion remains that compensated reductions in the workweek lessen international competitiveness and reduce profit margins on traded goods, with adverse effects on economic growth and ultimately on employment. But even in the absence of compensation, potential output – and hence the demand for labor – will be lower in the long run as a result of reductions in working hours.

Similar considerations apply to early retirement schemes that are in vogue in Western Europe. And while profit margins decline to a lesser extent if the cost of the scheme is paid partly by the government, this alternative raises questions of financing. In any case, early retirement reduces labor force participation rates and the rate of return on human capital. It may also lead to the loss of valuable skills. This appears to have been the case in the French automobile industry after 1981 when foremen and production supervisors retired in considerable numbers without equivalent replacements.

The retirement age is 60 years for men and 55 years for women in most socialist countries. It varies between 50 and 60 years in developing countries, with the most generous system applying in Uruguay where men can retire after 30 years and women after 25 years of work and receive a pension equal to 100 percent of average earnings in the last five years once they reach the age of 50. Finally, early retirement aside, the retirement age is generally between 60 and 65 in the developed countries.

Conversely, working hours are longer in the socialist countries (generally between 42 and 45 hours per week) than in the developed countries (usually 40 hours). The workweek is even longer in the developing countries; it is between 45 and 50 hours in Latin America and between 50 and 55 hours in much of Africa and Asia.

The next question concerns the effects of taxation on the supply of labor. While it is customary to distinguish between substitution and income effects, with the former reducing and the latter increasing the supply of labor, there are also income effects associated with the provision of goods and services financed by taxation that may offset the positive income effects of higher taxes. And, regardless of income effects, the taxation of labor involves a welfare loss that rises with the progressivity of the tax system.

There is considerable information on the progressivity of the tax system in developed countries; an extreme case being Sweden where the combined effects of all taxes may exceed 100 percent on the margin for some high income recipients. It is generally not recognized, however, that marginal tax rates are above 80 percent on relatively low labor incomes in several developing countries, much exceeding the highest tax rate of 50 percent in the United States.

As Lindbeck[10] has observed, high marginal tax rates have a variety of adverse effects. Apart from distorting the income-leisure choice, they affect decisions on the choice of the job and the intensity at which work is performed. They further encourage the pursuit of do-it-yourself work, production for barter, the search for tax loopholes, and outright tax evasion while discouraging investment in human capital and risk-taking by the entrepreneur.

The resulting distortions interfere with the efficiency of resource allocation in the countries concerned. This will be so even in the case when tax loopholes are sought, owing to the diversion of labor from productive activities. The deterioration of efficiency, together with the decline in human investment, then, lower the rate of economic growth.

In turn, minimum wage legislation will reduce the demand for labor. A review of available estimates pertaining to the United States has shown that a ten percent increase in the minimum wage lowers teenage employment by one to three percent and employment in low-wage manufacturing by one to four percent.[11] Furthermore, there are employment losses in the subminimum population (i.e. those with an unconstrained wage less than the minimum) both at the extensive (the probability of working), and at the intensive (annual hours worked), margin.[12] Finally, estimates for Canada show that the minimum wage significantly reduces employment in five out of six age–sex groups, with the effects being the largest for male teenagers. It further increases unemployment rates in all groups, with a one percent increase in the minimum wage being associated with an approximately one percent increase in the average rate of unemployment.[13]

Estimates for the United States relate to the postwar period of rapid increases in minimum wages. This period has since come to an end and the minimum wage has not been raised since January 1981. In turn, minimum wages have been increased to a considerable extent in Western Europe, and, in particular, in France. As a result, the minimum wage reached one-half of the average wage in manufacturing in France while it hardly exceeds one-third of the manufacturing wage in the United States.

In developing countries, as in developed countries, the original purpose of minimum wage legislation was to improve the conditions of low income groups. In practice, however, it benefits workers in the formal sector without affecting wages in the informal urban sector and in rural areas. Correspondingly, distortions are created in these seg-mented labor markets.[14]

Empirical estimates of the welfare cost of minimum wage legislation pertain to its effects on lowering employment. For the United States, it has been shown that if the elasticity of demand for low-wage is as low as 0.2, the reduction in national income is as large as the entire gain to the lower half of the income distribution when marginal taxation effects are ignored, and it is twice as large when marginal taxation effects are included.[15] At the same time, decreases in wage differentials associated with a rise in minimum wages will reduce the rate of return on human capital.

By lowering the marginal productivity of capital, the substitution of capital for labor in response to the setting of minimum wages will also reduce the rate of economic growth and, in extreme cases, it may lead to an absolute decline in national income.[16] As the results have been obtained by assuming labor to be homogeneous, they can be inter-preted as indicating the economic effects of exogenous increases in labor costs. This, in turn, leads to the question of social security regulations.

Social security schemes have assumed particular importance in the European Common Market, where the ratio of employer and employee contributions to wage varies between 37 percent in Belgium and 55 percent in the Netherlands, compared with 23 percent in Japan and 18 percent in the United States. Among developing countries, social security contributions exceed 20 percent in India and in several Latin American countries.[17]

In an early discussion of economic integration, the author examined the conditions under which the financing of social security schemes from employer and employee contributions would not create distor-tions in labor markets. He concluded that 'under perfect price and wage mobility, any increase in social charges would be shifted to the wage earners *if* they regarded the corresponding social benefits as part of their earnings'.[18]

Over a decade ago, Britain found support for the proposition that social security contributions are borne by the wage earner, irrespective of whether they are paid by the employer or the employee.[19] More recently, an elasticity of substitution of 7.7 was estimated between wages and employer-financed fringe benefits, although the estimated elasticity is only 1.6 between wages and health and life insurance alone.[20]

However, the study includes only voluntary contributions by employers to retirement, health insurance, and life insurance plans, all of which are subject to negotiations with the labor unions that cover wages as well as fringe benefits. It does not follow that wage-earners would consider the social benefits received through governmental institutions as part of their income. Also, they may not perceive a direct link between social security contributions, whether made by the employer or the employee, and their social benefits. Yet, in the United States, these schemes are nearly three times as important as the fringe benefits financed by the voluntary contributions of employers.

The moral hazard problem is of particular importance in Western Europe, where governmental programs of social security predominate. At the same time, increases in social programs do not appear to have induced unions to moderate their wage demands. It has been noted, for example, that in the United Kingdom 'workers did not acquiesce in the increased taxation that was needed to finance the extra-rapid growth of the non-market sector, and they therefore made every effort to increase their private consumption at rates almost as fast as public consumption was growing. [As a result,] the share of wages rose markedly at the expense of the share of profits.'[21]

These conclusions are supported by empirical evidence derived from country models of the growth of nominal wages, incorporating direct taxes and social security contributions, productivity growth, and the rate of unemployment as explanatory variables. The results show full forward shifting of direct taxes and social security contributions in the Netherlands and considerable shifting, with a regression coefficient of 0.7, for Germany, the coefficient being 0.4 for the United States. The estimates pertain to the 1960–80 period and are statistically significant at the 5 percent level.[22] There is further evidence that social charges raise the cost of labor to the firm in the developing countries.[23]

It appears, then, that social security schemes create distortions in labor markets by raising the cost of labor to the firm without the wage-earners considering the benefits financed by these contributions as a full addition to their incomes. At the same time, taxes and social charges establish a wedge between the cost of labor to the firm and after-tax labor incomes.

According to calculations made at the Institut der Deutschen Wirtschaft, the cost of social charges and fringe benefits is 80 percent of the wage in Germany. With marginal tax rates, including the social security contributions of employees, of 48 percent for unskilled labor and 61 percent for skilled labor,[24] the ratio of labor costs to after-tax income in the two categories is 2.7 and 2.9, respectively. Similar results for Sweden have led Assar Lindbeck to conclude:

> Market price distortions due to monopoly, monopsony, monopolistic competition, oligopoly, etc. – which have worried economic theorists so much for such a long time – are usually insignificant as compared to these *policy-implemented* factor price distortions. Whereas the former often seem to create a wedge between price and marginal costs of some 5 or 10 percent, the marginal wedges between wage costs for firms and the returns to the individual are, as we have seen, often about 200 percent and occasionally more than 500 percent.[25]

Distortions in labor markets will reduce the efficiency of resource allocation and depress the rate of economic growth. A further question, much debated in the literature, is whether pay-as-you-go social security schemes lower private savings. The flavour of the debate may be indicated by two quotations:

> In my opinion, the existing research indicates that social security does substantially depress private saving and therefore national saving in the United States. Each dollar of social security wealth appears to reduce private wealth accumulation by somewhat less than a dollar but more than 50 cents.[26]

> It is not clear whether a pay-as-you-go system reduces saving and the capital accumulation (measured against a relevant reference situation) below a defined level or not.[27]

Having surveyed the relevant literature, Janssen adds that 'the statistical results showing a negative effect of social security on saving are somewhat more convincing in the case of cross-section data than in time series analysis; nevertheless, the evidence does not seem to be conclusive and reliable.'[28] According to a recent study not covered by Janssen's survey, however, 'the empirical work of Feldstein and his critics has been flawed by a specification error. When this is corrected, the results – although still far from conclusive – appear to favor the existence of a depressing effect of social security wealth on household saving.'[29] Furthermore, 'government transfer programs in the United States may have lowered household saving by redistributing income to those with higher than average propensities to consume – the poor, the liquidity constrained and the old. In support of this approach, the tests that were conducted found a propensity to consume out of transfer payments that was close to unity.'[30]

IV POLICY-IMPOSED DISTORTIONS IN CAPITAL MARKETS

Policy-imposed distortions in capital markets may originate in credit policy, tax policy, and protection policy. To begin with, interest rates may be kept at below equilibrium levels, differential interest rates charged to different borrowers, and credit rationed among users. In turn, the system of taxation applied will affect the after-tax rate of return on capital. Finally, policies of protection will bear on the cost of capital goods.

In the United States, interest rate ceilings on personal savings were applied until recently and tax deductibility provisions continued to reduce after-tax interest rates on loans. In other developed countries, interest rate ceilings have often been combined with credit allocation among competing users.

In developing countries, in particular in Latin America, there has been a tendency to keep interest rates artificially low, giving rise to negative real interest rates. As the resulting excess demand for credit has necessitated rationing, governments have intervened in the allocation of credit. Also, a variety of credit preference schemes have been, in effect, providing better terms to favored users.

In socialist countries, interest rates have been kept low for savers as well as for users. Although under central planning the government allocates credit, its cost nevertheless enters into the calculations of the firm. In turn, in Hungary, real interest rates are positive and play a role in the allocation of credit.

Negative, or below equilibrium, real interest rates encourage capital-intensive activities and provide incentives for 'self-investment', including inventory building, at rates lower than those obtainable in the rest of the economy. Also, credit preferences and credit rationing create distortions among the uses to which capital is put, thereby reducing the efficiency of investment.

A further question concerns the effects of interest rates on savings. While earlier contributions suggested that the outcome is indeterminate, owing to conflicting income and substitution effects, in a structural estimation of the US aggregate consumption function by the use of instrumental variables, Boskin[31] obtained an interest elasticity of savings of 0.4. Utilizing a life-cycle growth model that incorporates the effect of interest rates on wealth, Summers subsequently derived elasticities of 1.9 to 3.4 in what he calls the 'plausible logarithmic case';[32] the lower value corresponds to Boskin's estimate if wealth effects are excluded. These results were subsequently challenged by Evans who obtained elasticities ranging between 0.1 and 1.9 for alternative parameter values.[33] In turn, according to Summers, 'empirical evidence casts doubts on the relevance of parameter values underlying Evans' low elasticity cases'.[34] Summers also suggests that introducing the bequest motive would raise rather than reduce the interest elasticity of savings as Evans claimed.

A review of available evidence for the developing countries by the International Monetary Fund has also led to the conclusion that 'the repression of interest rates produces lower rates of saving'.[35] It has further been observed that low interest rates contribute to the outflow of capital in search of higher returns abroad.

It would appear, then, that below-equilibrium interest rates reduce savings and investment while the attendant rationing of credit depresses the efficiency of investment. Correspondingly, the rate of economic growth will be lower than it would be in the absence of such distortions.[36]

Estimates of the interest elasticity of household savings are not available for the socialist countries. However, the recent experience of Hungary suggests that savers strongly react to higher interest rates. At the same time, the use of low interest rates in calculations made by firms in the socialist countries encourages the choice of capital-intensive activities.

Harberger[37] estimated the loss due to the misallocation of capital between the corporate and the non-corporate sectors in the United States, associated with the imposition of the corporate income tax, at 0.5 percent of national income. Subsequently, Feldstein estimated the welfare cost of capital taxation, exclusive of the misallocation between corporate and non-corporate business, to be of approximately the same magnitude if the alternative involves taxing consumption.[38]

These estimates do not include the effects of corporate taxation on private savings. The latter is incorporated in Summers' estimates, according to which steady-state consumption would rise by 17 percent if the corporate income tax were replaced by consumption taxation.[39] In turn, a wide range of possible results is shown by Evans' calculations: steady-state consumption would increase by 67 percent if the inter-temporal elasticity of substitution was assumed to be 1.0 and there were no bequests and it would be practically nil if the elasticity was 0.2 and there were inter-generational transfers.[40] However, the latter estimate rests on the unrealistic assumption that the interest elasticity of savings was negative.

In the King–Fullerton study of the taxation of income from capital, the effective marginal tax rate on US corporate income, derived from new investments, was estimated at 48 percent in 1960, 47 percent in 1970, and 37 percent in 1980, under the assumption of a 10 percent pre-tax rate of return and actual rates of inflation. Following the 1981 tax reform, the marginal tax rate declined to 26 percent, rising to 32 percent in 1982 when some tax benefits were again reduced. The comparable figures for 1980 are 4 percent for the United Kingdom, 36 percent for Sweden, and 48 percent for Germany.[41]

At the same time, there are considerable differences in tax rates among assets, among industries, as well as according to sources of finance and ownership. In the United Kingdom, for example, machinery receives a 37 percent subsidy, thereby substantially reducing the overall average. The effective tax rate on machinery is also low in Sweden and in the United States while it is 45 percent in Germany.[42]

Available evidence indicates that, owing to tax holidays and accelerated depreciation provisions, effective tax rates on business income are low in the developing countries. The over-valuation of the exchange rate associated with high protection, together with low tariffs on machinery, further reduce the cost of capital goods in these countries. In turn, taxes generally represent a fixed percentage of profits in socialist countries while there appears to be a tendency to underprice machinery in these countries.

V POLICY-IMPOSED DISTORTIONS IN THE RELATIVE PRICES OF LABOR AND CAPITAL

The impact of policy-imposed distortions in labor and capital markets on factor intensity will depend on the relative magnitudes of these distortions. Such calculations have been made for several developing countries in a comparative study directed by Anne Krueger. According to the estimates, policy-imposed distortions raised the wage-rental ratio by 316 percent in Pakistan, 87 percent in Tunisia, 45 percent in the Ivory Coast, 38 percent in Argentina, 31 percent in Brazil, 11 percent in Korea, and nil in Hong Kong.[43] The high ratios obtained in most of these countries indicate the effects of social charges on the cost of labor and the effects of low interest rates, tax incentives, and low machinery tariffs on the cost of capital.

Combining the cited estimate of the wedge between the cost of labor to the firm and labor's after-tax-income with the King–Fullerton estimate of the effective marginal tax rate on capital income, it is apparent that the measures applied raise the relative price of labor to a considerable extent in Germany. Distortions in factor markets may be even greater in some other European countries, such as France and Italy, where social security charges and fringe benefits account for a larger proportion of labor costs than in Germany. The outcome is less certain in the United States, where labor market distortions are much less prevalent than in Western Europe.[44]

These conclusions are supported by calculations that relate employer's contributions to public and private social security schemes to wages and revenue derived from the corporate income tax and from taxes on land and buildings to capital. The results obtained for 1980 show effective tax rates on labor and on capital of 40 and 10 percent in France, 23 and 10 percent in Germany, 35 and 10 percent in Italy, 17 and 10 percent in the United Kingdom, and 19 and 18 percent in the United States; the corresponding figures are 13 and 18 percent in Japan.[45] The overall results are not materially affected if one follows the *Economist* in adding employees' contributions, and deducting employers' private pension contributions, from taxes on labor and adjusting profit taxes for inflation.[46]

VI TAXES AND ECONOMIC GROWTH

In recent years increased attention has been given to the adverse effects of taxation on economic growth. This contention is far from new; Keynes is said to have expressed the view that Colin Clark's 'figure of 25 percent as the maximum tolerable proportion of taxation may be exceedingly near to the truth'. Any such argument must rest on the inefficiencies introduced by the wedges between the demand price and the supply price of particular factors, and on the responsiveness of the supply of factors – labor and entrepreneurship as well as savings – to the after-tax rate of return.

There have been several recent empirical studies on the relationship between taxes and economic growth. In regressing rates of economic growth on the ratio of taxes to GNP in a time-series analysis of 27 developed countries and in a cross-section analysis of the same countries, Peterson obtained negative coefficients in practically all cases but few of the results were statistically significant. Most of the regression coefficients were significant, however, at the 5 percent level, when the ratio of direct taxes to GNP was used as the explanatory variable.[47]

In turn, Marsden found the regression coefficient of the tax/GDP variable to be statistically significant at the 1 percent level in explaining inter-country differences in GDP growth rates in a twenty country sample as well as in low-income and high-income subsamples of equal size. And while significance levels declined when the rate of growth of domestic investment and that of the labor force were introduced as additional explanatory variables, these two variables were shown to be negatively correlated with the ratio of taxes to GDP.[48]

Finally, in a model that combines equations determining increases in nominal wages, the rate of inflation, the growth of private employment, and the ratio of net investment to GDP, Knoester found that simultaneous and equal increases in income taxes and social security contributions and in budgetary expenditures would have a negative long-run multiplier effect of 1.5 to 3.0 in Germany, Netherlands, United Kingdom, and the United States.[49] This effect is obtained because the forward-shifting of income taxes and social security contributions reduces profits that, in turn, lowers the rate of investment.

CONCLUSIONS

Certain broad conclusions emerge from the analysis of the effects of government directives and interventions in product factor markets on the efficiency of resource allocation and economic growth in developed, developing and socialist countries. These conclusions, in turn, have implications for future policies.

The cost of protection is especially high in developing countries. Apart from its adverse effects on the efficiency of resource allocation, the resulting decline in investment efficiency and savings, together with the lack of adequate stimulation of technological change, protection tends to lower the rate of economic growth. Levels of protection are lower in developed countries but its cost has been generally underestimated by neglecting economies of scale and the effects of foreign competition on technological change. Finally, in socialist countries, the adverse effects of import protection are aggravated by the lack of scarcity prices for use in the evaluation of foreign trade alternatives.

Among developed countries, social legislation has raised the cost of labor to a considerable extent in Western Europe and has contributed to unemployment by reducing both the demand for and the supply of labor. With some exceptions, labor market distortions have been less prevalent in developing countries; however, credit, tax, and protection measures substantially lower the cost of capital in many of these countries.

In raising the relative price of labor, the measures applied have encouraged the expansion of capital-intensive activities in the countries concerned. In socialist countries, such activities are encouraged by the low rate of interest and by rigidities that impede the efficient allocation of labor. The lack of scarcity prices further interferes with the efficient allocation of investment funds in socialist countries, lowering rates of economic growth, notwithstanding high savings ratios in these countries.

The conclusion emerges that improving the system of incentives through reductions in distortions in product and in factor markets would permit reaching higher levels of efficiency and raising the rate of economic growth in developed and in developing countries. Also, on the example of Hungary, the decentralization of decision-making, combined with the introduction of scarcity prices, would favor the efficiency of resource allocation and economic growth in socialist countries.

It has been objected, however, that in a world of the second best, removing a particular distortion may be welfare-reducing in the presence of other distortions. But, infant industry cases apart, free trade will contribute to efficient resource allocation in a small country that cannot affect world market prices and reducing distortions in the relative prices of labour and capital will also unambiguously improve welfare.

It has also been suggested that, in making policy recommendations, one should take account of non-economic, in particular social, objectives. This paper has had a more modest aim: to appraise the economic cost of distortions that may or may not find their origin in the pursuit of non-economic objectives. At the same time, it should be recognized that economic and non-economic objectives are not necessarily in conflict. In developing countries, for example, reducing distortions in product and in factor prices would promote equity by increasing demand for labor.

NOTES

1. J. N. Bhagwati, 'The Generalized Theory of Distortions and Welfare' in J. N. Bhagwati, R. W. Jones, R. A. Mundell and J. Vanek (eds), *Trade, Balance of Payments and Growth* (Amsterdam: North-Holland, 1971) pp. 69–90.
2. The paper builds on, and complements, the author's writings on policy-imposed distortions in developing (B. Balassa, 'Disequilibrium Analysis in Developing Countries', Essay 2 in this volume) and developed countries (B. Balassa, 'The Economic Consequences of Social Policies in the Industrial Countries', Essay 3 in this volume).
3. R. G. Harris with D. Cox. *Trade, Industrial Policy and Canadian Manufacturing* (Toronto: Ontario Economic Council, 1983) p. 115.
4. B. Balassa *et al.* *The Structure of Protection in Developing Countries* (Baltimore, Md.: Johns Hopkins University Press, 1971) p. 82.
5. J. de Melo, 'Estimating the Costs of Protection: A General Equilibrium Approach', *Quarterly Journal of Economics*, CXII (1978) pp. 209–26.
6. H. G. Johnson, 'The Possibility of Income Losses from Increased Efficiency or Factor Accumulation in the Presence of Tariffs', *Economic Journal*, CXXVII (1967) pp. 151–4.
7. B. Balassa, 'The Newly Industrializing Countries After the Oil Crisis', *Weltwirtschaftliches Archiv*, CXVII (1981) pp. 142–94; 'The Policy Experience of Twelve Less Developed Countries, 1973–1978', in G. Ranis, R. West, M. Leiserson and C. Morris (eds), *Comparative Development Perspectives*, Essays in Honor of Lloyd G. Reynolds (Boulder, Colorado: Westview Press, 1984) pp. 96–123; and 'Adjustment Policies in Sub-Saharan Africa, 1973–78', in M. Syrquin, L. Taylor and L. E. Westphal (eds), *Economic Structure and Performance*, Essays in Honor of Hollis B. Chenery (New York: Academic Press) forthcoming.
8. B. Balassa, 'Exports, Policy Choices, and Economic Growth in Developing Countries After the 1973 Oil Shock', *Journal of Development Economics* (forthcoming).
9. A detailed discussion of regulations affecting the supply of labor in developed countries is provided in Essay 3 of this volume where it is indicated that the measures applied in Western Europe find much less scope in the United States.
10. A. Lindbeck, 'Work Disincentives in the Welfare State', *Nationaloko-nomische Gesellscraft Lectures 79–80* (Vienna, 1981) pp. 27–76.
11. C. Brown, C. Gilroy and A. Kohen, 'The Effect of the Minimum Wage on Employment and Unemployment', *Journal of Economic Literature*, XX (1982) pp. 512–22.
12. P. Linneman, 'The Economic Impact of Minimum Wage Laws: A New Look at an Old Question', *Journal of Political Economy*, XC (1982) p. 468.

13. J. Schaafsma and W. D. Walsh, 'Employment and Labor Supply Effects of the Minimum Wage: Some Pooled Timed Series Estimates from Canadian Provincial Data', *Canadian Journal of Economics*, XVI (1983) pp. 86–97.
14. For a detailed discussion, see B. Balassa, 'Public Finance and Social Policy – Explanations of their Trends and Developments: The Case of Developing Countries', paper presented at the 39th Congress of the International Institute of Public Finance held in Budapest in August, 1983. To be published in the Proceedings of the Congress.
15. W. R. Johnson and E. K. Browning, 'The Distributional and Efficiency Effects of Increasing the Minimum Wage: A Simulation', *American Economic Review*, LXXVIII (1983) p. 211.
16. J. Z. Drabicki and A. Takiyama, 'Minimum Wage Regulation and Economic Growth', *Journal of Economics and Business*, XXXIV (1982) p. 232.
17. United States Department of Health and Human Services, Social Security Administration, *Social Security Programs Throughout the World 1981* (Washington, DC, 1982).
18. B. Balassa, *The Theory of Economic Integration* (Homewood, Ill.: Irwin, 1961) pp. 218–19.
19. J. Brittain, *The Payroll Tax for Social Security* (Washington, DC: The Brookings Institution, 1972) Ch. III.
20. S. A. Woodbury, 'Substitution between Wage and Non-wage Benefits', *American Economic Review*, LXXIII (1983) p. 179.
21. W. Eltis, 'How Rapid Public Sector Growth Can Undermine the Growth of the National Product', in W. Beckerman (ed.), *Slow Growth in Britain: Causes and Consequences* (Oxford: Clarendon Press, 1979) pp. 127–28.
22. The corresponding results for the United Kingdom are not reported on the grounds that with the inclusion of this parameter, 'the coefficients for prices and productivity would take on too high values', A. Knoester, 'Stagnation and the Inverted Haavelmo Effect: Some International Evidence', *De Economist*, CXXXI (1983) p. 564.
23. Balassa, 'Public Finance and Social Policy – Explanations of their Trends and Development: The Case of Developing Countries'.
24. The calculations relate a single worker with monthly pre-tax earnings of DM 2000 in the first case and DM 3000 in the second. Practically the same result is reached for a family of four, with two breadwinners each having the stated-earnings. A. Boss, G. Fleming, P. Trapp and N. Walter, 'Bundesrepublik Deutscheland: Trotz Krise noch Kein Undenken', *Die Weltwirtschaft*, II (1982) pp. 22–47.
25. A. Lindbeck, 'Work Disincentives in the Welfare State: The Case of Sweden', *European Economic Review*, XXI (1983) p. 245.
26. M. Feldstein, 'The Effect of Social Security on Savings' in D. Currie, R. Nobay and D. Peel (eds), *Macroeconomic Analysis: Essays in Macroeconomics and Econometrics* (London: Croom Helm, 1981) pp. 18–19.
27. M. Janssen, 'Social Insurance: Incentives and Disincentives to Save and to Work', paper prepared for the Conference on Economic Incentives, held at the Institute of World Economics of the University of Kiel on 18–22 June 1984, p. 24.
28. Janssen, p. 17.

29. O. Evans, 'Social Security and Household Saving in the United States: A Re-Examination', *International Monetary Fund Staff Papers*, XXX (1983) p. 611.
30. Evans, p. 611.
31. M. S. Boskin, 'Taxation Savings and the Rate of Interest', *Journal of Political Economy*, LXXXVI (1978), pp. S3–S28.
32. L. H. Summers, 'Capital Taxation and Accumulation in a Life Cycle Growth Model', *American Economic Review*, LXXI (1981) p. 536.
33. O. Evans, 'Tax Policy, the Interest Elasticity of Savings and Capital Accumulation: Numerical Analysis of Theoretical Models', *American Economic Review*, LXXIII (1983) Table 4.
34. L. H. Summers, 'The After Tax Rate of Return Affects Private Savings', *American Economic Review*, LXXIV (1984) p. 250.
35. International Monetary Fund, *Interest Rate Policies in Developing Countries*, Occasional Paper No. 22 (1983) p. 19.
36. It should be added, however, that excessively high real interest rates, resulting from the application of strongly restrictive monetary policies, will also have adverse effects by discouraging socially profitable investment and creating disturbances in capital markets.
37. A. C. Harberger, 'Efficiency Effects of Taxes on Income from Capital', in M. Krzyzahiak (ed.), *Effects of the Corporation Income Tax* (Detroit: Wayne State University Press, 1966).
38. M. Feldstein, 'The Welfare Cost of Capital Income Taxation', *Journal of Political Economy*, LXXXII (1978) p. 547.
39. Summers, 'Capital Taxation and Accumulation in a Life Cycle Growth Model', p. 541.
40. Evans, 'Tax Policy, the Interest Elasticity of Saving in the United States: A Re-Examination'.
41. M. A. King and D. Fullerton, *The Taxation of Income from Capital: A Comparative Study of the United States, Sweden and West Germany* (Chicago: University of Chicago Press, 1984) Tables 6.20, 6.27–28, 6.31–32, 7.1.
42. King and Fullerton, Tables 6.28 and 7.1.
43. A. O. Krueger, *Trade and Employment in Developing Countries 3. Synthesis and Conclusions* (Chicago: University of Chicago Press, 1983), p. 150.
44. B. Balassa, 'The Economic Consequences of Social Policies in the Industrial Countries'.
45. J. Kay and J. Sen, 'The Comparative Burden of Business Taxation', *Fiscal Studies*, IV (1983) pp. 23–28, Table 5.
46. The *Economist*, 10 December 1983.
47. H. G. Peterson, 'Taxes, Tax Systems and Economic Growth', in H. Giersch (ed.), *Towards an Explanation of Economic Growth* (Tubingen: J. C. B. Mohr, 1981) Tables 1 and 2.
48. K. Marsden, 'Links between Taxes and Economic Growth, Some Empirical Evidence', World Bank Staff Working Paper No. 605 (1983) Tables 3 and 4.
49. Knoester, p. 567.

Essay 2 Disequilibrium Analysis in Developing Economies: An Overview

INTRODUCTION

Following contributions by Haberler,[1] Bhagwati and Ramaswami[2] and Johnson,[3] Bhagwati[4] formulated a general theory of distortions in product and in factor markets. Bhagwati distinguished between 'endogenous' and 'policy-imposed' distortions, depending on whether departures from optimal resource allocation result from market imperfections or from policy actions.

While studies of distortions in product markets have continued to focus on policy-imposed distortions in the form of protection, the literature on distortions in factor markets has concentrated on endogenous distortions. Thus, Magee's survey article includes only two policy-imposed distortions in factor markets on a list of fifteen,[5] and in his subsequent book there are eight literature references to such distortions within a grand total of 244.[6]

This paper will analyze policy-imposed distortions in product and in factor markets of developing economies. Section I will describe briefly the principal policy-imposed distortions observed in developing economies, review recent estimates on the extent of discrimination in particular markets, and indicate their possible economic effects.[7] In turn, Section II of the paper will report on available estimates of the impact of these distortions on the efficiency of allocating existing resources as well as on savings, investment efficiency, and economic growth.

24

I POLICY-IMPOSED DISTORTIONS IN PRODUCT AND IN FACTOR MARKETS

Distortions in product markets

Protection, a ubiquitous phenomenon in developing economies, has received considerable attention in the theoretical literature on international trade. Furthermore, the introduction of the concept of effective protection in the mid-sixties has been followed by a spate of estimates, notwithstanding the conceptual and the measurement problems involved.

Protection introduces three forms of discrimination in the national economy: (a) discrimination among domestic products; (b) discrimination between domestic and foreign products; and (c) discrimination between domestic and foreign sales of a particular product. The first type of discrimination is indicated by relative rates of (gross) effective protection; the second by net effective rates of protection, with adjustment made for the effects of protection on the equilibrium exchange rate; and the third by the extent of the bias against exports and in favor of import substitution. The relevant formulas are shown in equations (1) to (3).

(1) gross effective rate of protection: $\quad z_i = \dfrac{t_i - \sum_j A_{ji} t_j}{1 - \sum_j A_{ji}}$

(2) net effective rate of protection: $\dot{z}_i = \dfrac{r_l}{r_o}(1 + z_i) - 1$

(3) bias against exports:

$$x_i = \frac{z_i^m - z_i^x}{z_i^x} - 1 = \frac{(t_i^m - \sum A_{ji} t_j^{mm}) - (t_i^x - \sum_j A_{ji} t_j^x)}{t_i^x - \sum_j A_{ji} t_j^x} - 1$$

In the equations, t is the nominal rate of protection, representing the effects of import tariffs (subsidies), or the tariff-equivalent of import restrictions, and export subsidies (taxes) on the price of the product. Subscripts i and j, respectively, refer to the product and its tradeable inputs; superscripts x and m refer to domestic and export sales of a particular product; A_{ji} denoted input–output coefficients under free trade; and r_l and r_o refer to the exchange rate under protection and under free trade, respectively.

Protection-imposed discrimination among domestic products, shown by (gross) effective rates of protection, reflects the existence of price distortions in regard to the product and its inputs. Positive (negative) net effective protection indicates the extent of discrimination between domestic and foreign products, i.e. import protection (subsidization) and export subsidization (taxation). Finally, there is discrimination between domestic and foreign sales of a particular product in the customary case observed in developing economies, when import tariffs (the tariff-equivalent of import restrictions) are not compensated by export subsidies.

The described forms of discrimination are illustrated in Table 2.1 by estimates for 12 developing economies. The estimates point to the existence of considerable inter-country differences in the extent of discrimination among economic activities, owing to differences in the structure of protection. At the same time, they show that the three forms of discrimination go hand-in-hand.

At one extreme, Argentina, Brazil, Chile, Pakistan, and the Philippines exhibit considerable discrimination against primary activities, against manufactured imports, as well as against sales abroad. At the other extreme, primary and manufacturing activities receive similar incentives, there is little discrimination against manufactured imports, and the bias against exports is small in Korea, Malaysia, Singapore, and Taiwan. Finally, Mexico, Colombia, and Israel occupy a middle position in regard to all three forms of discrimination.

There are also substantial differences in the inter-industry variability of the three forms of discrimination among the 12 developing economies studied. On the whole, the extent of discrimination and its dispersion among industries in the individual economies are positively correlated.[8]

Protection-imposed discrimination gives rise to inefficiencies in resource allocation that are aggravated due to a bias against exports. This conclusion is strengthened if we consider that tariff protection in developing economies leads to loss of economies of scale and/or a low level of capacity utilization in producing for limited domestic markets and failing to specialize within industries characterized by product differentiation. Also, tariff protection provides little incentive for technical change, in particular in cases when the domestic market can support only one or a few producers, and there may be a loss in the form of 'X-inefficiencies', owing to the failure of firms to use least-cost production methods. In turn, exports permit the use of large-scale production methods and need to meet the test of world markets, when

TABLE 2.1 Effective protection in 12 developing economies

	Gross effective protection (z_i)			Net effective protection (z'_i)			Bias against exports (x_i)		
	Primary	Manufacturing	Together	Primary	Manufacturing	Together	Primary	Manufacturing	Together
Brazil (1966)	52	113	83	20	68	44	na	122	na
Chile (1961)	21	182	84	−28	68	10	na	324	na
Mexico (1960)	1	26	12	−7	16	3	13	87	58
Malaysia (1960)	−6	−6	−6	−10	−10	−10	na	25	na
Pakistan (1963–64)	na	271	na	na	147	na	na	na	na
Philippines (1965)	−1	61	8	−14	41	−6	na	228	na
Argentina (1969)	0	112	47	−29	38	1	24	241	94
Colombia (1969)	−10	35	−2	−20	10	−15	13	42	23
Israel (1968)	48	76	62	−8	7	0	26	63	50
Korea (1968)	9	13	10	1	−11	−1	16	10	10
Singapore (1967)	9	4	6	5	−4	0	13	6	9
Taiwan (1969)	0	14	5	−8	9	−2	4	26	10

SOURCE: Bela Balassa, et al. *The Structure of Protection in Developing Countries* (Baltimore, Md., Johns Hopkins University Press, 1971), and Bela Balassa, *Development Strategies in Semi-Industrial Economies* (Baltimore, Md., Johns Hopkins University Press, 1982) et al.

the stick and the carrot of competition gives inducement for improvements in production methods.[9]

Apart from protection, distortions in product markets may result
from price control and underpricing by public enterprises, in particular,
public utilities. Price control may be applied in the production and/or
the consumption sphere, requiring increased imports or some form of
rationing. The adverse effects of price control on domestic production
have been observed, in particular, in Sub-Saharan Africa.[10] In turn, the
underpricing of public utilities, widely applied in developing economies, will increase the protection of manufacturing industries, such as
petrochemicals, chemicals, steel and aluminium, which are large users
of these utilities.

Protection also creates distortions in factor markets by affecting the
relative prices of labor and capital (the wage-rental ratio). As developing countries generally have a comparative advantage in labor-intensive products, the wage-rental ratio will tend to decline as a result of
protection. The distortions are aggravated by the oft-observed tendency in developing economies to discriminate against the domestic
production of machinery.[11] Other forms of interventions in product
markets, such as the underpricing of capital-intensive public utilities,
will introduce further distortions in factor markets.

Distortions in factor markets

Distortions in factor prices, with attendant inefficiencies in resource
allocation, further find their origin in policy interventions in factor
markets. The wage-rental ratio may be affected by credit and tax
policies that bear on the price of capital, as well as by tax policies,
minimum wage legislation, and the social security system that influence
the price of labor.

Policy-imposed distortions in factor markets may have a general or a
special incidence; in the latter case, their incidence varies among the
users of the factors of production. But measures of general incidence,
too, will affect the choice of techniques.

Capital markets

Among instruments of credit policy, interest rate ceilings and preferential credits have been widely used in developing economies. Interest rate

ceilings have been traditionally administered in Latin American countries, keeping real interest rates negative and necessitating the rationing of credit. Latin American, as well as Asian, countries have also provided considerable credit preferences.

The extent of credit preferences has been particularly large in Brazil, where real interest rates to preferred borrowers were in the − 30 to − 40 percent range in the late 1970s while nonpreferential borrowers paid inflation-indexed rates and savers received negative real interest rates. Credit preferences have been used in part to pursue particular objectives, such as import substitution in intermediate products, and in part to benefit otherwise disadvantaged sectors, such as agriculture.[12] In turn, in developing economies characterized by outward orientation, such as Korea, exports have benefited from preferential credits.[13]

Apart from adversely affecting the efficiency of resource allocation, credit preferences have detrimental effects on the development of financial intermediaries. Negative, or below-equilibrium real interest rates, too, hinder the development of financial intermediaries and provide incentives for 'self-investment', including inventory-building, at rates lower than those obtainable elsewhere in the economy.

More generally, credit rationing under below-equilibrium real interest rates, as well as credit preferences, lower the efficiency of investment, both by discriminating among the users of capital and favoring the application of capital-intensive techniques. Also, below-equilibrium real interest rates tend to discourage domestic savings and encourage the outflow of capital. McKinnon[14] and Shaw[15] speak of financial repression that ultimately adversely affects the growth of the economy.[16]

Excessively high real interest rates, resulting from the application of restrictive monetary policies, may also have adverse economic effects, however, by discouraging socially profitable investment and hindering the development of long-term capital markets. Such has been the case in Latin American countries of the Southern Cone, which have attempted to reduce the rate of inflation by not devaluing in line with differential rates of price increases at home and abroad.

A shift in interest rate policies has been observed in Turkey where real interest rates on non-preferential loans of one-year maturity were about − 80 percent in early 1980 but became strongly positive following the interest rate reform undertaken in July 1980. At the same time, differences in interest rates among borrowers have persisted. In mid-1981, interest rates on one-year non-preferential loans, including the cost of compensating balances, were about 70 percent compared to preferential rates of 32 percent on general investment credits, 24 percent on export credits, and 10 to 29 percent on agricultural credits. In the same period, wholesale prices rose at an annual rate of about 40 percent.[17]

Tax measures, including the double taxation of corporate income, lack of inflation accounting, accelerated depreciation provisions, and tax holidays, too, affect the price of capital. These measures as well as the taxation of private savings further bear on the system of financial intermediation, the efficiency of investment, and the volume of domestic savings in developing economies.

In 1981, in Turkey, for example, depreciation was calculated at historical values despite a four-fold rise in prices over the previous six years, thereby taxing 'phantom' profits. Nor were capital gains adjusted for inflation and, in mid-1981, interest rates paid to depositors barely covered the rate of inflation but were nevertheless subject to a tax of 25 percent. Financial transaction taxes and low interest rates paid on liquidity and reserve deposits further increased the cost of intermediation of the banking system, which totalled 30 percentage points on non-preferential loans financed from one-year time deposits in mid-1981.[18]

In turn, tax benefits to investments in particular sectors are generally linked to the value of investment in developing economies. They thus favor capital-intensive activities just as preferential interest rates do. A case in point is regional policy in Brazil that has provided inducements for capital-intensive investment in the Northeast, a region characterized by excess labor.

The effects of credit and tax measures on the price of capital have been estimated in the case of Pakistan. With tariffs and the overvaluation of the exchange rate bearing on the price of the capital asset; the cost of financing, depreciation provisions, and the corporate tax rate affecting the annual cost of owning capital assets; and tax holidays influencing net returns to capital; the ratio of the market to the equilibrium (shadow) price of capital in Pakistan varied between 0.23 and 0.34 between 1959–60 and 1971–2. The ratio subsequently rose to 0.79 as the overvaluation of the rupee was remedied and the tax holiday scheme was abandoned.[19]

At the same time, these measures were applied selectively and, until 1972, small investors faced capital costs more than twice those of large firms.[20] In turn, in the mid-seventies, the cost of capital to the private sector was about two-and-a-half times that for the public sector in Tunisia.[21]

Labor markets

Distortions in labor markets occur as high marginal income tax rates create incentives to reduce the work effort and to shift from payment in money to payment in kind. For example, in 1980 in Turkey minimum wage-income was subject to a tax of 28 percent. Under the new schedule introduced on 1 January 1981, the minimum wage is not subject to tax but the marginal tax rate is 40 percent on incomes immediately above this level.[22]

High marginal tax rates also discourage the movement of labor from lower to higher productivity industries. Labor mobility is further discouraged by redundancy payments that have particular importance in Latin American countries, often amounting to one year's wage. At the same time, high redundancy payments tend to reduce employment by discouraging new hiring. The prohibition to dismiss workers, applied in Turkey after 1980 will have similar effects.

Minimum wage legislation and social security charges, too, may increase the cost of labor. Such regulations are said to have raised the cost of unskilled labor by 23 percent in the Ivory Coast.[23] Furthermore, Guisinger suggests that in Pakistan 'the major part of the increase in wages [that] occurred in the 1970s appear to be due to non-market factors, particularly the wage policies introduced during the period'.[24]

Factor-market distortions lowering the cost of capital and raising the cost of labor much exceeded the effects of protection on the wage-rental ratio in Pakistan. According to Guisinger, until the 1972 devaluation, this ratio in market prices was on the average over five times the equilibrium ratio; it was two-and-a-half times greater afterwards.[25] Distortions were larger than the average in the large-scale sector that benefited from lower capital charges and was required to pay higher wages.[26] In turn, in the case of Tunisia, distortions in capital and labor markets are said to have resulted in a wage-rental ratio 2.4 times higher in the public sector than in the private sector.[27]

II THE ECONOMIC COSTS OF POLICY-IMPOSED DISTORTIONS

Effects on the efficiency of resource allocation

Harberger was the first to examine possible magnitudes of the (static) cost of protection (external distortions, in his terminology) and that of distortions in capital and in labor markets (designated as internal distortions). For the mid-1950s, in Chile, he estimated that 'the welfare costs of external distortions are less than 2½ percent of national income, the welfare costs of internal distortions among sectors less than 10 percent of the national income, and the welfare costs of within sector distortions less than 3 percent of the national income'.[28] On the assumption that these costs are additive, Harberger reached the conclusion that 'eliminating resource misallocations while maintaining existing production functions might raise the level of national welfare by some 15 percent, but probably not more'.[29]

Product markets

The present author suggested that Harberger had underestimated the cost of protection in Chile by understating the level of tariffs and the share of imports in national income, and by excluding the possibility that some inefficient industries may disappear under protection.[30] Subsequently, Bergsman estimated the cost of protection for Brazil by separating industries into two groups, depending on whether they can be expected to disappear or to survive under free trade. The savings in costs in the first group of industries following a move to free trade were considered to represent an improvement in allocative efficiency; in the second group, production costs were assumed to decline to competitive levels under free trade, representing an improvement in X-efficiency.[31]

Having further calculated the consumption cost of protection, the terms-of-trade loss due to reductions in export prices, and the cost of increased exports under free trade, the present author estimated the cost of protection, including monopoly profits, for several developing economies with relatively high levels of protection. The results, expressed as a proportion of GNP, were 9.5 percent in 1966 for Brazil, 6.2 percent in 1962 for Chile, 6.2 percent in 1963–4 for Pakistan, and 3.7 percent in 1965 for the Philippines.[32] In turn, in extrapolating the results obtained for a sample of industries to the entire Turkish manufacturing sector, Krueger,[33] concluded that the re-allocation of resources from import-substituting to export industries under free trade would lead to the doubling of the world market value of manufacturing output; with manufacturing industries accounting for one-seventh of GNP, this is equivalent to a cost of protection of 7 percent of Turkey's GNP.

The results cited so far were obtained in a partial equilibrium framework. Subsequently, de Melo estimated the cost of protection in 1970 for Colombia in a general equilibrium model, incorporating intermediate products, non-traded goods, as well as substitution among products and among factors. Excluding land re-allocation within agriculture and postulating an optimal export tax for coffee, the cost of protection was estimated at 11.0 percent of GNP, assuming labor to be fully employed, and at 15.8 percent of GNP assuming that additional supplies of labor are available at a constant real wage.[34]

The difference between the results indicates the importance of employment effects under surplus labor, which were not considered in earlier estimates of cost of protection. But the de Melo's estimates under the full employment assumption are also considerably higher than earlier partial equilibrium results, even though he does not allow for potential gains from X-efficiency and Colombia had a relatively low level of protection. Thus, effective protection rates, averaged 29 percent in the manufacturing sector in Colombia,[35] compared to 113 percent in Brazil, 182 percent in Chile, 271 percent in Pakistan, and 61 percent in the Philippines (Table 2.1). In Mexico which had a similar level of protection, with effective rates averaging 26 percent, the partial equilibrium estimate of the cost of protection was 2.5 percent of GNP.[36]

These results point to the under-estimation of the cost of protection in a partial equilibrium framework. The use of such a framework does not allow for the fact that the cost of protection rises more than proportionally with the rate of the tariff[37] and that this cost increases with the dispersion of tariffs.[38] Furthermore, the use of a general equilibrium framework permits to take account of the interactions among productive activities through factor prices and the allocative cost of distortions in factor prices that result from protection.

Factor markets

As regards the welfare cost of factor market distortions, on the basis of a computer analysis of hypothetical cases Johnson concluded that 'neither their existence nor their elimination is likely to be a strategic determinant of the level of national well-being'.[39] Subsequently, estimates derived in a partial equilibrium framework led Dougherty and Selowsky to the conclusion that, following the elimination of wage differences among five non-agricultural sectors in Colombia, 'output could not rise by more than one or two percent, a result which leads one to suspect that under any plausible set of assumptions the gain would be insubstantial'.[40]

These conclusions were not borne out by de Melo's results for Colombia, obtained in the general equilibrium model referred to earlier, consisting of two agricultural and 13 non-agricultural sectors. Thus, de Melo found that the intersectoral movement of labor in response to the elimination of wage differences among non-agricultural sectors would lead to a 5.7 percent rise in GNP if capital was immobile and to a 13.3 percent gain if capital was mobile among sectors.[41]

De Melo's use of a general equilibrium framework made it possible to allow for the interactions of product and factor markets through changes in relative prices, as well as the sectoral interdependence, which are absent from the partial equilibrium estimates. But while Dougherty and Selowsky distinguished among seven classes of labor, de Melo separated only skilled and unskilled labor, thereby overstating the welfare cost of factor market distortions associated with intersectoral wage differences.

In the second variant of his estimates, de Melo introduced capital mobility in addition to labor mobility. The welfare effects of the misallocation of both factors were considered by Syrquin in a study of Mexico. Utilizing a 17 sector model and assuming labor and capital to be homogeneous, Syrquin estimated that the misallocation of labor and capital entailed a loss of output of 15.5 percent in the Mexican manufacturing sector.[42]

The authors cited considered the welfare cost of factor market imperfections, reflected in intersectoral differences in factor prices, under the assumption that factor prices equalled marginal productivities in each. Harberger, however, assumed that a substantial part of factor market distortions originated in 'other influences, such as monopoly and taxes, which would cause differences between wages and the value of marginal product, and might make for more variance among sectors in marginal productivity than there is in wages'.[43]

As noted earlier, wage differences may also originate in government regulations other than taxes; they may be due, for example, to differences in legal minimum wages among sectors. Furthermore, in investigating wage differentials among Colombian industries, Schultz concluded that 'where economies of scale or market structure inhibited the development of competitive pressures in the protected domestic market, high levels of effective protection appear to have resulted in quasi-rents for factors employed in the more protected sectors'.[44]

In turn, following Harberger,[45] estimates have been made of the welfare cost of tax-induced distortions in the intersectoral allocation of capital in the US economy. Using a general equilibrium model and assuming a Cobb–Douglas production function, 'efficiency losses of over 10% of the value of production are reported for tax distortions (on net of tax returns) of 200%' by Whalley.[46] The losses are in the 3 to 5 percent range if the tax distortion (i.e. the tax on net corporate income) is 100 percent, corresponding to a 50 percent tax on gross income that was the case in the United States until recently. Similar estimates for developing countries are not available.

Effects on savings

The estimates reported so far take the amount of productive factors as given; they thus show the (static) cost of distortions in the allocation of existing resources. The assumption of given factor supplies is removed in studies that consider the effects of interest rates on savings. While it had earlier been assumed that savings tend to be insensitive to real interest rates,[47] several recent studies have established the positive interest elasticity of savings.

Brown found a positive correlation between the real interest rate and the ratio of savings to the gross national product in Korea, statistically significant at the 1 percent level.[48] A similar relationship was established for Portugal and for Turkey by Fry.[49] Domestic savings were also shown to be positively related to the real interest rate in 12 Asian developing economies, with the relationship being statistically significant at the 5 percent level in seven cases.[50] Subsequent work by Fry[51] has confirmed these estimates and a review of available evidence by the International Monetary Fund[52] also indicates the responsiveness of savings to interest rate.

Savings behavior is modeled by utilizing the notion of the target shock of wealth by Berger, who obtained statistically significant estimates of the interest elasticity of the asset–income ratio at the 5 percent level for Thailand.[53] It should be added, however, that the estimates pertain to financial savings, excluding unorganized money markets.

Effects on the efficiency of capital

The cited estimates show the direct effects of real interest rates on savings. As noted above, there will also be indirect effects through increases in the efficiency of investment. The direct and the indirect effects of real interest rates on savings were estimated for India and Korea in the framework of a dynamic savings-investment model by Sundararajan and Thakur.

The authors found that 'in India, the real interest rate had a significantly positive effect on total savings; while in Korea, the direct effect of the real interest rate, although positive, was not significant'.[54] However, in the latter case, there were strong indirect effects. Thus, 'although an increase in the interest rate does not have a significant direct influence on the average propensity to save in Korea, it does have a strong and significantly positive impact multiplier effect. This is so because the higher interest rate serves to raise the efficiency of capital and thereby stimulate economic growth which, in turn, stimulates savings'.[55]

Fry also found that improvements in the efficiency of investment are associated with higher real interest rates. Thus, the incremental output-capital ratio was positively correlated with the real rate of interest in all ten Asian developing economies for which calculations have been made, with the regression coefficient being statistically significant at the 5 percent level in five cases and at the 10 percent level in three cases.[56]

Furthermore, the efficiency of investment is adversely affected by protection-induced discrimination among economic activities that creates a wedge between financial and economic rates of return and limits the use of large-scale production methods as well as the utilization of capacity. This is shown in a study of 11 semi-industrial countries carried out by the present author for the 1960–73 period. Thus, incremental capital-output ratios were 5.5 in Chile and 5.7 in India – the countries which had the highest protection in the group during the period under consideration. In turn, incremental capital-output ratios were 1.8 in Singapore, 2.1 in Korea, and 2.4 in Taiwan – the countries with the lowest levels of protection; and declines in the ratios were experienced in countries such as Brazil (from 3.8 in 1960–6 to 2.1 in 1966–73) that reformed the system of protection during the period.[57]

The experience of the 1973–8 period of external shocks in the form of the quadrupling of oil prices and the world recession confirms these conclusions. Outward-oriented developing economies, characterized by a low degree of discrimination against primary activities, against manufactured imports, and against sales abroad, showed a higher level of investment efficiency measured in terms of incremental capital-output ratios than inward-oriented economies where this ratio increased during the period.[58]

Effects on economic growth

Increases in saving ratios and in the efficiency of capital in turn contribute to economic growth. Assuming that real interest rates are below their equilibrium level, Fry simulated the effects of increases in interest rates on economic growth by combining estimates of the impact of real interest rates on savings and on the efficiency of investment, represented by incremental capital-output ratios, in ten Asian developing economies. The results show a median increase of 0.3 percentage points in GNP growth rates for a one percentage point rise in the real rate of interest.[59] While such simulations are open to objections as for several countries they involve combining coefficient values which are not significant statistically, the results have been confirmed in a cross-section investigation of seven Asian developing economies.[60]

These estimates do not include the effects of increases in real interest rates on capital flows. Yet, there is evidence that real interest rates and changes in net foreign assets are positively correlated. In the case of 12 Asian economies, this relationship was statistically significant at the 5 percent level in five cases, at the 10 percent level in two cases, and the regression coefficient was positive but the level of significance was lower in five cases.[61]

The lowering of protection, too, tends to lead to the acceleration of economic growth. To begin with, Johnson[62] showed that, in a country that faces given world market prices and protects the capital-intensive sector, increases in the capital stock may lead to a fall in real incomes, measured in world market prices, through the transfer of labor from the labor-intensive to the capital-intensive sector. Subsequently, Martin[63] demonstrated that such immiserization through capital accumulation will occur if one plus the rate of protection in the capital-intensive sector exceeds the ratio of labor shares in the labor-intensive sector to that of the capital-intensive sector.

While immiserization through capital accumulation may represent an extreme case, there is evidence that protection adversely affects the rate of economic growth. Having shown that protection and exports are negatively correlated, the present author found a high positive correlation between exports and economic growth in the study of 11 semi-industrial economies cited above. This relationship was confirmed in a cross-section production-function type relationship, with exports added to the conventional explanatory variables of domestic and foreign capital and labor.[64] Applying a modified model specification to a sample of 31 semi-industrial countries, Feder found that the use of primary factors in export production, rather than in producing non-export products, accounted for a 1.8 percentage point difference in the rate of economic growth during the 1964–73 period.[65] The author's study of the 1973–8 period, indicating the superior growth performance of outward-oriented over inward-oriented economies, notwithstanding the greater external shocks they suffered confirms these conclusions.[66]

Interactions of savings, investment efficiency, and economic growth

Estimates of the effects of lowering protection on the rate of economic growth do not allow for the impact of higher GNP growth rates on savings. The potential importance of this relationship may be indicated in a hypothetical case, where capital is the only scarce factor of production, the incremental capital-output ratio is 4, the average savings ratio 16 percent, and the marginal savings ratio 33 percent. Eliminating protection, assumed to represent a loss of 6 percent of GNP, would now raise the rate of economic growth from 4.0 to 4.5 percent by increasing the amount saved. And, if population was growing at an average annual rate of 3 percent, the rate of growth of *per capita* incomes would rise from 1.0 to 1.5 percent. These savings effects, calculated under the assumption of unchanged incremental capital-output ratios, would thus augment the favorable impact of the lowering of protection on economic growth.

At the same time, the described effects will reinforce each other. Thus, increases in the savings ratio will raise the average efficiency of capital as new investments undertaken following the elimination of protection exhibit higher levels of efficiency. Also, as shown in the Sundararajan–Thakur study cited above, the direct effects of higher real interest rates on savings are reinforced by their impact on the efficiency of investment.

Another form of interdependence of the measures taken was observed by de Melo, according to whom removing distortions simultaneously in product and in factor markets would result in a larger increase in GNP than the sum of the effects of removing distortions in the two markets, taken individually.[67] It has further been shown that the elimination of corporate income taxes would result in a considerable welfare improvement through increases in savings as the (after-tax) real rate of return to capital rises. Boskin estimated the welfare loss associated with the existence of the corporate income tax in the United States at $60 billion a year[68] while Summers' estimates are $80 and $100 billion, depending on whether the capital gains tax is replaced by a consumption tax or by a wage tax.[69] It should be added, however, that these authors do not consider the welfare cost of consumption and wage taxes.

CONCLUSIONS

This paper has examined the existence of policy-imposed distortions in product and factor markets of developing economies and indicated their possible economic effects. Estimates have further been provided on the effects of such distortions on the efficiency of allocating existing resources as well as on savings, investment efficiency, and economic growth.

The findings show the importance of policy-imposed distortions in product and in factor markets of developing economies and indicate the cost of these distortions in terms of foregone incomes and economic growth. They thus point to the gains that may be obtained if such distortions are removed or alleviated.

At the same time, removing distortions in product and in factor markets reinforce each other. In particular, the favorable impact of trade liberalization is enhanced if distortions in capital markets are simultaneously removed and vice versa. On the one hand, increases in savings attendant on the rise of real interest rates permit undertaking investments in high-productivity industries as trade is liberalized; on the other, trade liberalization permits the efficient use of savings generated through higher real interest rates.

NOTES

1. G. Haberler, 'Some Problems in the Pure Theory of International Trade', *Economic Journal*, LX (1950) pp. 223–240.
2. J. N. Bhagwati and V. K. Ramaswani, 'Domestic Distortions, Tariffs, and the Theory of Optimum Subsidy', *Journal of Political Economy*, LXXI (1963) pp. 44–50.

3. H. G. Johnson, 'Optimal Trade Intervention in the Presence of Domestic Distortions', in R. Baldwin *et al.* (eds), *Trade, Growth and the Balance of Payments, Essays* in Honor of Gottfried Haberler (Chicago: Rand McNally, 1965) pp. 3–34.

4. J. N. Bhagwati, 'The Generalized Theory of Distortions and Welfare', in J. Bhagwati, R. Jones, R. Mundell and J. Vanek (eds), *Trade, Balance of Payments and Growth*, Papers in International Economics in Honor of Charles P. Kindleberger (Amsterdam: North-Holland, 1971) pp. 69–90.

5. S. P. Magee, 'Factor Market Distortions, Production and Trade: A Survey', *Oxford Economic Papers*, XXV (1973) pp. 2–3.

6. S. P. Magee, *International Trade and Distortions in Factor Markets* (New York: Marcel Dekker, 1976).

7. The analysis excludes however, aggregate demand effects by postulating that appropriate macroeconomic policies are applied, utilizing the exchange rate, the government budget, and the supply of money as instruments.

8. B. Balassa *et al. The Structure of Protection in Developing Countries* (Baltimore, Maryland: Johns Hopkins University Press, 1971) p. 72 and *Developing Strategies in Semi-Industrial Economies* (Baltimore, Maryland: Johns Hopkins University Press, 1982) Ch. 2.

9. B. Balassa, 'Reforming the System of Incentives in Developing Countries', *World Development*, III (1975) pp. 365–82.

10. World Bank, *Accelerated Development in Sub-Saharan Africa: An Agenda for Action* (Washington, DC, 1981).

11. This is the case for eight of the twelve developing economies studied. Cf. Balassa *et al. The Structure of Protection in Developing Countries*, and *Development Strategies in Semi-Industrial Economies*.

12. B. Balassa, 'Incentive Policies in Brazil', *World Development*, VII (1979) pp. 1023–42. Reprinted in B. Balassa, *The Newly Industrializing Countries in the World Economy* (New York: Pergamon Press, 1981) pp. 231–54.

13. W. Hong, 'Export Promotion and Employment Growth in South Korea', in A. Krueger *et al.* (eds), *Trade and Employment in Developing Countries 1. Individual Studies* (Chicago: University of Chicago Press, 1981) pp. 341–91.

14. R. I. McKinnon, *Money and Capital in Economic Development* (Washington, DC: The Brookings Institution, 1973).

15. E. S. Shaw, *Financial Deepening in Economic Development* (New York: Oxford University Press, 1973).

16. These adverse effects are mitigated if unorganized money markets assume the role of financial intermediation. It has been suggested that, in this event, the results will depend on the extent of substitution between time deposits, on the one hand, and unorganized money markets and 'unproductive' assets, on the other, as well as on bank reserve requirements and limitations imposed on bank lending (S. van Wijnbergen, 'Interest Rate Management in LDCs: Theory and Some Simulation Results For South Korea', *Journal of Monetary Economics*, XII (1983) pp. 433–52). It should be added, however, that informal credit markets tend to be fragmented; in rural areas, lenders often assume monopolistic positions; and transaction costs are increased by legal limitations on such credit.

17. Balassa *et al. Development Strategies in Semi-Industrial Economies*, Ch. 3.

18. Balassa *et al. Development Strategies in Semi-Industrial Economies*, Ch. 3.
19. S. Guisinger, 'Trade Policies and Employment: The Case of Pakistan', in A. O. Krueger *et al.* (eds), *Trade and Employment in Developing Countries 1. Individual Studies* (Chicago: University of Chicago Press, 1981) p. 332.
20. Guisinger, p. 333.
21. M. K. Nabli, 'Alternative Trade Policies and Employment in Tunisia', in Krueger, p. 468.
22. Balassa *et al. Development Strategies in Semi-Industrial Economies*, Ch. 4.
23. T. Monson, 'Trade Strategies and Employment in the Ivory Coast', in Krueger, p. 271.
24. Guisinger, p. 325.
25. Guisinger, p. 334.
26. Guisinger, p. 333.
27. Nabli, p. 468.
28. A. C. Harberger, 'Using the Resources at Hand More Effectively', *American Economic Review Papers and Proceedings*, XLIX (1959) p. 140.
29. Harberger, 'Using the Resources at Hand More Effectively', p. 140.
30. B. Balassa, 'Integración Regional y Asignación de Recursos en America Latina', *Comercio Exterior*, XII (1966) pp. 672–85. Moshe Syrquin pointed out to the author that Harberger has subsequently reconsidered his estimate removing the assumption that there would be some domestic production of each importable good in the absence of restrictions and assuming more realistic tariffs. With these modifications, he estimated the cost of protection at 10–15 percent of GNP in Chile. Cf. A. C. Harberger, *Taxation and Welfare* (Chicago: University of Chicago Press, 1974) p. 107.
31. J. Bergsman, *Brazil's Industrialization and Trade Policies* (London: Oxford University Press, 1970) Appendix 4.
32. Balassa *et al. The Structure of Protection in Developing Countries*, p. 82, Bergsman's revised estimate – derived by the use of the same methodology – was 7.1 percent for Brazil in 1967, following reductions in the extent of protection below the 1966 level. Cf. J. Bergsman, 'Commercial Policy, Allocation Efficiency and "X-Efficiency"'. *Quarterly Journal of Economics*, LXXXVIII (1974) p. 421.
33. A. O. Krueger, 'Some Economic Costs of Exchange Control: The Turkish Case', *Journal of Political Economy*, LXXXIX (1981) pp. 466–80.
34. J. de Melo, 'Estimating the Costs of Protection: A General Equilibrium Approach', *Quarterly Journal of Economics*, CXII (1978) p. 217.
35. De Melo's estimate of effective protection rates compares with an estimate of 35 percent reported in Table 2.1.
36. Balassa *et al. The Structure of Protection in Developing Economies*, p. 82.
37. H. G. Johnson, 'The Cost of Protection and the Scientific Tariff', *Journal of Political Economy*, LXVIII (1960) pp. 327–45.
38. H. G. Johnson, 'Factor Market Distortions and the Shape of the Transformation Curve', *Econometrica*, XXXIV (1966) pp. 686–98. Drawing on Johnson's results, Nugent estimated the cost of protection for a hypothetical country that cannot affect world market prices in a three-commodity general equilibrium model. Under the assumptions that the three commodities are consumed in equal quantities under free trade, that the elasticity of substitution in consumption is 1, and that the elasticity of substitution in

domestic production is 1.5, he found that the cost of protection would rise from 15.6 to 19.6 percent of GNP if importables had tariffs of 30 and 70 percent, rather than a 50 percent tariff on each. The cost of protection would rise further, to 29.8 percent of GNP, if the tariffs on the two importables were 0 and 100 percent, respectively. Cf. J. B. Nugent, *Economic Integration in Central America: Empirical Investigations* (Baltimore, Maryland: Johns Hopkins University Press, 1974) p. 66.

39. Johnson, 'Factor Market Distortions and the Shape of the Transformation Curve', p. 698.

40. C. Dougharty and M. Selowsky, 'Measuring the Effects of the Misallocation of Labor', *Review of Economics and Statistics*, LV (1973) p. 389.

41. J. de Melo, 'Distortions in the Factor Market: Some General Equilibrium Estimates', *Review of Economics and Statistics*, LIX (1977) p. 402.

42. M. Syrquin, 'Efficient Input Frontiers for the Manufacturing Sector in Mexico, 1965–1980', *International Economic Review*, XIV (1973) pp. 657–75.

43. Harberger, 'Using the Resources at Hand More Effectively', p. 138.

44. P. T. Schultz, 'Effective Protection and the Distribution of Personal Income by Sector in Columbia' in A. O. Krueger (ed.), *Trade and Employment in Developing Countries 2. Factor Supply and Substitution* (Chicago: University of Chicago Press, 1982) pp. 83–148.

45. A. C. Harberger, 'The Incidence of the Corporation Income Tax', *Journal of Political Economy*, LXX (1962) pp. 215–40.

46. J. Whalley, 'A Simulation Experiment into Properties of General Equilibrium Models of Factor Market Distortion', *Review of Economics and Statistics*, LIX (1977) p. 200.

47. According to a comprehensive review of savings behavior in developing countries, written a decade ago, 'the explanation of the responsiveness of saving to increases in the real rate of interest may lie in the effects of monetary reform on the level of investment and national income which in turn have a positive effect on saving', R. F. Mikesell and J. E. Zinser, 'The Nature of the Savings Function in Developing Countries'. A Survey of the Theoretical and Empirical Literature', *Journal of Economic Literature*, XI (1973) p. 19.

48. G. T. Brown, *Korean Pricing Policies and Economic Development in the 1960s* (Baltimore, Maryland: Johns Hopkins University Press, 1973) pp. 195–7.

49. M. J. Fry, 'Financial Instruments and Markets', in *Conferencia Internacional Sobre Economia Portuguese* (Lisbon: The German Marshall Fund of the United States and Fundacao Calouste Gulbenkian, 1977) p. 196 and 'The Cost of Financial Repression in Turkey', *Savings and Development*, II (1979) p. 132.

50. M. J. Fry, 'Interest Rates in Asia', mimeo (Honolulu: University of Hawaii, 1981) Table 9.

51. M. J. Fry, 'Savings, Investment, Growth and the Terms of Trade in Asia', Irvine Economic Papers No. 84–7 (1984).

52. International Monetary Fund, *Interest Rate Policies in Developing Countries*, Occasional Paper No. 22 (Washington, DC, 1983).

53. F. E. Berger, 'Thailand: Issues in the Financial Sector', mimeo (Washington, DC: World Bank, 1982).

54. V. Sundararajan and S. Thakur, 'Public Investment Crowding Out, and Growth: A Dynamic Model Applied to India and Korea', *International Monetary Fund Staff Papers*, XXVII (1980) p. 842.

55. According to the authors, 'an increase in interest rates – and hence the rental price of capital – increases the overall efficiency of capital by permitting a shift of resources to more productive sectors and by encouraging more productive use of capital within each sector', Sundararajan and Thakur, pp. 837–39.

56. Fry, 'Interest Rates in Asia', Table 11.

57. Balassa *et al. Development Strategies in Semi-Industrial Countries*, Ch. 3.

58. This result occurred despite the fact that exogenous influences, in the form of the external shocks they suffered, affected outward-oriented economies to a greater extent than inward-oriented economies. Cf. B. Balassa 'Structural Adjustment Policies in Developing Countries', Essay 4 in this volume.

59. Fry, 'Interest Rates in Asia', Table 16.

60. M. J. Fry, 'Money and Capital in Financial Deepening in Economic Development?' *Journal of Money, Credit and Banking*, X (1978) p. 470.

61. Fry, 'Interest Rates in Asia' Table 20.

62. H. G. Johnson, 'The Possibility of Income Losses From Increased Efficiency or Factor Accumulation in the Presence of Tariffs', *Economic Journal*, LXXVII (1967) pp. 151–4.

63. R. Martin, 'Immiserizing Growth for a Tariff-Distorted Small Economy: A Further Analysis', *Journal of International Economics*, VII (1977) pp. 323–8.

64. Balassa *et al.*, *Development Strategies in Semi-Industrial Countries*, pp. 52–5.

65. G. Feder, 'On Exports and Economic Growth', *Journal of Developmental Economics*, Vol. XII (1983) pp. 59–73.

66. B. Balassa, 'Structural Adjustment Policies in Developing Economies', Essay 4 in this volume.

67. J. de Melo, 'A Multi-Sector, Price Endogenous Trade Model Applied in Columbia', Ph.D thesis (Baltimore, Maryland: Johns Hopkins University, 1976) Chapter 8.

68. M. S. Boskin, 'Taxation, Savings and the Rate of Interest', *Journal of Political Economy*, LXXXVI (1978) p. 519.

69. L. H. Summers, 'Capital Taxation and Assumulation in a Life Cycle Growth Model', *American Economic Review*, LXXI (1981) p. 542.

Essay 3 The Economic Consequences of Social Policies in the Industrial Countries

INTRODUCTION

This essay will examine the economic consequences of the social policies applied in the industrial countries, with the exception of Japan, which has an institutional structure very much different from that of the other industrial countries. Correspondingly, the essay will concentrate on US–European comparisons.

With the European Common Market accounting for four-fifths of the combined gross domestic product of the countries of Western Europe and economic trends being very similar in the two cases, reliance will be placed on the more easily available data for the EEC. Furthermore, in cases when there are no data for the entire EEC, reference will be made to the experience of the four major European countries, France, Germany, Italy, and the United Kingdom, which account for two-thirds of the GDP of Western Europe (Europe, for short).[1] Thus, the essay excludes from its purview the case of the small Scandinavian countries, although some of them, such as Sweden, carried out instructive social welfare experiments.

The essay will begin by a review of trends in the gross domestic product, industrial production, employment, and unemployment in the industrial countries during the period preceding and following the quadrupling of oil prices in 1973 (Section I). Next, different facets of social policies will be considered that may have contributed to the observed developments. This will be done by examining factors that bear on the demand for labor (Section II) and the supply of labor (Section III). Finally, possible future policy changes will be briefly noted.

I MACROECONOMIC DEVELOPMENTS

In recent years, various commentators in the United States have decried the poor performance of the American economy, attributing this variously to the lack of an industrial policy, the slowdown of technological change, and union action. A comparison of US and European economic trends puts the American economy in a more favorable light, however.

To begin with, while the United States had a lower rate of economic growth than the major EEC countries other than the United Kingdom in the 1960–73 period, it has surpassed all of them in 1973–84. This has occurred as the United States has experienced a smaller decline in GDP growth rates (from 4.0 percent to 2.2 percent in 1973–84) than the Common Market countries (from 4.6 percent to 1.7 per cent, on the average).

The differences in the observed trends are even greater in regard to industrial production. In the 1960–73 period, the United States and the Common Market countries had practically the same growth rate of industrial production, slightly in excess of 5 percent a year. In turn, between 1973 and 1984, industrial production is estimated to have risen at an average annual rate of 1.8 percent in the United States while in the EEC the results range from an increase of 1.3 percent a year in Italy to a decline of 0.4 percent a year in the United Kingdom, with an overall average increase of 0.7 percent a year.

These data are of especial interest since trends in industrial production have been in the center of the discussion in recent years. At the same time, the differences in the observed results for the gross domestic product and for industrial production have been influenced by the expansion of the public sector that has been especially rapid in the EEC countries. Correspondingly, the advantage of the United States over the European Common Market is greater if we consider private, rather than total, GDP. And, to the extent that the expansion of the public sector has entailed greater bureaucratization, trends in private GDP offer an interest from the welfare point of view.

Unemployment rates provide another indicator of economic welfare.

In 1973, unemployment rates averaged 3.0 percent in the European Common Market, falling considerably short of the 4.8 percent rate of unemployment in the United States. By 1983, however, the EEC average (10.0 percent) surpassed the US figure (9.5 percent). Moreover, with the continued expansion of its economy, unemployment rates are expected to decline to 8.0 per cent in 1984 in the United States while they would average 10.5 percent in the Common Market, with each of the major EEC countries having substantially higher unemployment rates than the United States.

Nor can differential trends in unemployment be explained by differences in the growth of the labor force. In fact, the US labor force has increased much more rapidly than that of the EEC countries. Correspondingly, total employment has grown by over one-fifth in the United States between 1973 and 1984 while it has declined slightly in the Common Market taken as a whole, as well as in the four major EEC countries taken individually, the only exception being Italy.

At the same time, the United States has maintained industrial employment unchanged during the period under consideration and it has increased service employment by about one-third. By contrast, industrial employment has declined by one-eighth in the European Common Market and gains in service employment have been small, even though public sector employment has increased more rapidly in the EEC countries than in the United States.

II SOCIAL EXPENDITURES, REAL WAGE RIGIDITY, AND THE DEMAND FOR LABOR

The quadrupling of oil prices was an important factor contributing to the slowdown of economic growth in the industrial countries after 1973. This occurred as the resulting deterioration of the terms of trade reduced the availability of resources for domestic expenditures. With greater reliance on oil imports, the losses associated with higher import prices were greater in Western Europe (2–3 percent of GNP) than in the United States (less than 1 percent of GNP).

While the deterioration of the terms of trade would have required reductions in domestic expenditures, social spending increased to a considerable extent in European countries after 1973, exceeding increases in the United States by a substantial margin. Differential trends in social spending were, in turn, largely responsible for the observed inter-country differences in the growth of public expenditures.

The share of public expenditures in the gross domestic product rose from 40 percent in 1973 to 51 percent in 1982 in the European Common Market whereas the increase was only from 31 percent to 35 percent in the United States. Apart from the slowdown in the United Kingdom after the election of Margaret Thatcher, parallel developments are observed for this period in all the major EEC countries, with the ratio of public expenditures to GDP rising from 38 to 52 percent in France, from 40 to 50 percent in Germany, from 38 to 55 percent in Italy, and from 41 to 46 percent in the United Kingdom.[2]

Increases in social spending were associated with the rise in social security benefits and unemployment compensation. To the extent that wage earners consider these benefits as part of their income, they will accept commensurate reductions in wages and salaries. This does not appear to have been the case in the European Common Market, however.

In fact, the rise of real wages is estimated to have been 10 percent greater than that of GDP per worker in the EEC during the decade following the quadrupling of oil prices.[3] A change of equal magnitude but in the opposite direction occurred in the United States, where a 5 percent increase in GDP per worker in the non-agricultural private sector was accompanied by a 5 percent decline in real wages.[4]

The observed developments in the European Common Market reflect continued pressures for higher real wages, with formal and informal indexation providing the floor for increases in nominal wages. Rather than resisting this pressure, the governments of the EEC countries on the whole contributed to it by adopting indexation arrangements, rising public wages and statutory minimum wages in excess of the rate of inflation, and often siding with the unions in conflicts over wages.

In turn, apart from industries such as automobile and steel where strong labor unions faced accommodating oligopolies, wage determination in the United States generally responded to market forces. Correspondingly, declines in real wages occurred in response to the 1973–74 and 1979–80 increases in oil prices and the ensuing recessions.

The differential behavior of real wages and differential changes in social charges paid by employers, that financed part of the growth of social spending, are apparent in trends in unit labor costs. Taking the United States as the benchmark, the ratio of unit labor costs in manufacturing to industrial prices is estimated to have increased by 40 percent in France, 30 percent in the United Kingdom, 15 percent in Germany, and 12 percent in Italy between 1973 and 1983.

For the European Common Market, taken as a whole, preliminary calculations by the EEC Commission show labor costs to have increased at an average annual rate of 2.1 percent in real terms during the decade following the quadrupling of oil prices while the corresponding figure for the United States was 0.5 percent. Adjusting for labor quality and introducing data on the rate of return to capital, the relative price of labor to capital is estimated to have risen by 2.4 percent a year in the Common Market, with a decline of 0.6 per cent occurring in the United States.

In a seminal paper, Edmond Malinvaud has examined the effects of changes in the relative prices of labor and capital on unemployment. He has shown that a high real wage rate relative to the price of capital leads to high capital intensity and low labor requirements. In its effect on employment, this negative substitution effect will outweigh the favorable impact of higher wages on aggregate demand (the demand effect) as long as the long term elasticity of substitution is greater than labor's income share, which Malinvaud considers to be the likely outcome.[5] This conclusion is strengthened if we admit the possibility that profits are spent, which is excluded by assumption in Malinvaud's model. Moreover, as noted below, the redistribution of incomes from profits to wages will have adverse long-term effects on employment by reducing the amount invested.

Evidence on the substitution between capital and labor is provided by the preliminary estimates of the EEC Commission for the decade following the quadrupling of oil prices. According to these estimates, increases in capital intensity led to a decline in the productivity of capital at a rate of about 1 percent a year in the European Common Market while it remained approximately unchanged in the United States. There is further evidence on the effects of real wage rigidity on unemployment. The extent of real wage rigidity is indicated by comparisons of trends in actual wages and in feasible wages, when feasible wages are determined by changes in labor productivity and in import prices relative to domestic prices.

In examining changes between the 1960–72 and 1973–80 periods, it has been found that raising wages above their feasible level by one percentage point leads to an increase in the rate of unemployment by 0.5 percentage points in the industrial countries and that inter-country differences in wage rigidity explain a substantial part of the observed variations in changes in unemployment rates among the countries concerned.[6] Thus, greater wage rigidity in the face of a larger than average decline in the rate of growth of the feasible wage, associated with above-average increases in the prices of imports and decreases in productivity growth, contributed to a greater increase in unemployment rates in the European Common Market than in the United States.

Empirical estimates for individual countries also support the neoclassical paradigm. There is evidence that increases in real wages adversely affected employment in the major European countries during the 1961–81 period.[7] It has further been shown that, in German manufacturing, the unfavorable effects of wage increases on employment were much stronger after 1970 than beforehand.[8]

One may conclude that differences in policy responses to external shocks have importantly contributed to differential trends in employment and unemployment in Western Europe and in the United States. At the same time, the policies applied have led to declines in profit rates in Western Europe to an extent much exceeding the changes that have occurred in the United States.

To begin with, the after-tax rate of return on inflation-adjusted capital in private non-financial enterprises fell from 8 percent in 1973 to 2 percent in 1982 in France and increases in profits in 1983 and 1984 may not have raised this ratio above 3 percent.[9] Also, the average after-tax profit rate in the production activities of the private sector decreased from 8 percent in 1973 to 4 percent in 1983 in Germany, with little change occurring in 1984.[10] In turn, after moving in the 12 to 16 percent range between 1973 and 1981, the after-tax rate of profit in the US manufacturing sector declined to 9 percent in 1982, but it increased again to 11 percent in 1983 and it is expected to reach the 1973 level of 14 percent in 1984.[11]

Recent increases in profit rates have contributed to the rise of business investment in the United States, thus leading to the creation of new employment. Following declines in the early eighties, gross domestic investment is estimated to have regained its 1973 share in the gross domestic product in 1984. In turn, investment shares declined more or less continuously in the decade following the quadrupling of oil prices in Western Europe and little, if any, reversal appears to have occurred in 1984.

Lower investment shares, associated with the decline in profit rates, have had adverse effects on employment in European countries that have been reinforced by the capital-intensive nature of investment, associated with the rise in labor costs. Thus, statements made a few years ago in regard to the United Kingdom may find general application to Western Europe: 'The problem for economic policy at the present time is that profits, which initially bore the main burden of adjustment to higher raw natural and energy prices, have not recovered sufficiently to induce the rise in investment which is necessary in the long run to sustain demand and employment'.[12]

III LABOR LEGISLATION, TAXATION AND THE SUPPLY OF LABOR

It appears, then, that increases in the cost of labor have adverse effects on employment through the substitution of capital for labor and through reductions in investment owing to decreases in profits. These adverse consequences will obtain, irrespective of whether increases in the cost of labor are due to higher social charges or the actual wage exceeding the feasible wage.

The next question concerns the effects of government regulations on the supply of labor. For one thing, unemployment compensation and regulations aimed at ensuring job security may increase the rate of unemployment. For another, regulations on social benefits and the taxation of labor incomes may lower labor force participation rates.

It stands to reason that an individual's reservation wage, at which he will accept the job, will rise with the rate of unemployment compensation. In recent years, there have been estimates of the replacement ratio, defined as the ratio of after-tax unemployment compensation to after-tax income from work, and the relationship between the replacement ratio and the rate of unemployment.

Unemployment compensation has long been high in the United Kingdom, which fact may explain the large amount of empirical research devoted to estimating replacement ratios and their effect on unemployment. A careful study of replacement ratios, based on the annual Family Expenditure Survey, has provided estimates of average and marginal replacement ratios; the former indicates the incentive to accept unemployment of a certain duration rather than to take a job while the latter indicates the incentive to decline a job after a certain number of weeks of unemployment.

Adjusted for changes in the age composition of population, the results for 1968 show an average replacement ratio of 0.87 for a 13 week period and a marginal replacement ratio of 0.54 after 52 weeks of unemployment. The two ratios were 0.76 and 0.50, respectively, in 1975; they declined, following reductions in unemployment benefits, to 0.60 and to 0.50 in 1983.[13] The calculations are based on the discounted value of after-tax unemployment benefits and wages; no adjustment is made for work expenses, such as the cost of travel, clothing, and additional calorific intake.

The high replacement ratios observed until the late seventies underlie the concerns expressed as to their unfavorable effects on voluntary unemployment in the United Kingdom. At the same time, the UK is not alone among European countries in providing high unemployment benefits. In fact, unemployment compensation was increased to a considerable extent in France and Germany after 1973.

Before 1973, France provided unemployment compensation at 40 percent of the gross (pre-tax) wage for three months and at 35 percent of the gross wage for another three months. In 1974, both the rate and the duration of unemployment compensation was increased to a considerable extent. In cases when labor was discharged for economic reasons, the rate of compensation was set at 90 percent of the gross wage for a period of one year, with the rate of payment maintained for a second year to those who followed a program of course work in an accepted educational institution.

In Germany, the rate of unemployment compensation was raised from 63 percent to 68 percent of the net (after-tax) wage after 1973 for a period of one year, with compensation remaining at 58 percent of the net wage thereafter. At the same time, unemployment compensation is not taxable in Germany while it is taxable in France. And although the rate and duration of unemployment compensation have been reduced recently, they remain much above the 1973 level in both countries.

Estimates of the effects of unemployment compensation on the rate of unemployment in the United Kingdom vary to a considerable extent. Patrick Minford finds that the long-term elasticity of employment to the replacement ratio is 4.75; according to S. J. Nickell this elasticity is 1.4.[14] Minford has also made estimates for several European countries; the results obtained for Belgium and Germany are similar to those for the United Kingdom while the elasticity of unemployment to the replacement ratio is lower in France and in Italy.[15]

In the United States, unemployment benefits are considerably smaller, and they are limited to 39 weeks. As a result, the ratio of total unemployment compensation to the gross domestic product is substantially lower in the US than in Western Europe. In 1981, this ratio was 0.5 percent in the United States, 1.4 percent in Germany and the United Kingdom, and 1.9 percent in France.

Studies in the United States have concentrated on the effects of unemployment benefits on the duration of unemployment. Recent estimates show that increases in unemployment compensation of $10 per week are associated with an increase of three quarters of a week in the average length of unemployment.[16] Estimates for the United States also indicate that the system of unemployment compensation, paid in part by the government, contributes to temporary layoffs.[17] One may expect a similar situation to obtain in European countries where, the United Kingdom excepted, the government shares in the financing of unemployment compensation in the event of temporary layoffs.

The conclusion emerges that greater unemployment benefits and their longer duration have contributed to the higher rate of unemployment in Western Europe compared to the United States (In Germany a humorous reference is made to the 'Arbeitgeberabschreckungsanzug', a special suit to put off potential employers so as to remain on the unemployment rolls.)

The differences are even greater in regard to job security. While in the United States the employer can hire and fire labor practically at will, in European countries limitations apply to dismissing individual workers 'for cause' as well as to discharging labor for economic reasons. At the same time, these regulations have been strengthened since 1973.

In Italy it has been said that since the new divorce law, it is more difficult for the employer to separate himself from a worker than from his wife. In fact, a complicated legal procedure needs to be followed, and the authorities have given a restrictive interpretation of what is considered 'just cause' which the employer has to show for dismissing a worker. The situation is similar in Germany and in the United Kingdom while the threat of strikes is the principal constraint to dismissing individual workers in France.

In turn, a procedure of consultation with labor representatives is prescribed in France, followed by a decision of the Labor Inspectorate, in the event that the employer wishes to discharge labor for economic reasons. This process takes time, especially since the decision can be subject to appeal to the Ministry of Employment. And, following the election of the socialist government, there has been a tendency on the part of the authorities to postpone dismissals and to reduce their number as far as large firms are concerned. A case in point is Peugeot-Citroen that is apparently unable to discontinue uneconomic operations. Furthermore, although agreement has been reached on reducing the number of workers in the steel industry, this will be largely accomplished through attrition.

Consultation with labor representatives is also necessary in the other major European countries, with collective dismissal for economic reasons requiring authorization by the Federal Institute of Labor in Germany and by the Ministry of Labor in Italy whereas such authorization is no longer in the United Kingdom. At the same time, in all major European countries there are regulations under which workers with greatest seniority have to be retained, and – often onerous – redundancy payments have to be made to dismissed workers.

The effects of these regulations have been well described by Laidler:

> They discourage workers from quitting voluntarily to search for other employment. They make it expensive for an otherwise viable firm to close down a particular loss-making operation, thus perpetuating the existence of particular plants which consume more in the way of resources than they produce in output, and making it privately profitable for firms to inflict losses on society as a whole. Moreover, they inhibit employers from taking on new workers because of the prospective cost of declaring them redundant at some time in the future. Such schemes inhibit resource mobility, slow down the pace of economic change, and increase unemployment. They do not serve simply to redistribute wealth, but to reduce the total amount of wealth available for redistribution.[18]

Limitations on firing, redundancy payments, and seniority rights thus reduce labor mobility, and perpetuate the existence of inefficient plants. As Assar Lindbeck has noted:

> These effects have been accentuated by the tendency of politicians in some countries, mainly in North West Europe, to re-define full-employment: the full-employment target has increasingly been disaggregated into employment guarantees for specific regions, industries and firms, which forces the government to engage in strongly selective subsidies.[19]

Correspondingly, rigidities develop in the industrial structure, and the adjustment of firms to new situations is compromised. Such appears to have been the case in Western Europe, where adjustments to external shocks have been rather limited. By contrast, American firms have made vigorous adjustment efforts, leading to reductions in their break-even point. Chrysler, for example, now starts making a profit at one-half of the volume of output than a few years ago.

The process of adjustment has also involved the creation of new activities in the United States, leading to increases in employment and lower unemployment rates. In turn, the regulations applied in Western Europe have contributed to unemployment as firms are reluctant to hire labor that has increasingly become a fixed cost.

The implications of the limitations imposed on firing labor in Western Europe have been analysed by Paul Krugman who has estimated the real wage gap, defined as the extent to which real wages would have to fall to eliminate the disequilibrium between the firms' actual and desired labor force in France. His estimate is 14.6 percent for 1980, with an additional 1.6 percent wage cut required to restore full employment.[20] Krugman's estimate is based on changes in labor's share in GNP and it may exaggerate the real wage gap. At the same time, in the framework of an econometric model, Nickell has shown that the increased difficulties involved in firing labor have significantly contributed to unemployment in the United Kingdom.[21]

While unemployment compensation and regulations that limit the firing of labor have added to unemployment, the provision of certain social benefits and the taxation of labor income tend to reduce the number of labor hours and labor force participation rates. Among social benefits, sick leave and pension schemes are relevant in this context. Labor hours are affected more directly by legislation on the length of the workweek.

In the United States, there are no legal requirements for the payment of sick leave that is handled by private insurance, the cost of which may be shared by employers and employees. On the other hand in European countries sick leave is regulated by the government, and payments are generally made in the framework of the social security system. Correspondingly, in 1981, sickness cash benefits paid from social security funds equalled 0.1 percent of gross domestic product in the United States while accounting for 0.4 percent of GDP in the United Kingdom, 0.7 percent in Germany, and 1.2 percent in France.

At the same time, absences due to sick leave do not exceed 3 percent of potential labor hours in the United States whereas the ratio is 7 percent in Germany, having increased substantially as the benefits have been extended to blue-collar workers. It has also been observed that in Germany 70 percent of sick leave falls on a Friday or a Monday and only 4 percent on a Wednesday.[22] There is further evidence of fraud in Italy and the United Kingdom but, under existing regulations on labor dismissal, the employers find it.difficult to discipline the offenders. Finally, among the smaller European countries, sick leave accounts for 10 percent of potential working hours in the Netherlands and sickness cash benefits equal 1.9 percent of GDP. The Netherlands also leads in terms of the number of people with permanent handicap pensions: 12 percent of the labor force in 1978.[23]

In 1981, Germany (12.5) and France (11.1 percent) were not much behind the Netherlands (13.0 percent) in terms of the ratio of government-financed pension benefits to the gross domestic product. The corresponding ratio was 7.4 percent in the United States and the United Kingdom, where benefits were reduced following the election of the government of Margaret Thatcher.[24]

The differences in the cost of pensions will increase in the future, as the compulsory retirement age has been raised to 70 years in the United States while it has been reduced in most European countries. Also, incentives have been provided for early retirement, in particular in France and Germany. Finally, public employees may retire after twenty-five years of service with full pension in Italy.

Early retirement is encouraged in Western Europe on the grounds that it lowers unemployment; in fact, the replacement of early retirees is often a condition for the government sharing in the cost involved. This effect will operate only in the short run, however; over time the shortening of the working life will reduce potential output, and hence the demand for labor in the economy. In fact, with rising life expectancy, the burden on those working has been increasing rapidly in all industrial countries, and especially in Western Europe. At the same time, as long as part of the burden of early retirement is borne by the firm, labor costs will rise, with adverse effects on international competitiveness and on profits.

Reductions in working hours have also been rationalized on the ground that unemployment will decline as a result. The recent experience of France, involving a reduction from 40 to 39 hours a week in January 1982, shows little gains, however. Thus, increases in the permanent work force to replace lost hours is estimated to have added 0.2 to 0.4 percent to total employment, compensating for only 8 to 16 percent of the reductions in working hours. As workers have received full compensation through a 2.5 percent increase in hourly wages while output has declined in the majority of cases, the result has been an increase in labor costs for the firm.[25]

In 1981, the newly-elected socialist government in France declared its intention to reduce the workweek to 35 hours by 1985. While further reductions since January 1982 have not been made, there is again pressure from labor unions to move in this direction. In Germany, Willy Brandt, the Chairman of the opposition Social Democratic party has endorsed the demand of the metalworkers union – backed by strike

– to reduce the workweek to 35 hours without a cut in pay. At the same time, a report by the EEC Commission reportedly postulated that a general reduction in working time would greatly lower unemployment.[26]

Reductions in working hours, uncompensated by increases in hourly wages, would indeed reduce unemployment in the short run. However, labor unions in the EEC countries demand compensating wage increases, leading to a deterioration of international competitiveness and to declines in profit margins. The final outcome, then, will be negative as lower production and investment reduce the demand for labor.

In fact, the experience of the United States indicates that longer hours and higher employment may go hand-in-hand; thus, the length of the workweek in US manufacturing has reached a post-war peak while employment has been rising rapidly. Also, in Switzerland, the workweek in relatively long and unemployment rates are low.

The next question concerns the effects of labor taxation on the supply of labor. It has been traditionally assumed that these effects are indeterminate: while the supply of labor will decrease as leisure is substituted for other goods, reductions in their incomes will induce people to work more. However, to the extent that the tax revenue is used to supply public and even private (e.g. education) goods, and people consider these goods as part of their income, there is also a negative income effect on the labor supply which may compensate for the positive income effect of higher taxes, so that the net effect of taxation on the labor supply will be negative.

For the United States, it has been estimated that in 1975 the progressivity of the tax structure reduced the labor supply of husbands by 8 percent and that of wives by 30 percent. At the same time, the marginal cost of raising an additional dollar of tax revenue has been estimated to equal approximately 40 cents.[27] In this connection, it should be emphasized that progressive taxation would involve a welfare cost even if it did not lead to a reduction in the labor supply, owing to the deterioration in the efficiency of resource allocation it entails.

More recently, it has been estimated that in 1976 an increase of incomes in the lowest quintile of the distribution by one dollar involved a welfare loss of three-and-a-half dollars in the upper three quintiles in the United States, even though .the assumed labor supply elasticities were lower than in the previous case.[28] This estimate exceeds by several times the welfare cost of income redistribution assumed by earlier writers, but it may nevertheless understate this cost as the effects of progressive taxation on entrepreneurship could not be taken into account.

Since 1980, tax rates have been reduced by 23 percent in the United States. By contrast, tax rates have been raised in France as well as in Germany, so that the top marginal tax rates in three countries now exceed those in the United States. Despite recent reductions, this remains to be the case in the United Kingdom.

CONCLUSIONS

We have seen that, since 1973, the economic performance of the United States has been superior to that of the major European countries while the opposite had been the case in the preceding period. Thus, higher rates of growth of GDP and industrial production have been reached in the United States and total employment has increased, with unemployment rates declining in recent years, compared with stagnant employment and rising unemployment in Western Europe.

Policies that affect the demand for, and the supply of, labor have contributed to the poor performance of European countries as far as employment is concerned. For one thing, increases in real wages and social charges have led to the substitution of capital for labor, and the decline in profits attendant on risin₂ labor costs have had adverse effects on employment through lower investment. For another thing, high rates of unemployment compensation have engendered voluntary unemployment, and social measures together with progressive taxation have tended to reduce the supply of labor. At the same time, the adverse effects of these policies on economic efficiency may compromise future growth.

These considerations should not disguise the fact that there are distortions in labor markets in the United States as well. But such distortions are of much lesser importance than in Western Europe, and changes made since 1980 have facilitated the process of adjustment. Correspondingly, US industries have increasingly rationalized their operations. This has in turn contributed to their recent expansion and offers gains for the future.

One should further emphasize the unintended effects of social policies in Western Europe. In raising wages and social charges in the face of external shocks, the adverse consequences of these actions on international competitiveness and profits – and hence ultimately on employment and economic growth – have been largely disregarded.

Nor has there been sufficient recognition of the effects of high unemployment compensation on voluntary unemployment, or the impact of the regulations limiting the firing of labor on employment and on structural change. Also, the proponents of early retirement and reductions in working hours consider the short-term effects of these schemes to the neglect of their long-term consequences. Finally, the impact of the increasingly progressive tax system on the supply of labor and on efficiency has not been evaluated.

These considerations indicate the need to review the welter of policies that affect employment, efficiency, and, eventually, economic growth. As Herbert Giersch has noted, in European countries 'real wages will have to lag behind the growth of distributable output for manhour.'[29] There is further need to modify existing regulations, so as to encourage structural change and reduce the burden of social legislation on the working population. Finally, the progressivity of the system of income taxes would need to be reconsidered.

In the United States, steps have been taken in these directions in recent years. Nevertheless, more needs to be done to reduce the cost of social measures; to rationalize the existing social institutions such as Medicare, and to reform the tax system. Suggestions made for a flat rate of taxation above the poverty level, preferably on consumption rather than income, are particularly promising.

NOTES

1. Unless otherwise noted, the data derive from OECD statistics.
2. M. Albert and R. J. Ball, *Towards European Economic Recovery in the 1980s*, Report presented to the European Parliament, European Parliament Working Document 1983–84 (Brussels, 1983) Table 2.
3. Albert and Ball, Table 1.
4. *Economic Report of the President*, 1984 (Washington, 1984) Tables B–3, 9, 37, and 39.
5. E. Malinvaud, 'Wages and Unemployment', *Economic Journal*, XCII (1982), p. 7.
6. D. Grubb, R. Jackman and R. Layard, 'Wage Rigidity and Unemployment in OECD countries', *European Economic Review*, XXI (1983) pp. 11–39.
7. J. D. Sachs, 'Real Wages and Unemployment in the OECD Countries', *Brookings Papers on Economic Activity* (1983) Table 5.
8. G. Kirkpatrick, 'Real Factor Prices and German Manufacturing Employment: A Time Series Analysis, 1961 I–1979 IV', *Weltwirtschaftliches Archiv*, CXVIII (1982) Table 3.
9. E. Malinvaud, *Essais sur la théorie du chomage* (Paris, 1983) Table 1.

10. H. Dicke and P. Trapp, 'Zinsen, Gewinne, Nettoinvestitionen', Institute of World Economics, Kiel Discussion Papers, No. 99 (1984) Annex Table.
11. *Economic Report of the President*, 1984, Table B-86.
12. G. W. Maynard, 'Keynes and Unemployment Today', *The Three Banks Review* (1978) p. 20.
13. A. W. Dilnot and C. N. Morris, 'Private Costs and Benefits of Unemployment: Measuring Replacement Rates', *Oxford Economic Papers*, XXXV (1983) p. 332.
14. P. Minford, *Unemployment – Cause and Cure* (Oxford: Martin Robertson & Co., 1983), p. 92, S. J. Nickell, 'The Determinants of Equilibrium Unemployment in Britain', *Economic Journal*, XCII (1982) p. 565.
15. Minford, Part III.
16. G. Solon, 'Work Incentive Effects of Taxing Unemployment Benefits', National Bureau of Economic Research, Working Paper, No. 1260 (1984) p. 17.
17. R. H. Topel, 'On Layoffs and Unemployment Insurance', *American Economic Review*, LXXIII (1983) pp. 541–53.
18. D. Laidler, 'Entrepreneurship and Labor Market Mobility', in *Growth and Entrepreneurship: Opportunities and Challenges in a Changing World* (Paris: International Chamber of Commerce, 1981) p. 81.
19. A. Lindbeck, 'Emerging Arteriosclerosis of the Western Economies: Consequences for the Less Developed Countries', *India International Centre Quarterly* (1982) p. 43.
20. P. Krugman, 'The Real Wage Gap and Unemployment', *Annales de l'INSEE*, (1982) p. 67.
21. S. J. Nickell, 'The Determinants of Equilibrium Unemployment in Britain', *Economic Journal*, XCII (1982) p. 568.
22. J. Donges and D. Spinanger, 'Interventions in Labour Markets: An Overview', Institute of World Economics, Kiel Working Papers, No. 175 (1983) p. 18.
23. A. Maddison, 'Origins and Impact of the Welfare State, 1883–1983', *Banca Nacionale del Lavoro, Quarterly Review* (1984) p. 82.
24. The possible adverse economic effects of pension benefits provided in the framework of tax-financed social security schemes are considered in my 'Prices, Incentives, and Economic Growth', Essay 1 in this volume.
25. O. Marchand, D. Rault and E. Turpin, 'Des 40 heures aux 39 heures: processes et réactions des enterprises', *Economie et Statistiques*, No. 154 (1983) pp. 2–15.
26. The *Wall Street Journal*, May 14, 1984.
27. J. Hausman, 'Income and Payroll Tax Policy and Labor Supply', in L. H. Meyer (ed.), *The Supply-Side Effects of Economic Policy*, Proceedings of the 1980 Economic Policy Conference, Federal Reserve Bank of St Louis (1981) p. 175.
28. E. K. Browning and W. R. Johnson, 'The Trade-Off between Equality and Efficiency', *Journal of Politicial Economy* XCII (1984) p. 199.
29. H. Giersch, 'Prospects for the World Economy', *Skandinaviska Enskilda Banken, Quarterly Review* (1982) p. 107.

Part II
Policy Responses to
External Shocks

Essay 4 Structural Adjustment Policies in Developing Economies

INTRODUCTION

Structural adjustment policies may be defined as policy responses to external shocks, carried out with the objective of regaining the pre-shock growth path of the national economy. Regaining the growth path, in turn, will necessitate improvements in the balance of payments following the adverse effects of external shocks, since a country's balance-of-payments position constrains its economic growth.

The above definition reflects the importance of external shocks which developing economies have experienced since 1973. In the 1974–8 period, the experience of which is considered in the present essay, these shocks included the quadrupling of oil prices in 1973–4 and the world recession of 1974–5.

A broader definition will also include adjustments to internal shocks which may find their origin in inappropriate policies, such as the excessively expansionary fiscal measures taken in Mexico after 1972, or in political events, such as the April 1974 revolution in Portugal. Like external shocks, internal shocks adversely affect economic growth and the balance of payments, requiring the application of structural adjustment policies.

The expression 'structural' in the definition reflects the need for discrete, as compared to marginal, changes in policies in response to discrete shocks. Responding to these shocks will also necessitate a re-ordering of priorities as well as a reconsideration of policy instruments.

To begin with, growth objectives will need to be given greater weight as compared to income distributional objectives. This is because the shocks suffered impose limitations on the ability of the government to pursue several objectives simultaneously, and economic growth is necessary to provide the wherewithal for the alleviation of poverty that may be regarded as the appropriate income distributional objective.

The objective of regaining the pre-shock growth path also means that policies to alleviate poverty should give emphasis to measures that raise the productivity of the poor rather than increase consumption through the provision of public services or government subsidies. More generally, investment should be given priority over consumption, as raising the share of investment in GNP will reduce the time needed to regain the growth path.

The time horizon of structural adjustment policies will depend on the particular case; it may generally be set at 4–5 years. This will permit avoidance of abrupt changes which have a considerable human cost and give rise to disruptions in production, without however unduly extending the period of adjustment. The application of a gradual approach can be facilitated by foreign borrowing, provided that the proceeds of foreign loans are used in self-liquidating investments.

The general considerations described here may be applied in a variety of ways, depending on the circumstances of the situation in the particular case. But, in every case, the objective of regaining the growth path will be served by devising a policy package. The principal elements of such a package include production incentives, incentives to save and to invest, public investments, sectoral policies (in particular, energy and agriculture), budgetary and monetary policies, as well as foreign borrowing.

These elements of a policy package derive from the arsenal of development policies. They require modifications, however, in response to the character of the external or internal shocks. At the same time, external shocks increase the urgency of policy reforms, and may provide the opportunity to carry out overdue reforms as was the case in Chile and Uruguay after 1973.

This essay will consider the principal elements of a policy package for the case prevalent in developing economies where optimal policies have not been applied. Thus, the recommendations made in the essay aim simultaneously at responding to external (or internal) shocks and undertaking policy reforms. At the same time, the essay will not concern itself with the ways and means of remedying market distortions.

Section I will examine the policy experience of 28 developing economies following the quadrupling of oil prices and the world recession. While this group also includes four countries that experienced favorable external shocks, policy measures appropriate for such countries will not subsequently be considered in this essay. Nor will this essay concern itself with the case of countries in long-term economic decline, although the proposed policy reforms may find application in these cases, too.

The subsequent sections of this essay will consider possible reforms in production incentives (Section II), incentives to save and to invest (Section III), and public investments, sectoral policies (energy and agriculture), and budgetary and monetary policies (Section IV). In the conclusion, the interdependence of the various policy measures will be indicated, with further attention given to foreign borrowing. Also, comments will be offered on the international environment in which these policies operate.

I THE POLICY EXPERIENCE OF DEVELOPING ECONOMIES AFTER 1973

External shocks and policy responses to external shocks

The author has estimated the balance-of-payments effects of external shocks, in the form of the deterioration of the terms of trade and the slowdown in world demand after 1973, in 28 developing economies. He has further analyzed policy responses to external shocks in these economies and estimated the balance-of-payments effects of the policies applied, including additional net external financing, export promotion, import substitution, and (temporarily) reducing the rate of economic growth.[1]

Among the 28 developing economies, 12 belong to the newly-industrializing group, defined to include economies that had *per capita* incomes in excess of $1100 in 1978 and where the share of the manufacturing sector in the gross domestic product was 20 percent or higher in 1977. The investigation covers all newly-industrializing economies other than Greece, Hong Kong, and Spain.

All the newly-industrializing economies experienced adverse external shocks during the 1974–8 period but they differed in terms of the policies applied. The three Far Eastern economies – Korea, Singapore, and Taiwan – had adopted an outward-oriented development strategy, providing similar incentives to sales in domestic and in foreign markets, in the early 1960s and continued with this strategy after 1973. They were joined by Chile and Uruguay which had earlier applied an inward-oriented strategy, entailing the high production of domestic markets and a bias against exports, but turned outward following the external shocks of 1974. In turn, after earlier efforts to reduce the bias of the incentive system against exports, Brazil, Israel, Portugal and Yugoslavia again increased the degree of inward orientation while Argentina, Mexico, and Turkey maintained their relatively inward-oriented stance. At the same time, in three of the newly industrializing economies internal shocks predominated; they took the form of excessively expansionary policies in Argentina and Mexico and reflected the economic effects of the April 1974 revolution in Portugal.

Estimates have further been made for 12 less developed economies, covering the spectrum between newly-industrializing and least developed economies, which experienced adverse external shocks after 1973. Four of them – Kenya, Mauritius, Thailand, and Tunisia – may be characterized as having applied relatively outward-oriented policies, while the remaining eight followed an inward-oriented development strategy. Within the latter group, Jamaica, Peru, and Tanzania experienced internal shocks in the form of economic disruptions resulting from government policies; such was not the case in the other five members of the group, Egypt, India, Morocco, the Philippines and Zambia.

Finally, 4 of the 28 developing economies studied enjoyed favorable external shocks during the 1974–8 period. In these cases, improvements in the terms of trade due to the rise in the price of petroleum (Indonesia and Nigeria), coffee (Colombia), cocoa and coffee (the Ivory Coast) exceeded the adverse export volume effects due to the slowdown in world demand.

Outward- v. inward-oriented development strategies

The findings of the investigation point to the advantages of outward-oriented policies for export performance and for economic growth in the face of external shocks. To begin with, outward-oriented developing economies experienced an average gain of 14 percent, and economies characterized by inward orientation an average loss of 8 percent, in their export market shares in the 1974–8 period. A similar divergence in export performance was observed within the newly-industrializing and the less developed groups, with economies pursuing an outward-oriented development strategy experiencing gains in export shares of 15 and 10 percent while the inward-oriented economies experienced losses of 7 and 11 percent in the two groups.

There is further a positive relationship between export performance and economic growth. In the 1973–9 period, the Spearman rank correlation coefficient between the extent of reliance on export promotion in response to external shocks, defined as the ratio of export expansion associated with increases in export market shares to the balance-of-payments effects of external shocks,[2] and the rate of growth of GNP was 0.60 for this group. The estimate is statistically significant at the one percent level.

The results cannot be explained by differences in the extent of external shocks, market size, incomes per head, or the composition of exports (the share of manufactured goods in merchandise exports and the commodity concentration of exports). At the same time, there is a positive correlation between the extent of reliance on export promotion and the rate of growth of GNP for both newly-industrializing and less developed economies. The Spearman rank correlation coefficients were 0.59 and 0.66 in the two groups, respectively.

Economies applying an outward-oriented development strategy had a favorable growth experience after 1973, notwithstanding the fact that they suffered considerably larger external shocks than countries characterized by inward orientation. In the 1974–8 period, the balance-of-payments effects of these shocks averaged 7.5 percent of GNP in the first case and 3.8 percent in the second. A similar pattern is observed within the two groups, except that differences in the extent of external shocks as between outward- and inward-oriented economies was larger in the case of the newly-industrializing countries than for the less developed economies.

Various considerations may be introduced to explain these results. To begin with, imports include goods competing with domestic production under an outward-oriented strategy and extend from raw materials to final consumer goods. By contrast, economies pursuing inward-oriented policies generally preclude imports competing with domestic production and limit imports to material inputs and machinery. Correspondingly, there is greater latitude to reduce imports in response to external shocks under an outward-oriented than under an inward-oriented strategy, and the loss of production due to the decline in the capacity to import tends to be larger in the latter case than in the former. This observation is supported by an analysis of the effects of external shocks in archetypes of alternative development strategies in a general equilibrium framework.[3]

The flexibility of the national economy is also greater under an outward-oriented, than under an inward-oriented strategy. In the former case, firms have been exposed to competition in world markets and have acquired experience in changing their product composition in response to shifts in foreign demand. By contrast, under inward orientation, there is generally limited competition in the confines of the narrow domestic market and firms have little inducement to innovate, which is necessary under outward orientation in order to meet competition from abroad.

Finally, the low extent of discrimination against primary activities, the relatively low degree of variation in incentive rates, and cost reductions through the exploitation of economies of scale in export industries contribute to efficient exporting and import substitution in outward-oriented economies. In turn, under inward-oriented policies, import substitution behind high protection – aggravated by the variability of incentive rates – becomes increasingly costly and brings diminishing returns in terms of net foreign exchange savings.

In fact, in the 1974–8 period, economies pursuing an outward-oriented development strategy were more successful in import substitution than inward-oriented economies, with a 14 percent decline of import shares in the first case and 2 percent in the second. Again, broadly similar results are shown within the newly-industrializing and the less developed country groups.

At the same time, high-cost import substitution adversely affected the allocation of existing and incremental resources under inward-orientation while higher levels of efficiency were attained in economies pursuing outward-oriented development strategies. Efficiency differences have affected incremental capital-output ratios that averaged 3.3 in outward-oriented, and 4.8 in inward-oriented, economies during the 1973–9 period. These figures represent a small increase, from 3.0 in 1963–73, in the former group, and a rise from 3.5 in the latter.

A similar pattern is observed within the newly-industrializing and the less developed country groups. At the same time, in both groups, economies pursuing outward-oriented strategies reached higher levels of domestic savings ratios than economies characterized by inward orientation. Average savings ratios increased from 18.2 percent in 1963–73 to 23.3 percent in 1973–9 in outward-oriented economies, taken together, while a change from 18.9 to 20.2 percent occurred in inward-oriented economies.

These results may be explained by reference to the fact that interest rate policies and investment incentives were generally more conducive to savings in the former group than in the latter. The experience of individual economies will be briefly considered later, following a discussion of exchange rate policies. Consideration will further be given to budgetary policies and foreign borrowing.

Policies and performance

Note has been taken of the beneficial effects of outward-oriented policies for resource allocation and economic growth as compared to an inward-oriented strategy that entails a bias against exports and involves considerable dispersion in rates of incentives. The adoption of realistic exchange rates will also serve these objectives by improving the profitability of the production of internationally traded goods while the over-valuation of the currency leads to the opposite result.

Thus, the experience of the 24 developing economies studied shows that the over-valuation of the currency adversely affected exports as well as import substitution, unless compensating measures of export promotion or import protection were taken. During the period under consideration, the appreciation of the real exchange rate (the official exchange rate adjusted for changes in relative prices at home and abroad) gave rise to losses in export market shares and to increases in import shares in Colombia, Mexico, Egypt, Morocco, Peru, Nigeria and Turkey. In the same period, the effects of currency over-valuation on exports were largely offset by measures of export promotion in Korea, Thailand, Indonesia and the Ivory Coast while measures of import protection led to reductions in import shares in Israel, Yugoslavia, Kenya, Jamaica, Portugal, Tanzania and Zambia.

Domestic savings ratios are affected by changes in real interest rates that influence decision-making by consumers as well as by investment incentives that bear on firm decisions. In the group studied, the re-establishment of positive real interest rates immediately following the quadrupling of oil prices and increases in investment incentives led to a rise in the share of domestic savings in GDP in Korea, Singapore, Taiwan and Thailand. Positive real interest rates also contributed to higher savings ratios in Chile, Uruguay, India and Tunisia. Conversely, negative real interest rates adversely affected domestic savings in Argentina, Brazil, Israel, Morocco, Jamaica, Nigeria, Peru, Portugal, Turkey and Zambia.

In Argentina, Israel, Mexico, Jamaica, Peru, Turkey and Zambia, the rise in the government budget deficit contributed to inflation that was not fully offset by the devaluation of the exchange rate as interest groups attempted to maintain their real incomes unchanged. Apart from the adverse effects of the over-valuation of the currency on the production of traded goods, rapid rates of inflation in these countries created disruptions in the national economy. In turn, reductions in the government deficit contributed to lowering the rate of inflation and improved economic performance in Chile and Uruguay.

In all the cases under consideration, foreign borrowing increased immediately following the deterioration of the balance of payments due to the quadrupling of oil prices and the world recession. There were differences, however, as regards the extent of foreign borrowing and the uses to which it has been put. Among newly-industrializing economies, Singapore and Taiwan accepted a temporary decline in the rate of GNP growth in order to limit reliance on foreign loans and used the proceeds of these loans in productive investments. And, while Korea relied to a greater extent on foreign borrowing, it was subsequently able to reduce external financing as the amounts borrowed were productively used.

By contrast, in Brazil, Israel, Portugal and Turkey the proceeds of foreign borrowing were utilized in large part to maintain the rate of growth of consumption, and a substantial share of new investments was channeled into high-cost, import-substituting activities. The latter conclusion also applies to Mexico and Yugoslavia, where the rate of investment increased during the period under consideration. As a result, the debt service ratio rose to a considerable extent in all four countries while this ratio remained unchanged in the Far Eastern economies where the proceeds of foreign borrowing were more productively used.

The inflow of foreign capital was used largely to avoid (Tanzania) or to minimize (Jamaica and Peru) decreases in consumption per head in less developed economies experiencing internal shocks. In turn, with the exception of Zambia, foreign borrowing contributed to increases in investment shares in the other less developed economies studied, some of which experienced unfavorable and others favorable external shocks.

However, the beneficial effects of higher investment shares on economic growth were offset by the deterioration of the efficiency of investment in Morocco, Indonesia and Nigeria, and to a lesser extent in Egypt, Tunisia, the Philippines and the Ivory Coast, where public investments in high-cost capital-intensive industries were undertaken.

As a result, the debt service ratio increased in these countries while the ratio declined in Kenya and changed little in Mauritius and Thailand that placed reliance largely on measures of domestic adjustment.

Apart from indicating the effects of particular policies, the findings point to the usefulness of the simultaneous introduction of a package of policy measures. In this connection, reference may be made to the experience of Chile and Uruguay that have reformed their system of incentives, which had earlier been characterized by inward orientation, the use of non-market measures, and a considerable degree of government intervention in economic life. These countries reduced the bias against exports and in favor of import substitution by abolishing import restrictions, lowering tariffs, and/or providing export subsidies. They also devalued the exchange rate in real terms, abolished price control, set realistic prices for public utilities, established positive real interest rates, liberalized financial markets, practically eliminated budget deficits, and reduced the share of public consumption.

II PRODUCTION INCENTIVES

Having reviewed the policy experience of 24 developing economies after 1973, in the remaining part of this essay a policy package for structural adjustment will be presented. Such a policy package should include, first of all, production incentives that affect the allocation of resources and of increments in these resources. The relevant policy instruments comprise the exchange rate, import protection, export subsidies, and price control. Investment incentives also affect resource allocation but will be considered in Section III as they bear on the amount invested. In turn, public investment and sectoral policies will be taken up in Section IV.

Price control

The *desiderata* in regard to price control are relatively straightforward, inasmuch as the freeing of controlled prices will contribute to improvements in resource allocation and economic growth. In the private sector, price control results in higher consumption and lower production from existing capacity and reduces incentives for future expansion, necessitating formal or informal rationing and/or higher imports (lower exports) to remove the resulting excess demand. Price control also leads to increased demand for the goods and services produced in the public sector, where the production needed to provide for this demand may be undertaken at a loss.

Examples abound of the adverse effects of price control on production. In countries as different as Ecuador and Ghana, the control of agricultural prices has led to a decline in *per capita* food production, entailing an increase in imports and a decline in exports, respectively. Furthermore, in India and in Thailand, price control has given rise to a shift from exporting to importing cement as the expansion of cement production has become unprofitable, although it corresponds to the comparative advantage of the countries concerned. Finally, the underpricing of public utilities in many developing economies has had adverse effects through increases in the consumption of these highly capital-intensive commodities and the indirect subsidization of high-cost import substituting industries that are important users of public utilities.

Nor can price control be regarded as an effective means of increasing the welfare of the poor as it benefits all consumers. And, in cases when the prices of some agricultural staples are to be kept low for political or for social reasons, this should be done by subsidizing consumption while maintaining the price to the producer lest output declines.

The removal of price control in agriculture would also reduce distortions among alternative activities as well as in input-output relationships. In conjunction with the reform of the system of import protection and export subsidies discussed below, then, the prices of agricultural products and their inputs would approach world market levels.

The issue of price control is of particular importance in the case of energy. In a number of developing economies, domestic energy prices have fallen behind world market prices, and prices often vary among energy sources and users. Yet, inappropriate pricing unduly promotes the consumption of energy in both its final and intermediate uses, discourages the development of energy-saving devices and alternative energy sources, and results in inefficiencies in the production and uses of energy.

Apart from adjusting domestic energy prices to world market prices, an additional tax should be imposed on energy to the extent that the shadow price of foreign exchange exceeds the actual exchange rate. This will be the case even if the balance of payments is in equilibrium as long as there is import protection (export subsidization). In this event, the shadow exchange rate will equal the weighted average of 'commodity exchange rates', which are defined as the actual exchange rate augmented by import tariffs or export subsidies.[4]

Exchange rates, import protection, and export subsidies[5]

The exchange rate, import protection, and export subsidies are interdependent in their effects on productive activities, and they can be used in alternative ways to affect resource allocation and trade. For example, raising import tariffs (taxes) from 25 to 50 percent and granting a 20 percent export subsidy would have the same impact on productive activities as would a 20 percent devaluation.

There are differences, however, in the international acceptability of these measures. While the exchange rate can be varied on the country's own volition and import protection is generally considered to be within the purview of every developing country, foreign nations may apply retaliatory measures in response to export subsidies. The chances for retaliation will depend on the extent of injury to the competing industries of the importing countries as well as on the obligations taken by the exporting countries. An extreme case is Brazil that has committed itself to forego the use of export subsidies, so that the import tariff-export subsidy alternative is not practicable.

In turn, countries may forego variations in exchange rates by *de jure* or *de facto* joining a currency area. An example is provided by the member countries of the Franc area that are obligated to maintain fixed exchange rate parities vis-à-vis the French franc and therefore have to use import tariffs and export subsidies in the place of a devaluation. At the same time, the application of export subsidies by these countries is unlikely to trigger retaliation as the use of countervailing measures is conditional on the existence of material injury that will hardly result from the small exports of the countries concerned. More generally, small exporters have little to fear from retaliation in the event that they grant export subsidies.

An additional consideration is that complete equivalence between the two alternatives would require extending import taxes and support subsidies to all foreign transactions.[6] As noted later, this is of particular importance in countries where earnings from services (e.g. tourism), workers' remittances, and foreign capital inflow are considerable.

Reforming incentive policies

The described alternatives – a devaluation and an import tax-export subsidy scheme – may be utilized to remedy a balance-of-payments deficit due to an external or internal shock in a country that has followed optimal incentive policies prior to the shock. But, in most developing economies, there is excessive import protection of manufacturing activities, with a consequent bias against manufactured and primary exports and against primary activities in general. Reducing this bias, then, would result in improvements in resource allocation that would contribute to regaining the pre-shock growth path.[7]

Using tariff reductions for this purpose would, however, bring a further deterioration in the balance of payments, unless accompanied by compensating measures. Such measures may take the form of a devaluation that would offset the effects of tariff reductions on the domestic prices of imports while raising export prices. An alternative procedure that has been suggested involves producing explicit export subsidies while leaving import tariffs unchanged.

The two alternatives may be illustrated by an example. Assume that initially the exchange rate was 100 pesos to the dollar, all products were subject to a tariff of 50 percent, and export subsidies were not employed. Under the first alternative, a 25 percent tariff reduction, accompanied by a 20 percent devaluation, would leave the domestic prices of imports unchanged while raising export prices by 20 percent. Under the second alternative, the 20 percent increase in the prices of exports would be attained by granting a 20 percent export subsidy in the place of the partially-compensated devaluation (devaluation *cum* tariff reductions).

The described alternatives would also have identical effects on domestic prices and on the government budget. The inflationary effects of the devaluation would be mitigated by commensurate reductions in tariffs, so that these effects would be limited to increases in export prices just as in the case of export subsidies. And, under both alternatives, there would be a cost to the government budget – the loss of tariff proceeds in the first case and the budgetary cost of export subsidies in the second – that would in part be recouped through tax receipts on higher incomes and consumption following the expansion of exports.

The comparison of the two alternatives needs to be modified if account is taken of the use of imported inputs in export production. A devaluation would now raise export prices as well as the prices of direct and indirect imported inputs used in export production. To obtain equivalent results, export subsidies would need to be set on the value added in exports – the difference between the f.o.b. export value and the CIF value of imported inputs used directly and indirectly in the production process – rather than on the export value.

Deducting the CIF value of direct and indirect imported inputs from the export value may involve administrative difficulties, thereby favoring a devaluation that operates automatically. Extending export subsidies to service earnings and to workers' remittances, in order to match the effects of a devaluation on these items, may also encounter administrative difficulties. Finally, the repatriated dividends of foreign companies would need to be taxed, so as to offset the benefits these companies would derive from an export subsidy.

A further advantage of a partially compensated devaluation is that it would reduce discrimination against productive activities that are subject to tariffs at rates lower than the devaluation, or enter duty free.[8] This would be the case, in particular, in agriculture and in the production of energy, which are generally subject to low or nil tariffs in the developing countries. Efficient import substitution in these activities would be encouraged as a result.

Export incentives

The preceding considerations point to the advantages of a devaluation *cum* tariff reductions over an (explicit) export subsidy. The latter alternative would have to be utilized, however, if fixed exchange rates are maintained as in the Franc area or, on a temporary basis, if a devaluation is subject to political constraints. Finally, infant industry considerations may warrant subsidizing manufactured exports for a limited period.

In the event that export subsidies are to be employed, developing economies will wish to minimize the chance of retaliation on the part of developed countries. This objective may be served by applying measures that are accepted by GATT or have been used by the developed countries themselves.

Exempting exports and their domestic and imported inputs from indirect taxes and rebating duties on imported inputs are countenanced by GATT. At the same time, exemptions from indirect taxes do not represent an export subsidy; rather, the introduction of such exemptions is necessary to ensure tax neutrality by equalizing the tax burden on domestic and on foreign sales. This is accomplished under the so-called destination principle that entails levying indirect taxes on goods consumed domestically, irrespective of whether they are of domestic or of foreign origin, and exempting exports from indirect taxes.

Rebates of indirect taxes paid at earlier stages of fabrication are countenanced by GATT, which also permits the rebating of duties paid on imported inputs used directly (e.g. textile fabrics used in the production of clothing for export) or indirectly (e.g. thread and yarn used in the domestic production of textile fabrics embodied in exported clothing) in export production. Duty rebates on direct and indirect inputs reduce the bias against exports, although production for domestic markets continues to be favored in practically all cases.[9]

Among subsidy measures that have been used by the developed countries themselves, and therefore are not likely to encounter retaliation, preferential export credits and credit guarantee schemes are of importance. Apart from matching the conditions offered by exporters in the developed countries, the application of such measures would reduce the disadvantages of developing country exporters that are due to the undeveloped stage of domestic credit facilities and the riskiness of entering export markets for manufactured goods. Similar considerations apply to the collection of information, market research, the organization of trade fairs by quasi-governmental bodies, and the sharing of the cost of entering new markets through tax concessions.

Reforming import protection

A partially compensated devaluation would increase incentives to manufactured and to primary exports as well as to import substitution in productive activities, in particular agriculture and energy, which are subject to low or nil tariffs. At the same time, the profitability of import substitution activities which were subject to tariffs higher than, or equal to, the rate of devaluation would not be affected.[10]

In many developing economies, there is further need to reform the system of import protection, including reductions in tariffs; the rationalization of the tariff structure, and the replacement of quantitative restrictions by tariffs. In order to minimize dislocation, the reform of import protection should be carried out over a period of 4 to 5 years that is the time horizon of structural adjustment policies. At the same time, the measures to be applied should be made public in advance, so as to prepare firms for the necessary adjustments.

Rationalizing the structure of tariffs would involve reducing tariff disparities that entail a misdirection of resources and involve a cost to the national economy.[11] The rationalization of tariffs may be carried out in conjunction with tariff reductions that can be compensated by exchange rate depreciation if the balance-of-payments situation so requires.

Various considerations indicate the desirability of replacing quantitative import restrictions by tariffs in countries that rely on such restrictions to protect their domestic industry. While the extent of tariff protection can be easily ascertained, gauging the protective effects of quantitative restrictions, and their cost to national economy, would necessitate comparisons of domestic and foreign prices. Price comparisons, however, encounter practical difficulties in regard to differentiated products that assume increased importance in the process of industrial development. Case-by-case decision-making in the granting of import licences thus involves a considerable degree of arbitrariness and increases uncertainty to the user of imported inputs.

Also, tariffs have a lower administrative cost than import licensing and add to *government* revenue while the difference between the domestic and the import price accrues to the *importer* under licensing. Such quota profits, reflecting the scarcity of imports, may lead to 'overcrowding' in individual industries through the establishment of firms for the purpose of sharing in these profits and provide inducements for bribery.[12]

The question arises of whether tariffs should be raised in order to offset the loss of quota protection for domestic producers. This alternative is not recommended unless provisions are made for eliminating the additional tariff protection over a predetermined period. Failing this, there is the danger that the higher tariffs will become embedded in the system of import protection and will be difficult to reduce afterwards. Also, producers may clamor for tariffs in excess of the extent of protection provided by quotas, and their claims will be difficult to evaluate, given the problems encountered in measuring the tariff-equivalent to quotas.

It has further been suggested that reform of the system of import protection be made conditional on industry studies undertaken for the purpose of gauging the possible adverse effects of the elimination of quotas and reductions in tariffs in individual industries. Given the time involved in carrying out industry studies, however, the danger is that the reform of the system of protection may be postponed by several years as a result. At the same time, the studies involve considerable uncertainty, as one cannot anticipate the extent of improvements in efficiency on the firm level that would be made in response to increased import competition.

Industry studies may nevertheless be useful in carrying out reforms beyond the 4–5 year horizon of a structural adjustment program, as it will rarely be possible to reach desirable tariff levels during this period. Furthermore, use may be made of 'escape clauses', to be activated in the event of serious injury due to the elimination of quantitative restrictions or reductions in tariffs. Escape clause action should take the form of adjustment measures assisting the reconversion of the industry rather than the postponement of import liberalization.

Additional protection may be warranted on a temporary basis on infant industry grounds. At the same time, it would be desirable to provide infant industry protection to sales in domestic as well as in export markets, since reliance on tariffs alone risks the establishment of small-scale, inefficient firms catering to the narrow domestic market, which will find it difficult to make the subsequent transition to exporting. Subsidies may take the form of investment incentives, to be discussed later.

III INCENTIVES TO SAVE AND TO INVEST

In developing a policy package for structural adjustment, there will be need to review interest rate policy and investment incentives, which affect the volume of domestic savings and investment as well as the allocation of savings among alternative investments. The measures taken may further be accompanied by institutional reform aimed at improving the channelling of savings into investment.

Interest rate policy

Available evidence from a number of countries at different levels of economic development suggests that savings and the demand for financial assets are responsive to real interest rates.[13] To begin with, low and negative real interest rates tend to discourage savings and the holdings of financial assets. Thus, there will be an inducement to increase present consumption at the expense of future consumption, and the implicit tax on financial assets due to inflation will induce people to limit their holdings of such assets. Also, inventory accumulation and self-investment at low returns will be encouraged, diverting funds from higher-yielding uses. Finally, incentives will be provided for investing abroad where higher returns can be obtained, thereby lessening the availability of investible funds to the domestic economy.

While reductions in the holdings of domestic financial assets lessen the availability of funds to the banking system and to other financial intermediaries, low or negative real interest rates increase the demand for funds. The resulting excess demand will give rise to credit rationing, with the unsatisfied borrowers having to turn to unofficial or illegal curb markets where interest rates are substantially higher.

In developing economies, credit rationing by the banking system generally favors import-substituting investments, because of the lower risk due to the practical exclusion of foreign competition through high protection. Import-substituting investments often receive priority also in cases when credit allocation is undertaken, or influenced, by the government. At the same time, low or negative real interest rates provide inducement for the expansion of capital-intensive industries and for the use of capital-intensive production methods.

External shocks increase the urgency of reforming interest rate policies. Reductions in domestic consumption and the repatriation of foreign holdings in response to increases in real interest rates will augment the amounts available for investment and improve the balance of payments. Efficiency in resource allocation and economic growth will also be served as inventory holdings and self-investment are reduced; credit rationing is dispensed with, and the bias in favor of capital-intensive activities is removed. Finally, the lowering of consumption levels will increase the effectiveness of currency devaluations.

Portugal provides an example for the joint effects of a devaluation and increases in interest rates. Following the institution of these measures in May 1978, Portugal's balance-of-payments deficit declined from 8 percent of GNP to practically zero in the following year as exports rose rapidly and emigrants' remittance were repatriated. The expansion of exports further led to an increase in GNP by 3–4 percent while domestic aggregate expenditure remained unchanged as the rise of real interest rates contributed to increased savings.

Improving the financial system

Portugal and other newly-industrializing countries have a relatively developed financial system. In many other developing countries, reaping the full benefits of interest rate reform would necessitate improving the operation of the financial system. Some of these improvements may involve removing government-imposed restrictions on financial intermediaries; others would require institutional change. While these changes may not be fully effected within the time horizon of structural adjustment policies, their general direction can be indicated.

Reforms of the financial system should serve the twin objectives of ensuring that investors face identical credit conditions, with allowance made for differences in the riskiness of alternative investments, and that there is competition among banks and other financial intermediaries. Legalizing curb markets, easing the conditions of entry into commercial banking, and encouraging the establishment of other financial intermediaries would serve these objectives.

It would further be desirable to develop financial intermediation in long-term obligations, both to respond to the demand for such obligations on the part of savers and to provide loans for long-term investments. The form this may take – the extension of the activities of commercial banks to long-term finance; the establishment of investment banks, and the development of bond and stock markets – will depend on the degree of economic development and the financial sophistication of the countries concerned.

Investment incentives

While positive real interest rates would increase the amount of savings available for investment and improve the allocation of these savings, investment incentives would induce firms to increase the share of retained earnings for the purpose of new investment. Also, investment incentives are eminently suitable for promoting infant industries as they do not discriminate in favor of import substitution and against export activities. This is the case, in particular, in industries producing durable producer and consumer goods, where economies of scale and cost reductions through specialization in the production of parts, components, and accessories would be foregone, and the chances of subsequent exportation reduced, if measures of import protection were used to promote infant industries.

Infant industries apart, investment incentives should find general application, thus leaving the choice among alternative investments to private initiative. Investment promotion is not warranted, however, in the event of foreign market limitations, such as the application of quotas to textile exports from developing countries under the Multi-fiber Arrangement.

One should also avoid the bias often found in favor of capital-intensive activities. Accelerated depreciation provisions, low or nil tariffs on imported machinery and equipment, tax exemptions on domestically produced and imported machinery, and the imposition of minimum investment requirements as a condition for obtaining investment incentives create such a bias. These measures may be replaced by income tax exemptions that are neutral in their effects on factor intensity.

Finally, it would be desirable to provide equal treatment to domestic and to foreign investment. Foreign direct investment will benefit the national economy through the inflow of capital and the technological and marketing know-how associated with this inflow. Its balance-of-payments effects will also be favorable, unless profits are obtained through protection that raises domestic prices substantially above world market levels. This possibility, then, provides an additional argument against high import protection.

IV PUBLIC INVESTMENTS, SECTORAL, BUDGETARY AND MONETARY POLICIES

Public investments

Reliance on private incentives may not suffice in the case of large investments in basic industries, where the government can play a role as promoter and contribute to financing. In such instances, there will be need for economic project evaluation. This will also be necessary in regard to all public investments.

In countries where project evaluation machinery does not exist, it would be desirable to establish a separate entity charged with economic project evaluation. This would ensure uniformity in the methods and criteria applied in project evaluation and introduce a process of reviewing proposals prepared under the aegis of governmental agencies which would be concerned with the implementation of the project. Following a review of possible alternatives, final decisions on projects could then be made by an appropriate interministerial committee.

In the case of large projects, it would be desirable to make public the results of the evaluation prior to taking decisions, and to invite debate on the desirability of the projects in question. Information should also be made available on direct or indirect subsidies that may be provided to the project in the form of tariff protection, project-specific infrastructure, credit preferences, and the provision of inputs at less than world market prices.

Project evaluation is given special importance by reason of the need to rationalize the public investment program in the framework of structural adjustment policies. In particular, plans made for the implementation of energy-intensive projects would need to be reviewed, taking account of the higher energy prices.

Sectoral policies

The last point leads to the question of sectoral policies that supplement production and investment incentives, in particular in countries at lower levels of development. In these cases, institutional changes will contribute to the improved utilization of the country's productive powers and may be a condition for the efficient operation of the price system.

The following discussion will focus on two sectors: energy and agriculture, where policy reforms are of particular importance. For one thing, energy imports will have to be reduced in response to higher prices; for another, agricultural production will need to be increased in order to alleviate balance-of-payments difficulties and contribute to economic growth.

In the case of energy, governments may participate in the promotion and implementation of investments for increasing energý supply and take conservation measures while energy prices are being adjusted. However, over a period of time the rationalization of energy prices discussed in Section II will provide the most effective tool to ensure efficiency in energy use.[14]

At lower levels of economic development, institutional measures will also supplement production incentives in agriculture. Such measures may for example take the form of government-sponsored agricultural research; the establishment of extension services; the provision of high-quality grains, and improvement in transportation. However, the assuming by public agencies of tasks traditionally performed by the private sector, such as marketing, processing, and the sale of inputs, has often given rise to inefficiencies and high cost.

In fact, the role which incentive measures may play in economies at lower levels of development should not be underestimated. Thus, the provision of appropriate production incentives largely explain the rapid growth of agricultural activities in the Ivory Coast whereas, under similar natural conditions, production failed to keep pace with population in neighboring Ghana where the incentive system was strongly biased against exports and primary activities in general. As a result, *per capita* incomes, expressed in 1978 prices, increased from $540 to $840 between 1960 and 1978 in the Ivory Coast, while a decline from $430 to $390 occurred in Ghana.

Reference may further be made to the example of Tanzania, where inadequate production incentives led to the stagnation of the production of several agricultural staples in the face of rapid population growth. At the same time, as the examples of Hungary and Yugoslavia indicate, production incentives can also play an important role in a socialist economy.

In Hungary and Yugoslavia, state-owned firms operate in a market system and respond to price signals, with domestic prices being linked to world market prices through the exchange rate, import tariffs, and export subsidies. Of greater relevance to economies of lower levels of development, China also attempts to decentralize the process of decision-making, with increased use made of the market mechanism.[15]

These examples point to the importance of utilizing price signals with respect to state-owned firms, in countries at lower levels of development and in developing countries in general. Price signals are further necessary to ensure that decisions taken by private producers will conform to the requirements of the national economy, whatever the political system involved.

Budgetary policies

Government budget deficits increase the money supply and the balance-of-payments deficit if financed by borrowing from the central bank; reduce the availability of funds for private investment if financed through domestic borrowing; and add to the debt service burden if financed from the proceeds of foreign loans. Reducing the deficit through lower public spending, then, would support the implementation of a devaluation and would increase the availability of funds for private investment.

In view of the need to accelerate investment for the purpose of regaining the pre-shock growth path, reductions in government spending should generally be concentrated in current expenditures. At the same time, as noted above, the policy package should include a reappraisal of the public investment program. Apart from the introduction of rigorous project evaluation for investments in the productive sector, the utility of investments in non-productive sectors would need to be reviewed. This review, and the review of public investments in general, would provide an opportunity to establish a link between investment programs and budgeting procedures, for which multi-annual budgeting is a useful tool.

Monetary policies

Reducing the government budget deficit would need to be complemented by limitations on public borrowing from the central bank. However, the pursuit of an appropriate interest rate policy may obviate the need for credit ceilings for the private sector. At any rate, it is difficult to predict future credit needs, which depend on the rate of increase of real incomes, the rate of inflation, and changes in the income velocity of money. Relatively small errors in forecasting these variables can give rise to large errors in predicting required changes in the money supply. Nor can the inflow of capital be foreseen with any confidence.

The error possibilities of forecasting are particularly large following an interest rate reform that increases demand for financial assets. At the same time, to the extent that money creation responds to the increased demand for financial assets at higher real interest rates and provides the credit requirements of increased output, it will not have inflationary consequences. In turn, the imposition of strict credit ceilings in the private sector may hinder the expansion of output.

CONCLUSIONS

This essay has considered the elements of a policy package that may be applied in developing economies to reform their policies following external or internal shocks. These elements include production incentives, incentives to save and to invest, public investments, and sectoral, budgetary and monetary policies, when the particular combination chosen will depend on the circumstances of the country concerned.

Developing economies may also increase reliance on foreign borrowing to ease the adjustment to external shocks and to provide a cushion for undertaking the necessary reforms. However, in order to avoid undue increases in the debt service burden, foreign borrowing would need to be self-liquidating in the sense that it is invested at economic rates of return at least equal to the real rate of interest paid on the loans.

The changes suggested in regard to the various policy measures tend to reinforce each other in contributing to the efficient allocation of resources for economic growth. To begin with, in reducing the bias against manufactured and primary exports and against primary activities in general, and lessening disparities in rates of incentives among individual activities, the proposed reform of production incentives would contribute to exports as well as to efficient import substitution. At the same time, the exploitation of economies of scale through exports would permit lowering costs in production for foreign as well as for domestic markets.

Aligning domestic prices to world market price relationships would also contribute to efficient import substitution in agriculture and in energy. The expansion of production in these sectors may further be served through the implementation of institutional measures that are of particular importance in economies at lower levels of development.

Also, institutional reforms of the financial system would complement the proposed reform of interest rate policy and investment incentives. These measures would tend to increase the amount of savings available for investment and, together with production incentives, ensure greater efficiency in the allocation of savings among alternative investments.

Efficiency in investment allocation would further be served through the economic evaluation of investment projects promoted or financed by public authorities. In turn, reductions in the government budget deficit would increase the amount of investible funds and augment the effectiveness of exchange rate changes designed to improve the balance of payments. Reductions in the budget deficit would need to be complemented by credit ceilings for the public sector while the need for such ceilings for the private sector may be obviated through the adoption of realistic interest rates.

The recommendations made for reducing the bias against exports raise the question as to whether there will be sufficient foreign markets to absorb the expansion of exports that will be generated as a result. In particular, it has been suggested that protectionist measures taken by the industrial nations may obstruct the expansion of the exports of manufactured goods from developing economies.

Protection has indeed limited export expansion in some areas, such as textiles and clothing. Its effects should not be overstated, however. Thus, in the 1973–81 period, the volume of the manufactured exports of the developing economies to the industrial nations increased at an average annual rate of 9.5 percent, exceeding the 2.3 percent rate of growth at GNP in the industrial nations more than four times.

Following a slowdown in 1982, the growth of the manufactured exports of the developing countries to the industrial nations accelerated as economic conditions improved and further expansion can be expected.[16] For one thing, in accordance with the 'stages' approach to comparative advantage, economies at lower levels of development may take the place of the newly-industrializing economies in exporting simple manufactured goods, requiring mostly unskilled labor. For another, the newly-industrializing economies may minimize the possibility of adverse reactions on the part of the industrial nations by upgrading and diversifying their exports.

The developing economies also have excellent opportunities to expand their manufactured exports to the OPEC countries whose markets are not subject to protectionists or discriminatory measures. There are further possibilities for increased trade among the newly-industrializing economies as well as between these economies and economies at lower levels of development. Increased trade in manufactured goods will, at the same time, require the reducing of those trade barriers that tend to be the most restrictive on the actual and potential exports of other developing economies.

In turn, trade in primary products among developing countries may expand in response to the growing raw material needs of the newly-industrializing economies and the demand for food on the part of those with a food deficit. There are also rapidly growing markets for food in the OPEC countries. In fact, the principal constraint to this trade often lies in limited supply capabilities that may be improved by reforming the system of incentives.

At the same time, as noted earlier, the reform of the system of production incentives will permit efficient import substitution to proceed *pari passu* with the expansion of exports. For one thing, a partially compensated devaluation will increase incentives to activities that are subject to low or nil tariffs, in particular in the agricultural and energy sectors. For another, export expansion in manufacturing will permit reducing costs through large-scale manufacturing for export as well as for domestic markets.

More generally, the proposed reforms aim at adjustment in the form of increases in production through improved resource allocation and increases in the share of savings and investment in total expenditure. Nevertheless, the reforms would also tend to improve the distribution of income by reducing the bias against exports and against agricultural activities, which are generally labor-intensive in the developing economies, and by lessening the bias in favor of capital-intensive activities.

NOTES

1. This section draws on the author's 'Adjustment to External Shocks in Developing Economies', in B. Csikós-Nagy, D. C. Hague and G. Hall (eds), *Economics of Relative Prices* (London: Macmillan, 1984), which is itself based on his 'The Newly-Industrializing Developing Countries after the Oil Crisis', *Weltwirtschaftliches Archiv*, CXVIII (1981) 142–94, and 'The Policy Experience of Twelve Less Developed Countries, 1973–1979', in G. Ranis *et al.* (eds), *Comparative Development Perspectives* (Boulder, Col.: Westview Press, 1983) pp. 96–123.
2. External shocks and the ratios of policy responses to external shocks, including additional net external financing, increases in export market shares, import substitution, and lowering the rate of economic growth are averages for the years 1974–8, calculated on a 1971–3 basis.
3. J. de Melo and S. Robinson, 'Trade Adjustment Policies and Income Distribution in Three Archetype Developing Economies', *Journal of Development Economics*, X (1982) pp. 67–92.
4. In the case of quantitative import restrictions, the tariff equivalent of these restrictions will be relevant for the calculation. On the meaning of shadow exchange rate, see B. Balassa, 'Estimating the Shadow Price of Foreign Exchange in Project Appraisal', *Oxford Economic Papers*, XXVI (1974) pp. 147–68.
5. For a detailed discussion of alternative incentive schemes, see B. Balassa, 'Reforming the System of Incentives in Developing Countries', *World Development*, III (1975) pp. 365–82. Reprinted in B. Balassa, *Policy Reform in Developing Countries* (Oxford: Pergamon Press, 1977) pp. 33–46.
6. On the question of equivalence, cf. J. F. Laker, 'Fiscal Proxies for a Devaluation: A General Review' (Washington, D.C.: International Monetary Fund, Fiscal Affairs Department, 1980).
7. The following discussion considers the case when import protection takes the form of tariffs or tariff-type measures, such as important taxes and advance-payment requirements. Quantitative restrictions will be dealt with later.
8. A product subject to no tariff would enjoy the full benefit of the devaluation, for example.
9. The opposite result obtains if the ratio of tariff rebates to product value exceeds the rate of tariff on the product itself.
10. The latter statement abstracts from the possibility that the expansion of activities benefiting from increased incentives would lead to higher prices of productive factors.

11. Thus, it has been shown that, for a given average tariff, the economic cost of protection rises substantially with the extent of tariff dispersion. See H. G. Johnson, 'The Cost of Protection and the Scientific Tariffs', *Journal of Political Economy*, LXVIII (1960) pp. 327–45; and J. Nugent, *Economic Integration in Central America: Empirical Investigation* (Baltimore, Md.: Johns Hopkins University Press, 1974) pp. 60–7.
12. A. O. Krueger, 'The Political Economy of the Rent-Seeking Society', *American Economic Review*, LXIV (1974) pp. 291–303.
13. See Essay 2 in this volume.
14. In reporting on the findings of a World Bank Study, Raymond Goodman concluded: 'An essential tool in most countries, developing and industrial, for increasing energy efficiency in a pricing policy which ensures that, as far as possible, the price of energy in various uses reflects its real economic cost ... Governments can also use a variety of non-price controls, such as import restrictions, rationing or quotas for selective short-term intervention in the market for certain energy and energy-related products while fundamental price adjustments are being made', 'Managing the Demand for Energy in the Developing World', *Finance & Development*, XVII (1980) p. 10.
15. On the experience of Hungary and China, see Part IV of this volume.
16. B. Balassa, 'Trends in International Trade in Manufactured Goods and Structural Change in the Industrial Countries', Essay 18 in this volume.

Essay 5 Adjustment Policies in Developing Economies: a Reassessment

INTRODUCTION

In an earlier study, the author analysed policy responses to external shocks in the 1974–8 period in developing economies classified according to the character of these shocks; the level of industrialization, and trade policy.[1] In the present essay, the experience of the 1973–6 and 1979–81 periods of external shocks will be compared for the same group of economies.

Section I will describe the scheme of classification and the methodology of estimation utilized. The empirical results obtained in regard to the balance-of-payments effects of external shocks, including terms of trade effects, export volume effects, and interest rate effects will be presented in Section II. In turn, estimates of policy responses to external shocks in the form of additional net external financing and domestic adjustment policies of export promotion, import substitution, and deflationary measures will be discussed in Section III. The relationship between the policies applied and economic growth will also be considered in this section.

I ANALYSING ADJUSTMENT POLICIES IN DEVELOPING ECONOMIES

The scheme of classification

External shocks have been defined as large, unanticipated changes in world economic conditions. They include shifts in the terms of trade, associated to a considerable extent with increases in oil prices, and the slowdown in the growth of world export demand, associated with world recessions. In the second period, increases in interest rates in world financial markets may also come under this heading.

The investigation covers 28 developing economies, of which 24 suffered unfavorable external shocks in the 1973–8 period while the remaining four, on balance, benefited from the external shocks of the period. They have been classified according to the level of industrial development as newly-industrializing (NIC) or less developed (LDC), and according to the policies applied as outward-oriented or inward-oriented, economies.[2]

The latter classification scheme has been established on the basis of the policies applied in the 1974–8 period. Policy changes have occurred in several countries since. Among newly-industrializing economies, Portugal adopted a stabilization program in 1978, Turkey undertook a far-reaching policy reform in January 1980, while Chile and Uruguay introduced considerable distortions in the system of incentives by fixing their exchange rates in 1980–1. Among less developed countries, Jamaica and Peru carried out policy reforms towards the end of 1980. Nevertheless, in order to ensure comparability in the results, the earlier country classification scheme has been retained for purposes of the present study. At any rate, given the time lags involved, the policy changes appear to have had little effect before the end of the second period of external shocks, the exceptions being Portugal and Turkey.

Among the four countries that experienced favorable external shocks in the 1974–8 period, higher oil prices benefited Indonesia and Nigeria, and higher coffee prices benefited Colombia and the Ivory Coast. With the decline in coffee prices, Colombia and the Ivory Coast suffered unfavorable external shocks in 1979–81 while the emerging new exporters of petroleum – Mexico and Peru – experienced favorable shocks. Again, for reasons of comparability, the earlier classification scheme has been retained.

The methodology applied is the same as that employed in the previous study. It involves estimating the balance-of-payments effects of external shocks, resulting from changes in the terms of trade and the slowdown of foreign demand for exports. Also, in the second period, increases in interest rates, as well as the effects of policy responses to these shocks in the form of reliance on additional net external financing, export promotion, import substitution, and macroeconomic policies. The base year for the calculations pertaining to the 1974–6 period remains '1972' (the average for the years 1971 to 1973); it is '1977' (the average for the years 1976 to 1978) for the 1979–81 period.

External shocks

The balance-of-payments effects of external shocks have been derived by postulating a situation that would have existed in the absence of such shocks. Terms of trade effects have been estimated as the difference between the current price values of exports and imports and their constant price values, expressed in the prices of the relevant base period. They have further been decomposed into a 'pure terms of trade effect', calculated on the assumption that the balance of trade expressed in base year prices was in equilibrium, and an 'unbalanced trade effect', indicating the impact of the rise of import prices on the deficit (surplus) in the balance of trade, expressed in base year prices.

The balance-of-payments effects of the slowdown of foreign demand on the exports of the less developed countries, or export volume effects, have been estimated as the difference between the trend value of exports and hypothetical exports. The trend value of exports has been derived on the assumption that the growth rate of foreign demand for the country's traditional export products and for the exports of fuels, nontraditional primary commodities, and manufactured goods remained the same as in the 1963–73 period and that the country concerned maintained its base year share in these exports. In turn, hypothetical exports have been derived on the assumption that the country maintained its base year share in the foreign imports of these products and product groups during the period under consideration.

Finally, the balance-of-payments effects of increases in interest rates have been estimated as the difference between actual net interest payments and the payments that would have been made if interest rates remained at '1977' levels. The calculation has been made by utilizing London Euro-dollar rates for one year deposits. These rates averaged 6.83 percent in '1977'; they were 11.71 percent in 1979, 13.44 percent in 1980, and 16.05 percent in 1981.[3]

Adjustment policies

The balance-of-payments effects of adjustment policies have also been estimated by hypothesizing a situation that would have existed in the absence of external shocks. However, the methodology applied does not permit separating the effects of policy changes undertaken in response to external shocks from those of autonomous policy changes that may themselves constitute an internal shock. The distinction between the two necessarily becomes a matter of interpretation.

Additional net external financing has been derived as the difference between the actual merchandise trade balance and the trade balance that would have obtained if trends in imports and exports observed in the 1963–73 period continued and the prices of exports and imports remained at their base year level. Non-factor services and private transfers do not enter into the calculations as they are assumed to be unaffected by external shocks, except for the 1979–81 period when the financing of increases in interest payments has been separately estimated.

The effects of export promotion have been calculated as changes in exports resulting from changes in the country's base year export market shares. In turn, import substitution has been defined as savings in imports associated with a decrease in the income elasticity of demand for fuel and non-fuel imports by the country concerned, compared with the 1963–73 period. Finally, the effects of macroeconomic policies on imports have been estimated by taking the difference between actual GNP growth rates and the growth rate of the 1963–73 period and assuming unchanged income elasticities of import demand.

II THE BALANCE-OF-PAYMENTS EFFECTS OF EXTERNAL SHOCKS

Terms of trade effects

In the 24 developing economies experiencing unfavorable external shocks in 1974–6, adverse terms of trade effects averaged 4.2 percent of GNP in 1974–6 and 3.3 percent in 1979–81. Within these totals, there was an increase in pure terms of trade effects from 1.8 to 2.2 percent, and a decline in unbalanced trade effects from 2.4 to 1.1 percent, of GNP (Table 5.1).

The results for the two periods reflect increases in oil prices and

TABLE 5.1 External shocks and policy responses: summary results for groups of developing economies

Economy group	Period	Pure unbalanced total — Terms of trade effects		Pure unbalanced total	Export volume effects	External shocks Total	Interest rate effects	Together	Additional net external financing	Export promotion	Import substitution	Effects of lower GDP growth[a]
		As a Percentage of GNP							*As a Percentage of External Shocks*			
Newly Industrializing Economies	74–76	2.1	2.5	4.6	0.7	5.3	—	5.3	66.1	-1.2	24.4	10.8
	79–81	2.3	0.8	3.1	1.1	4.2	1.8	6.0	21.6	30.9	-3.4	50.9
Less developed economies	74–76	1.2	2.0	3.2	0.7	3.9	—	3.9	138.3	-10.3	-29.5	1.4
	79–81	1.9	2.0	3.9	0.9	4.8	0.7	5.5	85.9	-5.4	6.9	12.6
NICs and LDCs	74–76	1.8	2.4	4.2	0.7	4.9	—	4.9	84.7	-3.6	10.5	8.3
	79–81	2.2	1.1	3.3	1.1	4.4	1.5	5.9	40.7	20.2	-0.4	39.5
Outward-oriented NICs	74–76	7.4	1.0	8.4	1.7	10.0	—	10.0	1.1	31.6	40.4	26.9
	79–81	7.5	0.5	8.0	4.5	12.5	1.9	14.3	6.9	29.0	16.6	47.5
Outward-oriented LDCs	74–76	-1.4	5.6	4.2	1.0	5.1	—	5.1	52.9	24.8	21.9	0.6
	79–81	2.3	3.3	5.6	1.0	6.5	1.2	7.8	76.1	28.8	-15.4	10.5
Outward-oriented NICs and LDCs	74–76	4.9	2.3	7.2	1.5	8.7	—	8.7	9.7	30.5	37.3	22.5
	79–81	6.1	1.2	7.3	3.5	10.9	1.7	12.6	18.1	29.0	11.4	41.5
Inward-oriented NICs	74–76	1.2	2.8	4.0	0.5	4.5	—	4.5	91.3	-14.0	18.2	4.5
	79–81	0.9	1.3	2.2	0.5	2.6	1.7	4.4	35.3	32.8	-22.0	53.9
Inward-oriented LDCs	74–76	1.5	1.5	3.1	0.7	3.8	—	3.8	154.7	-16.9	-39.2	1.5
	79–81	1.8	1.8	3.5	0.9	4.4	0.6	5.0	88.6	-15.1	13.3	13.2
Inward-oriented NICs and LDCs	74–76	1.3	2.4	3.7	0.6	4.3	—	4.3	109.6	-14.8	1.6	3.6
	79–81	1.4	1.1	2.5	0.6	3.1	1.4	4.6	56.0	14.2	-8.3	38.1
NICs with internal shocks	74–76	0.4	1.8	2.2	0.3	2.5	—	2.5	108.6	-60.1	20.1	31.4
	79–81	-1.6	1.6	-0.0	0.5	0.5	2.0	2.5	491.3	260.7	-778.8	126.8
LDCs with internal shocks	74–76	0.7	3.4	4.1	1.5	5.7	—	5.7	116.7	-30.8	-5.5	19.6
	79–81	2.0	-0.0	2.0	1.7	3.6	2.1	5.7	-49.8	56.0	34.5	59.5
Economies with favorable shocks	74–76	-19.6	1.9	-17.7	2.0	-15.6	—	-15.6	-72.4	5.9	-32.2	-1.2
	79–81	-8.4	-0.1	-8.5	5.1	-3.3	0.1	-3.2	-170.1	16.6	-1.7	55.2

NOTE: [a] The signs have been reversed for the group that experienced favorable external shocks.

SOURCE: World Bank economic and social data base.

decreases in other primary product prices, relative to the prices of manufactured goods. The decline in the prices of non-fuel primary products was particularly pronounced in 1979–81, contributing to the deterioration of the pure terms of trade of less developed economies during this period. Nor did these economies experience an improvement in their unbalanced trade effects, so that their overall terms of trade deteriorated between 1974–6 and 1979–81. In turn, the adverse terms of trade effects declined in newly-industrializing economies, where the deterioration of the pure terms of trade was more than offset by improvements in unbalanced trade effects.

In both periods, terms of trade losses were much greater in outward-oriented than in inward-oriented economies, owing largely to differences in pure terms of trade effects, as unbalanced trade effects were of similar magnitude in the two cases. The differences in the results are explained by the substantially higher share of foreign trade in GNP under outward orientation (28 percent in 1974–6 and 39 percent in 1979–81) than under inward orientation (9 and 10 percent). In fact, terms of trade losses were a smaller proportion of the average value of trade in outward-oriented than in inward-oriented economies.

These conclusions also apply if newly-industrializing and less developed economies are separately considered.[4] Furthermore, between 1974–6 and 1979–81 outward-oriented NICs and LDCs experienced less favorable developments in their pure terms of trade than the corresponding inward-oriented groups. Finally, countries with favorable external shocks made substantial gains through improvements in their pure terms of trade that dominated the unbalanced trade effects; the improvements were particularly pronounced in the 1974–6 period when increases in oil prices were larger and coffee prices rose.

Export volume effects

Export shortfalls due to the deceleration of the growth of world trade averaged 0.7 percent of GNP in the developing economies studied in 1974–6 and 1.1 percent in 1979–81. The rise in the export shortfall suffered by the newly industrializing economies was of the same magnitude while it was smaller in the less developed economies.

At the same time, the adverse export volume effects remained unchanged in the case of inward-oriented developing economies (0.6 percent of GNP) while these effects rose from 1.5 to 3.5 percent in outward-oriented countries. The increase of the export shortfall, from

1.7 to 4.5 percent, was especially pronounced in outward-oriented NICs.

The observed differences are explained by differences in the product composition of exports and in the share of exports in GNP. For one thing, world trade in manufactured goods, exported chiefly by outward-oriented developing economies, and in particular the NICs, held up better than primary product trade in 1974–6 while the opposite occurred in 1979–81. Thus, the ratio of the export shortfall to exports rose from 5.7 percent in 1974–6 to 9.5 percent in 1979–81 in outward-oriented economies while there was a decline from 8.3 to 6.7 percent in inward-oriented economies. For another thing, the share of exports in GNP is substantially higher under outward- than under inward-orientation.

Among developing countries experiencing internal shocks in 1974–6, export volume effects were smaller than the average in the NICs and larger than the average in the LDCs in both periods under consideration. Finally, countries with favorable external shocks suffered increasing export shortfalls as world demand for petroleum declined.

Interest rate effects

The ratio of interest rate effects to GNP was considerably higher for newly industrializing economies (1.8 percent) than for less developed countries (0.7 percent) in the 1979–81 period. In both cases, the ratios were higher for outward-oriented than for inward-oriented economies.

External shocks combined

For the developing economies studied, terms of trade effects declined between 1974–6 and 1979–81, and were offset only in part by increases in export volume effects. At the same time, terms of trade effects continued to dominate export volume effects and the latter were also exceeded by interest rate effects in the 1979–81 period.

In 1974–6, the adverse balance-of-payments effects of external shocks were larger in newly industrializing than in less developed economies. The opposite result obtained in 1979–81 as the magnitude of external shocks declined in the former, and increased in the latter, group.

Within each group, outward-oriented economies suffered larger external shocks than inward-oriented economies, with the differential growing over time due to the increasing openness of outward-oriented economies, adverse changes in world demand for their manufactured exports, and the favorable effects of the rise of petroleum prices for Mexico and Peru among inward-oriented economies. In turn, the extent of improvement in the balance-of-payments of countries benefiting from favorable external shocks declined over time, in part because of the fall in coffee prices and in part because of the decrease in world demand for petroleum.

III ADJUSTMENT TO EXTERNAL SHOCKS

Additional net external financing

Developing economies relied to a considerable extent on foreign borrowing to cope with the external shocks of the 1974–6 period. In the cases studied, additional net external financing equalled 85 percent of the balance-of-payments effects of external shocks during this period. The ratio was 66 percent for newly-industrializing economies and 138 percent for less developed countries; in the latter case, losses in export market shares and negative import substitution aggravated the effects of external shocks.

Within both groups, inward-oriented economies placed much greater reliance on foreign borrowing than did outward-oriented economies, which made considerable efforts at domestic adjustment. Thus, in 1974–6, the ratio of additional net external financing to the balance-of-payments effects of external shocks was 91 percent in inward-oriented, and 1 percent in outward-oriented, NICs; it was 155 percent in inward-oriented, and 53 percent in outward-oriented, LDCs.[5]

The growing indebtedness of developing economies limited the extent of their foreign borrowing after 1978. Correspondingly, additional net external financing averaged only 41 percent of the balance of payments effects of external shocks in 1979–81 in the developing economies studied. Reliance on additional net external financing declined from 110 percent in 1974–6 to 56 percent in 1979–81 in inward-oriented economies, several of which encountered problems of creditworthiness. In turn, outward-oriented economies were able to step up borrowing abroad, with the ratio of additional net external financing to the balance of payments effects of external shocks rising from 10 percent in 1974–6 to 18 percent in 1979–81. Nevertheless, they continued to rely largely on domestic adjustment.

Domestic adjustment policies

The extent of reliance on additional net external financing indicates the paucity of domestic adjustment efforts in inward-oriented developing countries. In 1974–6, on the average, these countries did not undertake import substitution, while savings in imports owing to the deceleration of economic growth were offset several times by the loss in exports due to decreases in export market shares. In the same period, outward-oriented economies followed a balanced policy of export promotion and import substitution, to which should be added import savings due to the application of deflationary policies immediately following the quadrupling of oil prices.

The pattern of adjustment underwent little change in 1979–81 in outward-oriented economies, except that import substitution had lesser – and deflationary policies greater – effects during the period. In turn, import savings associated with the decline in economic growth rates largely compensated for the decrease in additional net external financing in inward-oriented economies.

As far as domestic adjustment policies are concerned, the principal difference between outward-oriented and inward-oriented economies lies in their export promotion efforts. In outward-oriented economies, the favorable effects of increases in export market shares offset about three-tenths of the balance of payments effects of external shocks in both periods. This result reflects the favorable treatment of primary and manufactured exports and the adoption of realistic exchange rates following external shocks.[6] Again, there is little difference in this regard between outward-oriented NICs and LDCs.

In turn, losses in export market shares added one-seventh to the adverse balance of payments effects of external shocks in inward-oriented economies in 1974–6. This result obtained as the countries in question biased the system of incentives against exports and, on the whole, maintained overvalued exchange rates. Nor was there any difference in this regard between inward-oriented NICs and LDCs. At the same time, declines in export market shares substantially exceeded the average for countries which experienced internal shocks that aggravated the effects of trade and exchange rate policies on exports.

Inward-oriented economies lost export market shares in 1979–81 as well, if one adjusts for increases in the petroleum exports of Mexico and Peru from newly-found deposits.[7] At the same time, inward-oriented NICs exhibited a better export performance than inward-oriented LDCs as policy reforms in Portugal and Turkey had their beneficial effects on exports during the period.

There were also differences between inward-oriented and outward-oriented economies as far as import substitution is concerned. While import substitution offset nearly four-tenths of the balance-of-payments effects of external shocks in 1974–6 and one-ninth of these effects in 1979–81 in outward-oriented economies, import substitution was, on the average, approximately nil in 1974–6 and became negative in 1979–81 in inward-oriented developing countries.

These results require explanation in view of the fact that inward-oriented economies had relatively high import protection that tended to increase further after 1973. Various factors have contributed to the observed results. To begin with, net foreign exchange savings in inward-oriented economies declined as import substitution was increasingly undertaken in industries that required imported inputs, when the smallness of domestic markets did not allow for full capacity utilization and/or hindered the exploitation of economies of scale. In turn, the expansion of exports in outward-oriented economies permitted efficient import substitution by removing the market constraint for the products in question. Furthermore, discrimination against agriculture and delays in adjusting domestic fuel prices limited the extent of import substitution in primary products in inward-oriented economies that was not the case under outward orientation. Finally, the overvaluation of the exchange rate hampered import substitution in inward-oriented economies while the adoption of realistic exchange rates encouraged the replacement of imports by domestic production in outward-oriented economies.

In the absence of output-increasing policies of export promotion and import substitution, inward-oriented developing countries had to adopt deflationary policies after 1978 as the possibilities for further borrowing diminished. Reliance on deflationary measures increased to a lesser extent in outward-oriented economies, which continued to apply output-increasing policies.

In the 1974–6 period, the favorable balance-of-payments effects of external shocks were offset by negative additional net external financing and, to a lesser extent, by increases in import shares associated with large investment programs in developing countries experiencing favorable external shocks. These programs came to a rather abrupt end in the late seventies and the countries in question further reduced import requirements through the application of deflationary policies, with a corresponding increase in negative additional net external financing.

The policies applied and economic growth

In order to limit reliance on foreign borrowing, outward-oriented economies initially applied deflationary policies during the first period of external shocks. The resulting deceleration of economic growth remained temporary, however, as output-increasing policies permitted these economies to reach – and even to surpass – earlier rates of growth. Thus, following a decline from 7.1 percent in 1963–73 to 5.1 percent in 1973–6, GNP growth rates in outward-oriented economies attained 8.4 percent in 1976–9. Practically the same pattern is observed in outward-oriented NICs as in LDCs.

In turn, despite extensive foreign borrowing for the sake of maintaining past rates of economic growth, these rates declined from 5.7 percent in 1963–73 to 5.3 percent in 1973–6, and again to 4.5 percent in 1976–9, in inward-oriented economies. The decline in growth rates was especially pronounced in inward-oriented NICs while inward-oriented LDCs experienced a temporary improvement.

In response to the deflationary measures taken, economic growth rates declined in both outward-oriented and inward-oriented economies after 1978. But the slowdown of economic growth in outward-oriented economies remained temporary whereas inward-oriented economies suffered further declines in growth rates as they applied deflationary policies. Thus, while the average difference in GNP growth rates between the two groups was less than one percentage point in the 1979–82 period, growth rates averaged 5 percent in outward-oriented economies in 1983 compared to stagnation in inward-oriented economies.

Finally, owing to inefficiencies in new investments and in resource allocation in general, countries experiencing favorable external shocks did not succeed in raising their GNP growth rates in 1974–6, even though they increased the share of investment in GDP by one-half. And growth rates declined to a considerable extent after 1978 as the effects of these inefficiencies came to be more strongly felt.

CONCLUSIONS

It has been shown that outward-oriented economies relied largely on output-increasing policies of export promotion and import substitution to offset the balance-of-payments effects of external shocks in the 1974–6 and the 1979–81 periods and accepted a temporary decline in the rate of economic growth in order to limit their external indebtedness. In turn, inward-oriented economies failed to apply output-increasing policies of adjustment. They financed the balance of payments effects of external shocks by foreign borrowing in the 1974–6 period and had to take deflationary measures in 1979–81 as their increased indebtedness limited the possibilities for further borrowing. The policies applied led to economic growth rates substantially higher in outward-oriented than in inward-oriented economies, with the differences in growth rates offsetting the differences in the size of external shocks several times.

These conclusions have been derived by classifying developing economies as outward- and inward-oriented. While such a binary classification necessarily involves a certain degree of arbitrariness, the results have been reconfirmed in an econometric study of 43 developing economies, in which initial trade orientation and policy responses to external shocks have been separately introduced. The results of this study are summarized in Essay 2.

NOTES

1. The results of this study are summarized in B. Balassa, 'Structural Adjustment Policies in Developing Economies', Essay 4 in this volume.
2. A description of the classification scheme applied is contained in Essay 4.
3. Adjusting for inflation rates does not modify the results as unit values for the manufactured exports of the developed countries, which can be considered as appropriate deflator, increased at the same rate (7.6 percent a year) between '1977' and 1981 as between 1975 and 1978 (United Nations, *Monthly Bulletin of Statistics*, various issues).
4. However, in 1974–6, the outward-oriented LDCs had favorable pure terms of trade effects and their terms of trade losses were entirely due to unbalanced trade effects.
5. For a discussion of the resulting changes in the external indebtedness of the countries concerned, see B. Balassa, 'The Problem of the Debt in Developing Countries', Essay 6 in this volume.
6. For a discussion of the policies applied by individual countries in the 1974–8 period, see Essay 4.

7. The effects of the rise of petroleum exports are apparent in the large contribution of increases in export market shares in 1979–81 in developing countries that experienced internal shocks in 1974–6 (Mexico among the NICs and Peru among the LDCs).

Essay 6   The Problem of the Debt in Developing Countries

INTRODUCTION

The problems associated with their growing foreign indebtedness have been in the focus of public discourse about the developing countries in recent years. The discussion has concerned the ability of these countries to service their external debt, the policies they may adopt to improve their debt situation, and the measures that may be taken by the international community to reduce the chances of future debt crises.

This essay examines the issues relating to the debt of the non-oil developing countries, defined to exclude countries whose oil exports provide at least two-thirds of their export earnings and represent at least one per cent of world exports of crude oil. This definition is employed by the International Monetary Fund whose statistics will be used to provide an overview of the debt situation during the last decade in Section I of the essay.[1] Next, Section II will analyze the policies applied by countries pursuing different development strategies and the effects of these policies on their debt situation. In turn, Section III will consider prospective future changes and Section IV will draw some policy conclusions.

I THE EXTERNAL DEBT OF THE DEVELOPING COUNTRIES, 1973–83

The following discussion will focus on two five-year periods characterized by external shocks – 1973–8 and 1978–83. The first period includes the quadrupling of oil prices and the world recession of

1974–5; the second comprises the two-and-a-half fold increase in oil prices and world recession of 1980–2, and increases in interest rates in world financial markets. Table 6.1 provides data for 1973 and 1978, the initial and the terminal years of the first period, as well as for each of the five years of the second period, during which considerable changes occurred in the debt situation of the developing countries. External borrowing rose rapidly in response to increases in oil prices and in interest rates after 1978, followed by a slowdown in the wake of the August 1982 Mexican financial crisis.

The table presents end-of-year data on the stock of the outstanding external debt of the non-oil developing countries (for short, developing countries), including medium-term and long-term debt, short-term credit, and credit from the IMF. It further provides information on their international reserves comprising holdings of SDRs and foreign exchange, reserve position in the IMF, as well as gold holdings valued at the London price. The net indebtedness of the developing countries is then derived as the difference between their total indebtedness and the value of their international reserves.

The outstanding medium-term and long-term debt of the developing countries nearly tripled in terms of current dollars between 1973 and 1978, followed by a doubling between 1978 and 1983. There appears to have been little slowdown in the growth of the debt, however, if adjustment is made for changes in prices. Thus, while the dollar prices of the developing countries' exports rose by three-fifths between 1973 and 1978, these prices increased by only one-fifth in the following five-year period.[2] Similar tendencies are observed in regard to import prices, except that in this case the absolute magnitude of the increase was somewhat greater in both periods (Table 6.1).

Although the developing countries made increasing use of IMF credit in recent years, the total remained relatively small compared to their outstanding medium-term and long-term debt. This conclusion applies also if comparisons are made with the short-term debt. After quintupling between 1973 and 1978 and rising one-and-a-half times beween 1978 and 1982, the current dollar value of the outstanding short-term debt declined by one-fifth in 1983, even though the estimates do not fully take account of the transformation of short-term debt into medium-term obligations. Finally, the stock of international reserves of the developing countries more than doubled between 1973 and 1978, increased by three-fifths between 1978 and 1980, declined by one-sixth in the following year, and remained at this level subsequently.

Combining available data on the medium-term and long-term debt,

TABLE 6.1 *Outstanding external debt, capital flows and debt service of non-oil developing countries*

1973	1978	1979	1980	1981	1982	1983	1984
Outstanding external debt							
end of year ($ billion)							
(1) Medium-term and long-term debt	96.8	282.7	336.2	390.8	455.8	508.2	566.4	622.8
(2) Short-term debt	11.3	51.6	59.1	84.5	103.8	125.1	102.2	88.2
(3) IMF credit	1.2	8.0	8.3	9.5	14.9	21.2	30.8	36.8
(4) Total indebtedness (1)+(2)+(3)	109.3	342.3	403.6	484.8	574.5	654.5	699.4	747.8
(5) International reserves	48.2	103.2	147.6	161.8	138.8	140.0	139.8	na
(6) Net indebtedness (4)−(5)	61.1	239.1	256.0	323.0	435.7	514.5	559.6	na
Ratio to GNP							
(per cent)							
(7) Medium-term and long-term debt	16.6	21.6	21.3	20.5	22.6	26.2	31.2	32.9
(8) Total indebtedness	18.7	26.2	25.5	25.4	28.4	33.7	38.5	39.4
(9) Net indebtedness	10.5	18.3	16.2	16.9	21.6	26.5	30.8	na
Ratio to exports of goods and services							
(per cent)							
(10) Medium-term and long-term debt	88.7	108.0	99.7	91.5	99.8	115.6	126.7	126.8
(11) Total indebtedness	100.2	130.7	119.7	113.5	125.8	148.9	156.4	152.2
(12) Net indebtedness	56.0	91.3	75.9	75.6	95.4	117.1	125.1	na
Net borrowings							
annual ($ billion)							
(13) Medium-term and long-term debt	11.7	36.6	48.5	58.4	73.5	43.9	65.7	58.3
(14) Short-term debt	0.2	10.0	5.0	22.2	19.6	14.0	−22.9	−14.0
(15) IMF credit	−0.1	−0.3	0.2	1.5	6.1	7.1	10.2	6.8
(16) Total (13)+(14)+(15)	11.8	46.3	53.7	82.1	99.2	65.0	53.0	51.1

Disbursements, debt service, and net transfers annual ($ billion)

(17) Disbursements[a] (13)+(18)	22.4	66.0	83.6	92.7	116.0	88.5	103.1	98.0
(18) Principal repayments (amortization)	10.7	29.4	35.1	34.3	42.5	44.6	37.4	39.7
(19) Interest payments	4.6	18.1	25.9	39.0	54.7	63.0	59.2	63.7
(20) Debt service (18)+(19)	15.3	47.5	61.0	73.3	97.2	107.6	96.6	103.4
(21) Net flows (16)−(19)	7.2	28.2	27.8	43.1	44.5	2.0	−6.2	−12.2
(22) Official transfers	5.4	8.3	11.5	12.8	13.5	12.9	13.2	13.8
(23) Net transfers (21)+(232)	12.6	36.5	39.3	55.9	58.0	14.9	7.0	1.2

Ratio to exports of goods and services (per cent)

(24) Debt service	14.0	18.1	18.1	17.2	21.3	24.5	21.6	21.0
(25) Debt service, adjustment for[b] the inflationary erosion of the debt	5.0	11.2	7.4	6.7	24.2	27.8	26.5	na

Changes in outstanding external debt[c] ($ billion)

(26) Medium-term and long-term debt	15.0	45.5	53.5	54.6	65.0	52.4	58.2	56.4
(27) Short-term debt	0.2	8.4	7.5	25.4	19.3	21.3	−22.9	−14.0
(28) IMF credit	−0.1	0.0	0.3	1.2	5.4	6.3	9.6	6.0
(29) Total (26)+(27)+(28)	15.1	53.9	61.3	81.2	89.7	80.0	44.9	48.4

Memorandum items

(30) Export price index (1980=100)	48.0	76.1	86.8	100.0	91.3	86.9	86.7	90.6
(31) Import price index (1980=100)	41.8	72.2	84.5	100.0	96.6	93.7	90.0	92.7
(32) Exports	109.1	261.8	337.3	427.3	456.8	439.5	447.2	491.3
(33) Gross domestic products	583.1	1305.8	1581.2	1908.4	2020.2	1942.6	1816.8	1895.7

NOTES: [a] Derived as the sum of medium term and long term net borrowings and principal repayment.
[b] The adjustment has been made by applying the import price index of non-oil developing countries to average outstanding debt in the particular year.
[c] Changes in year end position of external debt between two consecutive years.

SOURCES: IMF, *World Economic Outlook*, 1982, 1984, except for reserves that originates in IMF, *International Financial Statistics*, and exports and import price indices that are from the Economic Projections Department of the **World Bank**.

short-term debt, IMF credit, and international reserves, it is observed that the net indebtedness of the developing countries quadrupled between 1973 and 1978, nearly doubled between 1978 and 1981, but its growth decelerated afterwards. Thus, while the increment in the net indebtedness of the developing countries was $111 billion in 1981, it declined to $79 billion in 1982 and, rather precipitously, to $45 billion in 1983.

Data on the medium-term and long-term obligations of the developing countries originate from reports prepared for the World Bank; estimates on their short-term debt are made by the Bank for International Settlements, and statistics on their drawings from the International Monetary Fund are provided by the IMF. In turn, the balance-of-payments statistics of the developing countries, published by the IMF, provide information on their net foreign borrowings, repayments of principal (amortization), and interest payments.

A comparison of lines (13) to (16) and (26) to (29) in Table 6.1 shows varying discrepancies between these figures over time. In 1983, for example, the total external debt of the developing countries reportedly rose by $45 billion whereas, according to balance-of-payments statistics, their net foreign borrowings totalled $53 billion. These discrepancies are explained in part by changes in the valuation of the debt and in part by statistical error.

During the period under consideration, net foreign borrowings reportedly increased from $12 billion in 1973 to $46 billion in 1978, and to $95 billion in 1981, but declined to $65 billion in 1982. However, interest payments continued to rise until 1982, reflecting the growing indebtedness of the developing countries as well as rising interest rates after 1978. And albeit decreases in the rates reduced the interest obligations of the developing countries in 1983, this decline was much smaller than that of net borrowings.

Correspondingly, after rising from $7 billion in 1973 to $28 billion in 1978 and, again, to $45 billion in 1981, net flows (net borrowings less interest payments) to the developing countries decreased to $2 billion 1982 and turned negative in 1983. Net transfers to these countries nevertheless remained positive on account of (non-debt creating) official transfers to them (Table 6.1).

Making comparisons with net flows to the developing countries puts into focus the increasing importance of IMF credits. While borrowings from the International Monetary Fund were negligible until 1980, they equalled one-sixth of net flows to these countries in 1981, and offset much of the decline in net flows afterwards.

A number of indicators have been proposed to evaluate the debt situation of the developing countries. The indicators used in the present essay relate the stock of external debt to the gross domestic product (the debt-GDP ratio), and to the exports of goods and services (the debt-export ratio), and express the service of the debt as a percentage of the exports of goods and services (the debt-service ratio).[3]

The ratio of the net indebtedness of the developing countries to their gross domestic product rose from 11 per cent in 1973 to 18 per cent in 1978, declining to 16 per cent in 1979. However, the ratio increased rapidly afterwards reaching 31 per cent in 1983, when the current dollar value of the GDP of the developing countries fell as the dollar appreciated to a considerable extent.

In turn, the ratio of the net indebtedness of the developing countries to their exports of goods and services rose by one-third between 1973 and 1978, declined by one-sixth in the following year, and increased by two-thirds between 1978 and 1983. The differences in the results are explained by the fact that exports rose more rapidly than the gross domestic product between 1973 and 1981 and declined less than GDP afterwards. At the same time, as noted in Section II, there are considerable differences in this regard among developing countries applying different policies.

Finally, the ratio of the debt service (amortization and interest payments) to the exports of goods and services of the developing countries rose from 14 per cent in 1973 to 18 per cent in 1978, decreased to 17 per cent in 1980, but increased again to 25 per cent in 1982 as interest rates rose. In turn, the decline to 22 per cent in 1983 is explained by the fall in interest rates and, more importantly, by decreases in amortization as loan repayments were postponed.

A different pattern is shown if adjustment is made for the inflationary erosion of the debt.[4] The adjusted debt-service ratio was in the 7 to 8 per cent range between 1973 and 1980, jumped to 29 per cent in 1981 as import prices fell, changed little in 1982, and declined to 22 per cent in 1983 when import prices remained roughly constant.

Making such an adjustment assumes, however, that the actual inflation rate appropriately reflects expectations as regards future inflation. This does not appear to be a realistic assumption in view of the observed fluctuations in inflation rates. Adjusting for inflation also introduced extraneous factors in the determination of the debt-service ratio. As the ratio will be used in Section II of the essay to evaluate economic performance in the developing countries, an adjustment for the inflationary erosion of the debt will not be made in examining the experiences of various country groups.

Note further that the aggregate data do not provide an indication of the relative roles played by demand and supply factors in the growing indebtedness of the developing countries. A number of these countries increased their demand for foreign funds following the rise of oil prices in 1973–4 and 1979–80 while the commercial banks accommodated – and even encouraged – borrowing by most of them. And although a few countries, such as Turkey, were unable to borrow further after 1978, and some hardening of the terms occurred after 1980, a shift in the attitudes of the commercial banks came only in August 1982 when, in sharp contrast to the optimistic predictions made only days and weeks beforehand, Mexico plunged into a liquidity crisis.

Demand considerations are given emphasis if one examines the experience of developing countries applying different policies during the period preceding the Mexican crisis. This will be done in Section II of the essay that will analyze the consequences for foreign borrowing of the policies applied in response to external shocks by different groups of developing economies.

II POLICY RESPONSES TO EXTERNAL SHOCKS AND FOREIGN BORROWING

Reference has been made above to the external shocks the developing countries experienced since 1983. The external shocks evoked a variety of policy responses, including additional net external financing, export promotion, import substitution, and deflationary macroeconomic measures. In examining the extent of external shocks, and policy responses to these shocks, the author classified developing economies into two groups, depending on their policy orientation as regards international trade. Countries providing similar incentives to exports and to import substitution have been considered outward-oriented, and countries discriminating in favor of import substitution and against exports inward-oriented.[5]

Although the classification system is based on the trade policies applied, the distinction made between the two groups of countries may be generalized in terms of the extent and the character of public interventions. Outward-oriented economies by-and-large adopted realistic exchange rates and interest rates; gave similar incentives to industry and agriculture; eschewed price controls; limited the scope of public investments while giving attention to efficiency considerations in the choice of these investments; and had a relatively small deficit in the government budget. By contrast, inward-oriented economies tended to have overvalued exchange rates and negative real interest rates; biased the system of incentives against agriculture; made use of price controls; had a larger share of often inefficient public investment projects; and incurred relatively high budget deficits.

Furthermore, in the years following the first oil shock, outward-oriented economies limited reliance on foreign borrowing and accepted a temporary decline in the rate of economic growth in order to avoid substantial increases in their external debt. In turn, most inward-oriented economies relied to a considerable extent on foreign borrowing to maintain past rates of economic growth and to finance their growing budget deficit.

Outward-oriented economies soon re-established – and even surpassed – pre-1973 growth rates although, owing to their greater openness, they suffered greater external shocks than inward-oriented economies. This occurred as the policies applied contributed to the efficient use of investment funds as well as to higher savings. Productive investments led to increases in export market shares and import substitution that represented the principal policy responses to external shocks by outward-oriented economies, offsetting over two-thirds of the balance-of-payments effects of these shocks in the 1974–6 period (Table 5.1).[6]

In turn, the group of inward-oriented economies financed increases in the balance-of-payments deficit due to external shocks entirely by foreign borrowing. At the same time, the proceeds of foreign borrowing were partly used to increase public and private consumption and the funds devoted to investments were often not efficiently employed. Also, inward-oriented economies lost export market shares and were unsuccessful in replacing imports by domestic production, leading to a decline in the rate of economic growth.

The differences in the policies applied by outward-oriented and inward-oriented economies are apparent in the changes that occurred in their external debt. Table 6.2 presents data on debt-GNP, debt-export, and debt-service ratios for the years 1974, 1976, 1978 and 1981. The debt ratios have been defined in gross as well as in net terms, when the former refers to the sum of outstanding medium-term and long-term debt and IMF credit, and the latter makes adjustment for international reserves. In turn, gross debt service includes amortization and interest payments on all debt, while net debt service adjusts for interest receipts. In the following discussion, reference will be made to the net ratios only.

The debt-GNP ratio increased from 4 per cent in 1973 to 12 per cent

TABLE 6.2 *External debt indicators for groups of developing economies*

		Debt-GNP ratio		Debt-export ratio		Debt service ratio	
		Gross	Net	Gross	Net	Gross	Net
Outward-oriented	1973	19.0	6.3	47.8	15.7	10.2	8.2
NICs	1978	24.5	12.0	50.3	24.6	11.0	8.4
	1982	29.6	13.3	51.2	23.0	14.4	10.3
Outward-oriented	1973	10.6	−2.4	44.0	−10.0	14.7	11.7
LDCs	1978	20.4	10.5	79.3	40.9	14.8	12.4
	1982	29.7	22.5	103.9	78.9	28.0	25.6
Outward-oriented	1973	16.7	3.8	47.4	10.8	11.1	8.9
NICs & LDCs	1978	23.5	11.6	54.8	27.1	11.6	9.0
	1982	29.6	15.6	58.5	30.8	16.2	12.4
Inward-oriented	1973	10.5	2.0	79.4	14.9	17.5	14.7
NICs	1978	23.0	16.4	190.1	135.3	34.1	30.7
	1982	32.1	27.6	190.4	163.8	44.9	40.0
Inward-oriented	1973	14.3	10.3	132.9	95.7	18.0	16.4
LDCs	1978	26.1	19.3	179.8	133.1	22.9	20.3
	1982	28.5	22.9	190.1	152.9	27.1	24.0
Inward-oriented	1973	11.7	4.7	94.8	38.1	17.7	15.2
NICs & LDCs	1978	23.9	17.2	186.9	134.6	30.4	27.4
	1982	31.0	26.2	190.3	160.8	40.1	35.9

NOTE: For definitions and sources, see text.

in 1978 in outward-oriented economies. Larger-than-average increases occurred in outward-oriented LDCs that placed greater reliance on additional net external financing than outward-oriented NICs (the negative figures for the former group in 1973 indicate that their international reserves exceeded external debt obligations).

Increases were smaller, from 11 per cent in 1973 to 27 per cent in 1978, in the debt-export ratio of outward-oriented economies while their debt-service ratio remained unchanged at its 1973 level of 9 per cent.[7] The results reflect the fact that exports in outward-oriented economies rose more rapidly than the gross national product while their debt service obligations rose less than the external debt.[8]

All three indicators of external indebtedness were higher, and increased to a greater extent, in inward-oriented economies. Between 1973 and 1978, the debt-GNP ratio of these economies rose from 5 to 17 percent, their debt-export ratio from 38 to 135 percent, and their debt service ratio from 15 to 27 percent. Increases were much smaller than the average in inward-oriented LDCs that could rely to a considerable extent on foreign aid. This fact puts into focus the results for inward-oriented NICs, whose debt-GNP ratio base rose from 2 to 16 percent between 1973 and 1978 while the debt-export ratio increased from 15 to 133 percent and their debt-service ratio from 15 to 31 percent.

High levels of indebtedness limited the ability of inward-oriented economies to increase foreign borrowing at earlier rates after 1978. Whereas additional net external financing fully compensated for the balance-of-payments effects of external shocks in the economies in question in 1974–6, it offset only one-half of these effects in 1979–81. Reductions in imports associated with the application of deflationary policies accounted for much of the difference between the two periods as inward-oriented economies continued to be unsuccessful in raising output through increases in export market shares and import substitution.

By contrast, export promotion and import substitution, taken together, offset nearly one-half of the balance-of-payments effects of external shocks in outward-oriented economies in the 1979–81 period, even though import shares increased somewhat in outward-oriented LDCs. At the same time, outward-oriented economies slightly increased their reliance on additional net external financing and on deflationary macroeconomic policies in response to the greater external shocks they experienced in 1979–81 compared to 1974–6.

As in the previous period, outward-oriented LDCs placed greater reliance on additional net external financing, and lesser reliance on deflationary policies, than outward-oriented NICs. Correspondingly, their debt-GNP ratio increased more than that for outward-oriented NICs. The average ratio for the entire group was 16 per cent in 1981, compared to 12 per cent in 1978.

In the same period, the average debt-export ratio of outward-oriented economies increased only from 27 to 31 per cent, indicating their success in raising exports more rapidly than GNP. In turn, owing in large part to higher interest rates, the debt-service ratio of these economies rose from 9 to 12 per cent, with larger than average increases in outward-oriented LDCs.

Given their reliance on foreign borrowing, increases in the various debt indicators were much greater in inward-oriented economies. By 1981, the debt-GNP ratio of these economies reached 26 per cent while their debt-export ratio averaged 161 per cent and the debt-service ratio 36 per cent, even though continued foreign aid limited increases in the ratios in inward-oriented LDCs. High ratios of external debt and debt service to exports, in turn, set the stage for the financial difficulties inward-oriented economies came to experience once the commercial banks recognized the magnitude of the problem.

In response to their financial difficulties, inward-oriented economies adopted deflationary policies, and their gross national product stagnated in 1983. By contrast, outward-oriented economies had completed their, rather mild, deflationary phase by 1982 and reached average GNP growth rates of 5 per cent in 1983.

Successful adjustment in outward-oriented economies, notwithstanding the large external shocks they suffered, may be ascribed to their reliance on output-increasing policies of export promotion and import substitution, their judicious use of foreign borrowing, and in conjunction with these policies, the efficient use of borrowed funds. In turn, inward-oriented economies encountered financial difficulties as they failed to follow output-increasing policies, borrowed extensively, and used borrowed funds to increase consumption and/or invested them in projects that were often inefficient.[9]

Attention should further be given to the interdependence of the measures applied. In encouraging exports and import substitution, the adoption of realistic exchange rates reduced the need for external financing in outward-oriented economies. Conversely, in the absence of deflationary macroeconomic policies, the lack of export promotion and import substitution under inward orientation necessitated borrowing abroad and the inflow of capital contributed to the maintenance of overvalued exchange rates. Moreover, in creating expectations for a future devaluation, exchange rate overvaluation encouraged capital flight, thus further raising borrowing requirements.

A case in point is Mexico, whose real exchange rate – the nominal exchange rate adjusted for changes in relative price at home and abroad – appreciated by one-third between 1977 and 1981, with a further appreciation occurring in the first nine months of 1982. In turn, according to estimates made by the Manufacturers Hanover Trust, the outflow of private capital from Mexico totalled $12 billion in 1981 and $13 billion in 1982. In the latter year, the outflow is estimated at $3 billion from Argentina, $5 billion from Brazil, and $10 billion from Venezuela.[10]

Mexico also provides an example of a country where increases in the deficit of the public sector importantly contributed to external borrowing while reducing domestic saving. The deficit rose from 6 per cent of the gross domestic product in 1978 to 19 per cent in 1982. In the same period, the public sector deficit, expressed as a percentage of GDP, increased from 7 percent to 14 percent in Argentina, and from 6 percent to 14 percent in Brazil.[11]

The effects of government budget deficits on the external debt have further been investigated in an intercountry context by applying regression analysis to the data of 35 countries in the 1973–8 and in the 1978–82 periods. This has been done under two alternatives: by including official and private transfers (for short, transfers) with the change in the external debt as the dependent variable and by introducing transfers as an explanatory variable in the regression. In the first case, it is hypothesized that government budget deficits are financed through foreign borrowing and transfers; in the second case, it is hypothesized that transfers influence the extent to which the financing of government budget deficits entails foreign borrowing.

Equation (1) of Table 6.3 shows that the sum of the change in the external debt and cumulative transfers is highly correlated with the sum of government budget deficits in both the 1973–8 and the 1978–82 periods. The explanatory power of the regression equation rises – in particular in the second period – if *per capita* income is added as an explanatory variable. As shown in equation (2), this variable has a positive sign, indicating that the possibilities of financing budget deficits by foreign borrowing increase at higher levels of development.

In equation (3), the change in the external debt was regressed on the sum of government budget deficits, the sum of transfers, and *per capita* GNP. The level of statistical significance of the regression coefficients is relatively high and they have the expected sign, with the negative coefficient for transfers indicating that, for a given budget deficit, higher transfers give rise to less borrowing.

It appears, then, that government budget deficits have importantly influenced the debt situation of the developing countries in both the 1973–8 and 1979–83 periods. It further appears that the extent of reliance on foreign borrowing is positively correlated with the level of development and negatively correlated, with the official and private transfers to country receives.

III PROSPECTS FOR THE FUTURE

In recent years, the question has been repeatedly raised of whether the debt situation of the developing countries is sustainable. One may approach this question by making use of the model introduced by

TABLE 6.3 *Government budget deficits and the external debt*

Dependent variables	Independent variables			
Change in the external debt plus sum of transfers (percent of GNP)	Sum of Government budget deficits (percent of GNP)	Sum of official and private transfers (percent of GNP)	Per capita GNP initial year ($ million, logs)	R^2
(1a) 1973–78	1.082 (7.953)			0.657
(1b) 1978–82	0.719 (6.740)			0.594
(2a) 1973–78	0.899 (4.565)		1.328 (1.277)	0.664
(2b) 1978–82	0.421 (2.952)		2.120 (2.830)	0.669
Change in the external debt (percent of GNP)				
(3a) 1973–78	0.433 (3.688)	−0.208 (−2.352)	0.864 (1.545)	0.536
(3b) 1978–82	0.205 (2.026)	−0.228 (−1.838)	1.442 (2.823)	0.506

NOTE: The change in the external debt refers to the difference between terminal and initial year values; *per capita* GNP pertains to the initial year of the period; government budget deficits and transfers are cumulated values for each period; t-values are shown in parenthesis.

SOURCES: External Debt: Organization for Economic Cooperation and Development, *External Debt of Developing Countries*, various issues. Government Budget Deficit, Official and Private Transfers, Gross National Product, and Population: World Bank economic and social data base.

Evsey Domar.[12] Domar showed that the ratio of amortization and interest payments to the inflow of capital will asymptotically reach a limit, irrespective of whether the rate of growth of output exceeds, or falls short of, the rate of interest on foreign loans.

The debt situation will not be sustainable, however, if output continues to rise at a rate lower than the rate of interest. And sustainability is not necessarily ensured even when the rate of growth of output exceeds the rate of interest if consumption is related to national output, as in this case interest payments may eventually exhaust output.[13] In turn, if consumption is related to national income (i.e. output less income accruing to foreigners), the debt situation will be sustainable, provided that domestic resources are transformed into foreign resources for servicing the debt.[14]

The transformation of domestic into foreign resources requires that the necessary domestic savings are generated and they are translated into a surplus in the current account balance, exclusive of interest payments, through exports and/or import substitution.[15] All contributions to the problem have given emphasis to exports, implicitly assuming that the possibilities for import substitution in developing countries are limited.

The next question concerns the choice of indicators to gauge the sustainability of the debt situation in developing countries. Assuming that new debt is contracted only to pay interest, the debt will grow at the rate of interest. A comparison of output growth and the rate of interest can then be transformed into a comparison of the growth of output and that of the external debt. The latter indicator is, in fact, more general than the former, since it admits changes in the debt unrelated to the financing of interest charges.

But, using the ratio of the debt to GDP as an indicator of the sustainability of the debt situation does not take account of the problem of transforming domestic into foreign resources. Introducing the problem of transformation has, in turn, led to the use of indicators that take exports rather than output as the measure of comparison.

The ratio of interest payments and amortization to exports was introduced by Dragoslav Avramovic as an indicator of the strain the service of the debt represents for the balance of payments of the country concerned.[16] Avramovic emphasized the usefulness of this ratio for short-term analysis, noting that 'a higher ratio of fixed service commitments to external earnings implies a considerable short-run rigidity in the debtor country's balance of payments'.[17] He claimed, however, that 'the significance of the debt service ratio for long-run analysis of debt servicing capacity is virtually nil [as] the size of the debt service, and thus of the debt service ratio, is heavily influenced by maturities'.[18]

In turn, while admitting the statistical problems associated with the measurement of this ratio, David Roberts has suggested that 'the ratio of debt service to exports provides a rough measure of an economy's financial burden in [a] long-run sense. If this ratio is high, a large proportion of export earnings must be devoted to debt servicing, so that expanding imports, or even maintaining real imports as prices rise, may increasingly depend on uninterrupted flows of new loans.'[19]

It would, then, appear that high and rising debt-GNP and debt-service ratios provide an indication of the increasing precariousness of a country's debt situation, thus involving a risk for lenders. According to Jeffrey Sachs, the lenders will compensate for this risk by imposing an interest rate premium.[20] We thus have a testable proposition that the interest rate premium or spread, expressed as the margin over LIBOR, will be positively correlated with debt-GNP and debt-service ratios. This proportion has been tested by Sebastian Edwards who has found it confirmed in a model utilizing data for 19 countries in the years 1976-80.[21]

The use of the debt-service ratio as an indicator of the debt situation in developing countries implicitly assumes that all loans are reimbursed. But, as Avramovic noted, 'debt, whether of a corporation or of a country, is normally rolled over; and whenever it is repaid, it cannot be expected that a very large part of the total debt be repaid out of a year's income'.[22]

Assuming this to be the case, one may follow Mario Henrique Simonsen in using as an indicator of the sustainability of a country's debt situation the condition that the rate of growth of export earnings exceeds the rate of interest.[23] On the assumption that new debt is contracted only to pay interest, William Cline has transformed this condition into the requirement that the ratio of debt to exports declines or, at the least, does not rise.[24] Again, the condition can be generalized to the case when new debt is contracted independently from the financing of interest charges.

Having established the rationale for the use of alternative indicators to gauge the sustainability of a country's debt situation, one may utilize them to examine prospective changes in the debt of the developing countries. This will be done in the following by reviewing projections made in 1983 that employed the debt-service ratio,[25] the debt-export ratio,[26] or both ratios,[27] and by analyzing more recent developments.

The cited studies gave emphasis to the transformation of domestic into foreign resources by relating the external debt and the service of the debt to exports. This appears reasonable, considering that the estimates pertained to the medium-term, generally covering the years 1983 to 1986. Also, IMF programs usually involve the application of deflationary policies that lower rates of economic growth and may raise debt-GDP ratios for some years.

Projected changes in the debt situation of the developing countries will depend on the assumptions made as regards exogenous variables, including the prospects for the world economy, the foreign income elasticity of import demand, world market prices, and interest rates, as well as on the developing countries' own policies. The following discussion will concentrate on the assumptions made in regard to economic growth rates in the industrial countries, their income elasticity of import demand for goods originating in the developing countries, and the real rate of interest, neglecting changes in the relative prices of exports and imports.[28]

Under its base scenario, the IMF projected that a 1.6 percent average rate of GNP growth in the industrial countries in 1983 would be followed by a growth rate slightly below 3 percent in 1984–6. The corresponding increase in the volume of exports of the non-oil developing countries was estimated at 4.6 percent in 1983, reflecting in part a rebound from 1982, and 5.7 percent a year between 1983 and 1986. The growth of exports was to permit the avoiding of further increases in debt-service ratios of the non-oil developing countries while their debt-export ratio was projected to decline by 7 percent during this period. All in all, according to the Fund staff 'the non-oil developing countries as a group could improve their external positions substantially by 1986, provided that countries with serious imbalances implement comprehensive programs of adjustment'.[29]

Cline made projections for the 19 largest debtor countries for the same period. In the base case, he assumed that the gross domestic product of the industrial countries would rise by 1.5 percent in 1983 and by 3.0 percent a year between 1983 and 1986 while LIBOR would decline from 5 percent in 1983 to 4 percent in 1984 and 3 percent in 1985 in real terms. In turn, the industrial countries' income elasticity of demand for imports originating in the developing countries was taken to be 3 in all the variants. Cline concluded that, under the base case assumptions, 'the severity of the debt problem recedes substantially' in the non-oil developing countries.[30]

Enders and Mattione studied the case of the seven major borrowers in Latin America (Argentina, Brazil, Chile, Colombia, Mexico, Peru and Venezuela) that account for a substantial proportion of the indebtedness of the developing countries and where the problems of the debt are particularly pronounced. The authors projected the rate of economic growth to rise from 2.6 percent in 1983 to 4.8 percent in 1984 and to subsequently decline to 3.5 percent by 1986 in the United States, the corresponding figures for the four major European countries (France, Germany, Italy, and the United Kingdom) being 1.3 percent, 3.0 percent, and 2.1 percent. The authors further expected Eurodollar interest rates to average 11 percent during the period, corresponding to real rates of 4–5 percent.[31] However, they assumed lower income elasticities of import demand than Cline and the IMF, and thus projected smaller improvements in debt-export ratios than the other two studies.

Finally, the average debt-service ratio for six major Latin American countries (the countries studied by Enders and Mattione other than Colombia) would decline slightly between 1983 and 1986 under the base line estimates made by Adams, Sanchez, and Adams. These authors utilized forecasts developed by Wharton Econometrics on economic growth in the industrial countries, with average growth rates of 1.6 percent in 1983, 4.0 percent in 1984, subsequently declining to 2.3 percent in 1986, while LIBOR was assumed to be slightly positive in real terms. The authors further presented a crisis scenario, with the GDP of the industrial countries declining by 1.7 percent in 1983, increasing by only 0.5 percent in 1984, under which the debt-service ratio for the six Latin American countries would be one-fifth higher than under the baseline simulation.

In actual fact, the gross domestic product of the industrial countries rose by 2.4 percent in 1983 and, after projecting a growth rate of 3.5 percent for 1984 in December 1983, the OECD subsequently raised this projection by three-quarters of a percentage point. More importantly for Latin American countries, United States GDP rose by 3.4 percent in 1983 and it is projected to increase by 6 percent in 1984. Also, the volume of the exports of the non-oil developing countries increased by 7 percent in 1983 and it is expected to rise at the same rate in 1984, with export prices increasing by 5 percent.[32]

In April 1984, the IMF estimated that the dollar value of the exports of goods and services by the non-oil developing countries would rise by 10 percent in 1984, leading to a 3 percent decline in their debt-export and debt-service ratios (Table 6.1). Under its base scenario for the 1984–90 period, the IMF projects a further 14 percent decline in the debt-export ratio of the non-oil developing countries while, after a temporary increase, the debt-service ratio of these countries would regain its 1984 level. The temporary increase in the debt-service ratio would be due to higher debt repayments as the ratio of interest payments to the exports of goods and services would fall from 13 percent in 1983 and 1984 to 11 percent in 1987 and 9 percent in 1990.

Increases in amortization would be even greater for the twenty-five largest borrowers among developing countries (for short, major borrowers), a number of which postponed repayments in framework of large-scale reschedulings. Nevertheless, according to the report, 'the growth in exports and financing assumed between 1984 and 1987 leaves these countries in a much better position to pay for their required imports than was the case in 1982 and 1983'.[33] The described outcome is assumed to occur in the context of renewed economic growth in the non-oil developing countries, with their gross domestic product rising 4.6 percent a year between 1984 and 1990, following increases of 2 percent in the 1981–2 period and 3.5 percent in 1984.

These projections are based on the assumption that interest rates paid on the developing countries' debt would remain at the 1983 level in 1984 and in 1985, declining by 2 percentage points in 1986, and by another percentage point afterwards. It is further assumed that the dollar price of manufactured goods would rise by 4 percent and the gross national product of the industrial countries would increase by 3.25 percent a year throughout the period, with the volume of exports of the non-oil developing countries increasing at an average annual rate of 5.3 percent.

IV POLICY IMPLICATIONS

The latest IMF estimates reflect improvements in the debt situation of the developing countries. As economic growth in the industrial countries accelerated and most major borrowing countries undertook stabilization measures, the current account deficit of the major borrowers, exclusive of interest payments, declined from $24.2 billion in 1981 to $12.5 billion in 1982, turning into a surplus of $18.6 billion in 1983 and $34.0 billion in 1984. In 1983, the ratio of the surplus in the current account (exclusive of interest payments) was 5.9 percent of the exports of goods and services. After rising to 9.9 percent in 1984, this ratio is projected to decline to 7.2 percent in 1987 and to 4.5 percent in 1990.

The IMF projections may be considered as likely trend values. One would have to further consider, however, the implications of deviations from trend values for the debt situation of the developing countries. According to the report, an increase in LIBOR by one percentage point and a decline in the rate of economic growth in the industrial countries by one percentage point would equally raise debt-service ratios for the non-oil developing countries by one percentage point in 1987.[34]

While the IMF report, completed at the end of February 1984, assumed interest rates to remain unchanged in 1984, LIBOR rose by two percentage points between February and May of the same year. These increases have attracted considerable attention as have forecasts made in financial circles for further increases in US interest rates that are soon transmitted to the London Interbank Rate.

Deviations from the trend may also occur if increases in interest rates adversely affect economic expansion in the United States. There may also be year-to-year fluctuations around the trend and the debt situation of individual borrowing countries may vary to a considerable extent. At the same time, such variations as well as unforeseen events in one or the other of the major borrowing countries may have implications for other countries as well. The question arises, then, as to what are appropriate policies to cope with the problem of the debt in developing countries in a situation fraught with uncertainty.

Various policy alternatives have been suggested for the developing countries to deal with their external debt. One such alternative would involve their taking unilateral action that would substantially reduce the present value of the debt or extinguish it through outright repudiation. This would represent a break with the practice of recent years as the reschedulings have not occasioned losses to lenders.

Enders and Mattione examined the possible consequences for Latin American countries of consolidating all foreign loans outstanding on 31 December, 1982 into 22 year loans at a 6 percent interest rate, with a two-year delay before repayments begin, involving a reduction in the present value of outstanding loans by approximately one-half.[35] Assuming that commercial banks would extend no new loans to the countries concerned for five years, the authors concluded that 'such a restructuring would by 1987 make Latin America as a whole worse off than the current reschedulings and stabilization plans'.[36]

Enders and Mattione further considered the case of the repudiation of the external debt, assuming that this would entail the loss of foreign reserves, as well as decreases in export unit values and increases in import unit values, owing to actions by foreign suppliers and purchasers to insure themselves against losses and attempts by creditors to attach goods and bank accounts as was the case after the 1981 events in Iran. Assuming further that the countries in question would have to build reserves equal to four months of imports by 1986 and could not have negative reserves in the intervening period, a 10 percent loss in export receipts and a 10 percent increase in the cost of imports would leave only Argentina better off among the seven major Latin American borrowers, and even Argentina would be worse off if the cost in terms of exports and imports was 15 rather than 10 percent. At the same time, disruptions in foreign trade are likely to be greater than assumed, thus increasing the adverse effects of this alternative for the borrowing countries.

A further consideration is that any single developing country undertaking such actions would adversely affect the borrowing possibilities of other countries. In recognition of this fact Brazil, Colombia, Mexico, and Venezuela extended a $300 million bridging loan to Argentina to assure the payment of interest on its foreign debt in March 1984 and subsequently extended the loan to June 1984. The action taken may be explained by the fact that the unhindered operation of the international financial system is more important for these countries than for Argentina, which sends a large proportion of its exports to the Soviet Union and requires neither food nor oil imports.

Focusing on domestic policies, it is observed that the improvement in the current account balance of the major borrowing countries between 1981 and 1983 was brought about entirely through the compression of imports, with the volume of exports remaining unchanged. This was the result of the stabilization policies applied, mostly under programs negotiated with the IMF, that entailed the practical stagnation of economic activity in these countries.

CONCLUSIONS

While 1984 brought improvements, with both exports and imports rising, there is need for adjustment measures that focus on increasing domestic supply in the developing countries. This would necessitate policy reforms, in particular in the major borrowing countries that have pursued inward-oriented policies and often carried out extensive government interventions.

The proposed policy reforms would involve improving the system of incentives and giving a greater role to market forces. Apart from the adoption of realistic exchange rates and reductions in the deficit of the public sector, this would require reducing the bias of the incentive system against exports and agriculture, liberalizing prices, establishing realistic interest rates, and providing appropriate incentives for private investment.

Turkey provides an example of combining stabilization measures and policy reforms. The measures introduced in January 1980 aimed at turning the economy outward and increasing the role of market forces while reducing the rate of inflation and improving the balance of payments. They included a substantial devaluation of the exchange rate, incentives to exports, the liberalization of imports, the abolition of price control, together with reductions in the budget deficit and lowering the rate of growth of the money supply. Subsequently, interest rates were raised and incentives were provided to private investment.

While political and social uncertainties retarded the impact of the measures taken until political stability was established in September 1980, the data for 1981 and 1982 indicate the success of the reform efforts. To begin with, the dollar value of Turkish exports rose by 62 percent in 1981. While the expansion of exports to the Middle East was an important contributing factor, the dollar value of exports to the industrial countries also increased by 35 percent, even though the total non-oil imports of these countries fell by 10 percent in the same year. Turkish exports to the industrial countries increased again by 13 percent in 1982 whereas the non-oil imports of these countries declined by 6 percent.

Export expansion, in turn, contributed to economic growth in Turkey. The gross domestic product rose by 4 percent in 1981, followed by an increase of 5 percent in 1982. Furthermore, the rate of inflation declined from a peak of 133 percent in February 1980 to 20 percent by the end of 1982 as measured by the wholesale price index. Finally, notwithstanding increases in imports following the import scarcity of the years 1978–9, the deficit in the current account balance fell from $3.2 billion in 1980 to $2.1 billion in 1981 and, again, to $1.0 billion in 1982.[37]

Turkey provides an example of the success of reform efforts in increasing exports and national income, even though the reforms were undertaken in an unfavorable world environment and were carried out simultaneously with the application of stabilization measures. As a result, Turkey has again become creditworthy for borrowing in international financial markets after having been practically bankrupt in 1979.

The Turkish experience thus supports the evidence presented in Section II of this essay on the importance of policy choices in effecting adjustment. At the same time, as shown in Section II, apart from export expansion, appropriate domestic policies will contribute to efficient import substitution. In addition to import substitution in export industries, agriculture and energy provide possibilities for reducing imports if appropriate policies are followed.

Nevertheless, exports would have a crucial role to play in the adjustment as they have in the case of Turkey. Possibilities for exporting exist as the world economy is again expanding. Also, apart from some hardening of the Multifiber Arrangement and limitations imposed on steel imports from a few suppliers, protection in the industrial countries on their imports from the developing countries has not increased in recent years. Moreover, there are important markets in the OPEC countries and in the Far East.

Nevertheless, the industrial countries bear a special responsibility to liberalize their trade and to provide assurances that trade barriers will not be raised on their imports from the developing countries. The industrial countries should also reduce their budget deficits that contribute to high interest rates.

It would further be desirable to grant new credits and to return to more normal spreads above LIBOR in the case of developing countries that have undertaken serious adjustment efforts. The spreads on loans to the oil-importing developing countries averaged 1.0 percentage point in the first three quarters of 1982, but increased to 1.9 percentage points in the first three quarters of 1983.[38]

While the absolute amount involved may not be large, reductions in the spreads represent an important signal to countries that have undertaken adjustment. The commercial banks reduced spreads on Mexico's debt in January and again in June 1984; similar actions would need to be taken in regard to other borrowers carrying out adjustment, in particular Brazil. Nor would this jeopardize the profitability of the commercial banks that has not required increases in the spread.

The procedures used in rescheduling loans would also need to be modified. Apart from Mexico, rescheduling has been limited to loans falling due in a single year. This procedure does not appropriately serve the needs of either borrowers or lenders. Rather, one should take a longer-term perspective, involving the rescheduling of loans falling due over two or three years, with a stretching-out of the repayment period. This would reduce uncertainty for all involved and avoid having periodical reschedulings, with attendant costs for the lenders as well as the borrowers.

With the revival of the world economy and the pursuit of appropriate policies by the industrial and by the developing countries, then, the major borrowing countries may find a solution for their debt problem. At the same time, for reasons noted above, one has to prepare for contingencies. Rather than creating new institutions as it has been suggested in recent years, this may best be done in the framework of existing institutions although there may be need to assign new tasks to them.

US Treasury Secretary Donald Regan stated in testimony before the Banking, Finance, and Urban Affairs Committee of the US House of Representatives that, apart from domestic adjustment efforts in the developing countries, 'the second key element is a readiness to provide official financing on a transitional basis where that is needed to permit orderly adjustment to take place. The international institution best able to provide official support within the context of domestic economic adjustment is the IMF.' For the IMF to continue to effectively perform this role would, however, require increasing the financial resources available to it.

Following the rise in interest rates in early 1984, proposals have been put forward for a 'cap' on the rates, with the difference added to debt obligations. These proposals have been criticized on the grounds that the application of a cap may induce developing countries to slacken their adjustment efforts and that industrial country governments could not induce the commercial banks to forego interest receipts at present by adding these to the debt without a quid pro quo.

While these objections carry weight, it should be recognized that increases in interest rates create difficulties for the borrowing countries and may also give them an excuse to postpone payment on their debt. To avoid these adverse consequences, it would be desirable to devise a scheme that ensures the continuation of adjustment efforts in the developing countries while reducing uncertainties relating to interest rates.

It is proposed here to establish an Interest Equalization Scheme in the IMF, modeled on the Compensatory Financing Facility, for this purpose. The new facility would provide loans to compensate for a substantial part, say two-thirds, of the excess burden of interest payments on loans subject to variable rates, whenever LIBOR rises above a pre-determined benchmark. The use of this benchmark would mean excluding the effects of changes in margins above LIBOR that should reflect changes in the creditworthiness of individual countries. In order to allow for variations in inflation rates, the benchmark rate should be set in real terms.[39]

As in the case of the Compensatory Financing Scheme, the IMF would provide loans if real interest rates rise above the benchmark, to be repaid at the time when the rates fall below the benchmark. Furthermore, access to the facility would be limited to countries that have an agreed-upon program with the IMF.

These programs concentrate on stabilization measures that would need to be complemented by policy reforms as suggested above. Support for such efforts has been provided to a number of developing countries by the World Bank. In order to permit a larger number of countries to benefit from World Bank financing of their structural adjustment program, the funds available for this purpose would also need to be increased, possibly involving the establishment of a new facility.

NOTES

1. The countries outside the non-oil developing countries group are Algeria, Indonesia, Iran, Iraq, Kuwait, Libya, Nigeria, Oman, Quatar, Saudi Arabia, United Arab Emirates, and Venezuela (International Monetary Fund, *World Economic Outlook*, Occasional Paper 21, 1983, p. 167). Among these countries the debt statistics reported by the World Bank (*World Debt Tables, External Debt of Developing Countries*, 1983–84 Edition, Washington, DC, 1984) for the developing countries include Algeria, Indonesia, Nigeria, Oman, and Venezuela while excluding a number of small countries that are comprised in the IMF statistics. Thus, the number of countries covered in the World Bank's debt statistics totals 103, compared with 117 countries for the IMF.
2. Export prices are relevant because the service of the external debt involves the use of export earnings. In turn, information on import prices permits indicating changes in the purchasing power of the external debt.
3. The rationale for these indicators is discussed in Section III below.
4. Such an adjustment has been made by William Cline, who calculated the inflationary erosion of the year-end debt of the previous year by using the US wholesale prices index as deflator. Cf. W. R. Cline, *International Debt and the Stability of the World Economy* (Washington, DC: Institute for International Economics, 1983). In the present essay, the average outstanding debt in a particular year has been deflated by the import price index of the developing countries. This price index has been used on the grounds that the purchasing power of the debt is affected by changes in import prices. In turn, from the national accounting point of view, the appropriate deflator is the consumer price index as shown in R. Dornbusch, 'Consumption Opportunities and the Real Value of the External Debt', *Journal of Development Economics*, X (1982) pp. 93–101.
5. B. Balassa, 'Structural Adjustment Policies in Developing Countries', Essay 4 in this volume.
6. For a more detailed discussion of the balance-of-payments effects of external shocks, and of policy responses to these shocks, see B. Balassa, 'Adjustment Policies in Developing Countries: A Reassessment', Essay 5 in this volume.
7. Again, larger than average increases are shown in the debt-export ratio of the outward-oriented LDCs. However, debt-service ratios remained unchanged in both groups between 1973 and 1978.
8. Note that the external debt of the developing countries increased even in the absence of additional net external financing because foreign borrowings were in an upward trend before 1973. This is because, as noted in the Annex, additional net external financing represents above-trend inflows.
9. In May 1983 in Washington, DC the Institute for International Economics

organized a conference in 'The ABM Threat', making reference to the problems created by the external debt of Argentina, Brazil, and Mexico. In the course of the discussion, the author raised the rhetorical question as to why we do not speak of 'the KST Threat', referring to the fact that Korea, Singapore, and Taiwan borrowed judiciously and used the funds largely for efficient investments so that questions about their creditworthiness have not arisen.

10. *Financial Times*, 1 December 1983.
11. S. Edwards, 'LDCs' Foreign Borrowing and Default Risk. An Empirical Investigation 1976–1980', National Bureau of Economic Research, Working Paper, 1172 (1983) p. 65.
12. E. Domar, 'The Effect of Foreign Investment on the Balance of Payments', *American Economic Review*, XL (1950) pp. 805–26. Reprinted in E. Domar, *Essays in the Theory of Economic Growth* (New York: Oxford University Press, 1957) pp. 129–57.
13. B. B. King, *Notes on the Mechanics of Growth and Debt*, World Bank Occasional Papers, 6 (Baltimore, Md: Johns Hopkins University Press, 1968).
14. If foreign borrowing is the only source of investment as assumed by Domar, this condition will be fulfilled in the event that the rate of return on the projects financed by such borrowing exceeds the rate of interest. In turn, the rise in the debt-GNP ratio in inward-oriented developing economies after 1973 may be interpreted as an indication that the condition has not been met.
15. In the case of the public debt, a further condition is that private savings are transformed into public savings.
16. D. Avramovic, *Debt Servicing Capacity and Postwar Growth in International Indebtedness* (Baltimore, Md: John Hopkins University Press, 1958) p. 63.
17. Avramovic, p. 102.
18. D. Avramovic *et al. Economic Growth and External Debt* (Baltimore, Md: Johns Hopkins University Press, 1964) p. 42.
19. D. Roberts, 'The LDC Debt Burden', *Federal Reserve Bank of New York* (Spring, 1981) p. 38.
20. J. Sachs, 'LDC Debt in the 1980s: Risk and Reforms', National Bureau of Economic Research, Working Paper, 861 (1982) p. 33.
21. Edwards, p. 18.
22. Avramovic *et al.* pp. 44–5.
23. M. H. Simonsen, 'The Financial Crisis in Latin America', Rio de Janeiro, Getulio Vargas Foundation, 1983 (mimeo).
24. Cline, p. 18.
25. F. G. Adams, E. P. Sanchez and M. E. Adams, 'Can Latin America Carry Its International Debt? A Prospective Analysis Using the Wharton Latin American Debt Simulation Model', *Journal of Policy Modeling*, V (1983) pp. 419–41.
26. T. O. Enders and R. P. Mattione, *Latin America: The Crisis of Debt and Growth* (Washington, DC: The Brookings Institution, 1984).
27. Cline also uses a statistical model of debt rescheduling that includes additional variables, such as the ratio of reserves to imports and the current

account deficit; similar variables have been included by Edwards in estimating his model.

28. The International Monetary Fund (p. 207) assumed that the terms of trade of the non-oil developing countries would improve by 0.2 percent a year between 1983 and 1986, following an improvement of 1.5 percent in 1983; the assumptions made in regard to interest rates were not indicated in the report.
29. International Monetary Fund, p. 19.
30. Cline, p. 52.
31. Enders and Mattione, p. 36.
32. Organization for Economic Co-operation and Development, *OECD Economic Outlook*, 35 (Paris: OECD, 1984).
33. International Monetary Fund, *World Economic Outlook*, Occasional Paper 27 (1984) p. 70.
34. International Monetary Fund, *World Economic Outlook*, Occasional Paper 27 (1984) p. 221.
35. This alternative would involve a spread of about −4 percent for the commercial banks that roughly corresponds to the spreads that would obtain under several of the proposals made, including that by Felix Rohatyn. At the same time, according to Enders and Mattione, spreads of less than 0.5 percent would make foreign lending unprofitable for the commercial banks.
36. Enders and Mattione, p. 46.
37. For a detailed discussion and information on statistical sources, see B. Balassa, 'Outward Orientation and Exchange Rate Policy in Developing Countries: The Turkish Experience', Essay 10 in the volume.
38. World Bank, p. xiii.
39. Ideally, the adjustment should be made by utilizing the export price index for manufactured goods in the industrial countries, but delays in the preparation of this index may favor using a consumer price index.

Part III
Economic Policies in
Developing Economies

Essay 7 Trade Policy in Mexico

INTRODUCTION

This essay provides an evaluation of the trade policies applied in Mexico during the last quarter of the century and makes recommendations for the future. It follows the author's advisory reports for the Government of Mexico, which proposed introducing an export subsidy scheme[1] and reforming foreign trade and industrial policies[2] as well as his appraisal of the policies of the 1973–8 period and recommendations for modifying these policies.[3]

The essay will examine the policies applied in three, well-defined periods. The first period, from 1956 to 1971, is considered to be one of relative stability following the rapid inflation and devaluations of the first postwar decade, although it was characterized by the increasing overvaluation of the peso. The second period starts with the acceleration of government spending in March 1972 under President Echeverria and ends with the devaluations of September–December 1976. The third period covers the Presidency of José López Portillo (December 1976–December 1982).

The discussion of each of the three periods will begin with a description of the macroeconomic background that is necessary for understanding changes in Mexico's trade policy. This will be followed by an analysis of trade policy developments, with further attention given to industrial policy measures. Finally, changes in Mexican exports and imports and their contribution to industrial growth will be discussed.

131

I THE PERIOD OF 'STABILIZING DEVELOPMENT' (1956–71)

Macroeconomic background

In the first decade following the Second World War, prices rose rapidly in Mexico, giving rise to an inflation–devaluation cycle. With successive devaluations, the peso–dollar exchange rate more than doubled, from 4.85 in 1945 to 12.50 in September 1954; it was maintained at that level until September 1976.

Antonio Ortiz Mena, Secretary of Treasury from 1958 to 1970, called the decade following the establishment of the new exchange parity a period of 'Stabilizing Development' in Mexico.[4] This designation is appropriate to the extent that the rate of inflation declined from the preceding decade. Nevertheless, it continued to exceed inflation rates in the United States – Mexico's principal trading partner – accounting for two-thirds of its merchandise exports and imports. The US share reaches nine-tenths for service transactions and it is nearly 100 percent for border trade.

Gerardo Bueno calculated real exchange rates for the peso vis-à-vis the US dollar by taking 1956 as the base year, on the grounds that this year represented an approximate equilibrium position in Mexico's balance of payments.[5] A further argument in favor of his choice is that the price increases resulting from the September 1954 devaluation can be assumed to have run their course by this time.

In the event, wholesale prices rose by 32 percent in Mexico and by 10 percent in the United States between 1956 and 1967. With the nominal exchange rate remaining unchanged, the Mexican peso appreciated in real terms by 17 percent vis-à-vis the US dollar during this period (Table 7.1).

According to Leopoldo Solis, Head of the Economic Programming Group of the Secretary of the Presidency between 1971 and 1975 and long-time Director of Research at the Bank of Mexico, '1968 ... marked the beginning of the inflation period that became rampant in the 1970s'.[6] But, inflation accelerated in the United States as well, so that there was little further appreciation in the real value of the peso until 'the spending spree of 1972'[7] under President Echeverria. All in all, wholesale prices increased by 52 percent in Mexico between 1956 and 1971, compared to a rise of 26 percent in the US wholesale price index, while the peso–dollar exchange rate remained unchanged.

Increases in public consumption, with its share in the gross domestic product rising from 4.4 percent in 1956 to 8.1 percent in 1971,

TABLE 7.1 Changes in real exchange rates in Mexico, 1956–1980

	1956	1957	1958	1959	1960	1961	1962	1963	1964	1965	1966	1967	1968	1969	1970
Exchange rate (peso/$US)	12.5	12.5	12.5	12.5	12.5	12.5	12.5	12.5	12.5	12.5	12.5	12.5	12.5	12.5	12.5
Index of exchange rate	100.0	100.0	100.0	100.0	100.0	100.0	100.0	100.0	100.0	100.0	100.0	100.0	100.0	100.0	100.0
Domestic wholesale price index	68.4	71.4	74.6	75.4	79.1	79.8	81.3	81.6	85.1	86.8	87.8	90.3	92.1	94.5	100.0
US wholesale price index	82.3	84.5	85.7	85.9	86.1	85.7	85.9	85.6	85.7	87.5	90.5	90.6	92.9	96.5	100.0
Index of relative prices vis-à-vis US	83.1	84.5	87.0	87.8	91.9	93.1	94.6	95.0	99.3	99.2	97.0	99.7	99.1	97.9	100.0
Index of real exchange rate vis-à-vis US	120.3	118.3	114.9	114.3	108.8	107.4	105.7	105.3	100.7	100.8	103.1	100.3	100.9	102.1	100.0

	1971	1972	1973	1974	1975	1976	1977	1978	1979	1980	1981	1981IV	1982I	1982II	1982III
Exchange rate (pesa/$US)	12.5	12.5	12.5	12.5	12.5	15.43	22.57	22.76	22.80	22.95	24.51	25.68	34.34	46.7	65.5
Index of exchange rate	100.0	100.0	100.0	100.0	100.0	123.4	180.6	182.1	182.4	183.4	196.1	205.5	274.7	374.1	524.2
Domestic wholesale price index	103.8	106.7	123.6	151.3	167.2	204.5	288.6	334.1	395.3	492.1	613.7	701.4	743.0	858.4	1021.4
US wholesale price index	103.3	107.9	122.0	145.0	158.5	165.8	175.9	189.7	213.5	243.4	265.5	268.0	270.2	270.5	272.0
Index of relative prices vis-à-vis US	100.5	98.9	101.3	104.3	105.5	123.3	164.1	176.1	185.2	202.2	231.1	261.7	275.0	317.31	375.5
Index of real exchange rate vis-à-vis US	99.5	101.1	98.7	95.9	94.8	100.1	110.1	103.4	98.5	90.8	84.9	78.5	99.9	117.9	139.6

SOURCE: International Monetary Fund, *International Financial Statistics*.

importantly contributed to inflation in Mexico. The increased expenditures augmented the deficit of the public sector that equalled 5.1 percent of GDP in 1971. The deficit was financed in part through money creation, leading to the rise in the ratio of the money supply (money and quasi-money) to GDP from 15.1 percent in 1956 to 16.5 percent in 1971, and in part by the inflow of foreign capital, with Mexico's current account deficit rising from 1.4 percent of the gross domestic product in 1956 to 2.3 percent in 1971. Increased foreign indebtedness, in turn, gave rise to increases in the debt-service ratio (the ratio of debt-service charges to the value of merchandise exports) that reached 58 percent in 1971.

The increase in the ratio of the current account deficit to GDP was concentrated in the first several years of the period, when much of the deterioration of Mexico's competitive position occurred; the real value of the peso appreciated by 10 percent between 1956 and 1960. In turn, the ratio of the merchandise trade deficit to the gross domestic product increased from 2.8 percent of GNP in 1956 to 3.2 percent in 1960, subsequently declining to 2.5 percent in 1971. These changes occurred as export and import shares declined at different rates, in response to the incentives provided.

Trade policy developments

With the increasing overvaluation of the peso, pressures developed to raise protection levels. In the early part of the period, tariffs were raised in the framework of the 1956 revision of the general tariff classification and increased use was made of quantitative import restrictions. As shown in Table 7.2, the number of controlled import categories nearly doubled between 1956 and 1962, with their share in the total rising from 33 to 44 percent. In the same period, the share of controlled imports in import value increased from 28 to 52 percent.

Under the 1956 Regulation for the Granting of Import Permits, newly imposed import controls were often accompanied by agreements with firms on the replacement of imports in exchange for the free importation of parts, components, and accessories. This regulation was the counterpart of the Law of Promotion of New and Necessary Industries, which provided incentives to newly-established industries as well as to industries where domestic output supplied less than 80 percent of consumption. Both groups of industries were granted tariff exemptions on the importation of machinery and of inputs used in the

TABLE 7.2 *Import licensing in Mexico 1956–79*

	No. of import categories				Import value (percent)		
	Total	Controlled	Free	Percent	Total	Controlled	Free
1956	4 129	1 376	2 753	33	100	28	72
1962	5 204	2 313	2 891	44	100	52	48
1964	na	na	na	na	100	65	35
1966	11 000	6 600	4 400	60	na	na	na
1970	12 900[a]	8 400[a]	4 500[a]	65[a]	100	59	41
1971	na	na	na	na	100	57	43
1972	na	na	na	na	100	56	44
1973	16 000	12 300	3 200	80	100	64	36
1974	na	na	na	na	100	74	26
1977	7 340[b]	5 859[b]	1 481[b]	80[b]	na	na	na
1979	7 776[b]	1 866[b]	5 910[b]	24[b]	100[c]	60[c]	40[c]

NOTES: (a) L. Solis, *Economic Policy Reform in Mexico: A Case Study for Developing Countries* (New York: Pergamon Press, 1981).
(b) J. A. Abraham and G. del Rio, 'El Comercio exterior Mexicano. Análisis y perspectivas', *Comercio y Desarrollo*, VI (1981) p. 8.
(c) Direct communication.

SOURCE: Except as noted, Cárdenas Ortega, A., 'Algunos aspectos sobre instrumentos de control en la política de comercio exterior', *Investigación Económica*, XXXV (1976) Table 3.

production process, thereby increasing the level and the variance of effective protection.

The unification of customs classification in 1960 provided another opportunity for raising tariff rates. Subsequently, a surtax of 10 percent was imposed on luxury imports in 1962. Finally, all tariffs were increased by 6 percentage points in 1965.

The scope of import controls was also enlarged during the sixties, with approximately one thousand import categories added to the controlled list every year. By 1970, the number of controlled items reached 65 percent of the total (Table 7.2). In the same year, the share of controlled imports in total import value was 59 percent; while the ratio was lower than the peak of 65 percent in 1964, this is explained by the increased import share of raw materials and fuels, that were not subject to import controls.

Table 7.3 shows the extent of increases in effective protection rates in the Mexican manufacturing sector between 1960 and 1970. While the protection of durable consumer and capital goods appears to have risen the least, this was due to the decline in effective protection rates on automobiles from 255 percent to 111 percent which still remained the highest in any industry other than fertilizers. Effective protection rates increased from 45 percent to 67 percent on non-electrical machinery,

TABLE 7.3 *Effective protection in Mexico, 1960 and 1970*

	Effective rate of protection	
	1960	*1970*
Primary	2.7	− 2.7
− Agriculture, livestock, forestry and fishing	3.0	− 1.4
− Mining	− 0.3	− 12.3
Non-durable consumer goods	21.6	31.6
Intermediate goods	13.2	16.8
Durable consumer and capital goods	64.6	77.2

SOURCE: A. T. Kate and R. B. Wallace, *Protection and Economic Development in Mexico* (Rotterdam: Center for Development Planning, 1980) p. 135.

from 48 percent to 88 percent on electrical equipment, and from 49 percent to 90 percent on transport equipment.[8]

If we also consider the protectionist measures taken between 1956 and 1960, it will appear that increases in industrial protection outweighed the effects of the overvaluation of the peso, thereby contributing to lower import shares. Rising protection, in turn, increased the bias against manufactured exports as export incentives were negligible; only 20 percent of manufactured exports received preferential credits in 1969, the extent of credit preferences remained small, and tax rebates on exports were unimportant during the period. At the same time, exports suffered the effects of the overvaluation of the peso.

The effective protection of the primary sector turned negative during the sixties, with effective rates of − 1.4 percent in agriculture, livestock, forestry, and fishing and − 12.3 percent in mining (Table 7.3). In the first case, lower nominal protection and higher input costs (in particular, for fertilizer), in the second, the imposition of export taxes, contributed to this result.

Agricultural exports further suffered the effects of the price policy introduced under the aegis of CONASUPO (Compania Nacional de Subsistencias Populares), established in 1961, that fixed the prices of certain domestically-consumed goods above world market levels. With exports sold at world market prices, there was increased discrimination against export crops, in particular cotton.

Trade and industrial growth

The increased anti-export bias adversely affected the exports of both primary and manufactured products. The rise in discrimination against cotton explains the absolute decline in Mexican exports of this commodity between 1955–7 and 1970–2. With world exports continuing to rise, Mexico's share in the total fell from 11.4 percent to 4.9 percent during the period. Mexico's share declined in the world exports of beef and coffee as well. In turn, increases in its share in the world exports of cattle and sugar are explained by the rise of US demand in the case of the former and by the increased US quota allotment in the case of the latter.

Mexico further experienced an absolute decline in its exports of nonferrous metals (silver, lead, and copper) that accounted for 15 percent of total exports in 1955–7 but for only 4 percent in 1970–2. All in all, the volume of Mexican primary exports increased by altogether 2 percent during the sixties while these exports rose by 16 percent in Korea and 18 percent in Taiwan, both of which followed outward-oriented policies.[9]

Mexico also lost market shares in manufactured exports. Between 1960 and 1970, its manufactured exports grew at an average annual rate of 5 percent in volume terms, compared to increases averaging 16 percent a year in the exports of developing countries to developed country markets.[10] Korea and Taiwan much exceeded the average; manufactured exports rose 33 percent a year in the first case and 24 percent in the second.

With slow increases in manufactured exports, their contribution to the growth of industrial output was only 3 percent in Mexico while it was 45 percent in Korea and 51 percent in Taiwan. In turn, in response to protection, the contribution of import substitution to industrial growth was 11 percent in Mexico; it was −2 percent in Korea and 3 percent in Taiwan.[11]

II THE ECHEVERRIA EXPANSION (1972–76)

Macroeconomic background

Leopoldo Solis speaks of 'the loss of budget discipline ... as spending programs were directly promoted by the President [Echeverria]'[12] after

March 1982. The share of government consumption in the gross domestic product increased from 8.1 percent in 1971 to 8.5 percent in 1972, rising further to 10.0 percent in 1975. Increases were even larger in public investment, with its share in GDP rising from 5.0 percent in 1971 to 8.7 percent in 1975. As social transfers increased at a higher, and public revenues at a lower rate, the deficit of the public sector rose from 5.1 percent of GDP in 1971 to 8.8 percent in 1975.

The deficit was increasingly financed by foreign borrowing that provided 32 percent of the net financial requirements of the public sector in 1971 and 50 percent in 1975. Foreign borrowing made it possible for Mexico to maintain the exchange rate at 12.50 pesos to the US dollar until September 1976 while the current account deficit increased from 2.3 percent of GDP in 1971 to 5.3 percent in 1975.

The deterioration of the current account reflected largely the direct (through import leakages) and indirect (through rapid inflation) effects of expansionary fiscal policies on imports. The subsequent slowdown of import growth, associated with lower rates of growth of public expenditures, reduced the ratio of the current account deficit to GDP to 3.8 percent in 1976, but this ratio still remained substantially above the 1971 level. With higher foreign borrowing, Mexico's debt-service ratio reached 88 percent in 1976.

Expansionary fiscal policies led to increases in the money supply averaging 22 percent a year between 1971 and 1976, approximately double the rate of growth of the previous fifteen years. Nevertheless, the ratio of the money supply to GDP fell from 16.5 percent to 14.9 percent as inflationary expectations induced people to economize with cash reserves.

The macroeconomic policies applied contributed to inflation with a time lag. After rising by 3 percent in 1972, wholesale prices increased by 16 percent in 1973 and 22 percent in 1974. While inflation accelerated in the United States also, Mexico's real exchange rate appreciated by 4 percent vis-à-vis the US dollar between 1971 and 1974. The extent of appreciation reached 5 percent in 1975 and 13 percent in the second quarter of 1976, immediately preceding the September devaluation (Table 7.1). On 1 September 1976, the exchange rate was set at 20 pesos to the dollar, with a second devaluation taking place within a few months.

Trade policy developments

The increasing overvaluation of the peso led to pressures for higher protection. Increases in the scope of quantitative restrictions brought the share of controlled imports in total import value from 57 percent in 1971 to 64 percent in 1973 and to 74 percent in 1974 (Table 7.2). As the balance-of-payments situation deteriorated, import controls were tightened further in 1975. In the same year, a general increase of tariffs was undertaken.

While estimates of effective protection for 1975 are not available, it appears that the level of industrial protection was substantially higher in 1975 than in 1970. But, prior to the implementation of expansionary measures, an export promotion scheme was instituted following recommendations made by the author. This involved the introduction of the CEDI (Certificados de Devolución de Impuestos) scheme; the duty-free importation of inputs; the expansion of the scope of short-term export credits provided by FOMEX (Fondo para el Fomento de la Exportación de Productos Manufacturados); the establishment of FONEI (Fondo Nacional de Equipamiento Industrial) to finance export-oriented and efficient import-substituting investments; and the creation of IMCE (Instituto Mexicano de Comercio Exterior) to increase export promotion efforts.

Under the March 1971 regulations, a 10 percent tax rebate in the form of certificates, or CEDIs, was provided on the value of manufactured exports in cases when domestic content exceeded 60 percent; the rebate was 5 percent when domestic content was between 50 and 60 percent; it was nil below this threshold. Rebate rates were increased to 11 percent and 5.5 percent, respectively, two years later when indirect tax rates were raised.

Exporters whose products had at least 40 percent domestic content were eligible for the duty-free importation of inputs. Also, exporters with a 50 percent domestic content could receive preferential export credits; in 1973, one-third of manufactured exports received such credits, with the resulting subsidy averaging 1.5 percent of the value of these exports.

FONEI was to grant preferential credits for the purchase of machinery and equipment while IMCE was set up to provide information on export possibilities, to organize commercial missions, and to extend the network of commercial attachés. Also; in 1972 the export–import link system introduced for automobiles three years earlier was substantially revised, mandating automobile manufacturers to cover a rising proportion of their imports of automobile parts, components, and accessories by exports.

The CEDIs were discontinued on the occasion of the September 1976 devaluation, but were reinstated soon afterwards. In view of the cascade-type system of indirect taxes applied at the time, it is difficult to judge the extent to which the CEDIs represented reimbursement for taxes actually paid. But, the fact remains that their introduction increased incentives to manufactured exports.

The special treatment accorded to assembly – or maquila – industries in the border areas antedates the introduction of the CEDIs, but it was formalized in legislation only in 1971. These industries import materials, parts, and components duty-free from, and re-export the assembled product to, mostly the United States, where duty is paid on the value added only. After October 1972 maquila status was also granted to firms in the interior that exported under similar conditions.

Trade and industrial growth

The exports of assembly industries were first reported in Mexican balance-of-payments statistics in 1970. From a net value of $81 million in that year, maquila exports passed the half billion mark in 1976. In the same year, their gross value came to exceed that of (non-maquila) manufactured exports reported in trade statistics.

Under the impulsion of export incentives, Mexican manufactured exports increased rapidly between 1970 and 1974, rising by 60 percent in volume terms.[13] They declined, however, in 1975, in part because of the world recession and in part because of the increasing overvaluation of the peso. With the extent of overvaluation rising further until September 1976, the volume of Mexican manufactured exports in 1976 remained 18 percent below the 1974 level. By contrast, the 1976 manufactured exports of the developing countries to the developed countries exceeded the 1974 level by 25 percent.[14]

In the 1970–5 period, exports contributed to the growth of manufacturing output more than import substitution (8 percent v. 3 percent), although in this respect Mexico remained much behind Korea where the contribution of exports to output growth was 62 percent between 1970 and 1973.[15] While higher protection compensated for the increasing overvaluation of the peso, import substitution in Mexico was limited by the import leakages associated with expansionary fiscal policies.

Correspondingly, the share of imports in GDP rose from 6.3 percent in 1971 to 8.4 percent in 1975, subsequently declining to 6.8 percent in 1976 as the growth of public expenditures slowed down. In turn, after temporary increases, the share of exports in GDP returned to the 1971 share of 3.9 percent in 1976. As noted above, manufactured exports grew rapidly in the early sixties in response to the incentives provided, but declined afterwards when the overvaluation of the peso was increasingly felt. For the period taken as a whole, primary exports fell in absolute terms as the overvaluation of the peso was not offset by export incentives. The decline extended to most of Mexico's major primary export commodities while new primary exports failed to develop.

III THE LÓPEZ PORTILLO PERIOD (1977–82)

Macroeconomic background

The expansionary policies adopted by President Echeverria in March 1972 followed the application of deflationary measures in the first year of his Presidency, aimed at reducing the deficit in the current account of the balance of payments from the level of 3.2 percent of GDP reached in 1970. These measures involved a slowdown in the growth of public consumption and a reduction in public investment, both expressed in constant prices. In turn, the expansionary policies of 1972–5 led to rapid inflation and to the deterioration of the balance of payments, with the exchange rate remaining unchanged. They were followed by a slowdown in the growth of public consumption and a decline in public investment in 1976, and the exchange rate was repeatedly devalued later in the year.

Similar stages are observed in the policies followed by President López Portillo. In 1977, the volume of public consumption and investment remained virtually constant. In subsequent years, there followed a period of budgetary expansion, leading to rapid inflation while the nominal value of the peso was kept virtually unchanged. Finally, in the last year of López Portillo's Presidency, economies in public expenditures were made and the peso was devalued to a considerable extent. The following discussion will concentrate on the expansionary phase.

Between 1977 and 1981, public consumption increased by nearly one-half and public investment doubled in volume terms. But, data expressed in terms of constant prices do not appropriately indicate the extent of the expansionary policies, which occurred as the exchange rate was maintained between 22.5 and 23.0 pesos to the US dollar and the rate averaged 24.5 pesos to the dollar in 1981. In current prices –

and hence in terms of US dollars – public consumption increased threefold between 1977 and 1981 while public investment more than quadrupled.

It had been assumed that the tax paid by PEMEX from its rapidly growing oil revenues would finance much of the expansion of government expenditures. However, PEMEX undertook a large investment program and had to increasingly subsidize its domestic sales. As a result, its deficit approximately matched the amount of the tax paid to the government budget. At the same time, the deficit of the public sector, including PEMEX, rose from 6.8 percent of GDP in 1977 to 12.6 percent in 1981.

The deficit of the public sector was financed in part by money creation and in part by foreign borrowing. The growth of the money supply accelerated, reaching 27.9 percent of GDP in 1981 compared to 14.9 percent in 1976 and 21.0 percent in 1977. In turn, the rise in foreign borrowing brought the debt-service ratio above 100 percent.

The expansionary measures applied led to an acceleration of inflation with a time lag. Wholesale prices rose by 16 percent in 1977 and in 1978, 18 percent in 1979, 24 percent in 1980, and 25 percent in 1981. In turn, after maintaining the exchange rate in the 22.5–23.5 pesos to the dollar range until early 1981, the small devaluations in the remainder of the year brought this rate to only 26.2 pesos to the dollar at the end of 1981.

As a result, the peso appreciated to a considerable extent in real terms, more than offsetting the devaluations of 1976 and 1977. By the end of 1981, the extent of appreciation of the real value of the peso was 29 percent compared to 1977 and 8 percent compared to 1975; it was 21 percent compared to 1971 and 35 percent compared to 1956 (Table 7.1).

The devaluation of the peso was avoided through increases in oil revenues and in foreign borrowing. As far as the non-oil commodity sectors are concerned, it may be said that borrowing abroad added 'insult' to the 'injury' resulting from the rise of oil exports as these sectors increasingly suffered the effects of maintaining the nominal value of the peso unchanged in the face of rapid inflation.

Trade policy developments

The 1976–7 devaluations and the important oil discoveries of these years had promised a comfortable balance-of-payments position for

Mexico. In fact, with the tripling of petroleum exports and the favorable effects of the depreciation of the real exchange rate on non-oil exports, the ratio of the merchandise trade deficit declined from 4.6 percent of GDP in 1975 to 1.6 percent in 1977. These improvements, and the potential for future increases in petroleum exports, provided the basis for a campaign to lower levels of import protection. This campaign reflected the perception that import liberalization was necessary in order to reduce the existing bias against exports and to raise levels of efficiency by exposing Mexican industry to foreign competition.

In the event, the share of commodity categories subject to import licensing was reduced from 80 percent in 1977 to 24 percent in 1979 (Table 7.2). These changes were accompanied by increases in tariffs, so as to permit firms to adjust to the liberalized import regime. Tariff increases were supposed to remain temporary but, with the subsequent appreciation of the real value of the peso, the higher tariffs were maintained and were subsequently raised further.

The extent of import liberalization was more limited in terms of import value. It has been reported that about 60 percent of imports was subject to license in 1979. This share was substantially lower than the 74 percent share in 1974, but it was higher than in the early seventies. While the high share of capital goods imports raised the value of items subject to import license, it would appear that a substantial number of liberalized items had little importance in Mexican imports.

In fact, import liberalization in the years 1977–9 appears to have been concentrated on items where domestic producer interests were at stake to only a limited extent. In late 1979 and early 1980, the Secretaria de Comercio prepared plans for further import liberalization that would have increased foreign competition to a considerable extent. However, with the appreciation of the real exchange rate, further import liberalization was not undertaken. Rather, the decision taken by President López Portillo against GATT membership in March 1980 marks the beginning of a period of renewed import restrictions.

The reimposition of import restrictions assumed momentum in 1981 when tariffs were also increased. Restrictions were tightened further, and tariffs were raised again, in response to the foreign exchange crisis of 1982. Although export subsidies were increased by providing CEDIs averaging 8 percent on export value in addition to the rebate of the newly introduced value added tax, this was far from sufficient to offset the rise in import protection. As a result, the reduction in discrimination against exports in 1977–9 gave place to an increased anti-export bias. Manufactured exports further suffered the consequences of the overvaluation of the peso that was offset only in small part by the production subsidies provided under the March 1979 program of industrial development. Net subsidies to manufacturing value added rose by only 3 percentage points between 1975 and 1980, which is dwarfed by the increasing overvaluation of the peso.

The appreciation of the real exchange rate adversely affected primary exports also, and the introduction of the Sistema Agricola Mexicana (SAM) further discriminated against agricultural exports. Under SAM, support prices were raised on crops destined for domestic consumption, thereby giving further impetus to the shift of irrigated area from higher-value export crops to lower-value domestic crops.

Trade and industrial growth

The effects of the measures applied are apparent in the unfavorable developments experienced by several of Mexico's principal primary export products between 1975–7 and 1978–80. Furthermore, the dollar value of the exports of food, beverages and tobacco declined in absolute terms in 1981, falling 21 percent below the 1979 peak that represented the delayed effects of the 1976–7 devaluations.

The devaluations also gave a boost to manufactured exports which increased by 48 percent in volume terms between 1976 and 1978, compared to a 24 percent rise for developing country exports to the developed countries. The comparisons are much less favorable for Mexico if the entire 1973–8 period is considered, when the relevant figures are 16 percent and 63 percent.[16] Yet, this is a more appropriate comparison, since increases in Mexican exports after 1976 in part compensated for the declines of the previous years.

The volume of Mexican manufactured exports fell by 14 percent between 1978 and 1981, reflecting the adverse effects of the increased overvaluation of the peso and of rising import protection. In the same period, there was an increase of 13 percent in dollar terms as compared to a 58 percent rise in the manufactured exports of the developing countries to developed country markets reported by GATT. And, an absolute decline is shown in the dollar value of Mexico's manufactured exports if one excludes chemicals, based largely on petroleum, and automobiles and automobile parts, the exports of which are regulated under the export–import link system.

All in all, Mexicos exports other than petroleum and petroleum products stagnated in dollar terms between 1978 and 1981 while its exports of petroleum and petroleum products rose sixteenfold. This did not suffice, however, to avoid an increase in the current account deficit that reached 4.8 percent of GDP in 1981. For one thing, imports rose much more rapidly than the gross domestic product as the expansionary macroeconomic policies gave rise to large import leakages. For another thing, the balance of service transactions deteriorated to a considerable extent, reflecting the decline in the tourism balance brought about by the appreciation of the real exchange rate and the rising cost of servicing the foreign debt.

IV POLICY IMPLICATIONS

Macroeconomic policies and trade policy

This overview has shown the interdependence of macroeconomic and trade policies in Mexico. Under fixed exchange rates, expansionary fiscal policies repeatedly led to the overvaluation of the peso that, in turn, triggered the application of protectionist measures. And while trade was liberalized after the devaluations of 1976–7, improving the competitiveness of Mexican industries, this lasted only until the peso became overvalued again.

The results also indicate the sensitivity of imports and exports to the incentives provided. The overvaluation of the peso stimulated imports while higher protection had the opposite effect. Apart from the 1976–7 devaluations, the real value of the exchange rate continued to appreciate in Mexico, with the extent of appreciation attaining 35 percent at the end of 1981 compared to 1956. In turn, the 1977–9 import liberalization aside, import protection increased during the period. Changes in these variables largely explain variations in import shares over time, with spillover effects raising imports during periods of expansionary policies.[17]

Exports suffered discrimination through the effects of over-valued exchange rates as well as import protection. Discrimination against primary exports increased over a period of time, except for the period of the 1976–7 devaluations and the 1977–9 import liberalization interlude. In the case of manufactured products, the export incentives granted in the early seventies also reduced the extent of anti-export bias. However, by 1979, the adverse effects of the appreciation of the peso more than offset the resulting benefits, with a further deterioration in the competitive position of Mexican exports occurring in the following two years. For the period as a whole, Mexico exhibited poor performance as regards both non-fuel primary and manufactured exports.

The overvaluation of the peso was maintained by borrowing abroad. Foreign borrowing can provide only a temporary remedy, however, unless the proceeds are invested in efficient activities. This will not be the case if inefficient investments are made in the public sector and if inappropriate incentives are provided to the private sector through overvalued exchange rates and high protection. In such conditions, the accumulation of external debt will eventually give rise to a foreign exchange crisis.

Such crises occurred twice in Mexico, at the end of periods of expansionary policies under fixed exchange rates. The two occurrences provide remarkable parallels as deflationary policies were followed by expansionary fiscal measures, leading to the overvaluation of the exchange rate, increased foreign indebtedness, and higher protection.

Mexico missed an opportunity to escape this vicious circle at the beginning of López Portillo's Presidency, when the devaluation of the peso and increases in oil earnings permitted lowering protection and provided the basis for harmonious economic growth. The opportunity was missed and the policies applied led to the accumulation of foreign debts, reaching $80 billion in late 1982.

Policy alternatives for Mexico

In reviewing the situation created by the policies applied, in early 1980 the author suggested 'the need to reduce reliance on foreign borrowing and to accept exchange rate changes for the sake of improving the competitiveness of the non-oil sector in Mexico. This would require first of all reducing the budget deficit. It would further be necessary to introduce rigorous project evaluation for public investment.'[18]

The recent devaluations of the peso provide a basis for the adoption of appropriate policies. Also, with a considerable part of oil earnings utilized to service the debt, the exchange rate can be maintained at a level that does not discriminate against the non-oil sectors for years to come. In the following, consideration will be given to the choice of macroeconomic policies, improvements in the system of incentives, and the reform of trade policies.

Macroeconomic policy alternatives

Solis compares three possible courses of action as far as Mexican macroeconomic policies are concerned: '(a) inflation, with cyclical behavior of the "stop–go" type; (b) recession, with lower inflation rates and increasing unemployment; and (c) moderate growth, with declining inflation followed later by higher growth rates'.[19] He dismisses the first alternative, which led to unfavorable results over the past twenty-five years, criticizes the second, which he ascribes to the IMF, and endorses the third.

Solis' preferred alternative could not find application, however, in the period of foreign exchange crisis Mexico is experiencing today. Rather, the magnitude of the necessary adjustment to remedy existing imbalances in the Mexican economy has required the application of deflationary policies. At the same time, reducing the balance-of-payments deficit in a situation of stagnant output necessitates the cutting of aggregate expenditures.

Mexico is not alone in this regard. In Turkey, the balance-of-payments deficit was substantially reduced following the application of deflationary policies in 1980. Among socialist countries, Hungary effected a large shift in the balance of trade from deficit to surplus through expenditure reductions within a short period.

The first priority for Mexico is to reduce the deficit of the public sector that was translated into unsustainable domestic expansion and large-scale foreign borrowing. The government's agreement with the IMF reportedly stipulates lowering the deficit from 16.5 percent of the gross domestic product in 1982 to 8.5 percent in 1983 and to 4.5 percent by 1985. While the measures taken so far have largely involved increasing taxes and raising the prices of public goods and services, it has been proposed to cut public expenditures by 15 percent in real terms in 1983. This is indeed desirable as public spending has increased at a rate disproportionate with the capabilities of the Mexican economy. Also, the prices of public goods and services would need to be increased further and subsidies to consumer goods reduced.

Increases in the prices of public goods and services and reductions in subsidies to consumer goods, together with the price-raising effects of successive devaluations, lower real wages. Aiming at nominal wage increases to fully compensate for the rise in prices would be counterproductive, however, as it would engender an inflation–devaluation spiral, and decreases in real wages are necessary in view of the need to improve the balance of payments. Nor can profit margins be maintained, as weak domestic demand does not warrant increasing prices to fully compensate for a rise in costs, and lower profit margins are also necessary for improving the balance of payments.

While the private sector has to accept a decline in profit margins, it needs assurances that it will not be discriminated against in the allocation of foreign exchange and domestic credit. Rather than foreign exchange budgeting that considers allocations to the private sector as a residual, cuts in the foreign exchange requirements of the public sector should be commensurate with reductions in foreign exchange availabilities to the private sector. Furthermore, the nationalized banks should give equal treatment to the public and to the private sectors. It would be inappropriate to introduce noneconomic considerations in lending; such considerations should be left to the government budget.

There would further be need to delineate the scope of activities of the public and the private sectors in manufacturing industries, with distinction made between sectors that are in the public domain (e.g. basic petrochemicals), sectors where public and private enterprises co-exist and compete (e.g. steel), and sectors that are the domain of the private sector (e.g. clothing). This would involve the nationalized banks divesting themselves of the large bulk of enterprises they control, with consideration given to eventually privatizing public enterprises in industries alloted to the private sector.

Finally, one may welcome the intention expressed by the government to increase the attractiveness of Mexico for foreign direct investment. Such investment brings technological know-how and marketing expertise, together with capital, and it pays dividends from profits earned rather than giving rise to fixed income obligations.

At the same time, one should avoid a situation where profits are made as a result of high protection. Decreases in import protection would also be necessary in order to eliminate excessive profits in private business, to improve the efficiency of the Mexican manufacturing sector, and to reduce the bias against exports. Deductions in protection should be undertaken in the framework of a time-phased reform of the system of incentives.

Reforming the system of incentives

While the application of a deflationary policy has been necessary under present conditions, it would have to remain temporary lest excessive social tensions be created. Rather, the process of adjustment should increasingly involve raising output, so as to utilize the production capabilities of the Mexican economy while lowering unemployment. This would, in turn, require a substantial reduction in the extent of price distortions.

Again, Mexico is not alone in this regard. In Turkey, the January 1980 reforms involved a large devaluation and extensive price liberalization, with interest rates freed six months later.[20] In Hungary, deflationary policies were accompanied by the reform of producer prices and reductions in consumer subsidies, followed by a devaluation and the raising of interest rates.[21]

The extent of price distortions was especially large in Mexico in recent years. Apart from overvaluation of the exchange rate and high import protection, the prices of public goods and services, in particular transportation and energy, were kept at excessively low levels; consumer staples received substantial subsidies; and the prices of a large number of goods were controlled. Also, real interest rates became increasingly negative.

The devaluations effected in the course of 1982 have remedied the long-standing overvaluation of the peso, and it is now planned to adjust the exchange rate *pari passu* with domestic inflation. In this respect, one may refer to the example of Turkey, where a large devaluation was followed by exchange rate adjustments in line with domestic inflation, leading to rapid increases in exports.

The prices of public goods and services have also been raised in Mexico, but much remains to be done. While the price of gasoline was doubled in December 1982, with the subsequent devaluation of the peso a gallon of regular gasoline again costs less than a dollar. Also, the domestic price of fuel oil is only one-seventh of its export price and the average domestic price of petroleum products does not reach $10 per barrel at the present exchange rate of 96 pesos to the dollar. At the same time, the price of a subway ticket in Mexico City remains one peso and that of public telephones 20 centavos. Finally, the prices of the principal consumer staples are continued to be kept low through subsidies.

Rather than adjusting prices in instalments, an immediate and full adjustment was effected in Turkey in January 1980. This policy did not allow a build-up of political pressures that might have jeopardized subsequent price increases. In Mexico, further increases in the prices of public goods and services would need to be undertaken at an early date, lest pressures develop against such increases.

Subsidies to consumer goods would also need to be reduced and agricultural prices liberalized as the policies followed in the past had adverse effects on agriculture and contributed to migration to the cities and in particular to Mexico City, where living costs were kept low through subsidies. Finally, increasing economic efficiency would require the continuation of the process of liberalization of industrial prices that began in December 1982.

Interest rates were also raised in December 1982 but real interest rates continue to be negative. In order to encourage savings and to ensure the rationing function of interest rates for bank lending, it would be desirable to raise these rates above the expected rate of inflation.

Trade policy reform

As noted above, the reform of trade policy would have to be part of the general reform of the system of incentives. In the following, recommendations will be made for a medium-term reform program that may be carried out over a period of several years once the balance-of-payments situation improves.

For some years now, divergent views have been expressed as to desirable trade policies for Mexico. Following in the footsteps of the Cambridge School, some would opt for a protectionist policy that would increasingly isolate Mexico from world markets. Recommendations have also been made for increased state intervention in international trade.[22]

Protectionist policies have been advocated on the assumption that Mexico's large domestic market can support practically all industries. This argument conflicts with the experience of present-day developed countries. In fact, countries such as France and Germany, whose effective market size for industrial products is eight-to-ten times greater than Mexico's, rely on international specialization to ensure efficient production. And, in new, technologically advanced industries, US firms also derive considerable benefits from reliance on the world market.

In Mexico, the domestic market can rarely ensure the product specialization necessary for efficient production in non-traditional industries, such as capital goods and electronics. To attain this objective, domestic sales would need to be supplemented by exports. Export expansion, in turn, requires avoiding a bias of the system of incentives against exports. Correspondingly, to the extent possible, infant industries would have to be promoted by the use of subsidies rather than protection.

It would further be desirable to modify policies pertaining to existing industries. As suggested by Héctor Hernández Cervantes, there is need to rationalize protection when 'the rationalization of protection would contribute to the reversal of the conditions that discourage exports, and would create structural conditions that favor them . . .'.[23] The rationalization of protection would involve liberalizing imports and reducing the overall level of tariffs as well as tariff differentials among commodities. This may be accomplished according to a time-table determined in advance, so as to give business sufficient time for adjusting to lower protection.

To begin with, there is need to re-establish the program of import liberalization halted in 1980, with a view to abolishing import licensing over a predetermined period. Import licensing becomes increasingly inadequate in a modernizing economy: it raises the cost of production, with unfavorable repercussions for exports at the higher end of the production chain; it creates scarcity margins for the recipients of licenses that are difficult to measure, and it raises the danger of corruption as the decision-making process necessarily involves subjective elements. By contrast, the application of tariffs is automatic and decision on importation is made by the user who will take account of tariff-inclusive price differences between domestic and foreign products, as well as quality, specifications, and the conditions of sale.

The elimination of import licensing should begin with inputs, including capital goods, that affect the cost of commodities at higher levels of fabrication, including exports. Luxury consumer goods can be left to the last, but their importation may also be liberalized since government revenues would be increased by putting high taxes on the sales of luxury commodities.

High taxes are preferable to tariffs that encourage the domestic production of luxury goods. At the same time, levying taxes at the point of sale may also apply to smuggled goods which enter distribution channels. Such smuggling renders the import licensing of various luxury goods largely nugatory at present.

Greater reliance on excise taxes on luxury goods thus permits reducing tariffs on such goods. In general, one may set a tariff ceiling of 25 percent, that has traditionally been considered the maximum desirable price differential between domestic and equivalent foreign products in Mexico. Within this ceiling, tariffs may rise from products at a lower level to those at a higher level of fabrication for products using exportable inputs, with a view to equalizing the protection of value added (effective protection).[24] The proposed reform may be instituted in annual instalments over a period of, say, five years.

Notwithstanding the liberalization of imports and reductions in tariffs, there would remain a bias against exports. Correspondingly, there is need for export promoting measures as suggested by Hernández.[25] This would require re-establishing the CEDIs abolished in 1982 at rates that compensate for taxes on inputs used directly in exports and in the production of inputs for export. Exporters should also have access to imported inputs duty free, with the rebating of tariffs on direct and indirect imported inputs.

It would further be desirable to provide preferential loans for investment in exports, with the actual interest differential depending on the share of products exported. For reasons noted above, additional investment incentives may be provided to infant industries. The incentives should be granted in a form that does not favor capital-intensive industries and production methods as has often been the case in the past. Similar considerations apply to incentives for regional development.

Investment incentives are preferable to direct export subsidies that invite countervailing action. And while the taking of such action in response to investment incentives favoring exports may not be excluded, under GATT rules countervailing duties cannot be imposed unless injury to domestic industry is proven. At the same time, given Mexico's small share in sales of manufactured goods, a rapid expansion of its exports would rarely threaten injury even in the United States.

Until 1980, the United States invoked the 'grandfather clause' to impose countervailing duties without having to establish the existence of injury. In subscribing to the subsidy code under the Tokyo Round, the US gave up this privilege, except in response to export subsidization on the part of countries which are not members of GATT.

With the United States representing the principal threat of countervailing action for Mexico, the Tokyo Round agreements have greatly increased the benefits Mexico would derive from GATT membership. This conclusion is strengthened if we consider that membership is also a condition for the application of the other codes, including the government procurement code, adopted in the framework of the Tokyo Round. Also, under these codes, GATT members may take action against an offending party.

A further advantage of GATT membership for Mexico is that bilateral negotiations with the United States would be replaced by the application of multilateral rules. Last but not least, in cooperation with other developing countries, Mexico may influence the development of new rules in GATT. In so doing, Mexico would join countries, such as Brazil and India, that have become active in GATT affairs.

At the same time, the claims of the local adherents of the Cambridge School, that Mexico would seriously compromise its freedom of action by entering GATT, do not stand up to scrutiny. Several socialist countries, such as Hungary, are long-standing members of GATT as they have regarded the benefits of membership to far exceed the cost involved in applying GATT's rather flexible rules.

Mexico would further benefit from the expansion of maquila industries. At the same time, these industries would need to be increasingly integrated with the rest of the economy. This purpose would be served by allowing maquila industries to sell in domestic markets and by improving the transportation network so as to reduce the cost of using domestic inputs.

Under appropriate incentives, Mexican agriculture could undertake efficient exporting as well as import substitution. This would require approximating world market price relations in regard to both products and their inputs. Agriculture would also need to be provided with more investment funds than heretofore.

CONCLUSIONS

This review of Mexican trade policy over the last quarter of the century has shown that Mexico's present economic difficulties date back to the beginning of the period, when increases in public consumption contributed to inflation and to the appreciation of the peso in real terms under fixed exchange rates. The overvaluation of the exchange rate, in turn, led to the application of protectionist measures that permitted the establishment of inefficient activities oriented towards the domestic market while discriminating against exports.

The situation was aggravated by the excessively expansionary policies pursued by President Echevarria in 1972–5 and by President López Portillo in 1978–81. In both cases, deficits in the public sector necessitated substantial foreign borrowing as rapid inflation gave rise to the appreciation of the real exchange rate under the fixed rate regime and exacerbated protectionist pressures. Higher protection, in turn, added to the discrimination against exports inherent in the overvaluation of the exchange rate.

Recommendations have been made in this essay for remedying macroeconomic disequilibria, reducing price distortions, and reforming trade policy, with a view to moving towards an outward-oriented development strategy in Mexico. Such a strategy has been shown to be superior to inward orientation in developing countries during the 1960–73 period of rapid growth in the world economy as well as in the subsequent period of external shocks.[26]

In providing similar incentives to sales in domestic and foreign markets, an outward-oriented development strategy promotes exports as well as efficient import substitution. The capital goods industries and agriculture provide examples, where exports and import substitution could proceed in a parallel fashion in Mexico.

Maintaining the actual exchange rate constant in real terms would provide considerable incentives to exports and to import substitution, leading to improvements in the balance of payments through increases in output and employment in the present situation of large excess capacity. The experience of the last quarter of the century indicates the sensitivity of exports and imports to the exchange rate in Mexico. More recently, Turkey provides a case where exports grew substantially in response to increased incentives in a difficult world environment. In Mexico, exports should benefit from the economic recovery in the United States and Japan in 1983, and they may also be oriented to developing country markets.

Future growth would, however, require increased investments, in particular in export activities, that may be encouraged by appropriate incentives. Additional incentives may also be granted to new activities, preferably in the form of subsidies rather than protection so as to promote production for domestic as well as for foreign markets.

NOTES

1. B. Balassa, 'La Politica Comercial de Mexico: Analysis y Proposiciones', *Comercio Exterior*, XX (1970) pp. 922–30.
2. B. Balassa, 'Foreign Trade and Industrial Policy in Mexico', Published in B. Balassa, *Policy Reform in Developing Countries* (Oxford: Pergamon Press, 1977) pp. 31–55.
3. B. Balassa, 'Policy Responses to External Shocks in Selected Latin American Countries', presented at the Instituto Mexicano de Comercia

Exterior in Mexico, D. F., in January 1980, Published in W. Baer and M. Gills (eds), *Export Diversification and the New Protectionism: The Experience of Latin America* (Champaign, Ill.: National Bureau of Economic Research and the University of Illinois, 1981) pp. 131–64; reprinted in B. Balassa, *The Newly Industrializing Countries in the World Economy* (New York: Pergamon Press, 1981) pp. 83–100.

4. A. M. Ortiz, 'Desarrolo Estabilizador: Una Decada de Estrategia Económica en México', in *Mexico, El Mercado de Valores* No. 44 (1969).

5. G. M. Bueno, 'La Paridad del Poder Adquisitivo y las Elasticidades de Importación y Exportación en México', *El Trimestre Económico* XLI (1974) p. 315.

6. L. Solis, *Economic Policy Reform in Mexico, A Case Study for Developing Countries* (New York: Pergamon Press, 1981) p. 30.

7. Solis, p. 67.

8. A. Ten Kate and R. B. Wallace, *Protection and Economic Development in Mexico* (Rotterdam: Center for Development Planning, 1980) p. 136.

9. Data for Korea refer to 1963–70, those for Taiwan to 1961–71, and those for Mexico to 1960–70. They originate from the files of a research project on the sources of economic growth directed by Hollis B. Chenery, Sherman Robinson, and Moise Syrquin at the World Bank.

10. B. Balassa, 'Trade in Manufactured Goods: Patterns of Change', *World Development*, IX (1981) p. 265. Reprinted in Balassa, *The Newly Industrializing Countries in the World Economy*.

11. H. B. Chenery, 'Interactions Between Industrialization and Exports', *American Economic Review, Papers and Proceedings*, LXX (1980) p. 281. Increases in domestic demand and changes in input–output coefficients provide additional contributions to industrial growth.

12. Solis, p. 68.

13. Manufactured exports have been defined to exclude food, beverages, and tobacco, petroleum derivatives, and petrochemicals. The results are subject to considerable error as the deflator for all industrial exports, including the above commodities, has been applied to the narrower group.

14. Balassa, 'Trade in Manufactured Goods: Patterns of Changes', p. 265.

15. Chenery, p. 284.

16. Balassa, 'Trade in Manufactured Goods: Patterns of Changes', p. 265.

17. These conclusions are confirmed by the results of an econometric study by J. Salas, 'Estimation of the Structure and Elasticities of Mexican Imports in the Period 1961–79', *Journal of Development Economics*, X (1982) pp. 297–9. At the same time Salas interprets the upsurge of imports in 1978–79 to have been caused by import liberalizaton, neglecting the spillover effects of expansionary policies.

18. Balassa, 'Policy Responses to External Shocks in Selected Latin American Countries', p. 138.

19. Solis, p. 124.

20. B. Balassa, 'Outward Orientation and Exchange Rate Policy in Developing Countries: The Turkish Experience', Essay 10 in this volume.

21. B. Balassa, 'Reforming the New Economic Mechanism in Hungary', Essay 13 in this volume.

22. P. N. Ruiz, 'La Politica de Comercio Exterior de México', *Comercio Exterior*, XXXI (1981) pp. 1173–8.
23. H. C. Hernández, 'La Politica de Comercio Exterior de México', *El Economista Mexicano*, XVII (1981) p. 40.
24. For a detailed discussion, see Balassa, 'Foreign Trade and Industrial Policy in Mexico', pp. 44–6.
25. Hernández, p. 40.
26. B. Balassa, 'Export Incentives and Export Performance in Developing Countries: A Comparative Analysis', *Weltwirtschaftliches Archiv*, CXIV (1978) pp. 24–61, and 'Structural Adjustment Policies in Developing Economies', Essay 4 in this volume.

Essay 8 Policy Experiments in Chile, 1973–83

INTRODUCTION

The Chilean policy experience in the period following the fall of Allende in September 1973 has been the subject of much controversy, with views ranging from the unqualified defense of the policies applied to their wholesale rejection. The controversy has pertained to the interpretation of the evidence and to the empirical evidence itself. At the same time, there has been a tendency to evaluate the Chilean experience independently of the international context and to consider the entire period as a unit.

This essay will review the policy experiments carried out in Chile during the last decade on the basis of official and unofficial data which the author considers reliable. It will place the Chilean experiments in an international context by indicating the changing conditions in the world economy, the policies followed by other newly-industrializing countries, and the economic performance of these countries. The discussion will proceed by separating two sub-periods, the first of which was characterized by reductions in price distortions whereas in the second price distortions were increased again; another distinguishing characteristic of the second period was the liberalization of international capital movements.

The dividing line between the two sub-periods is provided by the June 1979 decision of the Chilean government to maintain the exchange rate fixed in terms of US dollars while liberalizing capital flows and making the 100 percent 'backward' (e.g. lagged) indexation of wages and salaries a minimum requirement for collective bargaining agreements. As a background to the discussion, the policies applied in the period prior to September 1973 and, in particular, under the Allende government, will also be briefly described.

I THE SYSTEM OF INCENTIVES PRIOR TO SEPTEMBER 1973

The incentive system in Chile was traditionally characterised by high import protection in the manufacturing sector and a considerable degree of discrimination against primary as well as manufactured exports. In 1961, nominal protection rates on manufactured goods averaged 111 percent and effective protection rates 182 percent. Protection rates in Chile were much higher than in the four large Latin American countries and, in a group of twelve developing countries, they were exceeded only in Pakistan.[1]

The results reflected the existence of high tariffs and prior import deposit requirements in Chile, although the estimates make adjustment for 'water' in the tariff. High import protection, in turn, discriminated against exports by giving rise to an unfavorable exchange rate that was not compensated by export subsidies. Also, rebates of indirect taxes and customs duties applied only to a limited range of products.[2] Correspondingly, the bias against exports in Chile exceeded that in the other developing countries studied.[3]

In response to the foreign exchange crisis in late 1961 and 1962, import prohibitions were introduced and import deposit requirements raised. However, imports were liberalized under the Frei government (1964–70). The scope of import restrictions was progressively reduced, with few items remaining on the prohibited list in 1970. Furthermore, prior import deposit requirements were largely eliminated by 1970, although they were in part replaced by higher tariffs. At the same time, subsidies were provided to non-traditional exports and the exchange rate was depreciated in real terms (i.e. adjusted for changes in domestic and in foreign prices) through a series of mini-devaluations, so as to provide incentives to exports and to reduce uncertainty for exporters. These policies led to a doubling of manufactured exports between 1965 and 1970.[4]

A policy reversal occurred immediately upon the Allende government's taking office in late 1970. Prohibitive prior import deposit requirements of 10.000 percent for 90 days were established for over 60 percent of imports, with subsequent extensions of the list,[5] and most products were subjected to import licensing. Also, a fixed exchange rate regime was instituted, with intermittent devaluations, thereby increasing discrimination against exports and creating uncertainty for exporters. Thus, the official exchange rate was maintained at 25 escudos to the US dollar between September 1972 and May 1973, and subsequent changes in the exchange rate failed to compensate for domestic inflation. At the same time, multiple exchange rate practices came into increasing use, with the ratio between the highest and the lowest rates reaching 33:1 in August 1973.[6]

Notwithstanding the 230 percent devaluation immediately following the fall of Allende, the real exchange rate vis-à-vis the US dollar appreciated by 32 percent between 1970 and 1973, if calculated by adjusting the nominal exchange rate for changes in consumer prices in Chile and in the United States. And while no appreciation is shown if adjustment is made for changes in wholesale prices, this may be explained by the fact that wholesale price indices reflected the effects of price control while consumer price indices have been adjusted to approximate price relations in the absence of controls (Table 8.1).[7]

Thus, following a short – and incomplete – import liberalization interlude under the Frei government, import protection and the bias against exports reached unprecedented heights in Chile on the eve of the quadrupling of oil prices in late 1973. By contrast, the four large Latin American countries, Argentina, Brazil, Colombia, and Mexico, reformed their system of incentives in the 1966-73 period. These countries lowered import protection and lessened the bias of the incentive system against non-traditional exports through the application of export subsidies and the adoption of realistic exchange rates while reducing uncertainty for exporters through the adoption of a system of crawling peg.[8]

The measures applied led to an acceleration of the growth of manufactured exports and output in the four large Latin American countries. Between 1966 and 1973, the dollar value of their manufactured exports increased at annual rates ranging from 20 percent (Mexico) to 39 percent (Brazil), with value added in manufacturing rising by 7 percent (Argentina) to 12 percent (Brazil) a year in volume terms. As increases under Frei were reversed under the Allende government, manufactured exports remained unchanged during this period in Chile while value added in manufacturing rose by less than 4 percent a year. Differences of a similar magnitude were shown in regard to the growth of non-traditional exports, agricultural production, and GNP.[9]

The situation was aggravated towards the end of Allende's presi-

TABLE 8.1 *Nominal and real exchange rates in Chile*

	1970	1971	1972	1973	1974	1975	1976	1977	1978	1979	1980	1981	1982
Nominal exchange rate													
Peso/US$	0.012	0.012	0.020	0.111	0.832	4.911	13.054	21.529	31.656	37.246	39.0	39.0	50.909
Index (1975 = 100)	0.24	0.24	0.41	2.26	16.94	100.00	265.81	438.38	644.59	758.42	794.14	794.14	1036.63
Chilean price indices													
Wholesale prices[a]	0.15	0.16	0.27	1.67	17.06	100.00	326.08	595.63	864.46	1307.60	1830.16	2015.37	2144.70
Consumer prices	0.22	0.27	0.59	3.49	20.87	100.00	334.50	715.16	1071.31	1463.41	1977.07	2366.55	2600.84
US price indices													
Wholesale prices	64.16	66.40	63.64	73.28	89.60	100.00	106.24	113.60	122.08	137.76	160.00	176.96	181.92
Consumer prices	72.13	75.19	77.79	82.54	91.57	100.00	105.82	112.71	121.29	134.92	153.14	169.07	179.33
Real exchange rate index vis-à-vis US dollar deflated by													
Wholesale price index	102.60	99.60	104.23	99.17	88.97	100.00	86.60	83.61	91.03	79.90	69.43	69.72	87.93
Consumer price index	78.69	66.84	54.06	53.45	74.33	100.00	84.09	69.09	73.00	69.92	61.51	56.73	71.48
Real exchange rate index vis-à-vis trading partners deflated by WPI	118.37	103.61	106.34	118.36	94.87	100.00	88.58	83.56	98.29	89.58	75.76	68.60	77.97

SOURCES: International Monetary Fund, *International Financial Statistics* (various issues) and Banco Central de Chile, *Indicadores Economicos y Sociales, 1960–1982*, Santiago, 1983; (for consumer price index) K. Schmidt-Hebbel and J. Marshall, 'Revision del IPC para el Periodo 1970–1980: Una Nota', 1981 Documento No. 1976, Departamento de Estudios Empresas BHC.

dency, when the gross domestic product declined in absolute terms, barely exceeding the 1970 figure. This contrasts with the experience of other newly-industrializing countries that reached high rates of economic growth under the boom conditions existing in the world economy.[10] Thus, Chile was not only unable to utilize the opportunities provided by the world boom of 1971–3, but its economic performance deteriorated during the Allende regime.

Apart from increased import protection and an anti-export bias, a number of policy measures applied under Allende contributed to these unfavorable results. To begin with, price controls were introduced and eventually applied to more than 3000 products, discouraging production and leading to shortages and to black market prices exceeding official prices up to ten times for most products.[11] Also, interest rates were set at low levels, giving rise to strongly negative real interest rates and to distortions in capital markets. In turn, labor costs were raised through labor legislation that regulated business-labor relations in great detail. These measures, and the takeover of a number of banks, industrial enterprises, and farms, adversely affected productive activity and created uncertainty for business.

At the same time, inflationary pressures increased as the public sector deficit reached 25 percent of the gross domestic product, credit to government came to account for 88 percent of total domestic credit and the rise of the money supply accelerated (Table 8.2). As a result, notwithstanding the price controls applied, inflation accelerated. Finally, with rising trade deficits, Chile's net foreign exchange reserves turned negative and its external debt reached 26 percent of GNP.

II REDUCING PRICE DISTORTIONS, SEPTEMBER 1973–JUNE 1979

One of the first actions taken by the newly-instituted military government was to liberalize prices. With the exception of 33 products, prices were freed in October 1973, with additional price liberalization occurring afterwards. Furthermore, interest rates were freed for capital market transactions in May 1974 and for commercial banks in December 1975 whereas the inflow of capital continued to be subject to limitations. In turn, cost-of-living adjustments were postponed from October 1973 to January 1974, although wage supplements and allowances were provided during this period.[12] The subsequent adjustments were made by using the official consumer price index that underesti-

TABLE 8.2 Monetary and fiscal indicators in Chile

	1970	1971	1972	1973	1974	1975	1976	1977	1978	1979	1980	1981	1982
Rates of change (percent)													
Reserve money	na	162.5	185.7	418.3	222.5	255.7	287.4	111.4	57.0	42.5	38.8	-9.2	-25.5
Money supply (M1)	na	110.0	157.1	314.8	273.2	256.3	195.2	108.2	67.0	64.5	56.8	-6.0	9.4
Money and quasi money (M2)	na	94.1	154.5	471.4	338.5	256.1	166.4	130.1	90.8	67.6	57.3	34.7	26.1
Wholesale prices (a)	36.1	17.9	70.1	511.4	1028.9	482.0	221.1	86.0	42.9	49.4	39.6	9.1	7.2
Interest rates (percent)													
Nominal interest rate	na	na	na	na	na	411.31	350.67	156.35	85.32	61.96	46.86	51.90	57.66
Real interest rate	na	na	na	na	na	-12.15	40.35	37.82	29.69	8.41	5.20	39.23	47.07
LIBOR (nominal/US$)	8.47	6.80	5.86	9.32	11.11	7.64	6.12	6.42	9.18	12.14	13.96	16.77	13.58
LIBOR (nominal/pesos)	39.63	14.72	66.22	521.63	734.26	535.29	182.05	75.65	60.53	31.90	19.31	16.77	48.26
LIBOR (real/pesos)	2.59	-2.70	-2.28	1.67	-26.10	9.16	-12.16	-5.56	12.34	11.71	-14.53	7.03	38.30
Domestic less foreign rates (nominal)	na	na	na	na	na	-123.98	168.62	78.70	24.79	30.06	27.55	35.13	9.40
Share of GDP (percent)													
Domestic credit	17.27	31.50	43.07	63.30	43.95	58.02	40.38	41.64	39.54	36.80	38.92	42.30	80.54
Private credit	8.13	9.45	9.81	7.76	6.72	8.67	10.19	17.25	23.84	26.42	34.75	41.29	74.66
Government credit	9.14	22.05	33.26	55.54	37.23	49.35	30.19	24.39	15.70	10.38	4.17	1.01	5.88
Changes in monetary base	3.79	6.26	22.18	24.92	8.10	8.59	8.57	4.97	3.37	2.69	2.30	-0.63	3.52
Domestic credit	3.48	5.98	18.82	23.62	7.65	2.05	0.80	2.06	-1.71	-1.33	-0.57	-0.43	12.63
Foreign exchange	0.31	0.28	3.36	1.30	0.45	6.54	7.77	2.91	5.08	4.02	2.87	-0.20	-9.11
Public sector deficit	2.7	10.7	13.0	24.7	10.5	2.6	2.3	1.8	0.8	-1.7	-3.1	-1.6	2.4

NOTE: (a) Home goods.

SOURCE: See Table 8.1.

mated the increases which occurred following the liberalization of prices.

In October 1973, the official exchange rate was devalued by 230 percent. Also, the multiple exchange rate system was progressively abolished, and a uniform exchange rate established by August 1975. At the same time, further devaluations were undertaken and the real exchange rate vis-à-vis the US dollar depreciated by 87 percent between 1973 and 1975, if calculated by adjusting for changes in relative consumer prices. However, little change is shown if adjustment is made for changes in wholesale prices that underestimated the rate of inflation in 1973 as noted above (Table 8.1).

The peso was revalued by 10 percent in June 1976 and in March 1977. As a result, the real exchange rate, calculated by making adjustments for changes in consumer prices in Chile and in the United States, appreciated by 27 percent between 1975 and 1978, although it remained 37 percent above its 1973 level. The extent of appreciation was smaller if adjustments were made for changes in wholesale prices.

Import protection was dramatically reduced during the period under consideration. Import restrictions and prior import deposit requirements were abolished soon after the establishment of the military government, and tariff rates were reduced by 40 percent, with a 200 percent ceiling. In June 1974, the Minister of Finance set a 40 percent tariff ceiling, to be reached over a three year period. Subsequently, in early 1975, the Committee on Tariff Reform proposed establishing tariff rates of 25 to 35 percent.[13] The tariff targets were subsequently lowered and, in December 1977, the government announced its new objective of a uniform 10 percent nominal tariff, the only exception being automobiles. This target was attained, as scheduled, in June 1979.

In line with the new government's economic philosophy, the re-privatization of banks and industrial firms nationalized during the Allende period was undertaken soon after September 1973, and the share of the public budget as well as that of the fiscal deficit in the gross domestic product were greatly reduced. The ratio of the public sector deficit to GDP fell from 25 percent in 1973 to 11 percent in 1974 and to 3 percent in 1975, giving place to a surplus by 1979 (Table 8.2).

The reduction in the fiscal deficit was also motivated by the desire to lower the rate of inflation that surpassed 1000 percent in late 1973 as the freeing of prices eliminated the repressed inflation of the preceding period. However, changes in credit to government were much slower, in large part to avoid the collapse of the Savings and Loan System.[14]

Thus, the share of credit to government in total domestic credit declined only from 88 percent in 1973 to 85 percent in 1975, and monetary growth still exceeded 250 percent. Nevertheless, as the rise of the money supply was considerably smaller than increases in prices, deflationary pressures were generated.

Apart from the desire to reduce the rate of inflation, the macroeconomic measures applied responded to the external shocks Chile suffered in 1974–75 as a result of the quadrupling of oil prices, the one-half decline in copper prices, and the world recession. And, notwithstanding the improvements that occurred in the world economy in subsequent years, the adverse effects of external shocks were hardly mitigated in Chile, which continued to experience low copper prices.

The unfavorable balance-of-payments effects of external shocks, in the form of the deterioration of the terms of trade and the export shortfall due to the world recession and the subsequent slow recovery, were estimated at 8.0 percent of Chile's gross national product in the 1974–8 period, on the average. This estimate was made on the assumption that world market prices would have remained at their 1971–3 level in the absence of external shocks. Under this assumption, the higher prices earned on Chile's balance of trade surplus, measured in terms of 1971–3 prices, reduced the adverse effects of external shocks.

In turn, the adverse balance-of-payments effects of external shocks averaged 19.4 percent of Chile's gross national product in the 1974–8 period, exceeding the comparable results for other newly-industrializing countries several times. The large external shocks which Chile suffered, then, need to be taken into account in evaluating its economic performance.

Consideration needs further to be given to the policies applied in response to external shocks. The methodology utilized distinguishes among the following policy responses: additional net external financing, export promotion, import substitution, and deflationary policies.[15] It should be added, however, that whereas in most other countries the policies applied responded to the external shocks suffered, Chile's policies to an important extent reflect decisions taken in late 1973 to reform the system of incentives.

III ECONOMIC PERFORMANCE, 1973–9

While initially deflationary policies were dominant, subsequently export promotion came to play a central role. In the 1974–8 period, on average, export promotion offset more than one-half of the balance-of-payments effects of external shocks.

Export promotion, representing the effects of increasing the country's world market share, was apparent in traditional as well as in non-traditional exports. Increases of 23 percent were observed in the case of traditional exports, with the gains being concentrated in copper, and 20 percent for non-traditional primary exports. Furthermore, manufactured exports were three times greater than the exports that would have been reached had Chile maintained its 1971–3 market share.

On the whole, Chile's exports surpassed the level calculated on the basis of unchanged export market shares by 34 percent. Among newly-industrializing countries, Chile's export performance was surpassed only by Korea whereas fully one-half of these countries lost export market shares.[16]

Exports were encouraged by the depreciation of the real exchange rate in the period following the establishment of the new government as well as by reductions in the anti-export bias of the incentive system through import liberalization.

In the 1974–8 period, on the average, Chile experienced positive import substitution, representing a 15 percent reduction in imports through the lowering of the income elasticity of import demand compared to the 1963–73 period. Import substitution was concentrated in agriculture, in response to the improved incentives provided through the depreciation of the real exchange rate. However, the extent of import substitution declined over a period, and eventually turned negative, in manufacturing. This occurred as tariff reductions on industrial goods largely involved eliminating the 'water' in the tariff and were accompanied by a depreciation of the real exchange rate at the beginning of the period, but the profitability of import substitution in manufacturing declined subsequently when tariffs were further reduced and the real exchange rate appreciated.

At the same time, the composition of imports according to broad categories remained largely unchanged. After a temporary decline in 1973–76, consumer goods imports regained their earlier share of 20 percent, capital goods imports remained at 20 percent, with materials and intermediate goods accounting for the remaining 60 percent. In the consumer goods category, however, the share of food imports declined *pari passu* with increases in agricultural production, while that of industrial imports increased.[17] Also, higher fuel prices led to a larger share of fuel imports at the expense of the imports of raw materials.

Chile did not rely on increased foreign borrowing to offset the adverse balance-of-payments effects of external shocks.[18] This contrasts with the case of Turkey, Singapore, Uruguay, Yugoslavia, Portugal and Israel, where additional net external financing represented the principal policy response to external shocks. Brazil and Mexico also stepped up borrowing abroad.

Correspondingly, Chile's external debt-GNP ratio increased only from 26 percent in 1973 to 31 percent in 1978, less than in other newly-industrializing countries, other than Turkey whose lack of creditworthiness did not permit further borrowing. Nevertheless, having reached high levels under the Allende government, Chile's debt-GNP ratio was exceeded only by Israel and Mexico in 1978. Also, with changes in the maturity of the debt, the debt-service ratio increased from 41 percent in 1973 to 60 percent in 1978 in Chile.[19]

Finally, while in Chile the adverse balance-of-payments effects of external shocks were initially offset by deflationary policies, economic growth accelerated after 1976. Thus, the average annual decline of 4.1 percent in *per capita* GNP between 1973 and 1976 was followed by a 7.3 percent rise in 1976–9, resulting in average increases of 1.9 percent a year for the entire 1973–9 period.

This result was achieved in an unfavorable world environment, and it contrasts with the slight decline of *per capita* incomes during the Allende period of 1970–73 when the greatest postwar boom occurred. In fact, apart from Korea and Uruguay, where reforms similar to those of Chile were instituted, Chile was the only newly-industrializing country whose growth performance improved after 1973. Improvements are shown, but differences in the results are smaller, if comparisons are made with 1963–73, although this period was characterized by rapid expansion in the world economy. Thus, the GDP of the industrial countries rose at an average annual rate of 2.3 percent a year between 1973 and 1979 compared to 4.6 percent in 1963–73.

The acceleration of economic growth was associated with the opening of the Chilean economy, with the exports of goods and services rising at an average annual rate of 17.5 percent in volume terms between 1973 and 1979 (Table 8.3). The growth of imports – 4.4 percent a year – was considerably lower during this period as Chile had to offset the deterioration of its terms of trade through increases in exports.

In response to the increased incentives provided through more favorable exchange rates, export expansion and import substitution led to rapid growth in agriculture. Mining exports also increased, resulting in higher output. At the same time, services grew slightly more rapidly than GDP while construction activity hardly increased between 1973 and 1979.[20]

TABLE 8.3 Rates of growth of national income aggregates in Chile

Growth Rates (per cent)	1970–3	1973–6	1976–9	1973–9	1979–82	1973–82
Gross Domestic Product	0.5	−2.9	8.8	2.7	−0.8	1.5
Agriculture	−5.9	9.3	4.1	6.7	2.3	5.2
Mining	−0.1	6.8	3.2	5.0	6.3	5.4
Manufacturing	2.3	−7.1	8.6	−0.2	−4.7	−1.7
Construction	−8.7	−6.9	9.9	0.5	2.1	1.1
Services	2.7	−2.1	8.8	3.1	−0.5	1.9
Import taxes	−2.4	−11.8	31.1	5.3	−4.2	1.9
Domestic Expenditure	1.3	−7.0	11.4	1.2	−2.9	−0.2
Private consumption	4.4	−8.4	9.9	−0.6	1.5	0.1
Public consumption	6.5	−0.6	6.6	2.9	−4.8	0.1
Gross fixed investment	−8.2	−6.8	16.6	3.7	−3.9	1.0
Inventory change	nd	nd	80.8	nd	nd	nd
Gross capital formation	−11.9	−4.5	23.1	8.2	−15.0	2.3
Exports of goods and services	3.9	23.0	12.4	17.6	6.3	13.7
Imports of goods and services	1.9	−10.2	25.0	4.4	−2.8	1.9
Domestic savings	nd	nd	5.8	nd	−7.2	nd
Foreign savings	7.0	nd	nd	−8.1	nd	nd

SOURCE: Banco Central de Chile, *Indicadores Economicos y Sociales, 1960–1982.*

In turn, the incentives provided encouraged manufactured exports *and* imports. To begin with, available estimates indicate the response of manufactured exports to the real exchange rate, with a short-term elasticity of 0.8 and a long-term elasticity of 3.9.[21] In turn, tariff reductions were shown to have had a negative effect on output in a cross-section framework.[22]

A disaggregation of factors affecting industrial output further indicates the positive contribution of exports (a growth rate of 15.3 percent a year) and the negative contribution of import substitution (−1.4 percent a year) and of changes in domestic demand (−0.6 percent a year), giving rise to 0.2 percent average annual rate of growth of output between 1969/70 and 1978.[23] By limiting attention to exports and import substitution, it is shown that the share of exports in the gross value of industrial output rose from 3 percent in 1969/70 to 8 percent in 1978 while the share of imports increased from 18 to 21 percent.[24]

It appears then, that the net contribution of exports and import substitution to industrial production in Chile during the 1969/70–1978 period was positive. Export expansion dominated output growth in resource based industries, with pulp and paper, wood products, molybdenum oxide, fish meal, and semi-wrought copper providing 63 percent of industrial exports. In turn, negative import substitution was especially large in the case of transport equipment, electrical machinery, and professional equipment that had particularly high rates of tariff protection in 1973.[25]

Among expenditure categories, the volume of private consumption declined slightly between 1973 and 1979, but this was offset by increases in public consumption – an unexpected result, given the philosophy of the government. At the same time, gross fixed investment increased, nearly compensating for the decline that occurred between 1970 and 1973. Inventory building also rose, following destocking towards the end of the Allende period, so that gross capital formation surpassed its 1970 peak.

Current price data, reported in Table 8.4, show a 10 percentage point decrease in the share of private consumption in GDP between 1973 and 1979, accompanied by an increase of identical magnitude in the share of gross capital formation. The share of gross capital formation in GDP more than doubled as a result, approximately offsetting the decline that occurred between 1970 and 1973.[26]

Increases in the share of domestic investment were largely financed by domestic savings.[27] This occurred although the relative shares of wages and salaries and of profits were practically the same in 1979 as in 1973 (Table 8.5). Income shares had fluctuated to a considerable extent in the preceding years, with the wage share rising from 52.3 percent in 1970 to 62.8 percent in 1972 and declining again to 47.2 percent in 1973.

National accounts data for wages and salaries also provide an indication of changes in real wages.[28] Between 1970 and 1973 real wages declined by 38 percent if the consumer price index, and by 14 percent if the GDP deflator is used in adjusting nominal values. In turn, increases of 47 and 7 percent are estimated to have occurred between 1973 and

TABLE 8.4 *The composition of gross domestic product in Chile (in current prices, as percent of GDP)*

	1970	1973	1976	1979	1982
Private consumption	70.4	80.8	68.9	70.7	76.9
Public consumption	13.3	13.2	14.0	14.3	14.9
Gross fixed investment	15.3	12.8	13.3	14.9	13.8
Inventory change	1.0	−4.9	−0.5	2.9	−3.9
Gross capital formation	16.3	7.9	12.8	17.8	9.9
Exports of goods and services	15.3	14.0	25.1	23.3	21.8
Imports of goods and services	14.3	15.9	20.8	26.1	23.5
Domestic savings	16.3	6.0	17.1	15.0	8.2
Foreign savings	−1.0	1.9	−4.3	2.8	1.7

NOTE: Domestic Savings have been defined as the difference between the gross domestic product and (private and public) consumption and foreign saving as the difference between the imports and the exports of goods and services.

SOURCE: See Table 8.3.

TABLE 8.5 *Wages and unemployment in Chile*

	1970	1973	1976	1979	1982
Share of wages and salaries in National Income (percent)	52.3	47.2	52.5	46.5	
Average wages and salaries (pesos)					
Nominal index 1975 = 100	0.39	2.87	420.13	2145.14	4504.22
Real index (a) 1975 = 100	177.27	82.23	125.60	146.59	173.18
Aggregate wages and salaries (thousands of pesos)	42029	427170	49335184	278585227	
Employment (thousands)	2766.1	2891.2	2783.3	3045.3	na
Average wages and salaries (pesos)	15.19	147.75	17725.43	91480.39	na
Nominal index	0.29	2.85	341.33	1761.59	na
Real index (a)	131.82	81.66	102.04	120.38	na
(b)	116.00	100.35	97.33	107.76	na
Unemployment rate (percent)					
National	3.5	4.8	12.7	13.6	19.4
Greater Santiago	7.1	4.7	16.8	13.6	22.1
Minimum employment program (percent)					
National			5.4	3.9	6.4
Greater Santiago			2.9	1.6	2.5

NOTE: (a) Derived by deflating with the consumer price index.
       (b) Derived by deflating with the GDP deflator.
SOURCE: See Table 8.1.

1979, depending on the choice of the deflator. Larger changes – a decline of 54 percent between 1970 and 1973 and an increase of 78 percent between 1973 and 1979 – are shown if the index of wages and salaries is adjusted by the consumer price index (Table 8.5).

It appears, then, that the general tendencies indicated by the data are rather similar, although the numerical results depend on the choice of the wage and salary data and on the price deflator utilized. Similar tendencies are shown in regard to old-age pensions and family allowances, except that increases after 1973 appear to have been smaller than for wages and salaries.[29]

Further interest attaches to changes in physical indicators. These relate to nutrition, health, education, and the availability of particular commodities and services. Data are also available on social expenditures by the government.

As shown in Table 8.6, calorie consumption and protein per head increased between 1970 and 1973. While some declines occurred between 1973 and 1976, by 1979 both calorie consumption and protein per head practically reached the 1973 level.

Among health indicators, the number of medical personnel per thousand population rose over a period of time; medical visits per

TABLE 8.6 *Nutrition, health, education, social, and consumption indicators in Chile*

	1970	1973	1976	1979	1982
Nutrition					
Calorie consumption per head	2282	2642	2565	2634	2627
Protein per head (grams)	67.1	70.7	66.3	68.6	70.2
Health					
Physicians per 1000 population	75	78	85	94	na
Nurses per 1000 population	7.5	7.8	8.5	9.4	na
Hospital beds per 1000 population	3.8	3.8	3.6	3.6	na
Medical visit per head	1.08	1.03	1.05	1.13	na
Adult visits per head	0.99	0.87	0.86	0.93	na
Pediatric visits per child	1.04	1.09	1.15	1.26	na
Obstetrical visits per woman of child bearing age	0.26	0.31	0.27	0.35	na
Crude death rate (percent)	8.9	8.2	7.8	6.8	na
Infant mortality rate (percent)	82.2	65.8	56.6	37.9	
Life expectancy (years)	64.2	65.1	65.9	66.7	67.5
Education (per age group)					
Pre-School (percent)	11.8	16.6	21.7	25.2	26.7
Primary School (percent)	107	120	117	120	111
Secondary School (percent)	39.6	50.9	48.9	54.9	54.8
Government expenditures per head (in 1976 US $)					
Health	1878	2876	1295	1400	1787
Social assistance	336	542	1446	1037	4059
Urbanization	1009	2281	715	628	239
Social security	2812	2671	2158	3183	5882
Education	4346	4541	3329	4076	5262
Regional development	78	194	549	416	491
Total	10459	13106	9492	10740	17718
Availability of goods & services per 10 000 population					
Automobiles	189	228	253	354	na
Television sets	138	129	139	459	na
Refrigerators	72	52	31	132	na
Washing machines	52	53	43	100	na
Telephones	415	461	475	536	na
Residential electricity consumption (thousand kw.)	988	1376	1344	1546	na
Liquid gas	302	387	393	411	na

SOURCE: See Table 8.3.

person also showed increases after a decline in 1973 and 1976; while the number of hospital beds per person fell after 1976. Increases in medical consultation was especially pronounced as far as pediatrician and obstetrician visits are concerned, presumably contributing to the decline in infant mortality rates. A decline was experienced in crude death rates as well, with corresponding increases in life expectancy.

All educational indicators show improvements, with the largest rise observed in regard to pre-primary school (kindergarten) enrolment. These increases were attained, despite a decline in government educational expenditures per head, in conjunction with the increasing privatization of education. Similar considerations explain the improvements made in health, notwithstanding decreases in government expenditure per head. In turn, expenditures on social assistance and social security rose while the fall in expenditures on urbanization was nearly offset by the increasing sums allotted to regional development.

The domestic consumption of electricity and liquid gas increased to a considerable extent between 1973 and 1979. Higher electricity consumption is in part explained by the increased availability of durable consumer goods, including television sets, refrigerators, and washing machines. These changes, together with the rise in the number of automobiles, reflect in large part increases in imports.

Finally, questions arise concerning changes in the distribution of incomes. According to the findings of a sample survey carried out by the Economics Department of the University of Chile for the Greater Santiago area, the share of the lowest 40 percent of income recipients increased temporarily between 1970 and 1973 and, despite a subsequent decline, it was slightly higher in 1979 (11.4 percent) than in 1970 (11.0 percent). In turn, after a temporary decline, the upper 20 percent of income recipients regained their 1970 share (58.5 percent) by 1979 (58.7 percent). At the same time, the Gini and the Theil coefficients do not show a change in income inequalities between 1970 and 1979.[30]

There was a slight increase in income inequalities, however, if family income rather than personal income is considered. Thus, the share of the lowest 40 percent of families declined from 11.5 percent in 1970 to 11.1 percent in 1979 while that of the upper 20 percent increased from 55.8 percent to 57.2 percent. Also, a small increase occurred in the Gini and the Theil coefficients.[31]

The differences in the results may be explained by increases in unemployment that occurred between 1970 and 1979. In the Greater Santiago area, the unemployment rate rose from 7.1 percent to 13.6 percent during this period. Furthermore, in 1975 a Minimum Employment Program was instituted that provides incomes below the minimum wage. Those participating in the program accounted for 1.6 percent of the labor force in 1979 in the Greater Santiago area (Table 8.5). They were 3.9 percent of the total (national) labor force while the national unemployment rate increased from 3.5 percent in 1970 to 13.6 percent in 1979.

Finally, the inequality of wealth appears to have increased as a result of industrial concentration that occurred after 1983. Large industrial groups were formed, as those with access to domestic and foreign credit were able to purchase denationalized enterprises at a relatively small downpayment during the recession, with purchases reportedly occurring at depressed prices. The control of banks by the conglomerates further increased their economic and financial power. This fact, the lack of supervision of the banks by the government coupled with the 100 percent insurance of their deposits, as well as the incentives provided for foreign borrowing in the subsequent period, contributed to the troubles that befell the banking system in 1982.

IV INCREASING PRICE DISTORTIONS, 1979-82

As noted above, following a large decline in 1975, the Chilean economy enjoyed rapid growth. As a result, notwithstanding the external shocks suffered after 1973, Chile's economic performance in the 1973-9 period was much superior to that of the 1970-3 period, when the biggest postwar boom occurred.

Parallel with the expansion of economic activity, inflation decelerated. By the second quarter of 1979, the rate of increase of wholesale prices fell to 40 percent, and that of consumer prices to 30 percent, a year. This was achieved by eliminating the fiscal deficit and reducing the annual rate of increase of the money supply (M1) to 50 percent a year.

Fiscal and monetary policies played a key role in lowering the rate of inflation until mid-1979, although the June 1976 and March 1977 revaluations were reportedly undertaken for purposes of price stabilization and, for the same reason, the rate of devaluation was reduced after December 1978. The break with reliance on domestic macroeconomic policies occurred in June 1979, when the exchange rate was fixed at 39 pesos to the US dollar, to be maintained at this level *ad infinitum*. At the same time, capital flows were liberalized by eliminating the global limit to external borrowing, which continued to apply until that time.

The theoretical underpinnings for these policy measures were provided by several authors, including Ronald McKinnon and Larry Sjaastad. According to McKinnon, 'with convergence to a fixed exchange rate and the liberalization of capital controls, the foreign exchanges completely dominate the country's monetary and financial policies. The supply of base money is endogenous to the demand for it through (nonsterilized) official purchases and sales of foreign exchange'.[32] McKinnon adds that as 'the monetary base is endogenized to the foreign exchanges ... the fixed exchange rate determines the domestic price level'.[33]

The effects of this policy on domestic prices have been considered in more detail by Sjaastad:

> In an economy in which all goods are traded internationally, it is widely held that the internal rate of inflation is determined by the external inflation and changes in the exchange rate. This proposition is merely an extension of the law of 'one price'. To the extent that this law holds at every moment in time, the price level is completely determined, as is its rate of change. In such an economy, exchange rate policy is obviously sufficient to determine the rate of inflation, and there can be little question concerning the efficacy of that policy as a stabilization tool.[34]

Sjaastad admits that 'the presence of "home" or nontraded goods complicates the analysis, as the exchange rate can affect the price of these goods only indirectly – by substitution effects and/or through expectations'.[35] But, he adds:

> The general idea is that, under normal assumptions concerning preferences and production possibilities, and given the state of overall demand relative to production, there is but one price of home goods, relative to that of traded goods, which will clear the home-goods market. Letting the nominal internal price of traded goods be determined by external prices and the exchange rate, this determines the *equilibrium* nominal price for home goods, and hence the equilibrium price level.[36]

A comparison of two equilibrium situations, before and after the adoption of a fixed exchange rate, fails to consider, however, the process of adjustment. Furthermore, the cited propositions reflect the presumption that the cost of adjustment, which would be associated with domestic deflationary policies, would not be incurred if inflation rates were to be reduced and stabilized through the fixing of the exchange rate.

To examine the validity of these propositions, one needs to consider the process of adjustment in regard to standardized and differentiated products in the traded goods sector as well as in regard to non-traded goods. The answer is simple in regard to standardized commodities: for importables, the domestic price will equal the international price plus transportation costs and the tariff while for exportables the domestic price will be the international price less transportation costs. The one price rule will hold in this case; the adjustment period will be short; and the rate of increase of domestic prices cannot exceed that of international prices.

Such will not be the case for differentiated products which dominate the manufacturing sector, including practically all consumer goods and investment goods as well as a substantial proportion of intermediate products. For these commodities, the relationship between domestic and international prices will depend on the elasticity of substitution between the domestic and the foreign variants of the products – in home markets for importables and in foreign markets for exportables. Correspondingly, prices – and their rates of increase – may diverge for a protracted period.

The slowness of the adjustment process is indicated by a comparison of US and Chilean wholesale price indices. Between June 1979 and December 1980, the wholesale prices of industrial goods rose by 22 percent in the United States while the wholesale prices of comparable home goods increased by 65 percent in Chile. Only in 1981 did the two price indices converge. By that time, however, Chile's current account deficit reached $4.8 billion, compared to $1.2 billion in 1979, and industrial growth came to a halt.

These results reflect the adverse effects of the depreciation of the real exchange rate on Chile's exports and imports.[37] Between 1978 and 1981, the peso appreciated in real terms by 22 percent if adjustment is made for changes in Chilean and US consumer prices. Practically the same result, an appreciation of 23 percent, is obtained if adjustment is made for changes in wholesale prices. The extent of appreciation is even greater (30 percent) if the real exchange rate is calculated by reference to changes in the wholesale prices of Chile's principal trading partners, most of whose currencies depreciated vis-à-vis the US dollar (Table 8.1).

The financial situation of firms producing traded goods was aggravated by increases in the prices of non-traded goods and of labor that provide inputs for these firms. In relating the non-traded goods component of the consumer price index to the weighted average of the prices of Chile's exports (excluding copper) and imports, it has been estimated that the relative prices of non-traded to traded goods increased by 21 percent between 1978 and, 1981.[38] At the same time, the divergence between the two indices accelerated in 1981 as the prices of traded goods stabilized while non-traded goods' prices continued to rise.

It appears, then, that the divergence in price trends for traded and for non-traded goods may be maintained over time. This is hardly surprising, given the low substitution elasticities in production and consumption between the two groups of commodities in the short run, and even in the medium run. At the same time, several influences contributed to the observed results in Chile.

Part of the explanation lies in the fact that the prices of certain non-traded goods were indexed on the past rate of inflation. The spillover effects of the expansion of the money supply further contributed to the rise in the prices of non-traded goods. M1 and the broader monetary aggregate, M2, increased by 65 and 68 percent, respectively, in 1979 and by 57 percent in 1980, reflecting continued increases in the monetary base as the increments of foreign exchange reserves, associated with the inflow of capital, were offset only in small part by the reduction in the domestic credit component of the monetary base.

While it had been assumed that, in an open economy with fixed exchange rates, increases in the money supply will be demand-determined, it appears that increases in the money supply contributed to excessive aggregate demand in Chile. There ensued an 86 percent rise in construction activity between 1978 and 1981, leading to a more than doubling in construction prices. In the same period, stock market prices nearly quadrupled and real estate prices also rose several-fold.

Foreign borrowing was motivated by negative real interest rates on foreign loans (Table 8.2). This was the case as the government virtually guaranteed the maintenance of fixed exchange rates and the domestic rate of inflation exceeded the foreign rate of interest. Negative real interest rates on foreign loans further provided incentives for increasing consumption and for investing in activities with a negative social rate of return, such as the building of luxury apartment houses that did not subsequently find takers. And while investment in traded goods was increasingly discouraged as the profitability of these activities declined, increases in non-traded goods' prices favored investment in such activities by the use of the proceeds of foreign loans.

Another factor contributing to increases in the prices of non-traded goods was the rise of wages and salaries. Thus, official wage adjustments based on the rate of inflation in the preceding period ('backward' indexation) cumulated to 66 percent between July 1979 and August 1981. Under the Plan Laboral, official adjustments provided a flow for wage increases; in fact, average wages and salaries slightly more than doubled between July 1979 and December 1981. With the exchange rate being maintained at 39 pesos to the dollar, wages and salaries expressed in terms of US dollars rose at the same rate, importantly contributing to the deterioration of the profitability of exports and of import substituting activities.[39]

In this connection, it may be added that a survey of a small sample of firms has led to the conclusion that firms successfully adjusted to the tariff reductions completed by June 1979, but encountered considerable difficulties after the fixing of the exchange rate. A producer of non-electrical home appliances, selling copper-based utensils abroad, had to abandon its exports as foreign sales became unprofitable, and even a producer of pulp and paper, where the availability of natural resources gives Chile a considerable advantage, lost market shares abroad as its costs increased 80 percent more than the sales price. Finally, increases in labor costs in the face of fixed exchange rates greatly burdened a domestic producer of stoves and refrigerators, favoring the imports of these commodities.[40]

It further appears that, notwithstanding reductions in tariffs, unemployment rates in manufacturing declined in 1976 and in 1977, and there was only a moderate increase in 1978. However, as the exchange rate became increasingly overvalued, national unemployment rates increased substantially, reaching 12.6 percent in the last quarter of 1981 compared to 6.8 percent in 1978.

These results indicate the effects of the increasing distortions introduced in product and factor markets by the simultaneous fixing of the exchange rate and the freeing of capital movements, accompanied by the 'backward' indexation of wages and of the prices of several non-traded goods. While the incentives created for the inflow of capital gave rise to an artificial boom in the construction industry as well as in the stock market, the production of traded goods in manufacturing and even in agriculture became increasingly unprofitable, contributing to a serious deterioration of the balance of trade.

The question arises as to what extent the deterioration of the trade balance may be explained by external shocks. Estimates made by the author indicate that, in contradistinction to the 1974–8 period, external shocks were a relatively minor influence in Chile in 1979–81. Although the price of copper declined, the adverse terms of trade effects amounted to only 3.0 percent in Chile's GNP and they were 0.4 percent if the pure terms of trade effects alone are considered. Pure terms of trade and export volume effects totalled 2.0 percent of GNP in

1979–81, compared to 19.4 percent in 1974–8. And while Chile also suffered increases in interest rates on foreign loans, the adverse effects of high interest rates were compounded by Chile's increased indebtedness, as additional net external financing was more than double of the balance-of-payments effects of external shocks.

By 1981, the net inflow of capital came to exceed 10 percent of Chile's GDP, providing financing for more than one-half of gross domestic investment as domestic savings declined. The decrease in domestic savings, in turn, may be explained in part by the use of borrowed funds for consumption and in part by the 'wealth effect' as the near-quadrupling of stock market prices led to increased consumption.

The capital inflow in turn increased Chile's indebtedness, which reached 42 percent of GNP at the end of 1981. In the same year, debt-service charges came to amount to 89 percent of export value. Increases in these ratios, together with the increase in the trade deficit, led to a decline in Chile's creditworthiness. Thus, foreign banks that willingly supplied funds to Chilean borrowers in earlier years, ceased to do so as the situation deteriorated.

The reversal began in the fourth quarter of 1981, when the overvaluation of the exchange rate and the resulting rise in the current account deficit became increasingly apparent. At the same time, the financial position of firms and banks deteriorated to a considerable extent. This was the case, in particular, for the large conglomerates, where the adverse effects of the overvaluation of the exchange rate were aggravated by their earlier overextension and the burden of interest charges on their foreign borrowing.

In the fourth quarter of 1981, Chile had a balance of payments deficit of $243 million, compared with surpluses in the preceding periods when the inflow of capital exceeded the current account deficit. At the same time, the overvaluation of the peso and the ending of the artificial boom fueled by the capital inflow led to a 3.2 percent decline in GDP between the fourth quarters of 1980 and 1981; the decline was the largest (9.0 percent) in manufacturing that had to bear the brunt of the appreciation of the exchange rate.[41]

The situation deteriorated further in the first half of 1982 and, according to data published in the November 1982 issue of *Economia y Sociedad*, the average rate of profit in the 44 largest private enterprises changed from + 11 percent in December 1980 to − 12 percent in June 1982. In June 1982 came the predictable consequence of a devaluation of the Chilean peso, followed by further devaluations. And, apart from the depreciation of the peso, the large balance of trade deficit and the need to service foreign loans necessitated the application of deflationary policies.

In 1982, the gross domestic product declined by 14.3 percent, with decreases of 29 percent in construction and 21.6 percent in manufacturing while gross domestic investment fell by 37.1 percent. In the same year, the national rate of unemployment reached 19.4 percent and that in the Greater Santiago area 22.1 percent; in 1981, the unemployment rate hardly exceeded 11 percent (Tables 8.3 and 8.5).

CONCLUSIONS

In the introduction to this essay, it was suggested that the 1973–83 decade of policy experimentation in Chile may be appropriately divided into two subperiods. The first subperiod, September 1973 to June 1979, was characterized by reductions in price distortions. In turn, price distortions increased after June 1979 – the beginning of the second subperiod.

In the first subperiod, the principal measures included the liberalization of prices, the freeing of interest rates, the elimination of import licensing and prior import deposit requirements, the reduction of tariffs to 10 percent, automobiles excepted, and the adoption of realistic exchange rates, although towards the end of the period devaluations did not fully compensate for domestic inflation. In turn, in June 1979, the exchange rate was fixed at 39 pesos to the dollar while capital flows were freed and the 'backward' integration of wages was institutionalized. The application of these measures led to the increasing overvaluation of the currency while the virtual guarantee to maintain the exchange rate constant in the face of continued inflation gave rise to an excessive capital inflow.

Notwithstanding the large external shocks it suffered, Chile had a superior growth performance in 1973–9, not only in comparison with the virtual stagnation under Allende in the period of the biggest postwar boom, but also compared to 1963–73, characterized by favorable world economic conditions. Rapid growth was associated with the opening of the Chilean economy that benefitted agriculture without adversely affecting industry, as increases in output due to export expansion more than compensated for negative import substitution following reductions in tariffs.

This is not to say that Chile's economic performance could not have been improved if certain policy errors had been avoided. To begin with, as the author suggested in an advisory report written in January 1975, 'reductions in tariffs would need to be accompanied by the depreciation of the exchange rate in order to prevent a deterioration of the balance of payments'.[42] While this was done in the earlier part of the period, subsequently exchange rate changes fell behind a rate of inflation. Yet, as recommended in the author's advisory report, 'Exchange Rates and Inflation in Chile', prepared in December 1974, the external shocks Chile suffered would have necessitated devaluations in excess of increases in domestic prices.[43]

Also, the provision of export subsidies, proposed in the same report, would have strengthened export-led growth by reducing discrimination against exports at a time when tariffs were still high. More generally, industrial adjustment would have been smoother, and unemployment rates lower, if incentives to export had preceded the dismantling of tariff barriers.

But the principal reason for the high unemployment in 1975, that was reduced relatively slowly in subsequent years, was the application of deflationary policies. Writing in December 1974, the author raised questions concerning the application of this policy under the conditions then existing in Chile: 'given pervasive indexing,[44] the time period necessary for reducing the rate of inflation to more normal levels, say 15 percent a year, would be very long. Also, the process of adjusting to a lower rate of inflation may involve a considerable cost to the economy in the form of output foregone'.[45]

Having indicated the possible costs involved, the author at that time suggested the need to radically change expectations in regard to the continuation of inflation. In making reference to Germany's experience with monetary reform during the nineteen-twenties, he suggested that Chile follow the German example. For this purpose, a combination of measures was proposed: exchanging the currency for a new 'hard' escudo; reducing public expenditures; imposing a once-for-all wealth tax; setting positive interest rates; providing credit to the private sector, and increasing incentive to non-traditional exports.[46] A comprehensive reform was not undertaken however, and with continued indexation, the deflationary policies led in large measure to a 'quantity adjustment', resulting in high unemployment, rather than to a 'price adjustment'. It is not surprising, therefore, that inflationary expectations persisted.

Slowing down the rate of devaluation and, subsequently, fixing the exchange rate was aimed at changing inflationary expectations. At the same time, it was not recognized that this alternative would involve an economic cost due to the adverse effects of the increased discrimination against the production of traded goods. And while the inflow of capital led to rapid expansion in the production of non-traded goods, this could not continue indefinitely. Thus, increases in Chile's foreign debt in the face of a substantial deterioration of its trade balance entailed a decline in its creditworthiness and, with the ending of the artificial boom in the non-traded goods sector, adverse changes in the production of traded and non-traded goods came to be synchronized. As a result, GDP fell in the fourth quarter of 1981, with further declines occurring as the balance-of-payments situation necessitated taking strong deflationary measures and the fixed exchange rate period came to an end.

Nor did external shocks account for these adverse developments, as the shocks which Chile experienced in 1979–81 were relatively small compared with the shocks suffered in 1974–78 when the economy grew rapidly. And, despite suggestions to the contrary, the appreciation of the dollar cannot be considered the culprit. While the extent of the appreciation of the real exchange rate was 30 percent vis-à-vis the currencies of Chile's major trading partners between 1978 and 1981, the peso appreciated in real terms by 23 percent vis-à-vis the US dollar as well.

Finally, although the Chilean rate of inflation converged to that of the United States in 1981, the distortions created during the process of adjustment continued. Thus, offsetting the appreciation of the real exchange rate would have required that Chilean prices fall below international levels. But even such an unlikely outcome may not have remedied the decline of the fortunes of the traded goods sector, as the loss of market positions involves a certain irreversibility.

In the presence of sluggish adjustment in prices, then, using the exchange rate as an instrument for reducing the rate of inflation imposes a real cost on the economy. This is because the appreciation of the real exchange rate during the period of adjustment is not undone at the time when domestic and foreign prices converge. The conclusion applies even in the absence of 'backward' indexation of wages since the adjustment process will take time.

It is paradoxical that, in the name of an untried – and basically unsound – theory, liberalization in Chile was perverted by increasing price distortions after June 1979. It will be inappropriate, however, to declare the experience of the entire decade a failure, when it is a policy reversal that led to the predicament in which Chile now finds itself.

NOTES

1. B. Balassa, 'Disquilibrium Analysis in Developing Countries: An Overview', Essay 2 in this volume. The countries in question included Argentina, Brazil, Chile, Colombia, and Mexico in Latin America and Israel, Korea, Malaysia, Pakistan, Philippines, Singapore, and Taiwan in other developing regions.
2. T. Jeanneret, 'The Structure of Protection in Chile', in B. Balassa *et al. The Structure of Protection in Developing Countries* (Baltimore, Md.: Johns Hopkins University Press, 1971) pp. 146–58.
3. B. Balassa, 'Disequilibrium Analysis in Developing Countries: An Overview', p. 1029.
4. F. D. Levy *et al. Chile: An Economy in Transition,* A World Bank Country Study (Washington, DC: World Bank, 1979) p. 35.
5. J. Behrman, *Foreign Trade Regimes and Economic Development* (New York: National Bureau of Economic Research, 1976), pp. 85–94.
6. R. Ffrench-Davis, 'Exchange Rate Policies in Chile: The Experience with the Crawling Peg', in J. Williamson (ed.), *Exchange Rate Rules* (London: Macmillan, 1979) p. 162.
7. The consumer price index used in the table is that reported by Schmidt-Hebbel and Marshall; K. Schmidt-Hebbel and J. Marshall, 'Revision del IPC para el Periodo 1970–1980: Una Nota', Document No. 176, Departamento de Estudios Empresas BHC, 1981 (mimeo). For the years 1970 and 1973–78, this index is practically identical to that derived by Cortazar and Marshall which, however, does not extend to further years; R. Cortazar and J. Marshall, 'Indice de Precios al Consumidor en Chile: 1970–1978', Santiago, CIEPLAN, 1980 (mimeo). It should be added that, notwithstanding the adjustments made, the error possibilities associated with the consumer price index for the years 1971–73 remain considerable. Correspondingly, all deflated figures for these years are subject to large errors.
8. The latter statement does not apply to Mexico where the fixed exchange rate system was maintained during this period.
9. B. Balassa *et al. Development Strategies in Semi-Industrial Economies* (Baltimore, Md.: Johns Hopkins University Press, 1982) pp. 45, 52.
10. B. Balassa, 'The Newly Industrializing Developing Countries after the Oil Crisis', *Weltwirtschaftliches Archiv,* CXVII (1981) 142–95. Reprinted in B. Balassa, *The Newly Industrializing Countries in the World Economy* (New York: Pergamon Press, 1981) pp. 29–81. The newly-industrializing countries were defined to include countries that had *per capita* incomes between $1100 and $3000 in 1978 and where the share of the manufacturing sector in the gross domestic product was 20 percent or higher in 1977. The countries in question are Argentina, Brazil, Chile, Mexico, Uruguay, Portugal, Spain, Yugoslavia, Israel, Hong Kong, Korea, Singapore, and Taiwan.
11. J. R. Ramoz, 'The Economics of Hyperstagflation: Stabilization Policy in Post-1973 Chile', *Journal of Development Economics* (1980) p. 472.
12. Levy, *et al.* p. 99.
13. B. Balassa, 'Tariff Reform in Chile', in B. Balassa, *Policy Reform in Developing Countries* (Oxford: Pergamon Press, 1977) pp. 70–2.

14. A. Harberger, 'The Chilean Economy in the 1970s: Crisis, Stabilization, Liberalization, Reform', *Carnegie – Rochester Conference Series on Public Policy* (Amsterdam: North-Holland, 1982) p. 118.

15. For a description of the methodology of estimating external shocks and policy responses to these shocks, see B. Balassa, 'Structural Adjustment Policies in Developing Countries', Essay 4 in this volume.

16. Balassa, 'The Newly Industrializing Developing Countries after the Oil Crisis'.

17. The rate of growth of imports was especially high for luxuries and conveniences, such as perfumery and cosmetics, radios and TV sets, cars and motorcycles, and toys and musical instruments, the importation of which was severely restricted during the Allende government, although their combined imports hardly exceeded 8 percent of Chile's total imports in 1980. The ratio was 13 percent if imports of textiles, clothing, and shoes are also added, compared to 4 percent in 1970; see R. Ffrench-Davis, 'Import Liberalization: The Chilean Experience, 1973–1980', *Coleccion Estudios CIEPLAN 4*, Table.

18. At the beginning of the period, this was the result of the difficulties Chile encountered in attempting to borrow abroad. In subsequent years, however, Chile became creditworthy for private lending, but there was a desire to limit foreign borrowing during the period under consideration.

19. For the explanation of concepts and estimates for groups of developing countries, see B. Balassa, 'The Problem of the Debt in Developing Countries', Essay 6 in this volume.

20. It should be added that the national accounts figures include only the profits of the banking sectors, which are likely to represent a relatively small fraction of imputed banking services that equalled 3.9 percent of GDP for 1979. Thus, the rapid expansion of the banking sector, with the ratio of imputed banking services to the gross domestic product nearly doubling between 1973 and 1979, contributed little to measured GDP growth. This conclusion applies *a fortiori* to import tax receipts that show the largest rise.

21. A. Solimano, 'Exportaciones Industriales en Chile: Un Modelo Annual para el Periodo 1960–81', Santiago, CIEPLAN, 1982 (mimeo).

22. L. Willmore, 'Economic Recession and Trade Liberalization: Chilean Manufacturing, 1975–1981', Santiago, United Nations Economic Commission for Latin America, 1982 (mimeo).

23. A. Foxley, 'Towards a Free Market Economy: Chile 1974–1979', *Journal of Development Economics* (1982) p. 19.

24. Ffrench-Davis, 'Import Liberalization.' The Chilean Experience, 1973–1980, pp. 25–7.

25. Ffrench-Davis, 'Import Liberalization.' These conclusions are confirmed by more recent data reported in S. Edwards, 'Economic Policy and the Record of Economic Growth in Chile: 1973–1982', in G. M. Walton (ed.), *The National Economic Policies of Chile* (Greenwich, Conn.: JAI Press, 1984).

26. The data of Table 8.3 permit deriving the corresponding shares in terms of 1977 prices. The results are, however, much affected by changes in relative prices that substantially raise the share of imports, and hence of foreign

savings, as well as that of investment, in GDP in the earlier years. At the same time, it is current price data that show the actual allocation of incomes and expenditures in any particular year.

27. Domestic savings have been defined as the difference between the gross domestic product and (private and public) consumption and foreign savings as the difference between the imports and the exports of goods and services. Adjusting for net current transfers (0.7 percent of GDP in 1979) would modify the results but little. In turn, the adjustment made in Chilean official publications, involving the deduction of net factor income from abroad from domestic savings, conflict with national accounts conventions.

28. Harberger.

29. R. Cortazar, 'Desempleo, Pobreza y Distribution: Chile 1970–1981', *Apuntes CIEPLAN*, No. 34 (1982) p. 12.

30. I. Heskia, 'Distribucion del Ingreso en el Gran Santiago, 1957–1979', Documento Serie Investigacion No. 53, Departamento de Economia, Universidad de Chile, 1980, p. 122.

31. Heskia, p. 92. Considerable attention has been given to the consumption surveys carried out in the years 1979 and 1978 by the Instituto Nacional de Estadisticas, which show larger changes in favor of the upper 20 percent at the expense of the lowest 40 percent (Cortazar, p. 5). However, this survey appears less reliable than the University of Chile surveys. The latter are carried out regularly every year; they provide information on incomes rather than on consumption, with incomes classified according to a variety of personal and family characteristics, and they are part of the widely-respected employment-unemployment survey, the results of which are utilized elsewhere in this study.

32. R. I. McKinnon, 'The Order of Economic Liberalization: Lessons from Chile and Argentina', Memorandum No. 251, Research Center in Economic Growth, Stanford University, 1982, p. 11.

33. McKinnon, p. 12.

34. L. A. Sjaastad, 'Stabilization and Liberalization Experiences in the Southern Cone', paper prepared for a World Bank Symposium held in May 1982 (mimeo), p. 6.

35. Sjaastad.

36. Sjaastad.

37. The results are in conformity with the estimates of the effects of relative price changes on exports and imports cited above. The sensitivity of the trade balance to relative prices is also shown by a macroeconomic model estimated for the 1974–81 period in Chile; see V. Corbo, 'The Relative Prices, Expenditures and the Trade Balance: The Case of Chile', paper presented at the Latin American Meetings of the Econometric Society held in Mexico City in July 1982, Table 4.

38. V. Corbo, 'Chile: An Overview of Macroeconomic Developments in the Last Twenty Years', in Walton (ed.), Table 8.

39. McKinnon and Sjaastad also criticized these wage adjustments, with Sjaastad arguing that 'Chile's wage policy really constitutes a second (and superfluous) *numeraire* (the first being the exchange rate) ...'; L. A. Sjaastad, 'Failure of Economic Liberalism in the Cone of Latin America',

The World Economy, VI (1983) p. 16. Carrying this argument to its logical conclusion would call for stopping wage indexation rather than establishing a fixed exchange rate as the absence of wage indexation would equally affect the prices of traded and non-traded goods and would not give incentives for an excessive inflow of foreign capital by providing a virtual exchange rate guarantee.

40. V. Corbo and J. M. Sanchez, 'Notes on Firm's Responses to the Reform in Chile: Some Case Studies', Santiago, Universidad Catolica de Chile, 1982.

41. R. Toso, 'El Tipo de Cambio Fijo en Chile: La Experiencia en el periodo 1979–1982', paper prepared for the Meeting of Technicians of Central Banks of America, held on 31 October–5 November 1982 in Vina del Mar, Chile, Tables 1 and 3. The results contrast with the statement made by Sergio de Castro, then Minister of Finance, on 'Public Finance and the Chilean Economy' in October 1981. De Castro declared that 'Chile has one of the healthiest, strongest and most dynamic economies in the world'. He further suggested that 'we must generate a deficit in the current accounts of our balance of payments, because this deficit constitutes precisely the reflection and the measurement of the foreign savings which we have been able to attract . . . We must strive to maintain it at the highest level and for the longest period possible' (advertisement in the *Wall Street Journal*, 9 October 1981).

42. Balassa, 'Tariff Reform in Chile', p. 77.

43. The report is available from the author upon request.

44. 'The indexing of wages on the consumer price index and the depreciation of the exchange rate over and above the rate of increase of this index tends to perpetuate inflation. If imported inputs and labor were the only inputs used by the firm, production costs would rise at a rate exceeding the consumer price index'; B. Balassa, 'Exchange Rates and Inflation in Chile', 1974 (mimeo), p. 4.

45. Balassa, 'Tariff Reform in Chile', p. 5.

46. Balassa, 'Tariff Reform in Chile', pp. 12–13.

Essay 9 Medium-term Economic Policies for Portugal

INTRODUCTION

This essay will examine the policies that may be applied to improve the performance of the Portuguese economy as the country becomes a member of the European Common Market. While the emphasis will be on medium-term policies, the essay will review the antecedents and the effects of the stabilization program adopted in June 1983.

Issues relating to the public sector are analyzed in Section I of the essay. Section II is devoted to trade policies while Section III examines the cost and the availability of credit to the private sector. Finally, sectoral policies regarding agriculture and industry are the subject of Section IV of the essay.

I THE JUNE 83 STABILIZATION PROGRAM AND ITS EFFECTS

Antecedents and objectives

Following excessive expansion during the post-Revolutionary years, Portugal successfully applied a stabilization program in 1978–79. The program included a 7 percent devaluation of the escudo, a rise in the crawling peg from 1.0 percent to 1.25 percent, increases in interest rates, and the imposition of credit ceilings. The application of these measures led to the rapid expansion of merchandise exports, tourist receipts, and emigrants' remittances, as well as to an increased savings effort in Portugal. The deficit in the current account of the balance of payments was practically eliminated while export expansion engen-

185

dered an increase in the rate of economic growth, notwithstanding the stagnation of domestic demand.

However, earlier trends towards a higher share of public expenditures were not reversed and these trends accelerated in subsequent years. With the rise of public consumption exceeding that of the gross domestic product and rapid increases in public investment, the cash deficit of the government budget surpassed 9 percent of the gross domestic product in 1980 and approached 12 percent in 1981. The poor performance of public enterprises and their overambitious investment program, involving large investment projects of doubtful economic viability, further added to the borrowing requirements of the public sector that reached 18 percent of GDP in 1980 and exceeded 21 percent in 1981.[1]

The public sector's borrowing requirements were increasingly financed by foreign loans that came to account for two-fifths of the total in 1981. This occurred as the appreciation of the real exchange rate, resulting from the revaluation of the escudo in February 1980 and the decrease of the crawl to 0.5 percent a month in the face of rapid inflation, led to the deterioration of Portugal's export performance. With increases in oil prices adding to the import bill, the deficit in the current account of the balance of payments approached 12 percent of GDP in 1981.

In April 1982, this author recommended reversing the appreciation of the real exchange rate through a devaluation of 14 to 16 percent and raising the crawling peg from 0.75 percent, established in December 1981, to 1.0 percent a month. It was further proposed to increase interest rates and to reduce the rate of growth of domestic credit creation. Within the overall total, the recommendations called for lowering the share of credit to the public sector, to be accomplished through a slowdown in the growth of public consumption and, in particular, public investment.[2]

In the event, the escudo was devalued by 9 percent in June 1982 while the crawling peg was maintained at 0.75 percent a month. A subsequent devaluation by 2 percent in March 1983, accompanied by an increase in the crawl to 1.0 percent a month, did not suffice to regain the competitiveness of Portuguese exports as prices continued to rise more rapidly at home than abroad.

At the same time, with the rise of public consumption exceeding that of the gross domestic product, the government budget increased further as did the deficit of the public enterprises. All in all, the borrowing requirements of the public sector (including general government and the so-called statutory public enterprises) came to surpass 22 percent of GDP in 1982, with one-half of the total being financed by foreign loans. In the same year, the current account deficit amounted to 13 percent of the gross domestic product.

With the service of the debt approaching 30 percent of total foreign exchange earnings, corrective measures became necessary. Soon after taking office in June 1983, the new government adopted a stabilization program in consultation with the IMF. The program included a 12 percent devaluation of the escudo in terms of effective exchange rates, increases in interest rates, lowering the rate of growth of domestic credit creation, lesser reliance on foreign loans, and reductions in government expenditures as well as in the deficit of public enterprises.

The measures applied led to a reduction in the borrowing require-ments of the public sector from 23 percent of GDP in 1982 to 15 percent in 1983, with the share of foreign loans decreasing to one-third of the total. At the same time, with improvements in the trade balance, the current account deficit declined to 8 percent of the gross domestic product.

Achievements and prospects

The data indicate the success of the June 1983 stabilization program. At the same time, with the gross domestic product remaining practi-cally unchanged, the counterpart of the improvement in the current account balance was a 7 percent decrease in total domestic expendi-tures in 1983. As public consumption rose by 4 percent, the decline was concentrated in the private economy. Real disposable incomes fell by 4 percent while private consumption decreased by 1 percent as the savings effort slackened. Lower savings and lesser reliance on foreign borrowing, in turn, contributed to a 8 percent fall in domestic fixed investment.

The decline in foreign borrowing by the public sector, however, led to increased reliance on domestic credit, thereby squeezing the private sector. Thus, domestic credit to the public sector rose by 25 percent between December 1982 and December 1983 while only a 17 percent increase occurred in credit to the private sector, falling considerably short of price increases of 34 percent in the same period.

Some improvement in credit conditions for the private sector oc-curred in the first half of 1984 as the public sector again increased reliance on foreign loans. At the same time, the overall borrowing requirement of the public sector is projected to decline only to 14 percent of the gross domestic product and even this target may not be met. This result reflects increases in public consumption and a lack of improvement in the financial situation of public enterprises. By contrast, private expenditures and, in particular, private investment have continued to decline.

A further consideration is that improvements in the current account of the balance of payments in 1983 involved a substantially larger decline in the dollar value of merchandise imports ($1.3 billion) than the rise in exports ($0.4 billion). Decreases in imports were concentrated in machinery, transport equipment, and metal products and were associated with the fall in investments that occurred. This trend continued in the first half of 1984, when investment activity declined again.

The revival of investment activity would thus require higher imports of capital goods and metal products, when the elimination of trade barriers following entry into the Common Market would further add to the amount imported. At the same time, new investments would be necessary to improve the competitiveness of the Portuguese economy and, in particular, to increase exports that are required to pay for the higher imports. As the large bulk of the export effort would continue to be made by the private sector, private investment would accordingly have to rise. Given the limited possibilities for foreign borrowing, this would require lowering the financial requirements of the public sector.

This essay will consider possible improvements in the public sector, both in general government and in public enterprises. Next, desirable changes in trade policy will be reviewed. The report will further analyze questions relating to the availability and the cost of credit. Finally, sectoral policies for agriculture and manufacturing industry will be considered.

II REFORMING THE PUBLIC SECTOR

Budgetary procedures

With rapid increases of public consumption and investment, government expenditures approached 43 percent of Portugal's gross domestic product in 1981, compared to 22 percent in the early seventies and 36 percent in 1978. In 1981, investment by the general government approached 14 percent of gross domestic fixed investment, with the statutory public enterprises accounting for another 19 percent.

The growth of public consumption continued to exceed that of GDP in 1982, and public consumption rose again in 1983 and 1984 while total domestic expenditures declined. In particular, public employment increased further, albeit to a lesser extent than beforehand. According to some estimates, employment in general government may have reached half a million compared to less than two hundred thousand ten years earlier.

Part of the growth in public employment relates to the increase of employment by the municipalities that was in part associated with the transfer of certain social and cultural functions to them. At the same time, the transfer has not entailed a decline of employment in the corresponding central agencies; rather, the size of the central government has continued to increase. The establishment of new governmental agencies has further added to the number of public employees.

Apart from impinging on scarce economic resources, increases in the size of the government have aggravated the long-standing problem of bureaucracy in Portugal. This has entailed additional costs, both by lengthening the time period needed to obtain various permits and licenses and by creating uncertainty as to whether they will eventually be granted.

The Programa de Recuperação Financeira e Económica, 1984–1987 (PRFE), made public in July 1984, calls for reducing the growth rate of public consumption below that of the gross domestic product. It also proposes abolishing several governmental agencies. While these recommendations are praiseworthy, several additional steps may be usefully taken.

For one thing, it would be desirable to introduce the application of the 'sunset' principle of budgeting, under which the desirability of various governmental functions and agencies is considered anew. This would replace the 'marginal' principle applied at present, under which budget negotiations concern incremental changes in the annual allocation of governmental functions and agencies. While this principle of budgeting could not be applied immediately across-the-board, a timetable may be set up for its application over, say, a five-year period.

The process of decision-making on public investments would also need to be reviewed. It would be desirable to prepare multi-annual budgets for public investment, with account taken of their implications for current expenditures. This would permit reviewing expenditures in particular areas, with cutbacks effected in cases such as education and health, where excessive expansion appears to have occurred in recent years.

Budgetary discipline for municipalities would also need to be strengthened. This purpose may be served by limiting transfers for current expenditures and investment programs and by circumscribing the ability of the municipalities to borrow. Also, plans to establish a large number of additional municipalities would need to be reconsidered.

The public enterprises

In 1982, the 51 statutory public enterprises, operating under Decree Law 26076, accounted for 5 percent of total employment, 15 percent of value added, and 18 percent of gross capital formation in Portugal. There are also public enterprises operating under the public holding company, IPE, as well as various public organizations producing goods and services, which altogether account for an additional 2 percent of employment, 3 percent of value added, and 6 percent of gross domestic investment.

The large investment programs of public enterprises have not brought commensurate benefits, as the productivity of the investments has been low. Part of the explanation lies in the inappropriate choice of investments, in particular in the Sines heavy industrial complex. Also, with the exception of pulp and paper, public enterprises are oriented towards the domestic market where they enjoy protection. At the same time, public enterprises have not been subject to market discipline but to largely uncoordinated, administrative guidance from the supervising ministries.

The PRFE puts emphasis on inefficient resource use by public enterprises, attributing this to the inadequacies of the system of evaluation, the multiple objectives applied, and the multiplicity of control. In order to remedy these deficiencies, it suggests establishing a unified system of control as well as a system of evaluation that would permit a greater decentralization of decision-making.

The last point requires particular emphasis as regards public enterprises in the so-called competitive sphere, i.e. that involving the production of traded goods. The objective should be to put these enterprises on the same footing as firms in the private sector, with profit maximization as their principal objective. Nevertheless, on the example of France, public enterprises in the noncompetitive sphere, such as electricity and gas, would also need to be given managerial autonomy.

In this connection, reference may be made to the fact that public enterprises have considerably less managerial freedom in Portugal than in Hungary, a socialist country, where profits are considered as the principal objective of the firm. Also, Hungary is in the process of establishing Boards of Directors that will determine the general orientation of the firm and will appoint and fire its managers. This would also be desirable in Portugal, so as to reduce the dependence of managers on the government administration. In turn, smaller public enterprises may come under holdings that would replace IPE, which has had too many enterprises under its control for effective operation.

One may avoid burdening the Board of Directors with political appointees, as has often occurred with respect to the Executive Committees of public enterprises in the past, if the government appointed only a minority of its members. Other members may be appointed by the banks, by organizations of employers, and by labor unions.

Transforming public enterprises into self-managed profit-making units will take time, particularly since a number of these enterprises have serious financial problems to contend with. In some instances, the financial problems find their origin in governmental arrears that have accumulated rapidly in recent years. This is a phenomenon unique to Portugal that has led to a cumulative process of building up arrears throughout the public sector.

A large part of the arrears originate in the government's having required certain public enterprises to borrow abroad instead of discharging its financial obligations to them. A possible way of dealing with the problem of these arrears is to utilize increases in the escudo value of the gold holdings of the Banco de Portugal to offset the budgetary cost of the government's paying its arrears to the public enterprises, which would in turn immobilize the proceeds by purchasing bonds of equivalent value from the Banco de Portugal in exchange for its assuming their foreign debt. In turn, a plan would need to be worked out to eliminate the outstanding balances of all other arrears over a predetermined period, with no further arrears allowed from now on.

Similar considerations apply to the arrears of municipalities that are of particular importance as far as payments for electricity to the public electricity company (EDP) are concerned. At the same time, the prices charged by EDP's would need to be reviewed, so as to avoid their profiting from the low price of fuel oil in Portugal.

It would further be desirable to eliminate the subsidy to fuel oil equalling approximately one-half of its domestic price. The subsidy has impeded fuel conservation efforts in Portugal, with energy consumption per unit of output continuing to rise while considerable declines occurred in the other OECD countries.

Several public enterprises that presently incur losses could operate efficiently if they were recapitalized. Some others, however, are not viable and would need to be closed down. Also, in the implementation of the PRFE, public enterprises may be sold to domestic and foreign interests in cases when no particular purpose is served by maintaining them in the public domain. And, even in the latter eventuality, joint ventures may be envisaged in order to obtain foreign technological, managerial, and marketing know-how.

At the same time, one should avoid the selection by the government authorities of privileged buyers of public enterprises. Rather, public enterprises should be sold at open auctions, with the participation of domestic as well as foreign private interests. And while the rate at which such sales may be undertaken is limited by the availability of private capital, IPE's program of divestiture would need to be accelerated. In turn, the remaining public enterprises should be put on an equal footing with private firms as far as the availability and the cost of credit are concerned.

Finally, the arrears of the public sector towards private enterprises, chiefly affecting construction, would need to be eliminated, with allowance made for over-invoicing in the face of the arrears. This would provide an example to the private sector to pay its own arrears, just as the past arrears of the public sector have provided an example to private firms to accumulate arrears.

III TRADE POLICY

Public enterprises producing traded goods are generally sheltered from foreign competition in Portugal. This is accomplished by utilizing the system of administrative restraint that requires the agreement of the Ministry of Industry for importation. Such agreement is not given if the product in question is manufactured by public enterprises.

Administrative restraint applies also to products manufactured by private enterprises. And while production at competitive prices and quality is supposed to be a precondition for denying an import permit, in actual practice this condition is often not fulfilled. At the same time, the application of administrative restraint may engender corruption. In one case, a firm reported that it could manufacture the product in question in the expectation of being able to make a 'deal' with the would-be importer.

The restrictive application of administrative regulations means that, notwithstanding free trade arrangements with the Common Market and EFTA, the Portuguese market is less open today than it was some years ago. And while administrative restraint might have been regarded as a response to the imposition of restrictions on Portuguese textile exports by European countries, it has led to the establishment and the maintenance of inefficient production activities and has discriminated against exports. Exports have been discouraged directly, as the importation of certain inputs has not been allowed; and indirectly, as the domestic market has provided profitable opportunities under protection.

In conjunction with Portugal's entry into the Common Market, administrative import restraints will eventually have to be abolished. It would be desirable to begin the process without delay by eliminating all restraints on the importation of inputs into export production, regardless of the availability of domestic substitutes.

Inputs should be defined in a wider sense, including raw materials, intermediate products, as well as machinery and transport equipment. At the next stage, the importation of all inputs, irrespective of their use, could be freed. This would leave durable and non-durable consumer goods to the last stage.

The most important export incentive, however, is a realistic exchange rate. Experience shows that merchandise exports as well as tourism are very responsive to changes in the real exchange rate in Portugal. At the same time, the exchange rate is a neutral instrument that provides inducements to increasing value added in exports as well as in import substitution.

The devaluation of June 1983 established the real exchange rate 8 percent above its peak level of early February 1980, if calculations are made by adjusting the trade-weighted exchange rate for changes in wholesale prices at home and abroad. Similar results are obtained if adjustment is made for changes in consumer prices or unit labor costs.

Owing to increases in domestic prices in excess of the rise in foreign prices, with allowance made for the 1 percent monthly crawl, the real exchange rate returned approximately to its early-1980 level by mid-1984. In view of the deceleration of wage increases, this was not however the case if the calculation is made by reference to unit labor costs, which provide a better indicator of export profitability. Thus, in the first quarter of 1984, wages in the manufacturing sector rose at an annual rate of only 17–18 percent.

It should be recognized that the deterioration of Portugal's terms of trade, due in large part to increases in oil prices, would require a real exchange rate more favorable than in the preceding period.[3] It would be necessary, therefore, to avoid a further appreciation of the real exchange rate. This objective may best be served by lowering the rate of inflation – a measure requiring fiscal discipline – and in particular, reducing the borrowing requirements of the public sector.

Apart from a realistic exchange rate and free access to imported inputs, the availability of foreign exchange for prospection and market research would contribute to good export performance. Existing regulations limit the availability of foreign exchange for such purposes and the practical application of these regulations often involves considerable delay. It is recommended that, on the example of several developing countries, the Banco de Portugal provides a foreign exchange allocation to exporters, based on report value or value added on exports, without requiring any supporting documentation.

It would further be desirable to increase the contribution of the government to the cost of prospection and market research by exporters, including participation at fairs, with a higher allowance made in the case of new products and new markets. Finally, on the example of Japan, Korea, and more recently Turkey, it would be desirable to grant incentives to trading companies that could channel the products of small and medium-size Portuguese enterprises into export.

IV AVAILABILITY AND THE COST OF CREDIT

Pursuing an appropriate trade policy would contribute to exports and to efficient import substitution in Portugal. At the same time, the continued expansion of exports, and economic growth in general, would require new investments. This is because the recent export expansion has occurred from existing capacity and in some areas capacity limits may soon be reached.

In the context of overall economic prospects, investment is conditioned by the availability and the cost of capital. Reductions in the financial requirements of the public sector would augment the availability of capital for private investments. Also, eliminating the interest preference to the public sector would permit reducing interest rates on private loans.

As shown in Table 9.1, interest rates were raised to a considerable extent in the course of 1983. However, the statutory rates shown in the table do not appropriately reflect either the level or the structure of interest rates. To begin with, a stamp tax of 0.25 percent is levied on the value of the loan and a tax of 6 percent on the amount of interest

TABLE 9.1 *Interest rates in Portugal*

	August 1977	May 1978	July 1981	April 1982	March 1983	August 1983
1. *Interest rates on deposits*						
– sight deposits at commercial banks	1.0	1.0	1.0	1.0	1.0	1.0
– sight deposits at Caixa General de Depositos and specialized loan firms						
. up to 70 000 esc.	4.0	—	—	—	—	—
. up to 100 000 esc.	—	4.0	4.0	—	—	—
. more than 70 000 esc.	2.0	—	—	—	—	—
. more than 100 000 esc.	—	2.0	2.0	—	—	—
. up to 150 000 esc.	—	—	—	4.0	4.0	4.0
. more than 150 000 esc.	—	—	—	2.0	2.0	2.0
– time deposits						
less than 90 days	6.0	8.0	10.0	11.0	15.5	17.5
from 90 to 180 days	9.0	12.0	14.0	15.0	19.5	21.5
from 180 days to 1 year	15.0	19.0	19.5	21.5	26.0	28.0
over 1 year	16.0	20.0	21.0	23.0	28.0	30.0
– savings deposits						
. 1 year	16.0	20.0	21.0	23.0	28.0	30.0
. 2 years	16.25	20.25	21.25	23.25	28.25	30.25
. 3 years	16.5	20.5	21.5	23.5	28.5	30.5
. 4 years	16.75	20.75	21.75	23.75	28.75	30.75
. over	17.0	21.0	22.0	24.0	29.0	31.0
2. *Interest rates on loans*						
– up to 90 days	14.75	18.25	19.0–21.0	23.0	27.0	29.5
– from 90 to 180 days	15.25	18.75	19.5–21.5	23.5	27.5	30.0
– from 180 days to 1 year	16.5	20.0	20.0–22.0	24.0	28.0	30.5
– from 1 year to 2 years	17.0	20.5	20.5–22.5	24.5	28.5	31.0
– from 2 to 5 years	17.75	21.25	21.0–23.0	25.0	29.0	31.5
– over 5 years	18.75	22.25	22.0–24.0	26.0	30.0	32.5
3. *Rediscount rate of the Central Bank*						
– 1st level	13.0	18.0	18.0	19.0	23.0	25.0
– 2nd level	15.5	20.5	20.5	21.5	25.5	27.5
– 3rd level	18.0	23.0	23.0	24.0	28.0	30.0

NOTE: The reported dates are the dates of change in interest rates.

SOURCE: Banco de Portugal.

payments, thereby raising the interest rate actually paid by approximately 2 percentage points. There are also surcharges on the interest rate that vary from 0 to 7.75 percentage points, depending on the destination of the loan. These taxes and surcharges apply to short-term as well as to medium-term loans.

On short-term loans, the effective interest rate is raised further owing to the fact that the interest is payable in advance. The resulting increase in the effective interest rate is the greater the longer is the original maturity of the loan. In turn, the renewal of a loan originally extended for three, or six, months adds to interest charges, both because the interest rate applies to the loan value augmented by interest payments at the previous stage (or stages) and because the stamp tax on the value of the loan is levied every time it is renewed.

Assuming the payment of statutory interest rates and the absence of surcharges, the effective interest rate for a loan with a total duration of one year will be 41, 43, and 48 percent, depending on whether it was originally extended for three months, six months, or a year. It follows that interest rates are considerably higher on short-term loans, representing 83 percent of the total, than on medium-term loans that account for the remaining 17 percent. And, while maturities of three months with subsequent renewals predominate among short-term loans, the banks have an interest to set maturities at six months and even for a year.

In the period between March 1983 and March 1984, the consumer price index rose by 32 percent. The increase was however partly due to the impact of the devaluation in import prices and the increase in the price of some public services. Thus, the staff of the Banco de Portugal projects consumer prices to rise by 25 percent between December 1983 and December 1984. The corresponding real interest rates would be in the 13 to 18 percent range on short-term loans, compared with rates of 7 to 12 percent in the March 1983–March 1984 period.

Real interest rates of this magnitude discourage investments, and they create liquidity – and eventually solveability – problems for private enterprises. The situation is aggravated by reason of the fact that firms in Portugal often have a high indebtedness because profits have been limited during much of the post-Revolutionary period, and a vicious circle may be engendered as high interest rates reduce profits or give rise to losses. At the same time, a large number of firms do not benefit from the deductibility of interest payments as they do not pay the Industrial Tax either because of a lack of profits or, in cases where profits are made, because of tax exemptions under the investment law (SIII).

It would thus be desirable to reduce over a period of time the effective interest rates paid by borrowers. This objective may be served by lowering stamp taxes on financial transactions, reducing reserve requirements, and/or lowering the 20 percent tax on interest payments to depositors, with a compensating reduction in the rate of interest on time and savings deposits. However, in order to encourage savings, it would further be desirable to increase after-tax interest rates on time and savings deposits, which will remain slightly negative in real terms even if one calculates with a 25 percent inflation rate. This may be accomplished through an uncompensated reduction in the tax rate on interest receipts.

Lowering reserve requirements would reduce the profits of the Banco de Portugal while the proposed elimination of the stamp tax on financial transactions and the reduction of the tax on interest receipts would lower budgetary revenues. A partial offset for this revenue loss could be provided by limiting the deductability of interest payments by business firms to the above-inflation portion of the interest rate. This modification would be the counterpart of the revaluation of assets that is now planned to take place every two years. Such periodical revaluations are highly desirable in order to avoid the loss of capital values to the firm but, for reasons of equity, they would need to be accompanied by corresponding action in regard to liabilities.

The proposed measures would lower interest rates on loans and increase after-tax interest rates on time and savings deposits, thereby reducing the excessive margin of 70 to 100 percent between the two rates while providing increased incentives to domestic savings. It would further be desirable to ensure the repatriation of a larger proportion of savings by emigrant workers than heretofore. Emigrant workers may respond to interest differentials at home and abroad, adjusted for expected changes in the exchange rate, as well as to domestic real interest rates.

From the continued decline of remittances, the recent devaluation notwithstanding, it would appear that sufficient incentives are not provided for the repatriation of savings by emigrant workers. Increases in interest rates could give inducements for repatriation as they recently have in Morocco, where raising interest rates paid on the emigrant workers' savings has led to a considerable rise in remittances. In Portugal, this may be achieved by maintaining the existing differential between after-tax interest rates for domestic residents and interest rates for emigrants, who do not pay the 20 percent tax, when the tax paid on interest payments to residents is reduced.

The PRFE further recommends the reactivation of financial markets in Portugal. Apart from institutional changes, this would require revising the taxation of bond interest and dividends. Under present conditions, neither the issue of bonds nor their purchase is profitable for economic agents in the private sector. At the same time, the example of Banco de Fomento indicates that cutting the tax on bond interest by one-half permits the offering of an interest rate on bonds that is attractive to buyers.

Extending the tax reduction to private bonds would permit setting interest rates at levels where they are attractive to issuers as well as to buyers. In turn, the purchase of shares may be encouraged by eliminating the double taxation of dividends. The issue of securities combining the features of bonds and stocks, proposed for public enterprises, may also be considered for private firms.

The described measures would promote the operation of capital markets in Portugal and furnish a larger menu of attractive assets for savers. Apart from increasing the efficiency of the financial markets, encouragement would thereby be provided for reversing the capital outflow that has occurred in recent years.

V SECTORAL POLICIES

Agriculture

Agriculture is a long-neglected sector of the Portuguese economy. In fact, the conclusions reached by this author on leading a World Bank mission to Portugal over fifteen years ago continue to apply today, except that in certain respects the situation has deteriorated since. Agriculture has been neglected in policy-making as well as in studies on the Portuguese economy that have largely concentrated on industry.

Yet, agriculture offers considerable scope for improvements. Such improvements are of particular importance since otherwise the cost of agricultural imports would rise to a considerable extent following entry into the Common Market. This is because the duties levied on the imports of commodities that come under the common agricultural policy are paid into the EC budget.

At the same time, as noted in a recent OECD report, the export–import ratio for agricultural products in Portugal is only 0.5 and the agricultural deficit accounts for nearly one-fifth of Portugal's trade deficit. Also, 27 percent of the population is employed in agriculture, but they produce altogether 8.5 percent of GDP as agricultural output failed to increase during the seventies.[4]

The OECD report further provides data on yields for the main agricultural products in Portugal, Greece, and Spain, expressed as a proportion of the EC average, which are reproduced in Table 9.2. The data show a considerable decline in the relative performance of Portuguese agriculture between the early and the late seventies, which contrasts with the substantial improvements that occurred in Greece and Spain, rice excepted.

The decline in relative yields can be only partly explained by unfavorable weather conditions. An important contributing factor has been continued uncertainty as regards ownership relationships in the South and the lack of full allocation of available land in this area. In turn, in the North and the Center, the fragmentation of land has not been conducive to improvements in productivity, and 'aid processes would appear to have failed to work because of excessive bureaucracy'.[5]

At the same time, one may disagree with the OECD report, according to which 'given the continuing surplus of agricultural labor, there is clearly little inducement for farmers to speed up the modernization of production',[6] since modernization through intensive cultivation would involve a greater, rather than a lesser, use of manpower. In fact, according to a World Bank study, the best possibilities for Portuguese agricultural exports lie in fruits, vegetables, olive oil, and wine – all labor-intensive products.[7]

Part of the reason for the inadequate exploitation of Portugal's agricultural potential traditionally was the relatively low price paid for agricultural products. This has since been remedied and wheat production has increased to a considerable extent as a result. In fact, the prices of wheat and of some other agricultural products are now above the

TABLE 9.2 *Comparative yields for the main agricultural products (expressed as a percentage of the EC average)*

	Portugal		Greece		Spain	
	1970–3	*1979–80*	*1970–73*	*1979–80*	*1970–73*	*1979–80*
Wheat	35.5	23.0	55.6	60.5	35.9	41.8
Rye	22.2	17.2	39.1	45.1	28.9	31.9
Barley	20.2	15.2	58.1	59.9	46.5	51.6
Oats	17.5	14.0	43.8	42.4	30.8	35.8
Maize	26.5	21.9	65.9	108.9	72.2	84.9
Rice	88.4	77.4	103.4	87.9	128.6	112.3
Potatoes	40.5	34.5	51.5	55.3	51.8	57.4

Sources: *Portugal,* OECD Economic Surveys 1983–1984 (Paris: Organization for Economic Co-operation and Development, 1984), p. 20.

Common Market level, so that they will have to be reduced relative to the price of industrial goods over time.

Following entry into the European Common Market, agricultural prices will not any more be subject to decisions by the Portuguese authorities. Correspondingly, the thrust of agricultural policy will have to be oriented towards the modernization of agriculture. The relevant conditions are of three kinds: the provision of complementary factors, improvements in production methods, and the establishment of facilities for the transformation of agricultural products.

As regards the first of these conditions, improvements in transportation facilities are of particular importance. Such improvements may be financed from the EC Regional Development Fund as noted below. There is further need to improve the system of agricultural credit that has become overly bureaucratized. Also, the reprivatisation of the marketing of farm products would be desirable, not only to comply with Common Market rules but also to reduce existing inefficiencies in marketing.

There is a vast storehouse of information that may be utilized to improve production methods in Portuguese agriculture, including the use of better seeds, planting materials, the increased application of fertilizer and pesticides, and the utilization of improved techniques. The shift from lower- to higher-yielding product varieties also comes under this heading.

In a broader sense, the transformation of agricultural products includes not only processing facilities, but storing and refrigeration as well. Apart from their importance in agriculture, improvements in these facilities would also be desirable in regard to fisheries.

The Agricultural Fund of the EC provides financing for agricultural improvements. At the same time, the preconditions of such financing include adequate problem formulation, program design, and execution. Judging from the experience of the last decade, the Portuguese central authorities may not be able to fully discharge these tasks. A possible solution may be decentralization, with reliance based on producers' co-operatives and associations and the use of foreign experts for this purpose.

Manufacturing industry

In examining the instruments of an industrial policy in Portugal, the question arises as to which industries will provide the best possibilities for expansion in the framework of the European Common Market and for exporting to other industrial countries, in particular the United States. Exports to the US offer considerable interest since the American economy is expected to attain higher rates of growth in the medium-term than the economies of the EC countries.

The situation in Italy during the nineteen-sixties may be taken as a point of departure. Like Italy at the time of the establishment of the European Common Market, Portugal offers relatively low-cost labor possessing basic skills that can be upgraded through training while it has little physical capital and limited technological sophistication.

Italy has developed industries relying on semi-skilled and skilled labor over the last quarter of the century. In particular, it has made progress in exporting good quality clothing, shoes, and other non-durable consumer goods that often incorporate new designs. Italy has also expanded its exports of automobiles and of relatively labor-intensive electrical and non-electrical machinery and machine tools, which do not involve highly automated processes and are mostly produced in small series. These exports have been oriented not only towards the EC but also to US markets.

Under present conditions, Portugal has a comparative advantage in products incorporating semi-skilled and skilled labor rather than unskilled labor or physical capital and are in the middle range in terms of technological sophistication. With its low wage level, Portugal offers advantages over Italy in these products, assuming that it can buy, and later develop, new designs.

At the same time, it would be a mistake to devote substantial resources to pursue the will-o'-the-wisp of advanced technology industries as it has been proposed. The industries in question require technological sophistication and scientific infrastructure as well as domestic markets of considerable size, which Portugal does not possess.

A further question relates to the choice between reliance on governmental institutions and on market incentives in pursuing Portugal's industrial development. The former approach seems to underlie the proposed Industrial Development Law and related regulations, which call for the establishment of an Industrial Development Fund, a Technological Innovation Agency, Technological Centers, Research and Development Enterprises, Industrial Development Centers for the Interior, and an Industrial Extension Network.

Italy's example is again relevant in this context. Rather than relying on governmental institutions, Italy has let market forces determine the direction of industrial development in the private sector. This will also be appropriate for Portugal, where government institutions do not have a particularly good record in promoting the efficient development of manufacturing industries. At the same time, the government would have to create the conditions for industry to develop along the lines of its comparative advantage by establishing an appropriate system of incentives and improving physical and human infrastructure.

Note has been taken above of the need for maintaining realistic exchange rates, liberalizing imports, providing export incentives, lowering interest rates, and developing capital markets. A further question relates to incentives that are presently granted under the investment law, known by its initials as SIII.

The extent of fiscal incentives provided under the SIII is based on three criteria: economic productivity (as measured by the output-investment ratio), sectoral priority, and regional priority, with weights of 35, 35, and 30 percent given to each. The implementation of the law has encountered bureaucratic difficulties, however, and the incentives are modulated on the basis of *ex ante* evaluations rather than the *ex post* results.

One may thus endorse recommendations made for abolishing SIII. At the same time, various suggestions have been put forward for instituting new incentive schemes in its place. The draft Industrial Development Law puts emphasis on the choice of priority industrial sectors, to be defined with respect to industrial policy objectives and comparative advantage criteria. The industrial policy objectives include the development of Portugal's natural resources; incorporating maximum value added; restructuring, modernization, and specialization of traditional industries; the expansion of industries with appropriate technology and development prospects; and the creation of new advanced-technology industries.

Apart from the issue of the appropriateness of advanced-technology industries for Portugal that has been raised above, it would appear that the stated objectives cover much of the manufacturing sector. But, at any rate, one could hardly depend on governmental institutions to make choices for private industry on the basis of Portugal's assumed comparative advantage. Such choices will have to be made by entrepreneurs on the basis of profit criteria.

It has also been suggested to place regional considerations in the center of a new investment law, on the grounds that this would permit drawing on the EC's Regional Development Fund. However, as in the case of Ireland, it can be expected that Portugal would be considered a development area in its entirety, in which case a special scheme of regional incentives is not necessary for drawing on the Fund.

At any rate, questions arise about the desirability of providing large subsidies to investment in remote areas, as has been proposed. Such incentives would entail an economic cost and contribute to the undue dispersion of industry. Apart from the lack of related industrial activities in remote regions, transportation from and to the ports and coastal cities would represent a substantial burden, thereby reducing Portugal's export possibilities.

Considering further the smallness of Portugal's territory, a more appropriate solution would be to expand industry from Lisbon and from Porto inwards. This would permit placing reliance on related industrial activities without adding to congestion; ensure the use of unemployed and underemployed labor, and allow the hiring of high quality managers who cherish the amenities of the city, not to speak of high-level education for their children. In turn, natural resource based industries, including the processing of food, agricultural raw material, and minerals, would locate near to these resources.

The proposed scheme would also have a lower cost in terms of physical infrastructure than would the dispersion of industries. Nonetheless, infrastructure needs are considerable, in particular as far as port facilities, roads, and telecommunications are concerned. This conclusion is strengthened if one considers the infrastructural needs of agriculture and those of mining, where Portugal has considerable possibilities.

It would seem appropriate, therefore, to orient a substantial part of the financial resources Portugal may obtain from the EC Regional Development Fund to the development of physical infrastructure. In order to exploit Portugal's comparative advantage in semi-skilled and skill-intensive products, it would further be desirable to develop human infrastructure. This may take the form of incentives to training and to research and development.

Government support is now given to specialized training programs, set up by industrial associations, that combine the acquisition of technical skill with on-the-job training. Transferring state-owned technical centers to these associations may also increase their effectiveness. It would also be desirable to grant tax benefits to firms that engage in on-the-job training.

Furthermore, it is incumbent on the government to improve the level of technical education. This purpose would be served by re-establishing technical high schools that have traditionally played an important role in technical education in other European countries. Technical education would further need to receive greater emphasis at the university level.

Research and development undertaken by firms or groups of firms may also be encouraged through the granting of tax benefits or by cost sharing on the part of the government. At the same time, if research and development centers are to be established in some fields, these should be closely linked to the industry associations.

As far as investment incentives are concerned, priority should be given to exports, the future development of which depends on the creation of new capacity. Incentives for investment in export industries are warranted because of their riskiness, which may lead to less investment than what is required for rapid export growth. Risks in exporting are only partly due to the variability of foreign market conditions and the possibility of adverse actions by foreign governments, which will lose their relevance in the framework of the European Common Market some years from now. There are also risks involved in connection with government policies in Portugal, in particular in regard to the exchange rate that has fluctuated to a considerable extent in real terms in recent years.

At the same time, one should avoid providing incentives on the basis of *ex ante* export objectives that may not be met. An appropriate solution may be to grant an interest preference on loans for investment in accordance with the actual share of exports in output from the increased capacity. Thus, if the interest preference is set at 4 percentage points and the firm exports only three-quarters of the incremental output, it would receive an interest reduction of 3 percentage points over the life of the loan. At the same time, exports of new products and to new markets may receive additional incentives.

Participation in the European Common Market further necessitates industrial concentration in order to confront competition in the markets of the EC countries as well as in Portugal's own home market. In this connection, reference may be made to the experience of France who, upon joining the Common Market, gave priority to industrial concentration, resulting in mergers on a large scale. This is even more important in Portugal, whose firms are smaller in size than were firms in France at the time of entry.[8]

On the example of France, Portugal may utilize credit as well as tax measures to encourage concentration. This would involve changing the present situation, under which the Banco de Fomento and the Caixa Geral do not provide credit for purposes of mergers, and the commercial banks are discouraged from doing so. Portugal should also follow France in granting tax exemptions for capital gains associated with the sale of firms involved in mergers.

As a result of the measures applied, the movement towards concentration accelerated in France following entry into the Common Market, with the value of assets of the absorbed companies rising from an annual average of 85 million francs during the 1950s to 1 billion francs in 1965 and 5 billion francs in 1970. Industrial concentration, in turn, resulted in increases in firm size and contributed to the improved competitive position of the French economy.[9]

Mergers may involve the purchase of some unprofitable firms that could be rendered profitable in the context of a larger unit. But, industrial transformation upon entry into the Common Market would also entail the disappearance of uncompetitive firms. This has rarely occurred in Portugal during the last decade as banks have continued to extend credit to unprofitable firms that could not meet their loan obligations. The continuation of such a practice would increasingly impinge on scarce credit and may eventually affect the viability of the banks.

One should accept, therefore, the need for some firms to disappear. In order to minimize the disruptions involved, bankruptcy laws would have to be revised. In particular, there is need for the rapid disposition of cases and for allowing the continuation of production while bankruptcy proceedings are under way.

At the same time, the viability of a number of unprofitable firms could be restored if the conditions for collective dismissals on economic grounds were eased. Existing regulations are cumbersome and the process is slow, which is also the case for temporary dismissals that were legislated several years ago. Correspondingly, few firms have made use of one or the other possibility.

Also, present regulations on temporary hiring should be retained. In recent years, much of the hiring has been done on this basis, so as to escape the cumbersome regulations on collective or temporary dismissals. The continuation of this practice is necessary in order to assure flexibility for the firms and to encourage new investment. In fact, experience indicates that restrictions on firing tend to limit new hiring and thereby new investment.[10] At the same time, in reducing the firm's working force, the jobs of those remaining would be saved.

Greater flexibility in labor conditions would also encourage foreign investment in Portugal. Also, the present conditions of granting investment licenses would need to be simplified and greater automaticity assured. While this will at any rate be necessary as far as investments by the firms of other Common Market member countries are concerned, the liberalization of the rules would be attractive for US and Japanese firms as well.

CONCLUSIONS

Following the review of progress achieved under the June 1983 stabilization program, this essay has considered the conditions for improving the competitiveness of the economy of Portugal as it enters the European Common Market. In this connection, recommendations have been made in regard to the public sector as well as concerning policies affecting the private sector.

To begin with, the financial requirements of the public sector would need to be reduced, so as to ease the pressure on the balance of payments and to increase the availability and lower the cost of credit to the private sector. Recommendations have further been made for limiting the scope of public enterprises in manufacturing industries, with decision-making decentralized in firms that would remain in the public domain.

The essay has further made recommendations for maintaining realistic exchange rates, liberalizing imports, providing export incentives, lowering interest rates, and developing capital markets. In agriculture, there would also be need for encouraging modernization and providing the necessary physical infrastructure. In manufacturing, improvements in physical as well as in human infrastructure would be needed.

Finally, it has been proposed that incentives be granted for investments in export activities and for industrial concentration, with modifications in labor legislation providing increased flexibility to the firm. The proposed incentives would replace the existing regulations or investment incentives. At the same time, it would be desirable to reduce the overall budgetary cost of incentives for new investment that has grown rapidly in recent years.

NOTES

1. Unless otherwise noted, all data cited in the report originate with the Banco de Portugal.
2. The advisory report was subsequently published under the title 'Economic Policies in Portugal' in *Economia*, VII (1983) pp. 111–34.
3. On a 1970 basis, the index of Portugal's terms of trade was 89 in 1978, declining to 74 in 1983.
4. *Portugal*, OECD Economic Surveys 1983–1984 (Paris: Organisation for Economic Co-operation and Development, 1984) p. 20.
5. *Portugal*, p. 21.
6. *Portugal*, p. 21.

7. Le-Si Vinh and Pasquale Scandizzo, 'Portugal and the EEC: Direct and Indirect Effects in the Rural Sector' (Washington, DC: World Bank, 1982) mimeo.
8. The following discussion draws on Balassa, 'Economic Policies in Portugal'.
9. B. Balassa, 'The French Economy under the Fifth Republic, 1958–1978', in W. G. Andrews and Hoffman (eds), *The Fifth Republic of Twenty* (Albany: State University of New York Press, 1981) pp. 204–27.
10. B. Balassa, 'The Economic Consequences of Social Policies in the Industrial Countries', Essay 3 in this volume.

Essay 10 Outward Orientation and Exchange Rate Policy in Developing Countries: the Turkish Experience

INTRODUCTION

Turkey had long pursued an inward-oriented development strategy but changed its policy orientation in January 1980 in response to the economic crisis which it experienced. This essay places the economic policies applied in Turkey in an international context, with a view to further our understanding of the changes that have occurred since 1980. The essay will also consider possible future reform measures in Turkey, with attention given to short-term as well as to long-term objectives.

Section I of the essay will examine the principal characteristics of inward-oriented policies and their economic effects; it will describe the policy content of reform efforts made by developing countries; and it will indicate the impact of outward-oriented policies on exports and economic growth. Section II will review the Turkish experience with inward orientation; it will describe the 1980–1 reforms; and it will analyze the economic effects of these reforms. In Section III, possible

208

future reform measures for pursuing short-term and long-term objectives will be discussed.

The essay covers the period until the summer of 1982, when Mr Turgut Ozal resigned as Deputy Prime Minister, with responsibilities for economic affairs. A postscript, originally prepared for a meeting of the Council on Foreign Relations, held in June 1984, reviews the events of the following eighteen months and examines desirable policy for the future.

I POLICY REFORM IN DEVELOPING COUNTRIES[1]

Policies of inward orientation

With the exception of Britain at the time of the Industrial Revolution and, more recently, Hong Kong, all present-day industrial and developing countries protected their incipient manufacturing industries producing for the domestic market. This first stage of import substitution involved replacing the imports of non-durable consumer goods, such as clothing and shoes, and their inputs, such as textile fabrics and leather, by domestic production. It has also been called the 'easy' stage of import substitution in view of the fact that the commodities in question suit the conditions existing in developing countries. Their manufacture largely involves the use of unskilled labor; the efficient scale of output is relatively low and costs do not rise substantially at lower output levels; production does not necessitate the use of sophisticated technology; and efficient operations do not require the availability of a network of suppliers of parts, components, and accessories.

In the course of first-stage import substitution, the domestic production of industrial goods rises more rapidly than domestic demand, since it not only provides for increases in consumption but also replaces imports. The rate of growth of output declines to that of consumption, however, once the process of import substitution has been completed.

Maintaining high industrial growth rates upon the completion of the first-stage of import substitution, then, necessitates moving to the second stage of import substitution or embarking on the exportation of manufactured goods. The first of these alternatives was chosen in the postwar period in several Latin American and South Asian countries, with Turkey providing the principal example of such an inward-oriented development strategy in Southern Europe.

Second-stage import substitution involves the replacement of the imports of intermediate goods, and producer and consumer durables, by domestic production. These commodities have rather different characteristics from those replaced at the first stage. Intermediate goods, such as petrochemicals and steel, tend to be highly capital-intensive. They are also subject to important economies of scale, with efficient plant size being large compared to the domestic needs of most developing countries and costs rising rapidly at lower output levels. Moreover, the margin of processing is relatively small, and organizational and technical inefficiencies may contribute to high costs.

Producer durables, such as machinery and equipment, and consumer durables, such as automobiles and refrigerators, are also subject to economies of scale. But, in these industries economies of scale relate not so much to plant size as to horizontal specialization, involving reductions in product variety, and to vertical specialization through the manufacture of parts, components, and accessories on an efficient scale in separate plants. At the same time, the production of parts, components, and accessories has to be done to a degree of precision for consumer durables, and in particular for machinery. This in turn requires the availability of skilled and technical labor and, to a greater or lesser extent, the application of sophisticated technology.

Given the relative scarcity of physical and human capital in developing countries that completed the first stage of import substitution, they are at a disadvantage in the manufacture of highly physical-capital intensive intermediate goods and skill-intensive producer and consumer durables. In limiting the scope for the exploitation of economies of scale, the relatively small size of their national markets also contributes to high domestic costs in these countries.

Correspondingly, the establishment of these industries to serve narrow domestic markets is predicated on high protection. In fact, rates of protection need to be raised as countries 'travel up the staircase', represented by ratios of domestic to foreign costs, in embarking on the production of commodities that less and less conform to their comparative advantage. This will occur as goods produced at earlier stages come to saturate domestic markets.

High protection, in turn, limits competition and discriminates against manufactured as well as primary exports and against primary activities in general. But, there is also discrimination within the manufacturing sector as protection rates tend to vary to a considerable extent in countries that embarked on second-stage import substitution.

High protection is generally associated with overvalued exchange rates, and there is a tendency in countries pursuing an inward-oriented development strategy to undertake devaluations only intermittently. With continuing inflation accompanied by periodic devaluations, then, real exchange rates (nominal exchange rates adjusted for changes in relative prices at home and abroad) fluctuate over time. Unforeseen changes in the domestic currency equivalent of foreign exchange receipts, in turn, create uncertainty for the exporter.

Protection and fluctuations in real exchange rates are often associated with price control, intended to keep the prices of consumer goods low and to limit variations in these prices. Price control of staple foodstuffs, however, engenders increases in the consumption of these commodities and discourages their production. In turn, price control of capital-intensive public utilities increases the demand for capital, which is a scarce factor in developing countries, while adding to the deficit of the public sector.

Countries engaged in second-stage import substitution also tend to keep nominal interest rates below the rate of inflation. The resulting negative real interest rates contribute to the adoption of capital-intensive techniques and the establishment of capital-intensive industries; discourage domestic savings; lead to capital outflow; and necessitate the rationing of credit. Credit rationing, in turn, is often accompanied by the application of credit preferences that favor particular users at the expense of others.

Second-stage import substitution thus generally involves overvalued exchange rates, with the extent of overvaluation varying over time; an anti-export bias; high and variable rates of industrial protection; price control of staple foodstuffs and public utilities; and negative real interest rates, accompanied by credit rationing and credit preferences. Apart from distorting the system of incentives, the measures applied have limited the role of market forces in countries pursuing such an inward-oriented development strategy.

After initially favoring industrial expansion, the described characteristics of second-stage import substitution adversely affected exports and economic growth. Primary as well as manufactured exports suffered as a result of the combination of high industrial protection, overvalued exchange rates, and variations in real exchange rates. In the primary sector, increases in domestic consumption at low prices aggravated the impact of the reduced profitability of domestic production. With the ensuing decrease in the exportable surplus, developing countries engaging in second-stage import substitution lost export market shares to developed countries, in particular the United States, Canada, and Australia, in products such as cereals, meat, oilseeds, and nonferrous metals. At the same time, the policies applied discouraged the development of manufactured exports.

The balance-of-payments effects of reductions in export market shares were aggravated by the decline in net import savings, due to the increased need for imported materials, machinery, and technological know-how at the second stage of import substitution. Correspondingly, economic growth in countries pursuing an inward-oriented strategy was increasingly constrained by the limited availability of foreign exchange, and intermittent foreign exchange crises ensued as attempts were made to expand the economy at a rate exceeding that permitted by the growth of export earnings.

Also, the savings constraint became increasingly binding as high-cost, capital-intensive production at the second stage of import substitution raised capital-output ratios, requiring ever-increasing savings ratios to maintain rates of economic growth at earlier levels. At the same time, negative real interest rates reduced the volume of available savings while credit preferences led to inefficiencies in the allocation of capital.

The turn towards outward orientation

The slowdown of economic growth that eventually resulted from the pursuit of an inward-oriented development strategy led to policy reform in several countries that had undertaken such a strategy. Policy reforms were carried out in the mid-sixties in Argentina, Brazil, and Colombia; around 1970 in Mexico; in the mid-seventies in Chile and Uruguay; and in 1980 in Turkey. The reforms generally involved establishing realistic exchange rates and subsequently maintaining real exchange rates constant; lessening the bias against exports; reducing the level and the variability of industrial protection; liberalizing prices as well as increasing real interest rates and limiting the scope of credit preferences. Apart from reducing distortions in the system of incentives, these measures also gave greater scope for the operation of market forces.

In the course of the reforms, the first step usually was to devalue the exchange rate to a considerable extent and to establish exchange rate flexibility. This took the form of a step-wise devaluation, followed by mini-devaluations based on changes in relative prices at home and abroad.

The devaluation was accompanied by export subsidies to manufactured goods and, in some instances, to non-traditional primary exports that lessened the bias against such exports. Subsequently, imports were liberalized, entailing the gradual replacement of quantitative import restrictions by tariffs as well as the lowering of tariffs. In the process of import liberalization, the variability of rates of industrial protection was also reduced.

Finally, the scope of price and interest rate controls was reduced, letting market equilibrium be increasingly determined by demand and supply. Interest rate reform in turn obviated the need for credit rationing and the scope of credit preferences generally decreased.

Measures of a similar character were taken earlier by countries that embarked on an outward-oriented strategy once the first stage of import substitution had been completed. The countries in question include Denmark and Norway in the years immediately following the Second World War; Greece, Portugal, Spain and, with certain limitations, Japan, in the mid-fifties, and Korea, Singapore and Taiwan in the early sixties.

In fact, outward-oriented economies have gone further in rationalizing their system of incentives and in providing scope to market forces, than have countries which undertook reforms only after having moved to the second stage of import substitution. Thus, in the three Far Eastern countries, a free trade regime has been applied to exports. Exporters are free to choose between domestic and imported inputs; they are exempted from indirect taxes on their output and inputs; and they pay no duty on imported inputs. The same privileges have been extended to the producers of domestic inputs used in export production.

The application of the described rules provides equal treatment to all exports. And while some additional export incentives have been granted in the three Far Eastern countries, these have not introduced much differentiation among individual exports. At the same time, the incentives have ensured that, on the average, exports receive similar treatment as import substitution in the manufacturing sector. Furthermore, there is little discrimination against primary exports and against primary activities in general; incentives are on the whole provided automatically; and the incentive system has undergone few modifications over time.

By contrast, countries that earlier moved to the second stage of import substitution do not provide exporters with a free choice between domestic and imported inputs. Rather, in order to safeguard existing industries, exporters are required to use domestic inputs produced under protection. In order to compensate exporters for the resulting excess cost, the countries in question have granted explicit export subsidies.

These subsidies do not suffice, however, to provide producers with export incentives comparable to the protection of domestic markets. Thus, there continues to be a bias in favor of import substitution and against exports, albeit at a reduced rate. The extent of discrimination is especially pronounced against traditional primary exports that do not receive export subsidies and, in some instances, continue to be subject to export taxes.

Furthermore, with the share of value added in export value and the protection of inputs used in export industries varying among industries, there is considerable variation in the ratio of export subsidies to value added in the countries in question. Despite the changes made, rates of protection on sales in domestic markets also continue to vary. At the same time, rather than being automatic, the incentives are often subject to discretionary decision-making.

Finally, the three Far Eastern countries have gone further in ensuring realistic exchange rates and in establishing positive real interest rates than countries that earlier followed an inward-oriented development strategy. And, through the liberalization of prices, they have given greater scope to the operation of market forces.

The economic effects of alternative development strategies

The economic effects of alternative development strategies are apparent in the periods preceding and following the quadrupling of oil prices. Countries applying outward-oriented development strategies had a superior record in terms of exports and economic growth; policy reforms aimed at greater outward orientation brought improvements in the economic performance of countries that had earlier applied inward-oriented policies; while countries that maintained an inward-oriented stance exhibited poor performance.

In the 1960–73 period, increases in manufactured exports were the most rapid in the three Far Eastern countries. As a result, the share of exports in manufactured output rose from 1 percent in 1960 to 14 percent in 1966 and to 42 percent in 1973 in Korea; from 11 percent to 20 percent and, again, to 43 percent in Singapore; and from 9 percent to 19 percent and, finally, to 50 percent in Taiwan. Notwithstanding their poor natural resource endowment, the three Far Eastern countries also had the highest growth rates of primary exports, and hence of total exports, among countries at similar levels of development.

In turn, following poor performance between 1960 and 1966, the growth of manufactured exports accelerated in the four Latin American countries that reformed their system of incentives in the mid-sixties. Thus, the share of exports in manufactured output rose from 1 percent in 1966 to 4 percent in 1973 in Argentina and in Brazil, with increases experienced also in Colombia and Mexico. Nevertheless, this share remained much lower than in the Far East, and the countries in question experienced a continued erosion in the world market shares of their traditional primary exports, although they made gains in non-traditional primary exports which received subsidies.

Finally, India, Chile, and Uruguay, which continued with an inward-looking development strategy during the period, did poorly in primary as well as in manufactured exports and showed a decline in the share of exports in manufactured outut between 1960 and 1973. India lost ground in textiles, its traditional export, and was slow to develop new manufactured exports. As a result, its share in the combined exports of manufactured goods of the ten countries under consideration declined from 69 percent in 1960 to 12 percent in 1973. In the same period, Chile's share fell from 4 percent to 1 percent, while in Uruguay it never reached one-fifth of one percent of the total.

Exporting involves resource allocation according to the comparative advantage; it permits the exploitation of economies of scale; it leads to increased capacity utilization; while exposure to foreign competition provides stimulus for improved operations as well as for technical change. Correspondingly, income increments were achieved at a lower cost in terms of investment in countries that consistently followed an outward-oriented strategy.

In the 1960–73 period, incremental capital-output ratios were 1.8 in Singapore, 2.1 in Korea, and 2.4 in Taiwan. At the other extreme, these ratios were 5.5 in Chile, 5.7 in India, and 9.1 in Uruguay. The four Latin American countries that undertook policy reforms represent an intermediate group, with incremental capital-output ratios declining after the institution of policy reforms. In Brazil, where the rate of capacity utilization increased to a considerable extent, the ratio fell from 3.8 in 1960–66 to 2.1 in 1966–73.

Outward orientation also appears to have been associated with higher domestic savings ratios. Lower capital-output ratios and higher savings ratios, in turn, ease the savings constraint to economic growth in developing countries. Export expansion also eases the foreign exchange constraint, thereby permitting increased imports of materials and machinery. A case in point is Brazil where the ratio of imports to the gross national product rose from 6.1 percent in 1966 to 11.1 percent in 1973.

The operation of these factors gave rise to a positive correlation between exports and economic growth in the 1960–73 period. The three Far Eastern countries had the highest GNP growth rates throughout the period; the four Latin American countries that undertook policy reforms improved their growth performance to a considerable extent after the reforms were instituted; while India, Chile, and Uruguay remained at the bottom of the growth league.

Some observers suggested, however, that the high share of exports in the gross national product associated with outward orientation increases the vulnerability of countries applying such a strategy to external shocks. Thus, predictions were made that countries following an outward-oriented strategy would fare poorly in the event that the world economic environment deteriorated.

The experience of the period following the quadrupling of oil prices in 1973–4 and the world recession in 1974–5 does not support this proposition. While the balance-of-payments effects of external shocks represented a larger proportion of GNP in countries following outward-oriented, than in those pursuing inward-oriented, policies, the superior growth performance of outward-oriented economies compensated for this loss several times over.

Apart from differences in the efficiency of resource allocation, the differential performance of countries applying alternative strategies in the period of external shocks may be explained by differences in the 'compressibility' of imports and in the flexibility of their national economies. While outward orientation is associated with high export *and* import shares that permit reductions in non-essential imports without serious adverse effects on the functioning of the economy, continued inward orientation often involves limiting imports to an unavoidable minimum, so that any further reduction will have a considerable cost in terms of economic growth. Also, the greater flexibility of the national economies of countries pursuing an outward-oriented strategy, where firms learn to live with foreign competition, makes it possible to change the product composition of exports in response to changes in world market conditions whereas inward orientation entails establishing a more rigid economic structure.

In addition to the three Far Eastern economies that continued to pursue an outward-oriented strategy, these conclusions apply to Chile and Uruguay that responded to the deterioration of their terms of trade and the slowdown in the growth of foreign demand for their export products by reforming the system of incentives. The reforms involved adopting realistic exchange rates, reducing the bias against exports, eliminating quantitative import restrictions, abolishing price control, and adopting positive real interest rates.

In Uruguay, which had a stagnant economy in the previous decade, the policy reforms led to rapid increases in exports and in the gross national product, with *per capita* GNP rising by 3.1 percent a year between 1973 and 1976 and by 4.3 percent a year between 1976 and 1979. Following a period of dislocation due to the application of a severe deflationary policy aggravated by rapid reductions in tariffs, the growth of exports and GNP accelerated also in Chile.[2]

By contrast, several countries, including Brazil, increased the inward-orientation of their economies, with adverse effects on exports and on economic growth. Thus, while growth rates of *per capita* GDP increased from 5.3 percent in 1963–73 to 6.6 percent in 1973–79 in outward-oriented economies, a decline from 4.9 percent to 2.3 percent occurred in inward-oriented economies. The data refer to the group of newly-industrialized countries to which Turkey belongs.

II THE TURKISH EXPERIENCE WITH ALTERNATIVE DEVELOPMENT STRATEGIES[3]

The period of inward orientation

Several reform efforts notwithstanding, Turkey maintained an inward-oriented stance during the 1960–73 period. While this policy permitted attaining relatively high rates of economic growth for a time, increases in *per capita* incomes were substantially lower than in the other Southern European countries (3.9 percent a year, compared to 6.8 percent in Greece and Portugal and 5.7 percent in Spain, between 1960 and 1973). The differences are even larger if adjustment is made for the overestimation of the rate of economic growth associated with high protection in Turkey.

Turkey continued with inward orientation following the external shocks of the quadrupling of oil prices and the world recession while attempting to maintain its rate of economic growth. This proved temporary, however, as the policies applied aggravated the adverse balance-of-payments effects of external shocks by giving rise to reductions in export market shares and increases in import shares.

Under the policies applied, the deterioration of Turkish economic performance continued after 1973. This is indicated by increases in incremental capital-output ratios (ICOR) that reflect the efficiency of using additional resources. With the rising cost of import substitution, the economy-wide ICOR estimated from official data increased from 2.3 in 1963–7 to 2.6 in 1968–72 and, again, to 3.8 in 1973–7. The increase was larger in the manufacturing sector, where inefficient import substitution was concentrated, from 1.6 in 1963–7 to 2.4 in 1968–72 and, finally to 4.7 in 1973–7.

Nevertheless, for a time, Turkey was able to avoid a decline in the rate of economic growth by raising the share of gross fixed investment in GDP. This share increased from 16.0 percent in 1963–7 to 18.0 percent in 1968–72 and, again, to 22.9 percent in 1973–7. The rise in investment, in turn, was made possible in large part by the inflow of funds from abroad, first in the form of workers' remittances and, subsequently, through foreign loans.

Workers' remittances increased from negligible amounts in 1966 to 5.6 percent of GNP in 1973, and recorded and unrecorded remittances combined may have reached 6 percent of GNP in 1977. In turn, the ratio of the net capital inflow to GNP, that was −2.8 percent in 1973, approached 7 percent in 1977. In the latter year, workers' remittances and the capital inflow combined were more than double the value of merchandise exports in Turkey.

As a result of increased foreign borrowing, the ratio of debt service (amortization and interest charges) to merchandise exports rose from 13 percent in 1973 and to 33 percent in 1977. At the same time, with the decline in export shares and increases in import shares, the Turkish economy did not generate the foreign exchange earnings (savings) that would have permitted to reduce foreign indebtedness.

By 1978, Turkey's borrowing possibilities were virtually exhausted and it became increasingly difficult to obtain the foreign exchange necessary to purchase the imports needed for the normal functioning of its industry. The situation deteriorated further in 1979, when the acceleration of inflation was only partially offset by increases in nominal interest rates, leading to an outflow of funds and reductions in workers' remittances. With increasing foreign exchange stringency, there were considerable shortages of energy, raw materials, and spare parts in Turkey. As a result, industrial production fell by 5.6 percent in 1979 and the gross national product also declined.

The 1980–81 reforms

It appears then that, rather than adjusting to the external shocks, the policies applied in Turkey after 1973 aggravated the situation. Employing the panoply of measures characteristic of inward-oriented economies, the policies applied included the overvaluation of the exchange rate; discrimination against exports; high and variable industrial protection; price control; as well as negative real interest rates.

Taking as the base year 1973 – the year preceding the quadrupling of oil prices and the world recession – by the end of 1978 the Turkish lira appreciated in real terms by 22 per cent vis-à-vis the US dollar and by 13 percent vis-à-vis the currencies of Turkey's major trading partners (measured as the average of the results obtained by alternative wholesale price indices for Turkey). The appreciation of the real exchange rate reflected the fact that rapid inflation in Turkey was only partially offset by changes in the nominal exchange rate. Yet, the lira should have been devalued in real terms in order to compensate for the effects of the deterioration of the Turkish balance of payments resulting from external shocks.

A substantial devaluation occurred in June 1979, but this was more than offset through rapid inflation in the remainder of the year. In the fourth quarter of 1979, the extent of appreciation of the real exchange rate was 30 percent vis-à-vis the US dollar and 22 percent vis-à-vis the currencies of Turkey's major trading partners, compared to its 1973 level. And although differential rates (47 instead of 35 lira to the US dollar) applied to manufactured exports, indirect tax rebate rates on these exports were simultaneously reduced by 5 to 8 percentage points.

In fact, the bias of the incentive system against manufactured exports increased in this period. With the same exchange rate applying to manufactured exports and imports, this occurred as export rebate rates were lowered while import protection was increased through the tightening of quantitative restrictions in response to intensified foreign exchange stringency.

Industrial protection had been traditionally high in Turkey, with tariffs on manufactured goods in the 30–60 percent range, to which customs surcharges (15 percent of customs duty), stamp duties (9–9.5 percent of cif import value) and pier duties (5 percent of the cif value of imports, customs duty and surcharges, and clearance expenses combined) were added. Furthermore, effective rates of protection on value added in the production process were often substantially higher than nominal rates as a number of imported inputs entered duty free.

Finally, there were considerable variations in effective rates among industries and products.

There was an even greater bias against primary exports. While manufactured exports benefited from indirect tax rebates that exceeded the taxes actually paid until June 1979, primary exports did not receive rebates. And, after June 1979, the exchange rate applicable to primary exports was much lower than that for manufactured exports.

Turkish agriculture also suffered the disadvantages of price control, aimed at keeping consumer prices low, that was offset only in part by the low price of fertilizer. Price control extended to most products of the state economic enterprises, resulting in considerable losses for the State Economic Enterprises (SEEs) that were financed from the government budget. At the same time, the artificially low prices of energy added to Turkey's balance-of-payments difficulties by keeping demand for energy high.

Also, with the acceleration of inflation, real interest rates became increasingly negative. In 1979, pre-tax interest rates were 15 percent on one-year savings deposits while interest charges were 24 percent on one-year nonpreferential loans. With a rate of inflation of about 70 percent, real interest rates were − 32 percent in the first case and − 27 percent in the second.

The January 1980 policy changes aimed at redressing the situation and changing the development strategy which Turkey had followed in the previous decades. They combined stabilization measures, with the twin objectives of reducing the rate of inflation and improving the balance of payments, as well as reform measures, with a view to turn the Turkish economy in an outward direction and give an increased role to market forces.

Stabilization objectives were pursued by reducing the rate of money creation. Both stabilization and reform objectives were served by a substantial devaluation, with the exchange rate set at 70 lira to the US dollar, that aimed at reducing the balance-of-payments deficit as well as improving the system of incentives.

With subsequent changes in the exchange rate, by the third quarter of 1980 the lira depreciated in real terms by 5 percent against the US dollar and 15 percent on the average against the currencies of Turkey's major trading partners, compared to its 1973 level. The lira depreciated further vis-à-vis the US dollar in subsequent months. However, with the rise of the US dollar, it appreciated vis-à-vis the currencies of Turkey's major trading partners, with the real exchange rate approximately returning to its 1973 level in June 1981.

The situation was subsequently remedied through the devaluation of the lira vis-à-vis European currencies and by reducing the excessive weight of the US dollar in the currency basket used in setting the exchange rates. Compared to its 1973 level, by May 1982 the Turkish lira depreciated in real terms by 27 percent against the US dollar and by 13 percent against the currencies of Turkey's major trading partners. Also, fluctuations in real exchange rates have been reduced.

Furthermore, the bias against exports has been considerably reduced. In January 1980, the administrative procedures used in providing export incentives were streamlined and recipients of export licenses were given the right to import materials and intermediate products duty free. In July 1980, the preferential margin on interest rates charged on loans to exporters was increased; in January 1981, income tax exemptions were granted on new exports and on increases in exports, and export-oriented investments were given additional benefits. Finally, in May 1981, indirect tax rebate rates were raised by five percentage points across-the-board and firms (mostly trading companies) whose exports exceeded $15 million a year received additional rebates.

Import regulations were also streamlined in January 1980, reducing the waiting period for licenses and providing foreign exchange allocation automatically once the licenses were granted. In January 1981, imports were liberalized to a considerable extent, involving the elimination of quotas as well as transfers from the restricted list to the free list. Subsequent measures of import liberalization, taken in January 1982, were of limited importance, however, and practically no change occurred in the system of tariffs.

Industrial prices were also liberalized in January 1980, with increases ranging up to 300 percent for paper and 400 percent for fertilizer, thereby reducing the deficit of the SEEs to a considerable extent. With few exceptions, the freedom of industrial prices has subsequently been maintained. The scope of central price determination has also been reduced in agriculture, and the prices of the remaining products subject to control have been annually adjusted.

Interest rates were freed in July 1980. While a gentlemen's agreement among banks initially limited increases in the rates, over a twelve-month period interest rates increased from 15 percent to 50 percent on one-year savings deposits and from 31 percent to 49 percent on one-year nonpreferential loans. However, the scope of preferential lending has undergone little change.

The economic effects of the policies applied after January 1980

The reform measures thus included a substantial devaluation in real terms; reductions in the bias of the incentive system against exports; the (partial) liberalization of imports; the elimination of much of industrial price control, and the freeing of interest rates. These measures represent important steps towards outward orientation and increased scope for the operation of market forces in Turkey.

In evaluating the economic effects of the policy measures applied, emphasis should be given to the simultaneous pursuit of stabilization and reform objectives in a situation characterized by economic disruptions and considerable distortions. This meant that the reforms had to be carried out in a deflationary environment and that reducing the existing large distortions necessarily involved dislocation. Also, political uncertainty and disruptions in production associated with declining labor discipline and increasing strike activity retarded the economic effects of the reform measures until after the military takeover of September 1980. Thus, particular interest attaches to the results for the years 1981 and 1982.

The dollar value of Turkish merchandise exports rose by 62 percent in 1981, following a 1 percent decline in 1979 and a 29 percent increase in 1980, much of which occurred in the last months of the year. Increases were even larger for industrial exports, 119 percent in 1981, raising their share in Turkey's merchandise exports from 35 percent in 1980 to 49 percent in 1981. Available data for the first four months of 1982 show continued rapid expansion in exports. Compared to the corresponding period in 1981, the dollar value of merchandise exports rose by 28 percent and that of industrial exports by 67 percent, with the share of the latter category reaching 53 percent of the total.

The rapid expansion of Turkish exports occurred in an inhospitable world environment. Part of the explanation for this favorable performance lies in the fact that Turkey increasingly exploited the market possibilities available in the Middle East and North Africa. As a result, exports to this area reached 41 percent of Turkish merchandise exports in 1981 compared to 10 percent in 1979.

But, Turkish exports to the OECD countries also rose to a considerable extent, with an increase of 35 percent in 1981, following a 4 percent decline in 1979 and a 16 percent increase in 1980. The increase in 1981 should be set against the 5 percent decline in the total imports of the OECD countries that occurred in the same year. And while OECD imports are projected to remain flat in 1982, Turkish exports are expected to rise by at least one-quarter (all figures are in terms of current dollars).

The rapid expansion of merchandise exports may be attributed to favorable exchange rates, the availability of export incentives, and the stability of the incentive system, although low capacity utilization associated with the stabilization policy also played a part. Favorable exchange rates and export incentives were the principal factors behind the rapid rise of construction activity in the Middle East, with the total value of contracts increasing from less than $4 billion at the end of 1979 to $12 billion two years later. In 1981, workers' remittances and repatriated profits from the Middle East approached $1 billion.

The dollar value of merchandise imports rose by 13 percent in 1981, following a 56 percent increase in 1980 and virtual stagnation in the previous three years. These changes reversed the decline in the ratio of merchandise imports to the gross national product from 11–13 percent in the years 1974–7 to 8–9 percent in 1978–9; the ratio rose to 15 percent in 1980 and to 16 percent in 1981. In the same period, the ratio of merchandise exports to GNP doubled, reaching 8 percent in 1981. Even larger increases occurred in the ratio of manufactured exports to manufacturing value added, from 5 percent in 1979 to 16 percent in 1981, while the export–import ratio in manufacturing rose from 20 percent to 53 percent.

With increases in the price of fuels, accounting for one-half of Turkish imports, the volume of merchandise imports rose by 13 percent in 1980. This increase occurred, notwithstanding the decline of GNP by 1.1 percent, as stocks were replenished following the foreign exchange shortages of the previous two years.

Apart from the stabilization measures applied, political uncertainty and disruptions in production in the first three quarters of the year contributed to the relatively low level of economic activity in 1980. Industrial production was particularly affected, with a fall of 5.9 percent in industrial value added, following a decline of 5.6 percent in 1979 that was occasioned by foreign exchange shortages.

Led by a 74 percent rise in the volume of the exports of goods and non-factor services, GNP grew by 4.3 percent in 1981. In the same year, industrial production (value added) increased by 7.2 percent. Projections for 1982 call for a 4.4 percent rise in the gross national product and for a 6.1 percent increase in industrial production. As a result, industrial production would return to its 1978 level, although production for domestic use would remain below this level, given the increased share of exports in manufacturing output.

While limiting the rate of economic expansion, the stabilization measures applied led to a substantial decline in the rate of inflation. According to the wholesale price index of the Ministry of Commerce, the annual rate of inflation peaked at 133 percent in February 1980, when the liberalization of prices gave rise to a jump of 19 percent in a single month; it subsequently declined to 35 percent by the end of 1981 and to 24 percent by June 1982. The latter figure, however, reportedly underestimates the rate of inflation, and the projected rise of the GDP deflator for 1982 had been revised from 25 percent to 33 percent.

The principal instrument of stabilization policy has been the reduction in the rate of growth of the money supply, defined as the sum of banknotes, sight commercial deposits, sight savings deposits, and deposits with the Central Bank, from a peak of 60 percent in 1980 to 23 percent in December 1981 on a twelve-month basis. In turn, positive real interest rates on savings, reflecting the joint effects of higher nominal interest rates and lower rates of inflation, contributed to the rapid growth of time savings deposits and deposit certificates.

With the consumer price index in Istanbul rising at an annual rate of 34 percent, the 50 percent interest rate on one-year savings deposits, adjusted for a 25 percent withholding tax, represents a real interest rate of 3 percent compared to the strongly negative real interest rates of earlier years. Correspondingly, time savings deposits and deposit certificates combined doubled between December 1979 and 1980 and tripled in the following twelve months. Including these forms of financial savings in a broader definition of the money supply, the growth rate of this aggregate was 67 percent and 61 percent in the two periods, respectively.

At the same time, the share of the financing requirements of the public sector in the total declined, although to a lesser extent than projected. The ratio of the budget deficit to the gross national product fell from 4.6 percent in 1980 to 1.6 percent in 1981, surpassing the original estimate of 1.0 percent that is now the target for 1982. And, the ratio of SEE financing requirements to GNP decreased only from 10.3 percent in 1980 to 9.4 percent in 1981, compared to a target of 8.1 percent, with a projected figure of 7.6 percent in 1982.

The public sector thus continues to impinge on private savings, albeit to a lesser extent than beforehand. The investment gap (gross investment less savings) of the sector declined from 10.3 percent of GNP in 1980 to 6.1 percent in 1981, compared to the original estimate of 3.3 percent that is now projected to be reached in 1982.

Apart from limitations on the availability of financing, high real interest rates on non-preferential loans have burdened the private sector. Adjusting for the approximate 30 percent compensating balance on loans held with commercial banks, the interest cost of non-preferential credit granted by these banks is 70 percent in Turkey, representing a real interest rate of 36 percent at an inflation rate of 25 percent and a real interest rate of 26 percent at an inflation rate of 35 percent. Non-preferential loans by commercial banks represent a secondary source of credit for firms that have access to preferential loans and finance inventory holdings and wage payments for others. At the same time, private industry has not been allowed to reduce its work force in response to the low level of domestic demand.

The financial situation was further aggravated by the failure of the so-called bankers (money lenders) that accepted deposits and provided loans at even higher interest rates to firms which were unable to obtain sufficient funds from commercial banks. As is well known, the situation culminated in the collapse of Kastelli, the largest money-lender in June 1982.

III POLICY PRIORITIES FOR THE FUTURE

Short-term objectives

The achievements of the Turkish economy in increasing exports in response to the incentives provided under an outward-oriented strategy have been remarkable, permitting reductions in the current account deficit from $3.7 billion in 1980 to $2.1 billion in 1981, with a deficit of $1.4 billion projected for 1982, the resurgence of imports notwithstanding. It is also remarkable that Turkey has been able to substantially reduce the rate of inflation in a relatively short period with only a small decline of its gross national product in 1980, followed by a considerable increase in 1981.

Nevertheless, with weak domestic demand, high real interest rates on non-preferential loans obtained from commercial banks, and even higher interest rates on non-bank credits which represent a marginal source of financing, various segments of private industry have encountered difficulties that are compounded by the inability of the firms to fire labor. At the same time, private investment has remained at low levels and, despite the government's stated desire to reduce the share of the public sector, public investment has gained at the expense of private investment.

After declining by 10.5 percent in 1979 and by 20.0 percent in 1980, private fixed investment stagnated in 1981 and, even with projected increases of 6.0 percent in 1982, it would remain considerably below the 1978 level. At the same time, in conjunction with increases in public investment of 7.0 percent in 1981 and a projected rise of 6.8 percent in 1982, the share of the private sector in total fixed investment declined from 48 percent in 1979 to 42 percent in 1981 and it is estimated at 41 percent in 1982.

The turn towards outward orientation necessarily involves a shift in industrial composition from firms operating under high protection to exporting firms. However, firms oriented towards domestic markets may rationalize their operations and modify their product composition if they can reduce their labor force and have access to financing at reasonable interest rates. In order to facilitate adjustment towards outward orientation, then, policies in regard to employment and credit would need to be reviewed.

It has been reported that military commanders in the various districts may give permission to firms to reduce their labor force. While such action will add to unemployment, it will be necessary in cases when operations are unprofitable. It would be desirable, therefore, to let firms make their own decisions on the size of their labor force.

An easing of monetary policy cannot be recommended lest inflation flares up again. This conclusion is of particular importance in view of the acceleration of monetary expansion at the beginning of 1982, associated with increases in reserves due to improvements in the balance of payments and the rise in the reserve money multiplier, as well as in June 1982, in response to the collapse of Kastelli.

Measures would need to be taken, however, to increase the availability and to lower the cost of nonpreferential credit to the private sector. This would require, first of all, reducing further the financial requirements of the public sector. Apart from economizing with current expenditures of government administration and the SEEs, one would need to reduce the public investment program and to raise the low interest rates charged on loans to the SEEs that encouraged stockpiling in 1981, leading to financial requirements much above expectations.

In order to put public and private industry on an equal footing, they should be required to pay the same interest rates. More generally, the scope of preferential credits would need to be reduced. The existing system creates inequities, leads to leakages, and gives rise to uncertainty as to the availability of preferential credit.

Last but not least, there is need to lower existing charges on bank lending that greatly increase the cost of financial intermediation in Turkey. This objective would be served by eliminating the 15 percent financial transaction tax. The proposed reform of preferential credit schemes could further permit reducing the 10 percent levy accruing to the Differential Interest Rebate Fund that is used to finance such schemes. At the same time, the cost of money to the commercial banks may be lowered by raising interest rates on compulsory deposits held with the Central Bank.

Reducing charges on bank lending would permit lowering interest rates on nonpreferential loans without however increasing their volume. Apart from reducing the public sector deficit, the volume of credit to the private sector could be increased by giving greater encouragement to private savings. For this purpose, it would be desirable to eliminate, or at least to reduce, the 25 percent withholding tax on interest earned by savers.

Long-term objectives

The exchange rate represents a link between policies designed to pursue short-term and long-term objectives. While the depreciation of the real exchange rate has contributed to improvements in Turkey's balance of payments, further changes would be necessary in order to permit liberalizing imports and limiting the extent of export subsidies.

Import liberalization is a priority task. For one thing, the eventual pick-up of domestic demand will increase the profitability of production for the protected domestic market at the expense of exports. For another thing, present levels of protection are not compatible with outward orientation, and import competition is necessary to promote adjustment in domestic industry.

The liberalization of imports would necessitate, first of all, establishing a list of items, the importation of which is effectively prohibited today, and eliminating these prohibitions at an early date. Furthermore, annual transfers of restricted items to the free list would need to be made, with priority given to liberalizing the importation of intermediate products and machinery and with a view to abolishing import restrictions by 1987.

The liberalization of imports would permit making the lira convertible once an atmosphere of stability is established in the Turkish financial system. In the meantime, existing regulations on international transactions would need to be eased by reforming the Law on the Protection of the Value of the Turkish lira.

Parallel with the abolition of import licensing, existing high tariffs would need to be lowered. This may involve establishing a tariff ceiling, to be reached in annual instalments over a transitional period of five years, and reducing inter-industry differences in tariff rates. The tariff ceiling may be set at 30 percent, with additional incentives granted to infant industries on a temporary basis. To the extent possible, this should be done in the form of subsidies rather than tariffs in order to avoid the establishment of high-cost industries producing for sheltered domestic markets.

Increasing the use of the exchange rate as a policy instrument to promote exports would also permit reducing reliance on export subsidies. At the same time, the remaining subsidies to exports would need to be simplified. Also, they should consistently be granted on a value added basis rather than on export value, so as to discourage import-intensive exports and to provide inducement for increasing the share of domestic value added in exports.

The described changes in exchange rate policy, import protection, and export subsidization would ensure continued progress towards outward orientation in the Turkish economy. Together with the proposed reforms in the financial system, they would also increase the scope of operation of market forces.

The objectives of the January 1980 reform would further be served by reforming the operation of the state economic enterprises. The implementation of proposals made by the government to increase the decision-making power of managers, and to make them responsible to an independent general assembly, would represent important steps in SEE reform. Additional steps would need to be taken, however, in order to fully integrate the SEEs in the market economy.

In this regard, Turkey may follow the example of Hungary in decentralizing decision-making and ensuring competition for public enterprises. This would require breaking up the industry-wide SEEs and giving firm managers the freedom to decide on production, prices, and employment. At the same time, with the elimination of credit and other subsidies and the establishment of an efficient pricing environment, profit maximization by SEE managers would appropriately serve the national interest.

In turn, the exploitation of Turkey's agricultural potential would necessitate rationalizing agricultural prices, strengthening research and extension services, and improving transportation facilities. The application of these measures requires a co-ordinated approach, aimed at raising agricultural productivity and at providing inputs for industry, in particular for fruit and vegetable processing.

As regards industry, the promotion of research and product development is an important task. This would permit, in particular, the exploitation of Turkey's long-term comparative advantages in the electrical and non-electrical machinery, machine tool, and electronics industries. The promotion of R&D could best be accomplished in the framework of a medium-term plan of science and technology that would also provide for the improved training of engineers and technicians. Apart from public programs, incentives for research and training by private industry would be necessary for this purpose.

The described policy measures, aimed at furthering the objectives of greater outward orientation and increased reliance on market forces, are interdependent and would need co-ordination. This, in turn, requires establishing a medium-term policy framework and creating an appropriate institutional structure to formulate and to implement policies within this framework.

CONCLUSIONS

This essay has reviewed the experience of Turkey with inward-oriented policies and has examined the effects of the reform measures of January 1980. The newly-introduced policies combined stabilization measures, with the twin objectives of reducing the rate of inflation and improving the balance of payments, as well as reform measures, with a view to turning the Turkish economy in an outward direction and giving an increased role to market forces. They included a substantial devaluation, increases in export subsidies, import liberalization, the elimination of price control, and the freeing of interest rates.

The measures applied led to rapid export growth that permitted increasing production, notwithstanding the deflationary measures applied. Furthermore, the balance of payments improved to a considerable extent, although imports rose substantially following the scarcities of earlier years.

However, private investment remained low and difficulties were experienced in the financial sector. The essay has made recommendations to remedy these shortcomings as well as to attain the objective of stable economic growth in Turkey through increased outward orientation and greater reliance on market forces.

POSTSCRIPT: ECONOMIC POLICIES IN TURKEY JULY 1982–DECEMBER 1983

This postscript, excerpted from a presentation made by the author at the Council on Foreign Relations in June 1983, will describe the events that occurred between Mr Turgut Ozal's resignation as Deputy Prime Minister in July 1982 and his return as Prime Minister in December 1983. Subsequently, the economic program of the new Ozal government will be described and suggestions will be made for further policy changes.

The 'interregnum' (July 1982–December 1983)

The one-and-a-half year period between Mr Ozal's resignation as Deputy Prime Minister and his return as Prime Minister may best be characterized as an interregnum. No clear conception of economic policy emerged during this period and not only was progress in economic reforms not made but some of the measures taken were counter-productive.

In the aftermath of the Kastelli affair, Mr Kafaoglu, the new Finance Minister, first proposed the establishment of a new entity to carry out financial rescue operations. As this proposal encountered opposition, the Ministry of Finance itself initiated such operations. Until mid-1983, however, no effort was made to distinguish between structural and financial causes of the difficulties firms experienced. Yet, a number of Turkish firms encountered difficulties because of inadequate management (in particular, worker-owned companies) or because they lacked competitiveness in the post-liberalization situation (enterprises established behind high protection during the period of inward-orientation). Efforts made to provide financial assistance to these firms reduced the availability of funds to others that suffered the effects of high interest rates but were otherwise viable.

Furthermore, in the first half of 1983, interest rates on six-month time deposits were reduced from 50 to 40 percent whereas interest rates on sight savings deposits were increased from 5 percent to 20 percent. While this switch helped to improve the financial position of the banks, it generated inflationary pressures because private consumption increased as incentives to save were reduced. With the acceleration of inflation, interest rates declined in real terms, further discouraging savings and fueling inflation. By the end of 1983, the rate of inflation, measured by the wholesale price index, reached 41 percent compared to 25 percent a year earlier and to the target rate of 20 percent.

Also, while in the preceding three years there was a tendency to devalue the Turkish lira by more than the difference between Turkish inflation and inflation abroad, thus improving the competitiveness of exports, this tendency was reversed in the course of 1983. Moreover, exports were discouraged by reductions in the availability of preferential export credits as funds were increasingly devoted to financial rescue operations.

These adverse developments aggravated the unfavorable effects on exports of the financial difficulties several of Turkey's major trading partners in the Middle East and North Africa experienced. In 1983, exports to this area declined in absolute terms and, with reduced incentives to export, the resulting shortfall was barely compensated by increases in sales to the OECD countries, even though some of these countries began a process of economic expansion. Correspondingly, the dollar value of Turkey's merchandise exports remained at the 1982 level of $5.8 billion in 1983 compared to the original target of $6.8 billion. In turn, the current account deficit reached $1.8 billion, or 3.4 percent of GNP, compared to the target of 1.5 percent.

The stagnation of export receipts was associated with increases in export volume and declines in export prices. But, export volume, too, rose less than projected. As a result, notwithstanding the increase in production for domestic consumption associated with the decline in personal savings, GNP growth at 3.2 percent fell short of the 4.8 percent target.

While the target of 0.6 percent budget deficit as a proportion of GNP was attained, the financial requirements of the public sector reached 5.7 percent of GNP as poor performance and inadequate price adjustments gave rise to increased losses in the SEEs. At the same time, the SEE reform of May 1983 failed to bring the necessary changes in the decision-making process. Nor was progress made in liberalizing imports.

The new reform measures

Mr Ozal announced a new economic program on 14 December 1983. The program re-establishes the earlier directions towards opening the economy and increasing the role of market forces. Furthermore, a number of important policy measures were immediately taken in pursuit of these objectives.

The need for a flexible exchange rate policy to encourage exports was re-emphasized and exchange rate devaluations exceeding the differential between domestic and foreign inflation rates were undertaken. Moreover, the allocation of preferential credits to exporters was increased while it was announced that export tax rebates would be reduced over a period of time.

Imports were liberalized on a wide front, involving about two-thirds of import value. Taking account of the liberalization measures undertaken in earlier years, only about one-eighth of imports remain subject to restrictions. In turn, tariffs were reduced to a considerable extent while an extra levy has been imposed on luxury imports, to be eliminated progressively over a five year period.

At the same time, foreign exchange transactions were extensively liberalized by freeing travel restrictions, giving Turkish citizens residing in Turkey the right to own foreign exchange accounts and allowing commercial banks to set the exchange rate within a 6 percent spread above and below the basic rate set by the Central Bank. Establishing such a spread effectively allows for a larger devaluation to the benefit of exporters.

Interest rates on six-month savings deposits were increased to 47 percent in order to encourage savings while interest rates on sight savings deposits have been reduced to 5 percent. Parallel with these changes, taxes on financial transactions were substantially lowered, so as to avoid increases in interest rates to borrowers. At the same time, apart from export credits, the scope of preferential credits was reduced.

Finally, the right of the SEEs to set their own prices was reaffirmed, the exceptions being fertilizer, coal, lignite, and sugar. Also, petroleum prices will be adjusted in small steps by the Ministry of Energy.

Future policies and prospects

The measures taken by the new Ozal government represent important steps towards opening the economy and increasing reliance on market forces. Practically at one stroke, imports and foreign exchange markets long subject to complicated restrictions have been liberalized. Also, the preconditions have been created for the reform of the financial system.

In the short term, the measures applied can be expected to lead to the renewal of the export drive and contribute to increased savings, thereby improving the balance of payments reducing inflationary pressures. In the medium term, they provide the basis for the establishment of a more efficient industrial structure.

In the short term, there are also risks of sudden increases in imports and capital outflow. But these risks are reduced by the imposition of the special levy on luxury imports as well as by the flexibility of exchange rates and they are worth taking for the sake of prospective gains from the policies applied. At the same time, in order to fully attain the objectives of opening the Turkish economy and giving full play to market forces, additional measures would need to be applied in several areas.

Firstly, while the level and the dispersion of tariffs have been reduced, additional changes are necessary to establish a rational tariff structure that provides similar incentives to all import-substituting activities and avoids discrimination against exports. The pursuit of this objective would require further reducing and harmonizing tariffs according to a consistent plan. The system of export subsidies would also need to be reformed, involving simplification and harmonization, as well as reductions in subsidy rates.

The reform of the incentive system would provide the pre-conditions for the establishment of an efficient economic structure in Turkey. There are several further steps that would need to be taken to pursue this objective. They include reforming the financial system, revamping decision making of the SEEs, ensuring sufficient private domestic investment, and attracting foreign direct investment.

According to some estimates, bad debts account for 15 to 30 percent of commercial bank portfolios. Under existing regulations, the liquidation of these loans involves a long and cumbersome legal process. At the same time, in refinancing bad debts with interest added, the commercial banks have to increase their liquidity deposits with the Central Bank, thereby reducing their lending power.

A solution to the problem of bad debts may be found in permitting the commercial banks to stop the accrual of interest payments on these debts and to write them off over a period of, say, 5 years. In this way, an incentive would be provided to the commercial banks to declare their bad debts. However, in order to avoid abuses, the application of these provisions would need to be made subject to certain conditions. The conditions may include the initiation of a legal process by the banks for the recovery of bad debts and an audit of the banks' portfolio by qualified accounting firms.

The application of this scheme would permit improving the financial situation of the commercial banks while leaving them the power of decision as to the loans they would cease to refinance. It would also reduce existing pressures on interest rates. To further reduce these pressures, the financial requirements of the public sector would need to be lowered. Apart from reducing the budget deficit by effecting economies in budgetary expenditures, this would necessitate reform of decision-making in the SEEs.

But, as long as real interest rates remain high, private investment will be discouraged. Yet, new investment is necessary to maintain the export momentum and to permit the transformation of Turkish industry. Correspondingly, on a temporary basis, there appears to be need to increase the scope of investment incentives.

Finally, Turkey needs foreign direct investment to complement its domestic capital and to bring technological know-how and marketing experience. Legislation introduced in 1980 has eased the conditions for foreign direct investment, but it has as yet attracted little new capital. To do so would require ensuring the complete freedom of the repatriation of dividends and capital.

The described measures would represent a continuation of the policies adopted in January 1980 and further strengthened in December 1983. While they can be expected to have favorable economic effects, they involve sometimes difficult political decisions. At the same time, taking such decisions would be necessary to ensure the continued progress in the Turkish economy.

NOTES

1. This section of the paper draws on the author's Grahm Lecture, 'The Process of Industrial Development and Alternative Development Strategies', *Essays in International Finance* (Princeton, NJ: Department of Economics, Princeton University, 1981) No. 141. Published in B. Balassa, *The Newly-Industrializing Countries in the World Economy* (New York: Pergamon Press, 1981) pp. 1–28.
2. Chile, however, subsequently introduced distortions in its economic system by fixing the exchange rate while official wage adjustments continued. Cf. B. Balassa, 'Policy Experiments in Chile', Essay 8 in this volume.

3. The Turkish experience with inward orientation was examined in B. Balassa, 'Growth Policies and the Exchange Rate in Turkey', in *The Role of Exchange Rate Policy in Achieving the Outward Orientation of the Turkish Economy* (Istanbul: Meban Securities, 1980) pp. 15–19. Reprinted under the title 'Policies for Stable Economic Growth in Turkey', in Balassa, *The Newly-Industrializing Countries in the World Economy*, pp. 297–328, and in B. Balassa, 'The Policy Experience of Newly Industrial Economies After 1973 and the Case of Turkey', *The Role of Exchange Rate Policy in Achieving the Outward Orientation of the Turkish Economy – II* (Istanbul: Meban Securities, 1981) pp. 1–35. The latter paper also considered the preliminary results of the 1980–81 reforms.

Essay 11 Korea in the 1980s: Policies and Prospects

INTRODUCTION

Korea has been considered as one of the success stories among developing countries. Starting from a small industrial base, it developed a modern industrial structure and achieved high rates of economic growth, based largely on export orientation, during the decade preceding the 1973–4 oil crisis. Also, Korea was able to rapidly surmount this crisis through the continued application of an outward-oriented strategy.

In 1979, however, Korea suffered a decline in the volume of merchandise export and in 1980 it experienced a 5.7 percent fall in its gross domestic product, together with a current account deficit of $5 billion. This contrasts with the case of the other Far Eastern economies, Hong Kong, Singapore, and Taiwan, which have maintained rapid rates of growth of exports and GDP and avoided substantial balance-of-payments disequilibria. In turn, improvements occurred in Korea after the measures taken from 1980 onwards.

This essay will attempt to explain recent economic developments in Korea by reference to the policies applied. It will consider developments in 1978–9, when various distortions were introduced as well as the changes that occurred in 1980 (Section I). The essay will further examine the growth potential of the Korean economy and make recommendations for policies that may be pursued to exploit this potential during the 1980s (Section II). The postscript to the essay reports on the government decision to re-establish an outward-oriented development strategy in Korea and describes the effects of the measures taken in the years 1981–3.

I POLICY CHANGES AND ECONOMIC PERFORMANCE, 1978 TO 1980

Economic developments in Korea, 1978–9[1]

With real GDP rising about 10 percent a year in the decade and a half following the policy reforms of the early sixties, Korea was one of the star performers of the world economy. Rapid economic growth was achieved under an outward-oriented strategy that led to increases in the volume of exports of goods and services at approximately 27 percent a year between 1963 and 1977.

Korea's high 'export elasticity', with a ratio of the rate of increase of exports to that of GDP of 2.7 in the period 1963–77, indicated the central role exports played in the growth process. In terms of 1975 prices, the exports of goods and services equalled 43 percent of GDP in 1977, compared with a ratio of 5 percent in 1963 and 17 percent in 1970. Exports contributed to economic growth by utilizing Korea's comparative advantage in labor-intensive industries, permitting the exploitation of economies of scale, ensuring the full use of capacity, and creating demand for domestically produced goods used as inputs in export production and consumed by workers engaged in export activities.

Its outward orientation made it possible for the Korean economy to quickly overcome the effects of the quadrupling of petroleum prices of 1973–4 and the world recession of 1974–5. With the volume of merchandise exports rising by 23 percent in 1975 and 36 percent in 1976, Korea was able to re-establish rapid rates of economic growth while eliminating its large balance of payments deficit.[2]

The slowdown in the world economy led to a decline in the rate of growth of the volume of Korea's merchandise exports to 19 percent in 1977. Nevertheless, it still exceeded the export growth rates of Korea's major competitors, Taiwan, Singapore and Hong Kong, by a considerable margin. The situation changed to the detriment of Korea in 1978 and, in particular, in 1979 when it experienced a 1 percent decline in the volume of its merchandise exports while exports increased by 7 percent in Taiwan, 20 percent in Singapore, and 17 percent in Hong Kong (Table 11.1).

The extent of the shortfall in Korean exports, associated in large part with the loss of market shares to the other three Far Eastern economies, can be indicated in different ways. Calculating the dollar value of exports that would have occurred if increases in Korea matched

TABLE 11.1 *Export performance in 1974–80: Korea, Taiwan, Singapore and Hong Kong (annual percent change)*

	1974	1975	1976	1977	1978	1979	1980
Korea							
Export value (US$ bil.)[a]	38.5	13.9	51.6	30.4	26.5	18.4	16.3
Export volume index	9.3	22.9	35.9	19.0	14.2	−1.1	10.9
Unit value index	26.6	−7.3	11.7	9.5	10.7	20.0	4.9
Taiwan							
Export value ($ bil.)[a]	25.2	−5.8	53.8	14.6	31.9	23.6	23.0
Export volume index	−4.3	0.2	50.2	7.8	24.1	6.6	10.6
Unit value index	30.9	−5.9	2.4	6.4	6.1	16.0	11.2
Singapore							
Export value ($ bil.)[a]	60.2	−7.9	21.8	24.9	23.5	39.9	36.0
Export volume index	10.1	−8.3	19.0	15.1	12.4	20.1	16.8
Unit value index	45.5	0.4	2.4	8.5	9.9	16.5	16.4
Hong Kong[b]							
Export value ($ bil.)	—	—	41.7	12.9	19.5	31.8	29.5
Export volume index	—	—	30.0	4.6	11.0	16.6	10.2
Unit value index[c]	—	—	9.0	7.9	7.7	13.0	17.5

[a] Based on balance of payments accounts.
[b] Trade figures from IMF data bank.
[c] Derived from export value and volume figures.

SOURCE: International Monetary Fund, *International Financial Statistics* and World Bank data bank.

average increases of exports by these countries in 1978 and in 1979, the export shortfall is estimated at $2.2 billion in 1979. And, 1979 exports would have been $8.2 billion higher had Korea maintained the advantage in export growth it experienced in 1976 and in 1977 vis-à-vis the three countries.

An important factor contributing to the deterioration of Korea's export performance was the decline in the competitiveness of its manufactured exports, which account for over 90 percent of the total. Following increases in 1973, Korea's real exchange rate, calculated by adjusting the nominal exchange rate for changes in wholesale prices relative to its principal trading partners, returned to the level observed in the early seventies by 1975. The real exchange rate fell afterwards, declining by 12 percent between 1975 and 1979 (Table 11.2).

At the same time, calculations of real exchange rates derived by the use of wholesale price indices underestimate the extent of the deterioration of Korea's competitive position. This is because increases in the prices of goods that enter international trade are limited by foreign competition, and hence they do not fully reflect the rise in production costs. Correspondingly, interest attaches to changes in unit labor costs, which show the extent of cost pressures on the firm due to increases in

TABLE 11.2 *Nominal and real exchange rates (1975 = 100)*

		1975	1976	1977	1978	1979IV	1980	1980	IV
Nominal and Real Exchange Rates, Korea									
(1) Nominal Exchange rate, Won per US$		484.0	484.0	484.0	484.0	484.0	484.0	607.6	652.1
(2) Wholesale Prices, Korea		100.0	112.1	122.2	136.5	162.1	175.4	225.3	245.9
(3) Unit Labor Costs, Korea		100.0	124.2	144.0	168.6	200.5	235.2	239.3	260.6
(4) Foreign Wholesale Price, US$		100.0	104.3	112.8	129.9	143.3	147.7	163.5	171.6
(5) Relative Wholesale Prices	(2):(4)	100.0	107.5	108.3	105.1	113.1	118.8	137.8	143.4
(6) Relative Unit Labor Costs	(3):(4)	100.0	119.1	127.7	128.6	139.9	159.2	146.4	151.9
(7) Real Exchange Rate (Wholesale Prices)	(1):(5)	484.0	450.2	446.9	460.5	427.9	407.4	441.0	455.1
(8) Real Exchange Rate (Unit Labor Costs)	(1):(6)	484.0	206.4	379.0	376.4	346.0	304.0	415.2	429.3
Unit Labor Costs, US Dollars									
(9) Korea		100.0	124.1	143.5	167.1	200.5	235.2	239.3	260.6
(10) United States		100.0	100.7	107.3	115.7	125.4	130.0	142.1	146.8
(11) Japan		100.0	99.4	113.2	144.0	133.7	121.7	129.1	142.9
(12) Taiwan		100.0	95.3	94.8	92.4	105.2	100.5	na	na
(13) Singapore		100.0	98.2	117.3	na	na	na	na	na
Unit Labor Cost and Real Wages, Korea									
(14) Nominal Wage		100.0	134.7	180.2	242.1	311.4	356.6	383.1	421.4
(15) Manufacturing Output		100.0	131.8	158.7	196.4	220.2	214.2	215.8	219.1
(16) Manufacturing Employment		100.0	121.5	126.9	136.8	141.8	141.2	134.8	135.5
(17) Labor Productivity	(15):(16)	100.0	108.5	125.1	143.6	155.3	151.7	160.1	161.7
(18) Unit Labor Costs	(14):(17)	100.0	124.1	143.5	168.6	200.5	235.2	239.3	260.6
(19) Consumer Prices		100.0	115.3	127.0	145.3	171.9	182.0	221.3	243.0
(20) Real Wages	(14):(19)	100.0	116.8	141.8	166.6	181.2	196.0	173.1	173.4

SOURCES: *International Financial Statistics* and Bank of Korea, *Monthly Economic Statistics*.

wages adjusted for variations in labor productivity. Differential changes in wholesale prices and in labor costs, in turn, provide an indication of changes in profit margins.

As shown in Table, 11.2, unit labor costs in Korean manufacturing rose less rapidly than wholesale prices until 1975, thereby raising profit margins. The situation was reversed after 1975; between 1975 and 1979, unit labor costs doubled while wholesale prices increased by 62 percent. The ensuing decline in profit margins reduced the profitability of exports and raised the spectre of bankruptcy over a number of firms engaged in export activities.

The reduced profitability of exports is also indicated by real exchange rate calculations made with respect to changes in unit labour costs in Korea (for lack of information, wholesale price indices rather than indices of unit labor costs have been used in the calculations for Korea's principal trading partners). The results show a decline in Korea's labor-cost-adjusted real exchange rate by 29 percent between 1975 and 1979.

Further interest attaches to comparisons of unit labor costs in Korea, in its major export markets, and in countries competing with Korea in these markets. The data of Table 11.2 indicate that unit labor costs, expressed in terms of US dollars, increased by 101 percent in Korea between 1975 and 1979 while increases were 34 percent in Japan and 25 percent in the United States and an increase of only 5 percent occurred in Taiwan.

Through its impact on exports, the deterioration of the competitiveness of Korean industry adversely affected economic growth, albeit with a time lag. This is indicated by the reversal of the pattern of year-to-year changes in real GDP between the four quarters of 1977 (9.7, 9.2, 11.2, and 13.7 percent) and those of 1978 (17.1, 16.7, 13.8, and 4.9 percent). The pattern observed in 1978 continued in 1979 (13.6, 9.2, 6.0 and 1.0 percent), when seasonally adjusted real GDP actually declined in the last two quarters.

Exports and economic growth were also adversely affected by the sectoral allocation of investment. The government favored capital-intensive industries producing intermediate goods and heavy machinery over labor-intensive export industries. This was done by the use of credit and fiscal measures as well as by 'moral suasion', after practically forcing firms in export industries to invest in the favored industries.

To begin with, capital-intensive industries producing intermediate products, such as ferrous and non-ferrous metals, petrochemicals, and chemicals, as well as heavy machinery, such as electrical power generators, heavy construction equipment, and heavy engineering, benefited from the decline in real interest rates after 1977. These industries were also given priority in the allocation of domestic credit and in providing access to foreign credit. 'Directed' credit assumed increased importance during the period and the cost of credit to the industries in question was further reduced through preferential interest rates. Finally, they benefited from fiscal incentives in the form of exemptions from corporate income taxes as well as accelerated depreciation provisions that, too, lowered the cost of capital.

While the availability and the low cost of credit and favorable tax treatment increased the profitability of the domestic production of capital-intensive intermediate goods and heavy machinery, the incentives alone did not suffice to ensure that investment in these industries was undertaken to the extent desired by the government. In order to obtain the desired pattern of investment, the government exerted pressure on firms in traditional export industries to invest in capital-intensive intermediate goods and heavy machinery. At the same time, the government had leverage over these firms through its control of much of the credit supply.

The effects of the measures taken were manifest in the pattern of investment during the Fourth Five-Year Plan period (1977–81). While the amount of industrial investment undertaken in the first three years was 80 percent of that planned for the entire five-year period, the relevant figures were 130 percent for basic metals and 101 percent for chemicals and other intermediate products. By contrast, only 50 percent of planned investment was undertaken in the textile industry and 42 percent in the other light industries. Machinery, electronics, and ships occupy a middle position, the relevant figure being 81 percent, with larger than planned increases for heavy machinery.[3]

At the same time, the investment targets for capital-intensive intermediate goods and heavy machinery in the Fourth Five-Year Plan much exceeded figures for earlier periods. With the overfulfillment of plan targets, then, in the 1977–9 period 27 percent of manufacturing investment was in basic metals, 29 percent in chemicals and other intermediate goods, 23 percent in machinery, electronics, and transport equipment, 13 percent in textiles and clothing, and 8 percent in other light industrial goods. This contrasts with the relative shares of the same industries in industrial production in the base year of the plan, 1975; basic metals, 8 percent; chemicals and other intermediate goods,

26 percent; machinery, electronics, and transport equipment, 15 percent; textiles and clothing, 25 percent; and other light industrial goods, 26 percent.

The emphasis given to investments in industries producing capital-intensive intermediate goods and heavy machinery lowered the productivity of capital in Korean manufacturing. This is evidence by the rise in the incremental capital-output ratio. This ratio was 1.34 in 1970–3 and 1.46 in 1973–6; it rose to 1.63 in 1976–8; and it reached 2.73 in 1979.

The rise in the incremental capital-output ratio reflects high costs in industries producing intermediate goods and heavy machinery. Apart from the capital-intensity of the production process, firms in these industries could not fully utilize their capacity in the confines of the domestic market and were not sufficiently specialized.

Unused capacity in capital-intensive intermediate goods and heavy machinery industries contrasted with the lack of sufficient new capacity in traditional labor-intensive export industries that were disadvantaged by the system of credit allocation and suffered the adverse consequences of the increased overvaluation of the won. The scarcity of new investments in these industries, in turn, hindered the expansion and the upgrading of Korea's labor-intensive exports.

Exchange rate changes and export performance in 1980

It appears, then, that the maintenance of the exchange rate at 484 won to the dollar from 1974 to 1979 in the face of rapid increases in labor costs reduced the competitiveness of Korean industry, with adverse effects on exports. Increases in labor costs resulted from the 81 percent rise in real wages between 1975 and 1979 in response to pressures on labor markets owing to the rapid expansion of construction activity in the course of the implementation of investments in industries producing capital-intensive intermediate goods and heavy machinery. These investments raised the share of gross fixed investment in GDP from about 25 percent in the mid-seventies to 32 percent in 1978 and 1979. At the same time, the capital needs of Korea's traditional export industries were not provided for.

Apart from reductions in export shares, the deterioration of the competitiveness of Korean industry gave rise to increased imports. The high import intensity of industries producing intermediate goods and heavy machinery further aggravated the situation. As a result, the rate of growth of the volume of imports accelerated, from 14 percent a year in the 1970–7 period to 21 percent a year between 1977 and 1979. The acceleration of imports was even greater if one excluded the import content of exports; the relevant figures were 11 percent in 1970–7 and 25 percent in 1977–9.

To improve the competitiveness of Korean industry, in January 1980 the won was devalued by 20 percent in terms of the US dollar. With small exchange rate adjustments in the remainder of the year, the exchange rate reached 656 won to the dollar at the end of 1980. Adjusted for change in wholesale prices in Korea and abroad, the real exchange rate depreciated by 12 percent between the fourth quarters of 1979 and 1980, but it was still 8 percent lower than in 1975.

Greater improvements occurred in labor costs as pressures on profit margins, relatively high unemployment, and exhortation by the government led to a slowdown of wage increases, with real wages declining by 3 percent between the fourth quarters of 1979 and 1980. Correspondingly, the real exchange rate, calculated by the use of unit labor cost indices, depreciated by 37 percent between the fourth quarters of 1979 and 1980, although it showed an appreciation of 14 percent compared with 1975. And, despite a decline in unit labor costs in terms of US dollars, their 1980 level exceeded the 1975 figure by 139 percent while comparable figures were 29 percent for Japan, 42 percent for the United States, and 10 percent for Taiwan.

The depreciation of the real value of the won led to increases in the volume of Korea's merchandise exports by 11 percent in 1980, approximately matching estimated changes in Taiwan and Hong Kong, although falling short of the 17 percent increase in Singapore (Table 11.1). With the depreciation limiting increases in export unit values,[4] the dollar value of exports however increased substantially less in Korea (17 percent) than in the other three economies (Taiwan, 23 percent, Hong Kong, 29 percent, and Singapore, 36 percent). Thus, Korea continued to lose market shares to its Far Eastern competitors in 1980.

Domestic policy measures

Simultaneously with the January 12 devaluation, various domestic policy measures were taken. The target growth rate of the broadly defined money supply was reduced to 20 percent a year as compared to increases in end-year values of 40 percent between 1976 and 1977, 35 percent between 1977 and 1978, and 25 percent between 1978 and 1979.

Also, interest rates were raised from 18.6 percent to 24.0 percent on one-year time deposits, from 18.5 percent to 24.5 percent on one-year loans to prime borrowers, and from 9.0 percent to 15.0 percent on export loans, with a rate of 12.0 percent applying until June 30.

In response to the deterioration of the economic situation, domestic expansionary measures were taken in June 1980. They included raising the target growth rate of the broadly defined money supply to 25 percent, reducing interest rates on domestic savings and loans by one percentage point, and postponing the scheduled increase of interest rates on export loans from 12 percent to 15 percent for another six months. At the same time, the government released 113 billion won, which had been withheld earlier in the year, for public works programs.

Expansionary measures were further taken in September 1980, involving the liberalization of selective credit controls, increases in the availability of loans for construction activity and for small- and medium-size firms, and reductions in interest rates to savers as well as to borrowers. Interest rates were set at 21.9 percent on one-year time deposits and at 21.5 percent on one-year loans to prime borrowers.

Additional expansionary measures were introduced in November 1980, providing special loan facilities to firms in difficulties, lowering consumption taxes on durable consumer goods, including automobiles, color TV sets, and electrical home appliances, and reducing interest rates. Interest rates were reduced by an additional two percentage points and were set at 19.5 percent on one-year deposits and loans.

In turn, wholesale prices rose by 44 percent and consumer prices by 35 percent between December 1979 and December 1980. And while these results were affected by the large oil price increase in the first half of 1980 and by the impact of the January devaluation, wholesale prices rose at an annual rate of 35 percent in the third quarter. Corresponding increases in consumer prices were 22 percent in the third quarter and 37 percent in the fourth quarter. The resulting negative real interest rates contrast with positive real interest rates established in Korea in the mid-sixties and re-established after the oil crisis.

Part of the increase in prices was due to the rise in food prices following the disastrous harvest in 1980. Still, excluding food, wholesale prices rose at an annual rate of 31 percent in the fourth quarter of 1980 while the increase in consumer prices was 7 percent. The expansionary measures taken were an important factor contributing to this increase. The consolidated public sector deficit reached 548 billion won in the fourth quarter of 1980, compared with a small surplus in the first three quarters and a deficit of 197 billion won in the fourth quarter of

1979. For the year 1980 as a whole, the consolidated public sector deficit reached 3.7 percent of GNP as against the originally estimated figure of 2.5 percent. In turn, the broadly defined money supply rose by 26.7 percent between December 1979 and December 1980.

II POLICIES FOR ECONOMIC GROWTH

The growth potential of the Korean economy

In analyzing desirable policy measures for Korea, one needs to consider their short-term as well as their long-term effects. To do so, in turn necessitates examining the growth potential of the Korean economy. In this connection, comparisons with Japan are of interest.

Notwithstanding its rapid economic growth, *per capita* incomes in Korea, expressed as a percentage of incomes in Japan and measured at the official exchange rate, changed relatively little, from 12 percent to 14 percent over the 1965–80 period. This is because economic growth was rapid in Japan as well, albeit it started from a much higher base, and its population was rising more slowly.

Korea would have to maintain high rates of economic growth in order to approximate Japan's present income level by the turn of the century. Rapid economic growth is also necessary in order to fulfill the aspirations of the Korean people. While considerable attention has recently been given to social goals in Korea, it is economic growth that permits attaining these goals.

At the same time, the experience of Japan indicates the possibilities for rapid economic growth in Korea, provided that appropriate policies are followed. Such policies would have to aim at the rapid expansion of exports as has been the case in the past. In participating in the international division of labor, exports permit the exploitation of Korea's comparative advantage, the full use of capacity, and production at an efficient scale. Also, exports provide inducement for technological change and supply foreign exchange to purchase the imports necessary for economic growth.

In order to provide impetus for rapid economic growth, exports would have to rise more rapidly than the gross national product. This is indicated by the experience of every successful economy, including that of Japan. Thus, over the past quarter century, exports in Japan grew more than one-and-a-half times as fast as its GDP.[5]

The need for continued export orientation was recognized in the

Proposed Guidelines for the Fifth Economic and Social Development Plan for 1982–6 prepared in July 1980. Under each variant, the export elasticity (the ratio of the rate of growth of exports to that of GDP) was assumed to be between 1.5 and 1.6, with GNP and export growth rates of 9.0 percent and 14.2 percent; 8.0 percent and 12.1 percent; and 6.5 percent and 9.8 percent under the three variants, respectively.

With population rising 1.6 percent a year, and the labor force by 2.7–3.0 percent a year during the Fifth Five Year Plan period, a rate of economic growth of 6.5 percent may not permit fulfilling the economic and social aspirations of the Korean people, however. Under the projections made, this variant would also give rise to unemployment, averaging 6.2 percent of the labor force.

At the same time, income differentials vis-à-vis Japan indicate the potential for increases in productivity that would permit attaining high rates of economic growth in Korea. Nor does the required expansion of exports face unsurmountable obstacles in foreign markets. According to estimates made by the author, the exports of manufactured goods by the developing countries to the industrial countries would rise by 12.5 percent a year between 1978 and 1990. And, manufactured exports may rise even more rapidly to other developing countries and, in particular to the Middle East.[6]

Through the upgrading and the diversification of exports, Korea may reach higher than average rates of export growth and regain losses in market shares in the industrial countries. Its increasingly sophisticated industrial structure would also permit exploiting the opportunities offered by the markets of OPEC and non-OPEC developing countries. The possibilities for export expansion are further indicated by the fact that, in *per capita* terms, Korea has only one-eighth of the exports of the smaller European countries, exclusive of intra-EEC trade.

Rapid export growth, and the acceleration of the growth of exports following the poor performance of the preceding two years, in turn, requires adopting appropriate policies. These will be considered under the following headings: incentive policies, investment allocation, and the accumulation of physical and human capital.

Incentive policies

Apart from the long-term requirements of economic growth, the rapid expansion of exports is necessary in order to regain the 'growth path' of the Korean economy. Rapid export expansion is also necessary in the short run, in order to reduce Korea's current account deficit that exceeded $5 billion in 1980, equalling 9 percent of its gross national product. At the same time, this deficit was associated with a 5.7 percent decline in GDP and, given the high import elasticity in Korea,[7] it would have been even larger if the economy continued to expand. This conclusion follows even though the poor harvest, which entailed a reduction in GDP by about four percentage points, necessitated increased food imports.

Attaining the goal of rapid export expansion would necessitate taking measures to improve the competitiveness of exports. At the same time, restoring the competitiveness of Korean industry is an urgent task since otherwise established export positions would be lost and new exports would not develop. In turn, a domestic expansionary policy would adversely affect the balance of payments both by drawing resources from export industries and leading to 'import leakages'.

The possible effects of alternative policies were indicated by simulations performed with the model of SRI International, developed by Sung Y. Kwack and Michael Mered.[8] Simulations of the effects of a 100 billion won increase in government expenditures in 1970 prices, amounting to 3.0 percent of GDP in the base year, and those of a 10 percent devaluation of the won, offer particular interest.

In this eventuality, increased government expenditures would raise Korea's gross national product by 2.1 percent in the first year, but part of this gain would be lost in subsequent years through rising imports and, by the fifth year, GDP would be only 1.4 percent higher than before the expansionary measures were taken. At the same time, such a policy would lead to a fall in export volume, and it would increase Korea's current account deficit.

By contrast, the volume of exports would rise by 7.8 percent in the first year, and by 12.6 percent by the fifth year, following a 10 percent devaluation of the won. As a result, Korea's gross national product would increase by 3.8 percent initially and by 6.2 percent after five years. Notwithstanding the rise in import volume by 3.6 percent, the current account balance would improve as a 6 percent increase in export prices expressed in terms of the domestic currency would limit the deterioration of the terms of trade.

Increases in export prices in terms of domestic currency are necessary in order to provide appropriate incentives to exporters through improvements in profit margins. Profit margins would increase substantially following a 10 percent devaluation as the consumer price index, heavily weighted with services, would rise by only 4 percent as a result, so that maintaining real wages at pre-devaluation levels would require only a 4 percent increase in nominal wages.

The devaluation of the won has been objected to in Korea by reason of its inflationary effects. But, as expansionary fiscal policy also contributes to inflation, and the inflationary effects of a devaluation may be mitigated by reductions in tariffs. Except for materials and foodstuffs that enter duty free, the prices of imports would not rise under a partially compensated devaluation, which would involve reductions in tariffs commensurate with the devaluation.[9] In turn, with the duty-free entry of imported inputs for export production being maintained, value added in exports would receive the full benefits of the devaluation.

Apart from their anti-inflationary effects, the compensating tariff reductions would contribute to efficient resource allocation and economic growth by lessening the extent of discrimination against exports, without however affecting the net protection of import-substituting activities. At the same time, with the devaluation and reductions in tariffs having offsetting effect on inflation and on import-substituting activities, the objections against each of these measures, taken individually, would weaken.

In addition to the proposed reductions in tariffs, the inflationary effects of the depreciation of the currency may be mitigated by the pursuit of disinflationary monetary and fiscal policies. In fact, the application of such policies is necessary for a devaluation to be effective, in the sense that it is not eroded by domestic price increases. This objective would be served by implementing the monetary target of 25 percent for 1981 and avoiding an unduly expansionary fiscal policy.

The depreciation of the won would reduce labor costs in terms of dollars, which rose rapidly between 1975 and 1979, undermining Korea's competitive position. This objective may be pursued in an alternative way through a slowdown of increases in wages compared with the growth of labor productivity. This alternative has the obvious merit that it would reduce the rate of inflation while the depreciation of the exchange rate has the opposite effect. Wage restraint would have the further advantage that it would reduce costs in labor intensive industries, where Korea's comparative advantage lies.

Restraining wages, however, has a social and political cost. Also, as noted above, the depreciation of the currency leads to lower labor costs even if real wages do not decline relative to labor productivity.

Nevertheless, following rapid increases in real wages between 1975 and 1979, a deceleration would be necessary in order to improve the competitiveness of Korean industry in world markets.

In view of these considerations, a combination of policies may be pursued, with wage restraint accompanying the depreciation of the won in real terms and disinflationary monetary and fiscal policies being pursued. At the same time, incentives would need to be provided for savings and investments and for improving the allocation of investment. Such a policy package would contribute to the rebuilding of confidence at home and abroad and it would have beneficial short-term and long-term effects on the Korean economy.

Investment allocation

The depreciation of the won improves the profitability of all industries producing internationally traded goods, while tariff reductions reduce discrimination against export industries and wage restraint further benefits these relatively labor-intensive industries. Apart from their favorable balance-of-payments effects, the described measures would improve the allocation of investment, with favorable effects on economic growth.

The efficient allocation of investment would further be served by lowering and rationalizing protection. Notwithstanding its large population (39 million) Korea has a relatively small economy, with its GNP being one-twentieth of that of Japan and one-half of that of Belgium, Sweden, or Switzerland. At the same time, present-day small developed countries traditionally followed a policy of low protection, with tariffs averaging 5–10 percent and excluding the use of quantitative import restrictions, in order to benefit from the international division of labor.

Lowering and rationalizing protection would necessitate tariff reform involving reductions in tariffs and in tariff disparities. The reform would follow the reductions in tariffs proposed to be undertaken in conjunction with the depreciation of the won. In order to prepare firms for tariff reductions, it would be desirable to carry out the reform during the period of the Fifth Five-Year Plan, according to a timetable made public in advance.

During the same period, quantitative import restrictions should be increasingly replaced by tariffs. Quantitative restrictions provide absolute protection, the incidence of which is not known with any confidence. They also tend to perpetuate inefficiencies and their replacement by tariffs would contribute to the modernization of the Korean economy.

The elimination of quantitative restrictions is of particular importance for the machinery industry. Experience shows that the application of such restrictions does not ensure adequate specialization in the production of machinery and its parts and components while allowing low quality production. A start in import liberalization may be made by eliminating quantitative restrictions on machinery parts and components.

More generally, the requirements of efficient scale and high quality operations in the machinery industry require the use of promotional measures, which do not discriminate between domestic and foreign sales, in the place of protection. Such measures may include tax benefits, preferential interest rates for investment and the sale of machinery, technical assistance, government-financed training, and support to research and development.

The use of promotional measures in the machinery industry is warranted because this is an infant-industry activity in Korea that has a long learning period. Nonetheless, the measures applied should remain temporary, so as to avoid the establishment and perpetuation of high-cost activities. Furthermore, identical incentives should be provided to all machinery firms, without favoring some firms and some activities over others. It is the firm that should decide if it wishes to make use of the promotional measures offered and should take the risks and reap the rewards of its production and export decisions.

One should also revise domestic content regulations that raise the cost of domestic production and limit the firm's choice among inputs. This is the case, in particular, in the automotive industry where domestic content is about 90 percent and the cost of domestic inputs, manufactured for several models on a small scale, is very high.

In this connection, one may welcome the recent decision taken by the government to consolidate the production of passenger automobiles in one firm. Further consideration should be given to participation in the international division of the production process, involving the production of some parts and components for domestic use and for export while importing others. A possible alternative is to take part in worldwide sourcing by General Motors, which has an interest in one of the Korean car-producing firms; another possibility is to establish links with Japanese firms.

While infant industry considerations warrant taking promotional measures in the machinery industry on a temporary basis, such does not appear to be the case for process industries producing intermediate goods where production techniques are well-known and the learning period is relatively short. Rather, these industries should receive the same investment incentives as light industries, which increasingly suffered discrimination in recent years although they have good possibilities for expansion through upgrading and product differentiation.

In turn, capital-intensive industries benefited from the policy of low interest rates that also favored the use of capital-intensive production methods. Following a decline from 18.0 percent in 1976 to 16.0 percent in 1977, interest rates on term loans of 3 to 8 years duration to prime borrowers were raised only to 19.5 percent in 1979 whereas the rate of inflation, as measured by the wholesale price index, increased from 12 percent to 19 percent. And while interest rates were raised to 25.5 percent in January 1980, they were subsequently reduced in three installments by five percentage points, notwithstanding the acceleration of inflation, with wholesale prices rising at a rate of about 35 percent a year.

It would be desirable to reverse these tendencies and to re-establish positive real interest rates. This would permit eliminating the existing subsidy to capital-intensive industries and production process. Market-clearing interest rates would also serve as a rationing device among would-be borrowers, thereby obviating the need for credit allocation. At any rate, one would need to reduce the scope of directed credit that was used in the past to benefit capital- (and energy) intensive industries in Korea.

More generally, there is need to reform the Korean financial system, so that it conforms to the requirements of a modern industrial economy. This would involve establishing a rational interest rate policy, eventually introducing flexible interest rates; limiting the scope of central credit allocation, transferring over a period of time responsibilities for lending to commercial and to investment banks; limiting the role of preferential lending, with the exception of exports and the machinery industry; and reducing the role of government in the banking system.

The accumulation of physical and human capital

A necessary precondition of rapid economic growth is the accumulation of physical and human capital. The former requires providing inducements to domestic savings and investment and encouraging the inflow of foreign capital; the latter necessitates educational and training efforts. These will be briefly considered in the following.

As the experience following the 1964–5 reform and after the re-establishment of positive real interest rates in 1975–6 indicates, household savings respond to interest rates in Korea. Correspondingly it would be desirable to again provide positive real interest rates to savers. At the same time, in order to generate sufficient amounts of business savings, one should not limit increases in prices through price control and the maintenance of low exchange rates.

Also, Korea should continue to borrow abroad since the marginal efficiency of domestic investment exceeds the real rate of interest on foreign borrowing by a considerable margin. But, borrowing may not continue at present rates without eventually jeopardizing Korea's creditworthiness.

Considerations of creditworthiness do not affect foreign direct investment in Korea. At the same time, such investment brings additional know-how and marketing experience. Foreign investment is of especial importance in the machinery industry that is characterized by rapid technical change. It may also bring benefits, however, in some consumer-goods industries with export potential.

In this connection, one may welcome the policy changes announced in September 1980, allowing foreign ownership up to 100 percent in various industrial branches. It would further be desirable to extend the applicability of these regulations to certain service industries, where foreign capital can make an important contribution to Korea's economic objectives.

To begin with, exporting would be helped by permitting foreign trading firms to hold inventories in Korea. Moreover, the modernization of the financial sector would require permitting greater participation by foreign interests in banking and in insurance. Finally, the speedy implementation of the proposal for the creation of a mutual fund, consisting of the shares of Korean companies for sale to foreign investors, would contribute to the development of capital markets in Korea.

The investment effort would further be helped by increasing and simplifying incentives to productive investment. The system of investment incentives presently applied is unduly complicated and introduces considerable discrimination among industries. Investment incentives may be simplified and unified by enacting the Investment Promotion Law that has been repeatedly proposed in the past.[10]

In turn, an increased educational and learning effort would contribute to the accumulation of human capital. Particular attention would need to be given to technical education and to vocational learning. Apart from government-sponsored learning programs, these efforts would be helped by providing tax exemption to firms who train workers.

Finally, Korea's research and development effort would need to be stepped up. Despite rapid increases, expenditures on research and development in 1978 amounted to only two-thirds of one percent of the gross national product in Korea while the number of researchers per 1000 population was 0.3; the comparable figures are 2.0 percent and 2.3 in Japan. At the same time, the growth of government support to research and development slowed down after 1975, with private industry providing an increased share.

It would be desirable to accelerate the expansion of government financing of research and development during the Fifth Five Year Plan period and to provide greater incentives to private industry for engaging in R & D activities. The co-ordination of existing research institutes and the expansion of university-based research may bring further benefits. Finally, there would be need for venture capital to ensure the application of new technologies.

CONCLUSIONS

This essay has examined the reasons for recent adverse developments in the Korean economy and has made recommendations for policies to redress the situation and to ensure rapid economic growth during the 1980s. The recommendations have concerned incentive policies, invest-ment allocation, and the accumulation of physical and human capital.

The major thrust of the recommendations made in the essay has been to re-establish an outward-oriented development strategy in Korea. This would require adopting realistic exchange rates and reducing the bias against exports through changes in the incentive system and in the allocation of investment funds. In particular, recommendations have been made for reducing and rationalizing tariffs, elimination quantita-tive import restrictions, abolishing credit preferences favoring capital-intensive industries, and simplifying and unifying investment incen-tives. Proposals have further been put forward for restoring positive real interest rates; relying on interest rates as a rationing device in the place of credit allocation; abolishing price control, and reducing government involvement in economic life in general.

There would further be need to rationalize industries producing intermediate goods and heavy machinery. The decisions taken to reduce the number of producers of passenger automobiles and electric generators represents the first step in this direction. In conjunction with import liberalization and the increased participation of foreign capital, the government should let inefficient, high-cost activities disappear, to be replaced by firms that produce on an efficient scale and are integrated into the world economy.

Efficient economic growth also requires the liberalization of prices. Agricultural price support systems, too, would need to be revised, with a view to reducing the burden on the government budget and encouraging shift toward higher-value products. The measures taken to increase agricultural efficiency would complement the policies of industrial expansion and modernization.

POSTSCRIPT: DEVELOPMENTS AFTER 1980

The Preliminary Outline of the Fifth Five Year Economic and Social Development Plan of the Republic of Korea (1982–6), issued in June 1981, called for a return to a full-fledged outward-oriented development strategy. It stated that 'the basic strategy Korea will follow will be to promote competition at home and liberalize its external economic policies' (p. 10). The document added that 'there is no escape from the conclusion that during the Fifth Five-Year Plan period export expansion should continue to be the major engine of growth for Korea' (p. 13). This conclusion is based on the perception that outward orientation is not only the best guarantee for long-term economic growth, but it also helps overcome the effects of external shocks. The rationale is spelled out in the preliminary plan:

It is true that the above assessment of the world economic environment expected to prevail in the 1980s does not spell an optimistic outlook for a trade-oriented economy such as Korea's. But one should be careful not to draw from such an assessment a policy conclusion that the country should in any way compromise its outward-looking development strategy. If anything, the only way for Korea to meet effectively the challenges posed by external uncertainties is to pursue a development strategy that is even more outward-looking than in the past. The validity of this view has been underlined by Korea's own experience in dealing with the severe impact of two rounds of oil price increases during the 1970s and also the experiences of such other countries as Japan. Both Korea's and other countries' experiences clearly show that an open, trade-oriented economy can alleviate the initial impact of higher oil prices first by increasing exports and then by shifting the burden of higher oil prices through subsequent improvement in terms of trade (pp. 12–13).

The preliminary plan further indicates the general orientation of policies to serve the above objectives:

In order to expand exports during the Fifth Five-Year Plan period, the government will make every effort to strengthen the competitiveness of Korea's export industries (p. 15).

In order to sustain long-term growth of exports and the economy as a whole, import liberalization is essential. There is a limit to which a country can improve its industrial structure without import liberalization. Furthermore, a country cannot possibly hope to improve its price competitiveness while its price cost of living rises due to import restrictions... (p. 17).

The single most important change in government industrial policy during the Fifth Five-Year Plan period will be the reduction of the government's role in promoting so-called strategic industries. Investment choices will be left to the initiative of the private sector and the government will provide only the general framework in which such choices will be made by private entrepreneurs in co-operation with their bankers and financiers. Stated differently, during the 1980s government industrial policy will aim at reducing preferential treatment for selected industries and expose domestic producers to foreign competition in order to enhance their international competitiveness (pp. 22–3).

During the Fifth Five-Year Plan period the government will make special efforts to make greater use of the market mechanism and private initiative for continued social and economic progress (p. 30).

In addition, special efforts will be made to maintain the real interest rate on bank loans and deposits at a positive level and gradually reduce the scope of policy preference loans (p. 31).

Making a greater use of the market mechanism also implies equalizing the terms of competition and policy incentives for all industries... During the Fifth Five-Year Plan period the government plans to gradually phase out specific incentives and provide instead generalized uniform incentives for investment in all industries (p. 31).

Various measures were taken to implement the objectives of the Fifth

Five-Year Plan. A combination of devaluations and wage restraint was used to improve the competitive position of Korean exports; imports and prices were liberalized in order to reduce protection levels and to introduce greater flexibility in the economy, a restrictive monetary policy was applied to restrain inflationary pressures; interest rates were raised and the scope of credit allocation reduced in order to improve the operation of the financial system; and government intervention in economic life was reduced in order to give increased scope to private initiative.

The measures applied had favorable effects on the Korean economy. To begin with, the volume of exports rose at an average annual rate of 13.5 percent between 1980 and 1983. This result was attained in an unfavorable world environment as Korea gained market shares vis-à-vis its competitors due to the improved incentives provided to exporters.

Rapid increases in exports contributed to economic growth with GDP rising at an average annual rate of 7.3 percent over the three-year period, greatly exceeding growth rates in other developing countries. Comparisons with countries pursuing inward-oriented policies are especially striking. With their large indebtedness, the economies of these countries; stagnated in 1983[11] while Korea's GDP grew by 9.3 percent. A related consideration in that rapid expansion of exports permitted Korea to service its debt that was put to good use in an outward-oriented policy environment.

With imports rising somewhat more rapidly than the gross domestic product, Korea succeeded in reducing its current account deficit from $3.5 billion in 1980 to $1.3 billion in 1983, i.e., from 9.3 percent to 2.1 percent of GDP. This in turn, permitted limiting increases in Korea's external debt.

At the same time, inflation decelerated. While the index of wholesale prices increased by 39 percent between 1979 and 1980, it rose by 20 percent in 1981, 3 percent in 1982, with no increase occurring in 1983. And while real wages rose less than labor productivity, the rapid growth of exports and GDP permitted raising real wages by 7 percent a year, on the average, between 1980 and 1983.

It may be concluded, then, that the return to outward-orientation and increased reliance on market forces permitted the Korean economy to advance rapidly in the midst of the world recession. The policies applied also allowed Korea to exploit the possibilities offered by the renewed expansion of the world economy in 1983.

NOTES

1. For an analysis of incentive policies in Korea, see the author's policy advisory reports: 'Korea's Development Strategy for the Fourth Five-Year Plan Period', and 'Incentives for Economic Growth in Korea', published in *Policy Reform in Developing Countries* (Oxford: Pergamon Press, 1977) pp. 119–65 and 'The 15 Year Social and Development Plan in Korea', and 'Inflation and Trade Liberalization in Korea', published in *The Newly Industrialized Countries in the World Economy* (New York: Pergamon Press, 1981) pp. 347–78. See also L. E. Westphal and K. S. Kim 'Industrial Policy and Development in Korea', in B. Balassa *et al. Development Strategies in Semi-Industrial Economies* (Baltimore, Maryland: The Johns Hopkins University Press, 1981) pp. 212–79. Unless otherwise noted, the data cited in this section orginate in *Economic Statistic Yearbook* and other publications of the Bank of Korea.
2. B. Balassa, 'The Newly Industrializing Developing Countries After the Oil Crisis', *Weltwirtschaftliches Archiv*, CXVII (1981) pp. 142–94. Reprinted in Balassa, *The Newly Industrializing Countries in the World Economy*, pp. 79–82.
3. The data have been provided by the Economic Planning Board of Korea.
4. By the end of 1980, however, average unit values in Korea relative to other countries nearly regained the 1975 level. The author is indebted to Sweder van Wijnbergen on this point.
5. For a more detailed discussion, see Balassa, 'The 15 Year Social and Development Plan in Korea', and 'Inflation and Trade Liberalization in Korea'.
6. B. Balassa, 'Prospects for Trade in Manufactured Goods between Industrial and Developing Countries, 1978–90', *Journal of Policy Modeling*, II (1980) pp. 437–55. Reprinted in Balassa, *The Newly Industrializing Countries in the World Economy*, pp. 211–30.
7. On the basis of past experience, it may be assumed that a one percent increase in GNP is associated with an approximately one-and-a-half percent rise in imports.
8. S. Y. Kwack and M. Mered, 'A Model of the Economic Policy Effects and External Influences in the Korean Economy' (Washington DC: SRI International, 1980).
9. The effects of a partially compensated devaluation are discussed in B. Balassa, 'Reforming the System of Incentives in Developing Countries', *World Development* III (1975). Reprinted in Balassa, *Policy Reform in Developing Countries*, pp. 7–30.
10. Cf. Balassa, 'Korea's Development Strategy for the Fourth Five-Year Plan Period', and 'Incentives for Economic Growth in Korea'.
11. Cf. B. Balassa, 'Adjustment Policies in Developing Countries: A Reassessment', Essay 5 in the volume.

Part IV
Economic Policies in Socialist Countries

Essay 12   The Hungarian Economic Reform, 1968–81

INTRODUCTION

This essay provides an evaluation of the Hungarian economic reform, introduced on 1 January 1968. The reform represented an important change in a centrally-planned socialist economy. Plan directives were abolished and decision-making was decentralized, with reliance placed on prices linked to world market price relations in the allocation process.

Following a discussion of the antecedents of the reform (Section I), the essay will describe the principal reform measures and the performance of the Hungarian economy under the reform (Section II). Next, subsequent tendencies towards recentralization and their economic effects will be analyzed (Section III). Finally, the essay will briefly review the reform measures introduced in 1980–1 and the role of agriculture and the 'second economy' in Hungary (Section IV).

I THE ANTECEDENTS OF THE ECONOMIC REFORM[1]

Along with other Eastern European countries after the Second World War, Hungary adopted with few modifications the system of centralized planning practised in the Soviet Union.[2] Planning was largely carried out in physical terms, with prices having mainly an accounting function. Decisions on investment and on foreign trade were made centrally and central plans served as a basis for the directives communicated by the supervising ministries to individual firms. The directives concerned, among others, output targets, material allocation, wages, and employment. Within the constraints imposed by the allocation of inputs, managers aimed at fulfilling the production plan that was the principal success criterion and the condition for obtaining bonuses.

In permitting the large-scale mobilization of resources, the system of centralized 'physical planning' was conducive to economic expansion in Hungary during the early postwar period, when a limited number of objectives was pursued. With the multiplicity of objectives and the growing complexity of manufacturing industry, however, the disadvantages of this system of planning assumed importance.

To begin with, in pursuing production targets, managers paid little attention to costs and often tried to increase output through shifts in product composition towards material-intensive commodities; disguised price increases, and quality deterioration. At the same time, users had practically no choice among suppliers and had to accept commodities that did not correspond to their needs.

The introduction of profits as a supplementary success criterion and condition for bonuses did not lessen these adverse effects to an appreciable extent. The basic features of centralized physical planning remained unchanged and, in the absence of scarcity prices reflecting resource scarcities, profits could not provide appropriate signals for the firm. Prices did not include an allowance for the use of capital and land; they did not equate domestic demand and supply; and they were divorced from world market price relations. Exporters received, and importers paid, the prices set domestically; the difference between domestic and world market prices was paid into, and financed from, an equalisation fund in the government budget.

Nor did the lack of scarcity prices permit the economic evaluation of investment projects and the appropriate choice of exports and imports. Correspondingly, additional increments in domestic consumption required increased efforts in the form of resources used for new investments and the rate of economic growth declined. According to official figures, the rate of growth of the net material product was 7.9 percent in 1958–60, 5.6 percent in 1960–3, and 4.3 percent in 1963–6. In the period taken as a whole, the volume of investment increased by 7.7 percent a year while total consumption (public and private) rose by 4.6 percent, and the net material product by 6.2 percent.[3]

A proposal for a comprehensive reform was first made by a committee appointed by the government and headed by Professor Stephen Varga in 1957. The recommendations of the committee were not implemented, however, and in the following decade only partial measures were taken that did not affect the basic character of the decision-making process.[4]

At the same time, the need for a comprehensive, rather than a piecemeal, reform came to be increasingly understood. The increased sophistication of the Hungarian economy and its extensive reliance on foreign trade, by reason of the small size of the domestic market and the limited availability of natural resources, favored the decentralization of decision-making. At the same time, decentralization could not provide appropriate results in the absence of profit incentives based on scarcity prices.

A comprehensive economic reform (the new economic mechanism) was introduced on 1 January 1968. The reform aimed at replacing plan directives by market relations among firms; limiting the scope of central price determination; linking the domestic prices of exports and imports to world market prices; and decentralizing a major part of investment decisions. At the time of the introduction of the reform, a variety of 'brakes' were applied for the ostensible purpose of easing the transition from the old mechanism to the new, although in some respects they reflected compromises between the supporters of the two. The following section briefly describes the principal features of the reform at the time of its introduction, further indicating some of the changes effected in the first years of its application.

II THE ECONOMIC REFORM AND ITS IMPACT ON THE HUNGARIAN ECONOMY

The introduction of the new economic mechanism

The reform of agriculture antedates the general economic reform in Hungary. Starting in the late fifties, obligatory plan targets and compulsory deliveries were abolished and the prices of agricultural products raised, with a number of products being sold in farm markets at freely determined prices. These reforms were supplemented by additional actions in 1968. To begin with, the rural co-operatives were provided with the legal and financial basis necessary for their operations. Also, limitations on livestock kept on household plots owned by co-operative, state farm, industrial and other workers were eliminated and a generally supportive attitude was taken in regard to cultivation on these plots. Finally, the establishment of ancillary activities, including construction and local manufacturing, by the agricultural co-operatives was encouraged.

Changes in the role of industrial firms under the new economic

mechanism were stated concisely in the resolution of the Central
Committee of the Hungarian Socialist Workers' Party of 7 May 1966,
which is the basic document of the introduction of the economic
reform:

> The development of an active role for the market requires that the
> laborious and bureaucratic system of the centralized allocation of
> materials and products . . . should give place to commercial relations,
> i.e.
>
> – producers should be able to decide, within their range of activities,
> what and how much they produce and offer for sale, as well as in
> what quantity and from whom they purchase the necessary inputs . . .
>
> – producers and users should be free to establish commercial or co-
> operative relationships – sellers and buyers should be free to agree on
> the conditions of sale and, within the limits of governmental price
> determination, also on the prices;
>
> – the buyers should be free to choose, within the limits dictated by
> the national interest, between domestic goods and imports, and the
> sellers between selling on domestic or on export markets.

The replacement of administrative directives by market relations was to
be supplemented by according greater freedom to the firm to carry out
new investments and to hire labor. At the same time, profits were to
become the measure of the firm's success, as well as the source of
incentive payments and of funds for new investment.

There is evidence that managers responded to changes in the
incentive system. According to a sample survey conducted soon after
the introduction of the reform, production as a target lost its pre-
eminence and increases in profits became the single major objective.
Some of the other objectives also bear on profits while repeated
references to the satisfaction of user needs may reflect the importance
of catering to demand by consumers and firms under the new mechanism. Increases in profits also appeared as the principal objective in the
short-term and medium-term plans prepared by firms.

The emphasis on profits contrasts with the objective of raising the *per
capita* incomes of workers in the Yugoslav system of labor-managed
firms. In fact, the Hungarian authorities decided against the introduction of workers' management that appeared to have adverse effects in

Yugoslavia by limiting the growth of employment and of output in individual firms.

Nevertheless, the high rate of taxation of increments in average wages[5] interfered with profit maximization by favoring expansion through increases in employment as against upgrading the labor force or rewarding wage-earners for productivity improvements, both of which raised average wages. These regulations were partially modified in subsequent years, when the wages fund became the principal criterion for taxation in some industries.

Changes in the system of incentives in 1968 were accompanied by the liberalization of prices. The major principles of the price reform were again indicated in the 7 May 1966 Party resolution. Having noted that prices should reflect the joint influences of the cost of production, valuation by the market, and state preferences, the resolution stated:

> Valuation by the market will have to find expression in prices so that, on the one hand, the resulting differences in profitability should influence the structure of production (supply) and, on the other, these prices should help to reach market equilibrium through their effects on increasing or reducing the quantity demanded. For this purpose, it should be made possible in the new price system to determine market prices over a wide area through the agreement of buyers and sellers.

Following the introduction of the reform, central price determination was abolished for 12 percent of agricultural goods, 28 percent of domestically-produced materials and semi-finished products, 78 percent of industrial end-products, and 23 percent of consumer goods and services. In turn, prices were fixed centrally, or were subject to an upper limit, for 70 percent of the products in the first two categories, 20 percent in the third, and 50 percent in the fourth. In the remainder of cases, prices were left free to fluctuate within predetermined limits.

Changes in producer prices brought these nearer to a system of scarcity prices. However, centrally fixed prices were equated to average rather than marginal costs. This procedure gave rise to distortions, especially for materials and for semi-manufactures, where a weighted average of domestic and import prices was taken, since domestic costs and the cost of importing from Western and from socialist countries often differed to a considerable extent. As a rule, prices were lowest on material imports from socialist countries, but the quantities available from these sources were limited under long-term trade agreements.

In 1969 and 1970, the scope of price fixing was further reduced for materials and for semi-manufactures, and it was practically eliminated for all finished products. But the Materials and Price Board retained its veto power over price increases on commodities accounting for about 5–10 percent of industrial production, and the rise of prices was restrained by limitations imposed on the rate of profit in cases where price determination required the agreement of the buyer and the seller. Also, differences between producer and consumer prices were maintained by the use of turnover taxes, albeit to a somewhat lesser degree than beforehand.

The central allocation of materials was also dismantled in 1968, although initially certain materials, semi-manufactures, and foodstuffs remained subject to quotas in one form or another. The scope of quota allocation was reduced in the following year when the value of the products subject to some kind of quota limitation accounted for less than 5 percent of total sales. Apart from meat, cereals, and fodder that were centrally allocated, there were in 1969 purchase quotas for 13 products, import quotas for 17 products (the two groups in part overlapped), and sales quotas for 8 products. Moreover, commercial monopolies handled the purchase or sale of 20 products.

Further liberalization occurred in 1970. The central allocation of cereals and fodder was discontinued; the number of products to which purchase quotas applied was reduced to 4 (iron ore; copper and copper products; newsprint; and autobuses), and only 5 products (electric energy; passenger automobiles; coking coal; fertilizers; and fodder) were subject to import quotas. The scope of quota allocation was again reduced and, with the exception of meat and scrap metal, commercial monopolies abolished in the following years.

The 7 May 1966 Party resolution also noted the need to improve efficiency in foreign trade:

The new economic mechanism should establish a close relationship between internal and external markets. It should increase the impact of influences originating in foreign markets on domestic production, sale and consumption, as well as on the structure of exports and imports. It should reduce the excessive protection to domestic production, thereby eliminating the complacency to which it gave rise.

The price reform should bring about the correspondence of domestic prices with prices in foreign trade transactions. For this purpose a conversion ratio should be determined on the base of the average domestic cost of foreign exchange, independently of the gold content of the forint.

Firms producing for export at a cost higher than the conversion ratio, subsequently renamed 'commercial exchange rate', were given export subsidies. In 1968, about two-thirds of exporting firms received subsidies averaging 29 percent in ruble trade and 33 percent in dollar trade. The subsidies were given on a firm-by-firm basis, thereby contributing to the maintenance of production for exports in high-cost firms while firms that received only the conversion ratio had little incentive to expand exports. In turn, imports were subject to tariffs, import quotas applied to certain products, and import licenses were required for others. Tariffs were reduced in subsequent years and the scope of import quotas also diminished.

Linking the domestic prices of exports and imports to foreign prices through the conversion ratio represented an important advance in the rationalization of the price structure in Hungary. Nevertheless, with the use of export subsidies and import protection, there were continuing differences between the domestic and foreign prices of exports and imports. Furthermore, on the average, incentives to import substitution exceeded incentives to export.

Public authorities retained decision-making power over infrastructural and social investments and over manufacturing investments that increased capacity by over 25 percent, necessitated substantial imports, or involved the establishment of new factories. Rather, it was suggested that there was a need to promote competition. For this purpose, some observers recommended breaking up all large trusts and firms while others proposed that this be limited to horizontal trusts and firms where no efficiency loss was involved. Again others emphasized the need for increased foreign competition through the liberalization of imports, arguing that in a number of industrial branches Hungary's small domestic market does not afford sufficient domestic competition.

Economic performance under the reform

Data for the period 1967–73 point to the success of the new economic mechanism in Hungary. The deceleration of economic growth was reversed, with the net material product increasing at an average annual rate of 6.2 percent between 1967 and 1973. Also, with improvements in the efficiency of investment, the rate of growth and consumption (5.7 percent) was only slightly less than that of the net material product.

Even greater improvements are shown if adjustment is made for changes in capital and labor inputs. Thus, according to an unpublished study undertaken by Márton Tardos at the Hungarian Institute for Market Research, the growth rate of total factor productivity in Hungary more than doubled between 1962–7 and 1967–72. Also, national income figures indicate reductions in inventory ratios as firms economized with the holdings of stocks. These results reflect cost reductions on the firm level that were made in response to profit incentives. There is further evidence – albeit fragmentary and impressionistic – that firms came to react more rapidly to domestic and foreign demand and made increased efforts to improve technology following the reform.

Manufacturing industry led the expansion, with growth rates averaging 7 percent a year during the entire period. Favorable developments were experienced also in agriculture, where the growth rate of gross output nearly doubled, approaching 3 percent between 1967 and 1973. With population rising only 0.3 percent a year, food production per head grew at nearly the same rate.

An important factor contributing to the growth of the Hungarian economy was the expansion of the volume of exports at a rate nearly double that of the net material product between 1967 and 1973. The value of exports to developed and developing market economies, including Yugoslavia, increased more than the average, raising their share in the total to 44 percent by 1973. Hungary's export performance in market economies was much superior to that of other socialist countries, the only exception being Romania whose oil exports increased during this period. Thus, as reported in United Nations trade statistics, the dollar value of these exports rose at an average annual rate of 24 percent between 1968 and 1973 in Hungary as against rates of growth between 14 and 18 percent in the other socialist countries and 28 percent in Romania.

III POLICY REVERSALS AND THEIR ECONOMIC EFFECTS

Tendencies towards recentralization

In the early seventies, a certain degree of recentralization occurred and measures were taken that reduced the incentive effects of prices and profits. The November 1972 Party resolution called for limiting the extent of profit sharing by managers for the sake of avoiding large income inequalities. Also, certain limitations were imposed on the movement of labor; investments by industrial firms came to be increasingly influenced by state preferences; and there were more frequent interventions on the part of the supervising ministries. More importantly, policy responses to external shocks, in the form of the inflationary 1972–3 world boom, the 1974–5 world recession, and the deterioration of the terms of trade after 1973, led to reduced use of market mechanisms and to increased central directions and interventions. This occurred as the policy-makers attempted to isolate the Hungarian economy from the impact of outside events.

Market economies also experienced sizeable external shocks during the 1973–5 period. Outward-oriented economies responded to these shocks by temporarily adopting deflationary policies in order to limit the deterioration of their balance of payments. As a result, average GNP growth rates declined to a considerable extent in Greece (1.2 percent in 1973–5), Japan (1.1 percent), and Taiwan (1.5 percent), although rapid increases in exports permitted economic growth to resume sooner in Korea, with average increases in GNP of 8.8 percent between 1973 and 1975.

By contrast, inward-oriented market economies, such as Brazil and Turkey, relied largely on foreign loans to avoid reductions in growth rates.[6] In Hungary, too, the decision was made to maintain past rates of economic growth. Growth rates of the net material product averaged 6.0 percent between 1973 and 1975, with slightly lower increases in domestic consumption (5.8 percent) and the rapid rise of net investment (34.2 percent in 1974 and 11.5 percent in 1975). Correspondingly, the export surplus of 1973 gave rise to a deficit, particularly in convertible currency trade.[7] This, in turn, necessitated foreign borrowing, with Hungary's indebtedness in convertible currencies more than doubling between 1973 and 1975 according to unofficial estimates (Table 12.1).

About two-thirds of the increased deficit in convertible currency trade reflected the deterioration of the terms of trade while the remainder represented an acceleration in the growth of the volume of imports and a decline in the rate of export expansion. Imports increased to provide for the growth of domestic consumption, the stockpiling of raw materials, and the rapidly rising investments that often required foreign machinery. In turn, the adverse effects of foreign

TABLE 12.1 Net Material Product and Foreign Trade in Convertible Currencies in Hungary

	(1) Net Material Product	(2) Aggregate Demand Expenditure	(3) Consumption	(4) Net Investment	(5) Import Volume	(6) Export Volume	(7)[a] Trade Balance	(8)[a,b] Net Foreign Debt
			Average Annual Rate of Growth in Volume Terms				(trade in convertible currencies) $ million	$ million
1971	5.9	11.3	5.4	30.4	15.8	-0.6	-243	900
1972	6.2	-3.7	3.1	-21.4	-5.9	12.5	-53	900
1973	7.0	2.0	3.7	-3.8	2.5	17.9	+114	900
1974	5.9	12.7	6.9	34.2	17.6	3.1	-582	1500
1975	6.1	6.4	4.7	11.5	-5.8	3.3	-531	2000
1976	3.0	1.2	2.1	-1.4	11.8	12.8	-347	2800
1977	8.0	6.2	4.6	11.0	10.1	10.4	-567	3400
1978	4.2	10.0	4.9	23.8	15.9	1.6	-1110	4600
1979	1.9	-5.5	2.9	-24.9	-9.6	15.6	-280	5000
1980	-0.8	-1.9	1.4	-12.3	-2.6	2.1	-15	5400
1970-1973	6.4	3.0	4.1	-0.5	3.8	9.7	-61	900
1973-1975	6.0	3.1	5.8	22.3	5.3	3.2	-557	1750
1975-1978	5.0	5.7	3.9	10.7	12.6	8.2	-675	3600
1978-1980	0.5	3.6	2.1	-22.7	-6.6	8.6	142	5200
1973-1980	5.2	4.0	3.9	4.4	4.8	6.9	-490	3530

NOTE: [a] excludes first year of period. [b] end of year data.

SOURCES: (1) to (7) Hungarian statistical sources cited in footnote 1 of p. 3. (8) Paul Marer, 'The Mechanism and Performance of Hungary's Foreign Trade', P. G. Hare, H. K. Radice, and N. Swain (eds) in *Hungary: A Decade of Economic Reform* (London: Allen & Unwin, 1980) p. 180 and, for 1979 and 1980, Hungarian National Bank, *Information Memorandum*, 1 April 1980 and *Economic Bulletin*, January 1981.

demand conditions on exports were aggravated by the buoyancy of the domestic market, the unfavorable product composition of Hungarian exports, and reductions in export incentives.

Export incentives were reduced through the withdrawal of subsidies to firms that made profits in exporting and the imposition of additional taxes on what were considered 'excess profits', while compensation was provided to firms that incurred losses in exporting. In turn, import subsidies were used to limit increases in the prices of imported products. This was the case in particular for petroleum, the domestic price of which was only one-third of the world market price in 1974. Yet, even though the Soviet Union – Hungary's main supplier – increased prices only with a time lag, the marginal cost of petroleum for Hungary is the world market price.

The described developments reflected the intention of the Hungarian authorities to minimize the effects of foreign inflation on domestic prices. Distinction needs to be made, however, between stability in the overall price level and in relative prices. While the former objective can be pursued by revaluing the currency, in Hungary reliance was largely based on export taxes and on import subsidies, thereby introducing firm-by-firm and product-by-product differences. These differences meant that the structure of domestic producer prices became increasingly isolated from world market prices. Also, for the sake of limiting increases in consumer prices, the rise in domestic producer prices was not fully transmitted to the consumption sphere, thereby exacerbating distortions between producer and consumer prices. Correspondingly, the usefulness of domestic prices as signals for decisions by consumers and by producers was reduced.

In the presence of distortions between world market and domestic producer prices, as well as between domestic producer and consumer prices, consumers had little incentive to adjust their consumption pattern to changes in world market prices. This was especially the case in energy, the consumer price of which was substantially lower than the producer price, that itself was a fraction of the world market price. Nor was inducement provided to producers to save energy, so that an energy-intensive pattern of production was maintained in agriculture as well as manufacturing. More generally, the use of import subsidies increased demand for imported inputs on the part of the firm. Also, notwithstanding the introduction of taxes on excess profits, import-intensive exports were encouraged since these taxes left domestic relative prices unchanged.

At the same time, the welter of taxes and subsidies on exports and on imported inputs, designed to offset changes in world market prices, discouraged adjustments in the export structure in response to changing foreign price relations. Moreover, measures taken in a particular area gave rise to measures in other areas in order to compensate for the effects of the former.

Thus, production taxes levied on a firm-by-firm basis came into increased use. Furthermore, the extent of central directions on the firms' product composition, and interventions on the part of supervisory ministries in the day-to-day operation of the firms, increased. But, the firms themselves turned to the supervising ministries for financial assistance in cases when they deemed to have been adversely affected by the measures taken, and production taxes and budget support – as well as export taxes and subsidies – became the subject of bargaining.

With lesser reliance on the price system, the scope of quantitative regulations also increased. The number of products subject to purchase quotas rose from 7 in 1971 to 22 in 1976; seller-buyer relationships were centrally determined in 41 cases in 1976 compared to 9 such cases in 1971; the number of import quotas was increased from 7 to 33 during this period; and foreign exchange restrictions were applied to limit the growth of imports. These measures, taken in conjunction with reductions in export subsidies and the imposition of export taxes, raised the level of import protection relative to that of export subsidies in Hungary.

Reduced reliance on price signals was accompanied by limitations on the freedom of the firm in making investment decisions. A rising proportion of investments undertaken by firms necessitated financing from outside sources, chiefly bank credit and budget support. At the same time, obtaining bank credit and budget support increasingly required the firm to conform to the priorities set by the government. Special credits assumed considerable importance, with credit quotas set for particular purposes and state preferences importantly affecting allocation within each quota. State preferences also had an important role in the allocation of budget support, and the supervisory ministries exerted increasing influence on the choice of investments by the firms.

The economic effects of the policies applied

Following the application of deflationary policies as an immediate response to external shocks, outward-oriented market economies experienced rapid increases in exports and in national income. In the

1975–8 period, GNP growth rates averaged 5.5 percent in Greece, 5.2 percent in Japan, 11.7 percent in Korea, and 10.9 percent in Taiwan.

In turn, reliance on foreign borrowing permitted inward-oriented economies to maintain past economic growth rates only for a time. As the borrowed funds were used largely to increase consumption and to carry out costly investments behind high and often increasing protection, these countries did not generate the foreign exchange necessary to service foreign loans and to maintain high rates of economic growth after the mid-seventies. An extreme case is provided by Turkey, who had to apply strong deflationary policies as additional borrowing became practically impossible.[8]

Hungary accepted a decline in the rate of growth of aggregate domestic expenditure in 1976, when consumption rose by 2.1 percent and net investment declined by 1.4 percent, compared to a 3.0 percent increase in the net material product. The resulting improvement in the balance of payments proved temporary, however. In 1977 and in 1978, the rate of growth of aggregate domestic expenditure again exceeded that of output, leading to an acceleration of import growth and a slowdown of export expansion in convertible currency trade. Correspondingly, the deficit in this trade rose from $0.3 billion in 1976 to $0.6 billion in 1977 and to $1.1 billion in 1978, and Hungary's net indebtedness in convertible currencies reached $5.0 billion at the end of 1979 compared to $0.9 billion six years earlier.

Deflationary policies were applied anew in subsequent years, with domestic consumption rising by 2.9 percent in 1979 and 1.4 percent in 1980, after having increased by nearly 5 percent a year in the preceding two years. Furthermore, large increases in investment (in particular, inventory accumulation) in 1977 and 1978 gave place to substantial declines in the two years afterwards (Table 12.1).

As a result of these changes, Hungary's deficit in convertible currency trade declined to $0.3 billion in 1979 and was practically eliminated in 1980. Nevertheless, the servicing of foreign loans contracted earlier led to a further increase in Hungary's net debt in convertible currency to $5.4 billion at the end of 1980.

All in all, the data show that Hungary postponed cutbacks in consumption growth and experienced substantial fluctuations in investment activity in the period following external shocks. Furthermore, available evidence indicates the influence of the level of domestic activity on exports and points to the existence of a high short-term income elasticity of demand for imports in convertible currency trade.

Fluctuations in investment activity may be explained by the lack of use of macroeconomic policy instruments and the excessive investment demand that gave way only to quantitative measures. Excessive investment demand, in turn, reflected an accommodating stance on the part of public authorities in the event of losses by firms and in provision of investment funds.[9]

Until 1976, the role of profitability considerations on the firm level was further reduced by reason of the fact that there was no repayment obligation for the amounts received in the form of budget support. Since that time, firms had to repay budget support with interest for their pre-tax profits.

Also, in January 1976, domestic producer prices were brought nearer to world market price relations and export incentives were increased by abolishing export taxes and raising export subsidies. Subsequently, a fund was established to provide financing for investment aimed at increasing convertible currency exports. The National Bank grants credit on a competitive basis to firms whose net foreign exchange earnings over five years at least equal the amount invested, and the exports of which are profitable at the existing commercial exchange rate.

Increased incentives to exports contributed to the growth of exports in convertible currencies. These incentives did not suffice, however, to regain earlier export growth rates. Thus, the volume of exports in convertible currencies rose only 7 percent a year between 1973 and 1978 as compared to an increase of 10 percent a year between 1968 and 1973. Also, with average annual increases of 15 percent in the dollar value of exports to developed and developing market economies, including Yugoslavia, Hungary fell behind the Soviet Union (21 percent), Romania (19 percent), East Germany and Poland (18 percent), and surpassed only Czechoslovakia (13 percent) among socialist countries. At the same time, exports were given further impetus by the deflationary measures applied in 1979 when the volume of Hungary's convertible currency exports increased by 16 percent.

IV THE 1980–1 REFORMS, AGRICULTURE, AND THE 'SECOND ECONOMY'

The reform measures introduced in 1980 and 1981

While domestic producer prices were brought nearer to world market price relations in January 1976, substantial differences remained; the price of petroleum, for example, was still only 60 percent of the world market price. Also, notwithstanding some reductions in consumer subsidies, there continued to be large differences between the structure of producer and consumer prices.

With continuing differences between domestic and world market prices, firm-by-firm production taxes and budget support were retained. The introduction of selective tax exemptions and wage preferences provided to firms that undertake an obligation to expand exports also added on element of voluntarism in the decision-making process, further reducing the role of profit incentives for the firms.

It became increasingly understood that the existing regulations would need to be thoroughly revamped in order to ensure that Hungary will best utilize its opportunities in exploiting its comparative advantage for economic growth. It was further recognized that this will require resuming the process of decentralization of decision-making, giving greater role to profit incentives, and rationalizing producer and consumer prices.

The October 1977 resolution of the Central Committee of the Hungarian Socialist Workers' Party re-emphasized the central role of exports in Hungarian economic growth and stated the need to let firms decide on the product composition of their exports as well as on changes in their production structure. Subsequently, the December 1978 Party resolution called for giving increased emphasis to the profit motive, reducing the scope of government preferences and central interventions, and rationalizing the price system. These guidelines underlie the reform measures introduced on 1 January 1980.[10]

The lynchpin of the reforms was the introduction of 'competitive' prices in the industrial sector. The purpose was to increasingly align domestic producer prices with world market prices, thereby undoing the adverse effects of measures taken after 1973 and re-affirming the objectives enunciated at the time of the 1968 reform.

Firms have also been given greater freedom in their investment decisions. The large number of credit quotas have been consolidated into a few categories, permitting greater competition based on the profitability of the investment. At the same time, the availability of credit for export production has been increased, with additional facilities provided for import substitution.

As noted in Section I, the high degree of industrial concentration reduced competition in Hungary. In order to increase competition, 137 new firms have been established by breaking up horizontal trusts and large firms. These changes have occurred in coal mining and in the production of wine, sugar, confectionery, cigarettes, construction materials, shoes, and, to a lesser extent, machinery.

The organizational changes were carried out on 1 July 1980 and on 1 January 1981. The consolidation of industrial ministries took place on 1 January 1981. On the same date, some changes in the regulations affecting industrial firms also occurred, generally aimed at futher simplification.

All in all the measures introduced on and after 1 January 1980 have reversed the process of recentralization observable since the early seventies, and have carried the decentralization of decision-making beyond that existing beforehand. Decentralization has been linked to the greater role given to profitability on the firm level that will be increasingly determined by world market price relationships.

Developments in agriculture and the 'second economy'

The producer prices of agricultural products are set on the basis of production costs in Hungary, with certain adjustments made in accordance with world market price relations. Agricultural prices exceed world market prices, although they are substantially lower than domestic prices in the European Common Market where much of Hungary's exports were sold.

Agriculture continues to play an important role in the Hungarian economy, accounting for 14 percent of the net material product and for 23 percent of exports, including processed food, in 1980. Gross output in agriculture grew at an average annual rate of 3.5 percent between 1970 and 1980, exceeding the increase shown in any other European country.

With food consumption rising at an average annual rate of 1.5 percent during the seventies, exportable production rose at a rate much exceeding that of gross output. In the second half of the decade, about 50 percent of the increment in gross output was exported, with over 25 percent of agricultural output and 30 percent of processed food destined for export towards the end of the decade.[11] As a result, the share of agricultural products in total exports declined only slightly, from 25 percent in 1970 to 23 percent in 1980, with processed food accounting for two-thirds of the total. More generally, a shift occurred towards the exportation of higher value products, such as livestock, meat, poultry, wine, and processed fruits and vegetables. Of further interest is the emergence of new export products, including rabbit meat and eggs for poultry raising.

Rapid increases in exports and the transformation of the export structure in part reflects the response to incentives by agricultural co-operatives that are profit-making units. Another important factor has been the development of small-scale agriculture, consisting of household plots owned by co-operative, state farm, and industrial employees, retirees, and to a lesser extent, private farms.

Apart from 1975, when a hardening of the tone on the part of Party officials led to the wholesale slaughter of pigs, small-scale agriculture has been increasingly supported by the government. Recent measures include a threefold increase in the threshold of taxable income derived from small-scale agriculture, greater investment in this sector, and the lease of land not suitable for large-scale farming by state farms and co-operatives. Such leases would permit members of agricultural co-operatives to double the size of their household plots from the 0.6 hectares that is provided free to all members; other small-scale cultivators could increase the area they cultivate to an even greater extent.[12]

Small-scale agriculture, characterized by intensive cultivation, provides 36 percent of agricultural output, compared to 30 percent in 1970.[13] It accounts for over four-fifths of the production of eggs, and over one-half of pigs, poultry, wine grapes, fruits, and vegetables.[14]

The new economic mechanism has also contributed to the expansion of the ancillary activities of agricultural co-operatives that were discouraged prior to the 1968 reform.[15] The volume of output of these activities rose by 115 percent from 1970 to 1980, when they came to account for 35 percent of the total output of agricultural co-operatives; in the same period, the gross agricultural output of the co-operatives increased by 59 percent.

A study of 86 agricultural co-operatives further indicates that ancillary activities are more profitable than agricultural activities, with the average profit margin being 11.5 percent in the first case and 2.4 percent in the second in 1979. In the same year, these co-operatives derived over 90 percent of their profits from ancillary activities.[16] While the ratio is not representative of all agricultural co-operatives, since those in the sample had a higher share of ancillary activities than the average, it is noteworthy that in the 86 co-operatives output per asset value and output per worker were several times higher in ancillary activities (4.60 and 436 thousand forints) than in agricultural activities (0.55 and 157 thousand forints).

Ancillary activities provide for the needs of the co-operative itself and of other co-operatives, for which the large industrial firms are unable or unwilling to provide in sufficient quantities. They involve, in particular, the manufacture of simple agricultural implements, wood products, and construction materials, as well as local construction. Their activities further extend to agricultural processing and to the manufacture of parts and components for large industrial firms. The production of parts and components by agricultural co-operatives is a reflection of the excessive concentration of the Hungarian engineering industries, where the network of small and medium size firms producing parts and components exists only in a rudimentary form. In fact, the share of firms with over 1000 workers in the total employment of the engineering industries was 88 percent in Hungary, 66 percent in the Soviet Union, 38 percent in West Germany, and 28 percent in the United States.[17]

Industrial co-operatives play an increasing role in producing parts and components for large industrial firms in Hungary. They also manufacture a variety of products for consumption and even for export. An oft-cited example is the joint venture formed by Radelkisz of Budapest with Corning Glass of the United States for the production of blood analyzers.

In 1980, the industrial co-operatives employed 14 percent of the industrial labor force but had only 3 percent of the industrial capital stock, reflecting the fact that they largely produce labor-intensive items in response to consumer and export demand. And while these co-operatives are reported to have provided 6 percent of gross industrial output, with the low share of material inputs they accounted for a much higher proportion of value added.

Industrial co-operatives have the advantages of flexibility in deciding on their product composition, setting prices, and undertaking investment. Similar considerations apply to construction co-operatives that accounted for 22 percent of the labor force in the construction industry in 1980 but had a share in fixed assets of only one-third as much. And, again, the 17 percent reported production share may understate their contribution to construction activity.

The so-called 'second economy' possesses even greater flexibility than the co-operatives. As defined by Gábor and Galasi, it includes small-scale agricultural production, officially recognized and registered private non-agricultural activities, and not officially registered activities, generally on the part of those whose main occupation is in the large-scale socialist sector.[18]

According to a well-known Hungarian sociologist, 'the economic reason for the existence of the second economy is evident. The socially-organized production is not able to satisfy all the emerging needs in appropriate quantity and/or quality.'[19] At the same time, the existence of the second economy has been accepted as 'the integral part of the socialist economy'.[20]

It has been estimated that work performed on private agricultural plots is equivalent to 750–800 thousand man-years and that 250 thousand people have their main occupation in the private non-agricultural sector. Furthermore, private construction activity is said to involve the annual work time of 150–200 thousand people, and it is responsible for the building of one-half of all dwellings.[21]

Altogether 1.2 million man-years are expended in these branches of the second economy, compared to an economically active population of 5.2 million. The numbers do not include work done in the evening and during weekends as a part-time second job, although about one-third of building maintenance and two-thirds of television, automobile, and other repairs are said to be performed in the second economy.[22] Each of these activities involves about 100 thousand people.[23] According to one estimate, in 1979 hourly earnings in such activities were about five times higher than in the large-scale sector.[24]

It appears, then, that Hungary has established an economic system which combines the large-scale socialist sector, co-operatives, and small-scale private activities in a flexible manner. The success of this formula may explain the availability of a wide range of consumer goods and services that is unique in the CMEA area. New legal structures in effect from 1 January 1982 concerning the establishment of small and medium-size firms in the socialist sector, including subsidiary enterprises of existing firms, the creation of small co-operatives and smaller groupings in existing co-operatives, the founding of private partnerships, the leasing of equipment to private interests, and the liberalization of regulations affecting private artisans will further contribute to the expansion of the second economy.

CONCLUSIONS

This essay has received the economic reform measures applied in Hungary since 1 January 1968. The original reforms introduced on that date represented an important departure for a socialist economy, inasmuch as centralized physical planning was to be replaced by decentralized decision-making, involving the use of prices linked to world market price relations in the allocation process.

The implementation of the 1968 reform led to improvements in Hungary's economic performance. In turn, the partial recentralization of decision-making that occurred after 1972 had an unfavorable economic impact. Having recognized these adverse effects, the Hungarian authorities introduced new measures in 1980–81 that carried forward the original reform effort. Also, the operation of the agricultural, industrial, and construction co-operatives was liberalized and greater scope was given to private interests in the Hungarian economy.

NOTES

1. For source material used in Sections I to IV, the reader is referred to the following three articles by the author: 'The Economic Reform in Hungary', *Economica*, (1970) pp. 1–22; 'The Firm in the New Economic Mechanism in Hungary', in M. Bornstein (ed.), *Plan and Market* (New Haven, Conn.: Yale University Press, 1973) pp. 347–82; and 'The Economic Reform in Hungary, Ten Years After', *European Economic Review*, IX (1978) pp. 245–68; Reprinted in B. Balassa, *The Newly Industrializing Countries in the World Economy* (New York: Pergamon Press, 1981) pp. 329–46.
2. For a detailed description, see B. Balassa, *The Hungarian Experience in Economic Planning* (New Haven, Conn.: Yale University Press, 1959).
3. Unless otherwise noted, all data relating to the Hungarian economy originate from the *Statistical Yearbook* and the *Foreign Trade Statistical Yearbook*, both published by the Hungarian Statistical Office. The former publication is available in Hungarian and English; the latter in Hungarian only.
4. As noted below, agriculture provides an exception to this statement – an excellent discussion of the reform proposals and the surrounding controversy is provided by T. I. Berend, 'Gazdaságirányitási reformtervek 1956–57–ben' (Plans for Reforming Economic Management in 1956–57), *Valóság* (Reality), XXIV (12) (1981) pp. 1–2.
5. A system bearing a resemblance to the so-called TIP proposals by American economists.
6. B. Balassa, 'The Newly Industrializing Countries After the Oil Crisis', *Weltwirtschaftliches Archiv*, CXVII (1981) pp. 142–94. Reprinted in B. Balassa, *The Newly Industrializing Countries in the World Economy* (New York: Pergamon Press, 1981) pp. 29–81.
7. Trade with developed and developing countries, including Yugoslavia, as well as trade in convertible currencies with socialist countries, which latter amounted to above 15 percent of the total in recent years.
8. Balassa, 'The Newly Industrializing Countries After the Oil Crisis'.
9. J. Kornai, 'Resource-Contrained versus Demand-Constrained Systems', *Econometrica*, XLVIII (1979) pp. 801–19 and *Economics of Shortage*

(Amsterdam: North Holland, 1980) speaks of a 'soft budget constraint', under which the firm's activities are not limited either by its financial position or by the risk of bankruptcy.

10. For a detailed discussion, see B. Balassa, 'Reforming the New Economic Mechanism in Hungary', Essay 13 in this volume.

11. F. Biró *et al.* Merre tart a magyar mezögazdaság? (What are the Prospects for Hungarian Agriculture?), (Budapest: Kossuth Könyvkiadó, 1980).

12. N. Swain, 'The Evolution of Hungary's Agricultural System since 1967', in P. G. Hare, H. K. Radice and N. Swain (eds), *Hungary: A Decade of Economic Reform* (London: Allen & Unwin, 1981) pp. 225–51.

13. R. I. Gábor and P. Galasi, 'A második gazdaság' (The Second Economy), (Budapest: Közgazdasági es Jogi Könyvkiadó, 1981).

14. B. Pálovics 'Mezögazdasági termelésünk a hetvenes évtizedben' (Our Agricultural Production during the Seventies), *Közgazdasági Szemle* (Economic Review) XXVIII (1981) p. 428.

15. L. V. Nagy, 'A termelöszövetkezetek kiegészitö tevékenységének hatása a munkaerögazdálkodásra' (The Impact of the Ancillary Activities of the Co-operatives on the Management of Labor), *Közgazdasági Szemle* (Economic Review), XX (1973) pp. 1210–18.

16. F. Vida, 'Nyolcvanhat tsz melléktevékenysége' – A gazdálkodás stabilitását szolgálja' (The Activities of Eighty-six Co-operatives Serve the Interests of the Economy's Stability), *Figyelö* (Observer), 13 May 1981.

17. K. Bossányi, 'Elötérben a háttéripar' (Putting Forward the Background Industries), *Figyelö* (Observer), 20 June 1979.

18. Gábor and Galasi, pp. 17–18.

19. Z. Ferge, 'Keresetek, jövedelem, adózás (Revenues, Incomes and Taxation) *Valóság* (Reality), XXI (1978) p. 12.

20. O. Lukács, 'A kiegészitö gazdaság' (Supplementary Economy), *Figyelö* (Observer), 18 February 1981.

21. Gábor and Galasi, pp. 47–9.

22. Nor do the figures allow for the so-called 'third economy' that includes illegal and extralegal activities, such as the use for private profit of material or work-time of socialist firms; see O. Lukács, 'Kenni vagy nem kenni' (To Grease Their Palms), *Budapest*, I (1981) pp. 29–30.

23. Lukács, 'Kenni vagy nem kenni' (To Grease their Palms).

24. M. Marrese, 'The Evolution of Wage Regulation in Hungary', in P. G. Hare, H. K. Radice and N. Swain (eds) *Hungary: A Decade of Economic Reform* (London: Allen & Unwin, 1981) p. 58.

Essay 13 Reforming the New Economic Mechanism in Hungary

INTRODUCTION

On 1 January 1968, Hungary introduced the New Economic Mechanism (NEM), in order to respond to the needs of an increasingly sophisticated economy characterized by considerable reliance on foreign trade. The NEM aimed at replacing plan directives by market relations among firms; limiting the scope of central price determination; linking the domestic prices of exports and imports to world market prices; and decentralizing a major part of investment decisions.[1]

At the time of the NEM's introduction, a variety of 'brakes' were applied, in part to smooth the transition from the old to the new mechanism and in part as a compromise between the supporters of the two. While several of these brakes were eased in the next few years, steps towards recentralization were subsequently taken in the wake of the Party resolution of November 1972. Furthermore, policy responses to external shocks, in the form of the inflationary 1972–3 world boom, the 1974–5 world recession, and the deterioration of Hungary's terms of trade after 1973, led to reduced use of market mechanisms and to increased central directions and interventions.

These measures weakened the link between domestic and world market prices, reduced the scope of application of the profit motive, and increased the role of governmental preferences in investment decisions. They aggravated the problems resulting from the predominance of large firms, the maintenance of the supervisory organizations established during the period of central planning, and from the fact that the firms had little to fear from bankruptcy and could have recourse to the state in the event of financial difficulties.[2]

282

This situation could not fail to have adverse effects on the balance of payments and on the efficiency of resource use in Hungary. As these adverse effects came to be recognized, the October 1977 and the December 1978 Party resolutions called for re-establishing the original directions of the NEM. Newly adopted guidelines aimed at the transformation of the price structure so as to correspond to world market price relationships; the acceptance of profits reflecting performance at these prices as the sole success criterion for the firm; and reductions in the scope of government interventions in the firms' operations and in their investment decisions.

This essay will evaluate the reform measures taken in 1980 and in 1981[3] and will consider possible future changes. It will examine price setting (Section I), the exchange rate and protection (Section II), wage determination and personal incomes (Section III), investment decisions (Section IV), and the organizational structure (Section V).

I THE PRICE REFORM

The lynchpin of the 1980–81 reforms was the introduction of 'competitive' prices in much of the industrial sector. This involved equating the domestic prices of raw materials, fuels, and basic intermediate products to the tariff-inclusive import price in convertible currency trade; providing exporters with the FOB export price, supplemented by tax rebates; and setting prices for the domestic sales of the bulk of industrial products on the basis of profit margins, reflecting the domestic cost of earning foreign exchange in exports.

Equating the domestic prices of raw materials, fuels, and basic intermediate products to import prices paid in convertible currency trade involves the application of the marginal cost principle, with compensation by taxes and subsidies for the differences vis-à-vis the prices of imports from socialist countries. On 1 January 1980, the average prices of raw materials and basic intermediate products were raised by 30 percent while energy prices were increased by 57 percent.[4]

Following these adjustments, the domestic prices of raw materials and basic intermediates were free to vary with the changes in prices paid in convertible currencies and in the exchange rate, while energy prices were fixed centrally and modified intermittently in response to changes in world market prices.

Industrial exporters received the price obtained in convertible currencies, times the exchange rate, plus a rebate for imputed indirect taxes that was set at 10 percent of export value (except for light industrial products, originally 16 percent, but subsequently reduced to 13 percent, and for iron and steel, originally nil, but subsequently set at 5 percent). Exceptions were made, however, in cases when the domestic cost of earning foreign exchange exceeded the sum of the exchange rate and the tax rebate. In such instances, compensation continued to be provided for a period of five years on a decreasing scale. Also, production taxes for individual firms were abolished and while firms continued to receive budget support, this was done on a temporary basis.[5]

As of 1 January 1980, firms that exported more than 5 percent of their output in convertible currency trade were required to set the prices of their domestic products, adding to the cost of production an allowed profit margin established on the basis of the domestic cost of earning foreign exchange in exports. Where the domestic cost ratio equaled the exchange rate adjusted by the 10 percent tax rebate, firms could apply a profit margin of 6 percent, on the sum of their fixed capital and the wage bill; the allowed profit margin rose to 12 percent for firms that had a domestic cost ratio one-fourth lower than the exchange rate; and it declined to nil in the case of firms that earned foreign exchange through exports at a cost one-third higher than the exchange rate.[6]

Firms were not allowed to subsequently raise their average domestic prices to an extent greater than the increase in their average export prices; they were obligated to reduce domestic prices if export prices declined, with changes in the profitability of exports providing a further constraint to price setting. Finally, firms that exported less than 5 percent of their output but manufactured products similar to those produced by firms having an export share in excess of 5 percent were to follow the price-setting procedures applied by the latter.

The rules for competitive pricing found application in about two-thirds of Hungarian industry, with the share varying between 75–80 percent in machine building, 50 percent in the chemical industry, and 15–20 percent in food processing. In turn, firms in the so-called noncompeting sphere were allowed to calculate with a profit margin of 6 percent in setting their domestic prices as of 1 January 1980, with subsequent changes in prices determined by changes in costs.

The regulations introduced on 1 January 1980 provided incentives to firms to raise their export prices, since they could then increase their domestic prices accordingly. However, the regulations discouraged the expansion of export volume in cases when this would have involved lower than average export prices and/or export profitability. Moreover, inducements were provided to reduce the volume of exports when this permitted raising domestic prices.

In fact, the current price value of manufactured exports (excluding processed food) in convertible currency trade increased by only 1 percent in 1980 in terms of forints, representing a decline of 2 percent in volume terms.[7] This followed increases of 29 percent in value terms and 17 percent in volume terms in 1979. It contrasted with trends in processed-food exports, which were not subject to the same regulations and experienced an export increase of 13 percent in value and 9 percent in volume in 1980, nearly matching the results for 1979.

Within the manufacturing sector, the exports of steel, transport equipment, and clothing declined in current price terms as well, while machinery exports fell in volume terms; among major product groups, only chemicals experienced an increase in export volume in 1980. These results cannot be explained by the pressure of domestic demand since the domestic sales of industrial products declined by 1.5 percent in 1980. Nor do unfavorable business conditions in Western Europe provide an adequate explanation, the principal exception being steel. In fact, the volume of manufactured exports from developing countries to the OECD increased by approximately 10 percent in 1980, following a rise of 15 percent in 1979.

A survey of 38 firms, representing 80 percent of manufactured exports in convertible-currency trade,[8] and an investigation of the structure of machinery exports,[9] show that the expansion of exports was positively correlated with profits made in exporting. And while this involved in part reducing exports that were not socially profitable, both authors report that socially profitable exports, too, were foregone. Such is also the conclusion of a paper provocatively entitled: 'The Firm's Export Dilemma: Only the Best – or the Good as Well'.[10]

The observed adverse consequences led to changes in the regulations in 1981. As the changes did not have the desired effects, further modifications were made as of January 1982. If a firm is able to earn foreign exchange in convertible currency trade at less than the official exchange rate, while raising its exports by a predetermined percentage,[11] it does not have to lower domestic prices even if its average export prices or export profitability decline. Also, firms have to report increases in their domestic prices to the Material and Price Bureau in cases when their exports decline in terms of forints.

Changes in the regulations can only alleviate, but not eliminate, the adverse effects of incentives on export volume. Fluctuations in export prices and in the profitability of exports due to events outside the firms' control also tend to discourage exports and may induce firms to reduce their exports below the 5 percent limit that triggers the application of competitive pricing rules. In general, firms may be inclined to play it safe, avoiding risky exports and the introduction of new export products or entry into new markets where initial costs are high and/or price concessions need to be made to obtain a foothold.

Apart from variations in prices expressed in terms of foreign currency, fluctuations in export prices may result from changes in exchange rates among convertible currencies, exemplified by the gyrations of the dollar-mark relationship in recent years. Fluctuations in the foreign currency prices of industrial materials also lead to variations in the profitability of exports. While firms may establish reserves in the event of variations in export and import prices, this has in practice proved insufficient to cope with the actual magnitude of price fluctuations.[12]

The above considerations have led some observers to suggest replacing export-oriented pricing by import-oriented pricing, with domestic prices equated to the tariff-inclusive import price. This price presently represents a ceiling for domestically sold products, but a survey has shown that firms often do not know the relevant import price.[13] And while import prices are easily ascertainable in the case of raw materials, fuels, and basic intermediate products, which are standardized commodities, price comparisons encounter considerable difficulties in the case of differentiated products, owing to differences in product specifications and quality. Quality differences are of particular importance since the products Hungary does not export tend to be lower in quality. In the absence of import competition, then, import-oriented pricing would not have the desired effects.[14]

The question remains as to how existing regulations could be modified in order to provide incentives for efficient export expansion in the present situation, when the conditions of import competition have not been established. As far as new export products and export markets are concerned, this could be done by excluding them from the calculations for an initial period of, say, two years. For the remaining products two-year averages could be used in the place of annual data, or alternatively, firms could be allowed to establish a reserve to even out fluctuations in profits.[15]

It would further be desirable to adopt a single criterion of price setting for domestic sales in the place of the double criterion based on changes in the prices and in the profitability of exports. The price criterion has the disadvantage that it disregards differential changes in input prices between products destined for export and for domestic sales. Reliance placed on the profit motive under decentralized decision-making also favors the use of the profit criterion. But this should be defined in terms of profit rates rather than the margin of profit on the sum of fixed capital and wages, which has no economic significance and conflicts with the use of the rate of profit on invested capital in making decisions on new investments.[16]

Apart from contributing to increased exports and improved efficiency, the proposed changes would lessen the possibility of intervention on the part of the authorities in price setting. This possibility has been acknowledged by László Rácz, Department Director at the Material and Price Bureau, according to whom 'the firm will not have an interest in practicing a low price domestically when it can obtain a high price abroad, or vice versa. If it does so, it would not any more belong to the group of well-regarded firms and would lose all the advantages this entails.'[17] Apart from the ambiguity of the reference to the advantages 'well-regarded' firms enjoy, the statement does not appear to recognize the need for lowering domestic prices in the event of excess supply. In turn, in the more frequent case in Hungary that sufficient quantities are not available at the 'constructed' prices, imports should be permitted.

More generally, adjustments in prices or in import quantities would need to be made whenever domestic supply and demand are not equated at the constructed prices. The lack of market equilibrium, then, adds to the difficulties associated with constructed prices. Thus, while the new price regulations represent a step towards aligning producer prices in the manufacturing sector to world market prices, full alignment would require the freeing of imports. Although this could not be done overnight, steps would need to be taken to gradually free imports, with first priority given to raw materials, intermediate products and machinery.

The liberalization of imports would also encourage efficient import substitution. This is apparent in the case of industrial materials where alignment to world market prices has led to efforts to save on imported materials and to make increased use of substitutes. At the same time, as noted in Section II below, there is need to reduce import protection so as to lessen discrimination against exports.

Consideration should finally be given to the relationship of consumer and producer prices. Disparities in the structure of consumer prices and producer prices were reduced through decreases in subsidies and the imposition of turnover taxes in 1979 and 1980. But tax rates vary among commodities, with higher taxes applying to products the consumption of which is to be discouraged (e.g. tobacco and alcoholic beverages), and tax exemptions (e.g. children's clothing and construction materials) or subsidies (e.g. certain drugs and services) provided for social reasons. The subsidies are especially large for services, including housing, heating materials, and public utilities.

Consumption subsidies continue to be applied to major agricultural staples where producer prices are determined on the basis of production costs, with certain adjustments made according to world market price relations. Also, processed agricultural exports receive higher tax rebates (28 percent) than manufactured exports.

It would appear then that, notwithstanding recent changes, the system of consumer prices in effect does not ensure the satisfaction of consumer needs at least cost to the national economy; also, consumer prices lack sufficient flexibility to transmit changes in demand to the producer.[18] Consumption subsidies are largest for heating materials (73 percent) and public utilities (41 percent) while, apart from taxes on luxuries and semiluxuries, the highest taxes (19 percent) apply to clothing.[19] At the same time, free price formation occurs in only 50 percent of retail trade, albeit representing an increase from a share of 37 percent in 1978.[20] It would be desirable to further reduce differences between producer and consumer prices, while ensuring the flexibility of the latter, more rapidly than is now foreseen.[21]

II THE EXCHANGE RATE AND PROTECTION

Prior to and immediately after the introduction of the NEM, there was a debate about whether the commercial exchange rate (then called 'the foreign-exchange conversion ratio') should be equated to the average cost or to the marginal cost of exports, which was defined as the domestic cost of earning foreign exchange in 10–15 percent of the highest cost exports. In the end, the average cost principle was applied, necessitating the subsidization of about four-fifths of exports.[22]

Data exist for the period 1970–80 on export prices in convertible currency trade for Hungary that are comparable to export price data for other countries. The calculations show that changes in export prices in Hungary relative to its major trade partners exactly matched the appreciation of the exchange rate from 60 forints to the US dollar in 1970 to an average of 32.5 forints to the dollar in 1980, thus maintaining the exchange rate constant in real terms.[23] And while the introduction of indirect tax rebates in 1980 benefited exports, a substantial part of exports in convertible currency trade continue to require compensation payments.

At the same time, the focus of the debate has shifted, with the holders of opposing views suggesting that the exchange rate be used to combat imported inflation or that its main function be to equilibrate the balance of payments. The first view, prominently held by János Fekete, First Deputy President of the National Bank,[24] is based on the relative version of the purchasing power parity doctrine[25] and it assumes low import and export elasticities.[26] This view received support from Marer,[27] according to whom 'the elasticity conditions were unlikely to be satisfied for a devaluation to improve the BOP in Hungary. However, the empirical basis for this conclusion is weak.

It has been suggested that the import demand elasticity is low because Hungary's convertible currency imports consist mainly of material inputs that have no domestic substitutes. Yet, 15 percent of imports in convertible currency trade are producer goods, 6 percent industrial consumer goods, and 13 percent foodstuffs. Also, the estimates have been derived by the use of least-squares techniques that are known to have a downward bias. Finally, the low elasticity of import demand in the past may have reflected the large profits made in using imported inputs, the prices of which were kept artificially low,[28] as well as the fact that the profit incentives were blunted by the pervasiveness of taxes and subsidies in the second half of the seventies. In fact, there is evidence that firms have attempted to reduce their demand for imported raw materials in response to the rise of their prices and the increased importance of the profit incentives after 1 January 1980, and that consumers have economized with energy as increases in world market prices have been partially transmitted to the consumption sphere.[29]

In turn, in a simultaneous equation analysis of Hungarian exports to West Germany – its largest trading partner among capitalist countries – statistically significant results with the correct sign have been obtained for the supply of exports in regard to about one third of the products, with the elasticities clustering around two.[30] This has been the case in particular for products where *a priori* considerations indicate that profit-maximizing behavior predominated. After 1980–81, such behavior is expected to be the general rule, and the positive correlation between export expansion and the profitability of exports, noted above, points to the responsiveness of export supply.

At the same time, the system of incentives introduced in January

1980 puts a premium on setting a realistic exchange rate in Hungary. Failing this, the firms will be discouraged from undertaking exports that are produced at a domestic cost that exceeds the actual exchange rate but falls short of the equilibrium rate. The latter is defined as the rate that would keep the balance of payments in equilibrium without the application of export subsidies and with foreign borrowing not exceeding desirable levels.

Under the reforms introduced in January 1980, compensation payments to industrial exports would be phased out within five years. The elimination of these payments would require devaluing the exchange rate in real terms, i.e. after adjustment for changes in relative prices, since otherwise, unacceptable balance-of-payments deficits would occur.[31] Changes in real exchange rates spread over a five-year-period would also permit the expansion of exports through increases in capacity, thereby raising the elasticity of export supply.

It should not be assumed, however, that the equilibrium exchange rate would exceed the average exchange rate for all exports, when the exchange rate for individual activities is defined as the sum of the official exchange rate and the rate of export compensation. Rather, the opposite is likely to be the case as the same export total will require fewer domestic resources.

With the devaluation of the real exchange rate, import protection rates would need to be lowered, lest the bias against exports increases. In fact, it would be desirable to reduce the existing bias against exports, as the transfer of resources from higher-cost import substitution to lower-cost exports would improve the efficiency of the allocation of existing resources and contribute to the use of incremental resources in activities that have relatively low domestic costs per unit of foreign exchange earned or saved.

Tariffs averaged 24 percent in Hungary, with further import charges of 4 percent. While tariff rates are scheduled to be lowered under obligations assumed in GATT, it would be desirable to liberalize import licensing that has led to investments in the manufacture of products that cannot compete abroad, either because of high cost or low quality. Examples are the production of cleaning materials, the manufacture of gearshifts, and the making of automobile windshields.[32]

It would also be desirable to modify existing regulations that allow the same profit margin for firms in the non-competing sphere as for firms that export at the existing exchange rate adjusted for the tax rebate. The absence of exports in convertible currency trade can be taken as *prima facie* evidence of the lack of competitiveness of firms in the non-competing sphere. An additional consideration is that these firms can raise their profits above the allowed margin more easily than firms that are subject to the discipline of the world market. This has in fact been the case following the January 1980 price reform, when non-competing firms increased their profits substantially more than firms that competed abroad.[33]

The decline in the average export exchange rate would have an anti-inflationary effect. The price of products subject to import protection would also decline following the liberalization of imports. And while these changes would be more than offset by increases in the domestic prices of imported materials that are subject to low tariffs, the resulting average increase should be manageable within the limits of the 4–5 percent annual rate of inflation foreseen for the period of the sixth five-year plan as long as continued adjustments are made in the exchange rate to offset higher inflation abroad.

In 1968, the commercial exchange rate exceeded the tourist exchange rate by 100 percent. This difference was reduced over time, contributing to improvements in resource allocation. The unification of the two rates in mid-1981, however, has involved an economic cost. This is because tourism is effectively subsidized in Hungary through artificially low consumer prices, thereby raising the domestic cost of earning foreign exchange in this activity.

It may be added that while the unification of exchange rates for merchandise exports has been objected to on the grounds of the allegedly low elasticity of export supply, the limitations of tourist facilities – in particular, hotels – have apparently been neglected in unifying the commercial and the tourist exchange rates. The result has been unsatisfied demand, coupled with the effective subsidization of those tourists who have been able to obtain hotel accommodation.

The unification of the commercial and tourist exchange rates has, however, been seen as a step towards convertibility and membership in the International Monetary Fund. Under the IMF definition, convertibility requires that there be no restrictions on the use of currency balances acquired by non-residents for current-account transactions (external convertibility). This means financial convertibility (the conversion of forint balances into another currency) as well as commodity convertibility (the use of forint balances to purchase Hungarian goods and services). Both of these forms of convertibility could be established under present regulations once foreigners are empowered to hold balances in forints.

In fact, apart from conforming to the IMF conditions of external convertibility, the principal purpose of the unification of exchange rates appears to have been to induce foreigners to hold forint balances, thereby increasing the availability of foreign exchange to Hungary. The question is, however, at what rate of interest the holding of forint balances would be sufficiently attractive to foreigners, taking account of the exchange rate risk. It may in fact be cheaper for the National Bank to offer deposits denominated in terms of foreign currencies that would not be subject to the exchange rate risk in forints, especially since foreigners may not anticipate the continuation of the policy of currency appreciation to offset inflationary developments abroad.

Marer nevertheless suggests that the adoption of external convertibility would be beneficial to Hungarian firms: 'If the forint had external convertibility, commercial contracts could be concluded and payments made in forints, eliminating the ER [exchange rate] risk for Hungarian enterprises.'[34] But this may well be a will-o'-the-wisp, since small countries generally denominate their foreign exchange transactions in US dollars or in the currency of a large trading partner. It is difficult to see that foreigners would be willing to denominate their exports in forints, and Hungarian firms may not wish to weaken their competitive position by denominating their exports in forints.

III WAGE DETERMINATION AND PERSONAL INCOMES

In the years immediately following the introduction of the NEM, the regulation of wages generally took the form of limiting increases in average wages at the firm level. It soon became apparent, however, that this so-called relative wage-level regulation was not conducive to raising productivity through reductions in the labor force of the firm, improved work performance, or upgrading of the labor force. Rather, an incentive was provided to reduce average wages through the hiring of low-wage labor. These factors, in turn, contributed to a slowdown of labor productivity growth in Hungarian industry.[35]

To correct these shortcomings, wage regulations were modified in subsequent years. In sectors where relative wage-level regulation was maintained, allowable increases in average wages were tied to the growth of the sum of wages and profits per worker; in a number of sectors increases in the wage bill were regulated on the basis of changes in value added (relative-wage-bill regulation) with additional limitations imposed on the extent of increases in average wages, however; and in several sectors increases in the wage level or in the wage bill were centrally determined. By 1978, the percentage distribution of workers among the four types of wage regulations was as follows: relative wage bill, 55 percent; relative wage level, 14 percent; central wage bill, 15 percent; and central wage level, 15 percent.[36]

Under both the relative wage-level and the relative wage-bill regulations, increases in average wages in excess of 6 percent a year were made subject to a progressive tax at rates starting at 150 percent. In the large majority of cases, the rise of average wages reached or approached the 6 percent limit; but few firms raised average wages by more than 6 percent to avoid the 150 percent tax.

The increased use made of wage-bill regulations apparently contributed to saving manpower[37] and labor productivity increased on the national economy level. However, this mode of regulation is also subject to the shortcomings associated with the application of the basis principle, under which changes in particular indicators compared to base-period trigger wage increases.

Thus, firms already operating at high levels of efficiency were unable to substantially raise wages because they had few possibilities for productivity increases, whereas firms having such possibilities were motivated to utilize these opportunities slowly so as to avoid 'bumping' against the ceiling. At the same time, the imposition of a ceiling for increases in average wages penalized firms that experienced fluctuations in profits due, for example, to changing world market conditions. This was the case even though the regulations permitted setting aside wage reserves, because of the uncertainty associated with the utilization of these reserves; thus, the reserves accumulated in 1977 and 1978 were eliminated in 1979.

The elimination of wage reserves in 1979 may have responded to the situation existing at the time, as improvements in measured performance much depended on the ability of the firm to negotiate its prices, taxes and subsidies with the supervising authorities. The price reforms introduced in 1980–1 have reduced the scope of discretionary measures, but only few changes have been made in the system of wage determination.

The scope of wage-bill regulations has been extended to a larger number of sectors and the limit for tax-free increases in average wages has been raised to 9 percent (12 percent after 1 January 1982), with a 150 percent tax rate applying above this limit. The tax rate rises up to 800 percent, with the size of the increment depending on the ratio of profits to the sum of fixed capital and wages. Finally, wage preferences have been introduced to the benefit of firms whose actions, aimed at pursuing long-term objectives, have entailed temporary reductions in profits or whose special circumstances have led to deterioration of performance.

Apart from the introduction of wage preferences, the changes in the system of wage determination have not affected the application of the basis principle. At the same time, the system applied is rather complicated and involves discretionary action on the part of the supervising authorities in applying wage preferences. It also discourages structural changes in the firm if these would involve increased labor intensity, even though such changes may be in the national interest as in the case where they are conducive to an increase in exports in convertible currency trade. Reliance on value added as a performance criterion in wage setting represents an additional shortcoming of relative wage-bill regulation.

Lajos Faluvégi, Deputy Prime Minister and President of the National Planning Office, has stated the need for an overhaul of the system of wage determination while adding that this could not be accomplished overnight, lest disruptions occur in the national economy.[38] In recent years, various proposals have been made to reform the system of wage determination in Hungary. They include further increasing the scope of wage-bill regulations;[39] taxing wages above a certain level and applying lower taxes to increments in profits than to the base-period profit;[40] and regulating wage increases centrally, with a small additional distribution made from profits.[41] Instead of providing a detailed evaluation of these proposals, recommendations will be made below for establishing a new system of wage regulations that would conform to the principles underlying the 1980–1 price reforms.

In accordance with the 1980–1 price reforms, emphasis should be placed on the profitability of the firm rather than on changes in profits, or, for that matter, changes in value added. At the same time, it should be recognized that, through decisions made on product composition, market orientation, and investments, it is the management rather than individual workers who are responsible for the profitability of the firm. This conclusion has implications for the remuneration of both management and workers.

To encourage the profitable operation of the firm, the financial interest of management in profitability would need to be increased. This would require establishing a stronger link between the remuneration of management and the firm's profits and phasing out bonuses based on the evaluation of the management by the supervising authorities that introduce subjective elements and reduce the managers' independence.

Increasing the financial interest of management in the profitability of the firm would also provide the basis for realistic wage setting. While, for reasons noted above, linking wage increases to increases in profits is not warranted, the profits of the firm could be increased if wages were linked to the productivity of the worker.

If wages were based on labor productivity and labor were mobile among competitive industries, efficiency wages would tend towards equalization across industries and firms. Such is not the case under the existing system of wage regulations, thereby creating inequities among workers performing equivalent tasks. At the same time, for labor migration to equalize efficiency wages, it would be necessary to establish competitive conditions and to eliminate the present excess demand for labor that creates pressures for wage increases. Measures that may be taken to pursue these objectives will be considered in Section V below.

The necessary conditions could not be established overnight, however, hence there would be a need for transitional measures. These could take the form of extending the scope of productivity-based wage determination, with wage increases being constrained by the profitability of the firm rather than by changes in value added or in profits.[42]

IV INVESTMENT DECISIONS

Firms can finance investments from their own resources, including after-tax profits and 60 percent of depreciation allowances, from credits, and from government budget support. While at the time of the introduction of the NEM it was assumed that the importance of budget grants would decline over time, the opposite occurred and in 1976 budget support was provided for the financing of 61 percent of investments undertaken by industrial firms. The corresponding percentage for bank credit was 75 percent, with three-fifths of the credits given to firms that also received budget support. Correspondingly, only one-tenth of industrial investments were carried out from the firms' own financial resources alone.[43]

Bank credits were often made on the condition of availability of budget support which, in turn, was increasingly made available in accordance with state preferences. There were 60 classes of preferences that were formulated in most part in physical terms[44] and practically excluded the possibility of competition for state funds. At the same time, competition for bank credit was reduced by reason of the existence of 29 classes of credit preferences.[45] Yet, the sharing of responsibility for the investment decision was not conducive to efficiency and it provided firms with the opportunity to request government aid in the event that the investment proved to be unprofitable.[46]

For the future, an important question relates to the extent which investment by the firm will be self-financed or centrally financed. In recent years, recommendations were made to limit the extent of self-financing and the 1980–1 price reforms envisaged substantial reductions in profit margins.[47] In this connection, reference was made to the need to avoid the expansion of firms that have low social profitability and to moderate investment demand in general.

As long as the firms' profits were much influenced by selective taxes and subsidies, and hence did not appropriately reflect social profitability, there may have been cause for criticizing the financing of their expansion from profits. However, the role of selective taxes and subsidies has been reduced under the 1980–1 reforms, which aim at aligning domestic prices to world-market prices. As a result, the firms' profits will better correspond to social profitability and will show greater differentiation than in the past. High profits will be made by efficient firms whose expansion is desirable from the economic point of view while the low profits of inefficient firms will not permit their expansion.

These considerations indicate the desirability of reducing central financing of investments under the conditions created by the 1980–81 reform. An additional consideration is that large reductions in profit rates would make it difficult for firms to repay credits they obtained at the time when higher profit margins were allowed.[48] This is the case especially since actual profits are overstated by the use of historical depreciation and FIFO (first-in-first-out) accounting of inventories.

Central financing of investments also limits the responsibility of the firm for its own investments and increases the chances of central interventions. Such intervention often led to uneconomic investments in the past and reportedly lowered the average profitability of industrial investments.[49]

It would further be desirable to ensure transfer of funds from firms with low, to those with high profitability. This objective would be served through establishment of appropriate financial institutions: separating central-bank and commercial-bank functions, extending the range of operations of existing banks, establishing new banks, and creating conditions of competition among banks.

Competition and application of the profit principle to the banks would make them interested in attracting deposits from individuals as well as from firms and in providing self-liquidating loans. There would also be need to utilize additional financial instruments such as bonds and to ensure participation of individuals in the financing of co-operatives.

Transformation of the banking system would represent a further step in the implementation of the 1980–1 reforms, which are intended to limit the application of credit preferences and to give greater role to economic considerations in granting credits. The new regulations establish a minimum profitability level of 14 percent for most industrial borrowers, 10 percent for production of industrial and construction materials, food processing, mining, internal trade, transportation, and communication, and 8 percent for agriculture and services.

At the same time, preferential credits for exports in convertible currencies will continue, and their share in total credit allocation during the sixth five-year plan is expected to increase.[50] One third of the interest on export credits is repaid by the National Bank if the credit conditions, generally requiring net foreign exchange earnings to total the amount of the loan in the first three years, are met. In turn, one fourth of the interest is repaid on loans for import substitution as well as on loans that lead to energy savings equal to the amount of investment over a five-year period.

Granting preferential credits to exports in convertible currencies is warranted because of continued discrimination against these exports in the incentive system and the risk they involve. Questions arise, however, about the desirability of introducing preferential credits for import substitution. Such credits should be subject to the condition that they finance the manufacture of internationally competitive products. As in the absence of import liberalization the only way to judge competitiveness is that exports actually take place, the application of this principle would necessitate financing manufacturing facilities that simultaneously provide for exports and for domestic markets, thereby ensuring efficient import substitution.

Interest rates on credits granted before and after 1 September 1981 are 8–9 percent, and 9–10 percent, respectively, on investment credits, and 10 and 11 percent on credits for variable capital. In conjunction with increased profit margins, these rates would need to be raised to market-clearing levels. Higher interest rates would also encourage the inter-firm transfer of funds as well as private savings.

The 1980–1 reforms have also brought improvements in regard to regulations on budget support for investment. Such support will be provided only in cases when the firms' profitability is adversely affected by centrally imposed deviations from world market prices and the choice among claimants will be made on the basis of profitability at undistorted prices. It will be given in the form of a loan, repayable in ten years. The same procedure will be applied in cases where large investments are financed from the budget.

The government may also make contributions to the capital of individual firms whose profitability exceeds the limit set for bank credits. Contributions will be made on the basis of competitive bidding, with firms paying a 15 percent interest from their pre-tax revenue over a period of ten years.

Finally, the government plans to limit its actions aimed at altering the industrial structure. According to István Hetényi, the Minister of Finance, 'the sectoral and subsectoral structure of our industry is much nearer to the international level than the competitiveness of our firms. Correspondingly, adaptation to market possibilities and improvements in productivity are the principal objectives and the introduction of sectoral priorities will be warranted in exceptional cases only'.[51] There will be no new programs for large industrial complexes during the period of the sixth five-year plan and outside basic industry only two priority sectors have been identified, pharmaceutical products and selected electronics products; in both cases, the government will finance basic research that may be warranted on external economies grounds. Assistance will further be given to investments aimed at effecting savings in materials and in energy, and funds will be provided for the development of the production of parts and components.[52]

These guidelines represent a welcome change from the previous two five-year plans when changes in the industrial structure were to a considerable extent centrally determined, involving investments in several large complexes some of which (e.g. petrochemicals) were highly capital- and energy-intensive. Nevertheless, a concern has been voiced that the volume of state-financed investments, including the considerable investments begun during the previous plan period, will be too large to allow for a sufficient amount of investment by individual firms within the constraint imposed on total investment.[53]

V ORGANIZATIONAL STRUCTURE

Industry in Hungary is highly concentrated by the standards of capitalist as well as socialist countries.[54] The extent of concentration observed today is largely the result of the mergers of independent firms during three separate periods – the late 1940s and the early 1950s; the first half of the 1970s; and between 1972 and 1979.

The concentration movement was particularly strong in the first half of the sixties, increasing the share of industrial firms employing more than 1000 workers from 14.7 percent in 1960 to 35.4 percent in 1970. After a temporary reversal following the introduction firms of the NEM, this process continued following the Party resolution of November 1972. By 1979, the share of firms employing more than 1000 workers reached 44.8 percent while that of firms with less than 100 workers fell to 7.1 percent from 10.7 percent in 1970. The corresponding ratios in Western Europe and Japan are 30–40 percent and 20–30 percent, respectively.

The process of industrial concentration involved reducing the number of firms from 1368 in 1960 to 812 in 1970 and to 702 in 1979; by comparison there are 6830 industrial firms in Austria. The extent of concentration is even greater if allowance is made for the fact that nearly one half of Hungarian industrial firms are organized into trusts. If the 24 trusts and the 364 independent firms were considered to be separate decision-making units, then in 1977, 12 such units accounted for 40 percent of fixed capital and 8 of them received 50 percent of total government subsidies to Hungarian industry.[55] At the same time, trusts and most large independent firms were characterized by horizontal integration; they consisted of a number of plants – often relatively small – producing identical or similar products. This may explain that in a variety of industries plants were not of efficient size.[56]

Also, Hungarian industry was oriented towards the production of final goods to the neglect of what has been called 'background industries', consisting of small- and medium-size firms producing parts, components, and accessories.[57] Yet, in modern industry, and in particular in the manufacture of machinery and transport equipment, specialization on an efficient scale requires a network of subcontractors that produce these inputs to precision.

In the United States, General Motors provides an example in having several thousand subcontractors. And specialization increasingly cuts across national borders, leading to the international division of manufacturing activities. Countries where skilled and unskilled labor is available at a relatively low cost play an important role in this process by producing parts, components, and accessories for assembly elsewhere.[58]

On the basis of availability and cost of skilled and semiskilled labor, Hungary is well-placed to produce parts, components, and accessories for export. Yet, these products equalled only 22 percent of the exports of machinery and equipment in convertible currency trade in 1980 while they constituted 72 percent of the corresponding imports. In fact, the lack of domestic availability of adequate parts, components, and accessories made rapid growth of their imports necessary. This was the case, in particular, for the protection of machinery and transport equipment exported in convertible-currency trade.[59]

The lack of an adequate network of subcontractors led to backward integration, with firms engaged in the production of the final product also manufacturing their own parts, components and accessories, thereby incurring excess costs. The same applies to service inputs, such as preparation of production designs.[60]

It appears then, that the Hungarian industrial structure combined the disadvantages of small numbers, thus limiting competition; the existence of relatively small plants producing identical or similar final commodities, thus foregoing economies of scale; and the lack of adequate specialization, thus leading to inadequate and high-cost production of parts, components, and accessories, and failing to exploit Hungary's comparative advantages in these products. The 1980–1 reforms have introduced several measures aimed at improving the situation.

To begin with, 137 new firms have been created by breaking up horizontal trusts and large firms. Besides increasing competition, this is expected to reduce the need for an administrative bureaucracy and to simplify the decision-making process. The newly established firms will be responsible for their own performance, in contrast with the past when incentives for improvements on the plant level were rarely provided.

While the reorganization has not been without difficulties, the findings of a survey covering over one half of the newly established firms have shown the beneficial effects of independence through modernization of product structure, technological development, and market research, as well as through revision of investment plans in favor of less costly alternatives. In fact, the officials of the firms have stated that 'considerable energies have been freed because of the fact that they can directly experience the impact of the market, that they have come under the pressure of the economic climate, and that they have to bear the consequences of their own actions'.[61]

The sixth five-year plan is expected to promote development of the production of parts and components. This reportedly involves almost exclusively large firms that would receive financial benefits in exchange for agreeing to manufacture some of the two dozen products included in the plan.[62] However, the number of products involved is small and their choice has apparently not been made on the basis of social profitability calculations. At the same time, in selecting chiefly large firms, the advantages of flexibility that small- and medium-size firms possess may be foregone. Furthermore, apart from 'hardware', there is need to increase the availability of 'software' in the form of technical marketing and other services. Finally, export possibilities need to be considered since the limited domestic market often does not allow for the production of parts and components on an efficient scale.

These needs will be served by the practical implementation of the measures in effect since 1 January 1982, that provide for the establishment of new small- and medium-size producers and the expansion of existing ones. By easing the limitations imposed on their operations, the new regulations improve conditions for the development of co-operatives and private producers who in recent years have increasingly contributed to the availability of parts and components. They promote more flexible forms for small- and medium-size activities – public, co-operative, and private – in agriculture, industry, and services.

Private artisans can now operate in the entire industrial sector. They may hire up to three workers and employ six family members. They may also let out piecework up to one half of their production value and may establish partnerships in which the total number of workers can reach 30.

Existing co-operatives may set up specialized subgroups to carry out production and service activities on their own account but in the name of the co-operative as well as special units that pay a fixed fee to the co-operative based on estimated revenue and costs. Furthermore, individuals may set up small co-operatives, subject to simplified regulations, with up to 100 members, who share in the income on the basis of their labor as well as their capital contribution.

State firms may enter into contractual relationships with an entrepreneur who manages on his own account, for payment of a fee, a unit of the firm employing no more than 15 workers. Also, individuals may establish partnerships, provided that their main occupation is in a state firm or co-operative.

State firms and public agencies may under simplified regulations establish small firms. A state firm, individually or jointly with other state firms, may establish subsidiaries which may engage in a variety of activities, including foreign trade. Existing firms may diversify their activities, entering into new areas for domestic sales and exports.

In exporting machinery, and increasingly other commodities, producers may now choose among trading firms. This creates conditions of competition among trading firms, and it is linked to greater freedom of the producing firm to choose its own sphere of operation. At the same time, increasing numbers of firms and co-operatives, actually about 120, have been given the right to export directly to capitalist countries; some 90 foreign-trade partnerships have been established with the participation of trading firms and of altogether 170 producing enterprises.

Another important organizational change has been the consolidation of the three industrial ministries into a single ministry, involving a reduction of the total number of employees by about one half. With the transfer of responsibilities concerning price setting and material allocation to the Material and Price Bureau, and the lack of sectoral departments in the new ministry, the opportunities for intervening in day-to-day affairs of the firms have been much reduced.

The possibilities for intervention by the supervising authorities could be reduced further by separating the functions of the state as the source of regulations and as the owner of the means of production.[63] This purpose could be served by establishing independent boards for each individual firm, with responsibility for hiring (and firing) its managers, for overall supervision of its decisions on major changes in the range of its activities and, if necessary, for ending its operations. The initial members of the board could be appointed by the Council of Ministers for fixed terms while co-optation could provide an appropriate procedure to replace those whose terms have expired. The members of the board could include the representatives of the firm's management and workers, with further representation from government, banks, Chamber of Commerce, and independent experts.[64]

In recent years, consideration has been given to the need to weed out firms that are not economically viable. Earlier, this was practically impossible as the government rescued failing firms by providing additional capital, subsidies, or permission to raise prices. At the same time, such rescue efforts often proved to be temporary, necessitating another rescue operation soon afterwards.[65]

Bankruptcy proceedings could be initiated in cases when the price does not cover variable costs while restructuring could provide a solution in cases when firms are profitable in the short run but cannot recover capital costs. The latter could involve closing down some units, or financial restructuring that could be handled by banks on the basis of profitability considerations; i.e. loans provided would have to be repaid from future profits.

The possible need to close down firms, or some of their units, and the implications for the reallocation of labor, are now apparently accepted in Hungary. Thus, János Kádár, the General Secretary of the Hungarian Socialist Workers' Party is quoted to have said that 'the development and expansion of economical production, the contraction and finally cessation of uneconomical production, require the appropriate regrouping of labor'.[66] Introduction of this possibility would induce firms to be more selective in their investments and to limit wage increases.

The measures applied, or proposed, are interdependent. The possibilities for making profits, together with the risk of bankruptcy, would provide inducement to the firm to improve productivity and to be cost-effective. This, however, would require that the firm has full responsibility for its actions, thus excluding central interventions in the firm's operations. At the same time, for profitability on the firm level to correspond to social profitability, there would be a need to adopt world market price relationships. The logical conclusion would be liberalization of imports which would ensure full transmission of world market prices to the domestic economy as well as import competition. Competition would, moreover, be served by continuing in the direction of breaking up large firms where economic consideration so warrant and by establishing new firms.

Import liberalization, together with the elimination of export compensation, would necessitate devaluing the exchange rate in real terms so as to establish its equilibrium level. Also, interest rates would need to be raised in order to eliminate credit rationing and to encourage inter-firm transfers of funds as well as private savings. These measures would have to be accompanied by the use of macroeconomic policy instruments, both to ensure the effectiveness of changes in exchange rates and interest rates and to avoid the investment cycles of the past.

CONCLUSIONS

This essay has reviewed changes in the Hungarian economic mechanism in 1980 and in 1981, which have reversed the process of recentralization of the preceding years and have reestablished the original course of the reforms introduced on 1 January 1968. In fact, in various respects, the new measures go beyond the initial reforms.

Apart from analyzing the reform measures of 1980–81, the author has made recommendations on further steps to be taken in the future. The proposed measures concern pricing, the exchange rate and protection, the determination of wages, decisions on investment, and the organization of economic decision making. In order to minimize economic disruptions, it is suggested that these measures be taken over a period of several years.

NOTES

1. The author examined the introduction and the practical implementation of the new economic mechanism in 'The Hungarian Economic Reform, 1968–81', Essay 12 in this volume. Unless otherwise noted, the data cited originate from the *Statistical Yearbook* and the *Foreign Trade Statistical Yearbook*, both published by the Hungarian Statistical Office. The former is available in Hungarian and in English; the latter only in Hungarian.
2. J. Kornai, 'Resource-Constrained versus Demand-Constrained Systems', *Econometrica*, XLVII (1979) pp. 801–12 and *Economics of Shortage* (Amsterdam: North-Holland, 1980).
3. A detailed description of the reforms is provided in B. Csikós-Nagy, *A magyar árpolitika – Az 1979/80 évi árrendezés* (Hungarian Price Policy – the 1979/80 Price Adjustment), (Budapest: Kozgazdasági és Jogi Könyvkiadó, 1980); and L. Horváth (ed.), *Gazdasági szabályozók 1980* (Economic Regulations 1980), (Budapest: Közgazdasági és Jogi Könyvkiadó, 1980).
4. L. Rácz, 'Az uj árrendszer' (The New Price System), *Közgazdasági Szemle*, XXVII (1980) p. 133.
5. Still, in 1981, the various subsidies were estimated at 42 percent of the profits of industrial firms, compared to 58 percent in 1977. (O. Gadó, 'Economic Policy Problems in Hungary in 1981', Paper prepared for the Meeting of American and Hungarian Economists held in Budapest on 26–31 October 1981, mimeo, p. 9).
6. At the same time, the payment of a charge on fixed assets was abolished and social-security contributions were reduced from 35 percent to 24 percent of wages; they were set at 27 percent starting on 1 January 1982.
7. I. Garamvölgyi, 'Vállalati exportdilemma: csak a legjobbat – vagy a jót is' (The Firm's Export Dilemma: Only the Best – or the Good as Well), *Figyelö*, 22 April 1981.
8. K. K. Fazekasné, 'Jövedelmezöség és növekedés a nem rubel exportban' (Profitability and Expansion in Non-Ruble Exports), *Figyelö*, 15 July 1981.

9. J. Csobay, 'Müködésben az ármechanizmus' (The Price Mechanism in Operations), *Figyelö*, 9 September 1981.

10. Garamvölgyi.

11. The value of exports in terms of forints has to rise by 8 percent for firms that export 5 to 12 percent of their production in convertible currency trade; the required export expansion is 6 percent for firms with an export share of 12 to 25 percent; and it is 4 percent for firms exporting more than one-fourth of their output. The required increases are 14, 12 and 10 percent, respectively, in the case of firms that earn foreign exchange in convertible currency trade at less than the official exchange rate, adjusted for the tax rebate.

12. A. Kováts, 'Vállalkozni – nyereségtartalékolással' (Be Enterprising – with Profit Reserves), *Figyelö*, 18 November 1981.

13. G. Réti, 'Arellenörzési tapasztalatok' (Experience with Price Reviews), *Figyelö*, 15 April, 1981.

14. It has been noted, for example, that, due to the higher quality of consumer goods imported in small quantities, the price of imports in no way limits increases in the prices of domestic products. The authors add: 'our price mechanism presupposes the market mechanism, and much of our problems are due to this fact or to the situation that in practice we have a simulated rather than a real market. We can expect an appropriate solution only if steps are taken to establish a real market mechanism and competition'; J. Berényi and S. Holé, 'Tapasztalatok az ármechanizmusról' (Experiences with the Price Mechanism), *Figyelö*, 18 November 1981.

15. For a similar proposal, see J. Deák, 'Külkereskedelmi szabályozás – idei tapasztalatok, 1981 évi módositások' (The Regulation of Foreign Trade – This Year's Experience, Modifications in 1981) *Figyelö*, 26 November 1980. Beginning in 1983, averaging is in fact to be used in determining changes in the forint value of exports referred to above.

16. In fact, as of January 1982, the export price condition has been eliminated in the case of firms that earn foreign exchange in convertible-currency trade at less than the official exchange rate adjusted for the tax rebate and increase in the forint value of their exports in the proportions indicated above; however, the profit criterion continues to be defined in terms of profit margins rather than profit rates.

17. L. Rácz, 'Erdekeltség az árkockázat vállalásában' (Financial Interest in Assuming a Price Risk) (Interview), *Figyelö*, 6 May 1981.

18. O. Gadó, 'Szabályozás módositás – mechanizmus-továbbfe-jlesztés' (Modifications in the Regulations – The Further Development of the Mechanisms), *Gazdaság*, XIII (2) (1979) p. 75.

19. Rácz, 'Az uj árrendszer', p. 141.

20. Csikós-Nagy, *A magyar árpolitika – Az 1979/80 évi árrendezés*, p. 224.

21. Rácz, 'Az uj árrendszer' (The New Price System), p. 141.

22. B. Balassa, 'The Economic Reform in Hungary', *Economica*, XXXVII (1970) p. 16.

23. This result represents a devaluation in real terms vis-à-vis the French franc and the West German mark, an appreciation vis-à-vis the US dollar and the Italian lira, and no change vis-à-vis the Austrian schilling (Hungarian exports to these countries were used as weights in the calculations, with the

West German mark taken to be representative of the currencies of the smaller Common Market countries participating in the snake).

24. Fekete expressed the view that 'the forint exchange rates of foreign currencies should correctly reflect – individually and in their totality – domestic and foreign price ratios; in other words, they should provide a realistic picture of the relationship between the purchasing power of the forint and that of the foreign currencies and they should adequately keep up with changes in these relationships, thus ensuring the stability of the forint'. J. Fekete, 'Exchange Rate Policy in a Planned Economy', *New Hungarian Quarterly*, Autumn 1976, p. 58; cited in P. Marer, 'Exchange Rates and Convertibility in Hungary's New Economic Mechanism', in *East European Economic Assessment, Part I, Country Studies*, Joint Economic Committee, US Congress (Washington, DC: US Government Printing Office (1981) p. 538).

25. The relative version of the purchasing power parity doctrine requires the exchange rate to parallel changes in relative prices at home and abroad. For a critical appraisal, see B. Balassa, 'The Purchasing Power Parity Doctrine: A Reappraisal', *Journal of Political Economy*, LXXII (1964) pp. 584–96.

26. Csikós-Nagy (*A magyar árpolitika – Az 1979/80 évi árrendezés*, p. 92) also makes reference to the experience of West Germany, Japan and Switzerland which revalued their exchange rate for the sake of keeping the prices of imported inputs low. As Csikós-Nagy notes, however, these countries have a particular export pattern dominated by products that have few substitutes, at least in the short run, which is not the case in Hungary. Furthermore, following the quadrupling of oil prices in 1973–4, these countries initially revalued their exchange rate in nominal but not in real terms and, once revaluation occurred in real terms, their balance of payments were adversely affected.

27. Marer, p. 539.

28. Marer (p. 532) refers to Hungarian press reports, according to which it was profitable to export in convertible-currency trade even if net foreign-exchange earnings were small and, in extreme cases, negative.

29. P. Medgyessy, 'A pénzügyi szabályozás uj vonásai és a vállalatok' (The New Features of Financial System and the Enterprises), *Gazdaság*, XV(3) (1981) p. 40.

30. T. Wolf, 'Foreign Trade Prices and Other Determinants of Hungarian Manufactures Exports to the West', paper prepared for the Meeting of American and Hungarian Economists, held in Budapest on 26–31 October 1981, mimeo. Also, substitution elasticities were mostly between two and three, had the correct sign, and were statistically significant for about one third of Hungarian export products to Germany. At the same time, as the author notes, difficulties of estimation may have contributed to the lack of statistical significance of the remaining estimates.

31. Werner suggests that, in the absence of a devaluation in real terms, the new price mechanism will be overshadowed by the application of discretionary measures aimed at increasing exports; R. Werner, 'Közgazdasági egyensúly és az árfolyampolitika' (Economic Equilibrium and Exchange Rate Policy), *Figyelő*, 15 October 1980.

32. A. Török, 'Importhelyettesités és megtakaritás' (Import Substitution and Import Savings), *Figyelö*, 17 December 1980.
33. P. Medgyessy, 'Gazdasági szabályozás' (Economic Regulations), *Figyelö*, 5 November 1980.
34. Marer, p. 546.
35. B. Balassa, 'The Firm in the New Economic Mechanism in Hungary', in M. Bornstein (ed.), *Plan and Market* (New Haven, Conn.: Yale University Press, 1973) pp. 351–3.
36. J. Lökkös, 'A keresetszabályozás néhány problémája és a továbbfejlesztés lehetöségei' (Some Problems of Regulating Earnings and Possibilities for Further Improvement), *Közgazdasági Szemle*, XXV (1978) p. 178.
37. Lökkös, p. 181.
38. L. Faluvégi, 'Az ötéves tervet formáló szándékok, viták és tapasztalatok' (Intentions, Discussions, and Experiences Shaping the Sixth Five-Year Plan), *Gazdaság*, XV(1) (1981) p. 25.
39. Lökkös; and L. Pongrácz, 'Elgondolások a bérszabályozás továbbfejelsztésére' (Thoughts on the Further Development of Wage Regulations), *Munkaügyi Szemle* (1979) pp. 84–99.
40. S. Balázsy, 'A keresetszabályozás megoldhatatlan dilemmája' (The 'Unsolvable' Dilemma of Regulating Earnings), *Közgazdasági Szemle*, XXV (1978) 154–73; and S. Balázsy, 'A megoldható dilemma még mindig megoldatlan' (The Solvable Dilemma is Still Unsolved), *Közgazdasági Szemle*, XXVI (1979) pp. 1063–70.
41. G. Révész, 'Keresetszabáályozásunkról' (On the Regulations of Earnings), *Közgazdasági Szemle*, XXV (1978) 917–34; and G. Révész, 'Keresetszabályozás és gazdaságirányitási (-szabályozási) koncepció' (The Regulation of Earnings and Guidelines for Economic Directions-Regulations), *Közgazdasági Szemle*, XXVI (1979) pp. 1086–92. These proposals are summarized in the 3 June 1981 issue of *Figyelö*.
42. Szakolczai also proposes linking wage increases to the profitability of the firm, but the implementation of this proposal would lead to larger interfirm wage differences than could be considerable desirable. See G. Szakolczai, 'Nyereségérdekeltség és bérszabályozás' (Profit, Interest and Wage Regulation), *Figyelö*, 28 October 1981.
43. A. Deák, 'Vállalati beruházási döntések és a gazdaságosság' (Firm Investment Decisions and Economic Efficiency), *Gazdaság*, XII(1) (1978) pp. 17–36.
44. I. Wiesel, 'Az önfinanszirozás labirintusa' (The Labyrinth of Self-financing), *Figyelö*, 7 October 1981.
45. M. Barát, 'A beruházásirányitási rendszer elemzése: javaslatok a továbbfejlesztésre' (Analysis of the System of Investment Regulations and Proposals for its Further Development), *Közgazdasági Szemle*, XXVIII (1981) pp. 140–57.
46. J. Mocsáry, 'A beruházási mechanizmusnak a nagyberuházások hatékonyságát gátló ellentmondásai' (Contradictions in the Investment Mechanism Impairing the Efficiency of Major Investment Projects), *Közgazdasági Szemle*, XXVIII (1981) pp. 158–71.
47. It was originally planned to reduce the average profit rate from 15 to 6 percent under the 1980 price reform; see B. Csikós-Nagy, 'Az 1980 évi

árrendezés' (The 1980 Price Reform), *Figyelö*, 20 June 1979. However, profits in 1980 were considerably higher than expected. Thus, profits in the manufacturing sector exceeded calculated magnitudes by one-fourth, with a difference of over 100 percent shown for 180-200 industrial firms out of a total of about 700.

48. According to a study carried out at the National Bank, difficulties of repayment were observed even before 1980, with nearly one-half of firms with profit rates between 10 and 30 percent experiencing such difficulties; see L. Weöres, 'A bankhitelezés lehetöségei és korlátai a fejlesztési politikában' (Possibilities and Constraints of Bank Credits in Development Policy), *Gazdaság*, XIV(1) (1980) pp. 57–69. Another study shows that, taking account of taxes on profits, a 20 percent profit rate would permit repayment only if the firm received one half of its external funds from bank credit and one half from budget support, thereby reducing servicing costs; see I. Cseresznyák, 'A vállalati beruházósok finanszirozása vegyes forrásokból' (The Financing of the Firm's Investments from Mixed Sources), *Pénzügyi Szemle*, XXV (1981) pp. 523–31.

49. J. Sári, 'Eszközáraramlás – irány: a nagyobb jövedelmezöség' (The Transfer of Funds – Direction: Higher Profitability), *Figyelö*, 20 May 1981.

50. L. Faluvégi, 'A müszaki haladás és a VI ötéves terv fejlesztési politikája' (Technical Progress and the Development Policy of the Sixth Five Year Plan), *Közgazdasági Szemle*, XXVIII (1981) p. 783.

51. I. Hetényi, 'A magyar gazdaság a 80-as években' (The Hungarian Economy during the 1980s), *Közgazdasági Szemle*, XXVII (1980) p. 1300.

52. Faluvégi, 'A müszaki haladás és a VI öteves terv fejlesztési politikája' (Technical Progress and the Development Policy of the Sixth Five Year Plan) pp. 776–7.

53. I. Belyácz, 'A beruházási elkötelezettségröl' (On Investment Commitments), *Figyelö*, 27 May 1981.

54. J. Mocsáry, 'A hazai vállalatrendszer centralizációjának hatása a termelésirányitás és szabályozórendszer hatékonyságára' (The Impact of the Centralization of the Hungarian Enterprise System on the Efficiency of Directing Production and Regulating Industrial Activities), *Közgazdasági Szemle*, XXVII (1980), p. 1311.

55. G. Varga, 'Vállalati méretstruktura a magyar iparban' (Enterprise Size in Hungarian Industry), *Gazdaság*, XIII(1) (1979) p. 28.

56. Z. Román, 'A magyar ipar szervezeti rendszere' (The Organizational Structure of Hungarian Industry), *Ipargazdasági Szemle*, (1978) pp. 225–38.

57. K. Bossányi, 'Elötérben a háttéripar' (Putting Forward the 'Background Industry'), *Figyelö*, 20 June 1979.

58. B. Balassa, 'Industrial Prospects and Policies in the Developed Countries', in F. Machlup, G. Fels and H. Muller-Groeling (eds), *Reflections on a Troubled World Economy*, (London: Trade Policy Research Center, 1983) pp. 257–78.

59. An example is provided by IKARUS, a major exporter of buses, whose domestic suppliers are reported to be 30 years behind requirements; see G. Nagy, 'Rugalmas gazdasági változások az Ikarusnál' (Flexible Economic Changes at IKARUS) (Interview), *Pénzügyi Szemle*, XXV (1981) p. 517.

60. It has been reported that the 200 largest Hungarian industrial firms producing final goods design and manufacture 90 percent of their own tools; see Varga, p. 36.
61. G. Varga, 'Leválasztás – Tanulságokkal' (Separation Experiences), *Figyelö*, 15 April 1981.
62. M. Laki, 'A "háttéripar" fejlesztése' (The Development of 'Background Industry'), *Gazdaság*, XIV(1) (1980) p. 66.
63. For an early proposal to this effects, cf. M. Tardos, 'A gazdasági verseny problémái hazánkban' (Problems of Economic Competition in Hungary), *Közgazdasági Szemle*, XIX (1972) pp. 911–22.
64. Retired high-level civil servants and managers could well be utilized in such a capacity as the retirement age is 60 years in Hungary.
65. M. Laki, 'Az állam szerepe as uj termékek gyártásában, as uj technologiák alkalmazásában' (The Role of the State in the Introduction of New Products and in the Application of New Technologies), *Közgazdasági Szemle*, XXV (1978) p. 822.
66. E. Hewett, 'The Hungarian Economy: Lessons of the 1970s and Prospects for the 1980s', in *East European Economic Assessment, Part I, Country Studies*, Joint Economic Committee, US Congress, (Washington, DC: US Government Printing Office, 1981) p. 521.

Translation of journal titles *Figyelö*, – Observer: *Gazdaság*, – Economy; *Közgazdasági Szemle*, – Economic Review; *Mundaügyi Szemle* – Labor Review; *Pénzügyi Szemle* – Financial Review, and *Valóság* – Reality.

Essay 14   Economic Reform in China

I REFORMING A CENTRALLY PLANNED ECONOMY

Reform efforts in socialist countries

After the Second World War, the newly-established socialist states of Asia and Europe adopted, with few modifications, the system of centralized physical planning practised in the Soviet Union. Under this system, the authorities set output targets, material allocation, employment, and other objectives for the producing units and determined the pattern of investment, exports, and imports. The principal targets were established in physical terms, with prices serving chiefly an accounting function.[1]

The system of centralized physical planning permitted the large-scale mobilization of resources in pursuing selected objectives, in the manner of a war economy. However, the shortcomings of this system became apparent as multiple objectives were to be pursued. As all details could not be perceived from the center, the plan objectives of output, material allocation, employment, and production costs often came into conflict, and the producing units had to abandon some targets in order to attain others. Also, the lack of scarcity prices for products, factors (capital, labor and natural resources), and foreign exchange did not permit making appropriate choices in production, investment, and foreign trade. Finally, the system of incentives was not conducive to technological improvements.

The workings of the system of centralized physical planning are exemplified by the Soviet Union, where it has been applied since the nineteen-thirties. As long as a few, selected objectives such as the development of heavy industry were followed, rapid rates of economic growth could be attained by mobilizing labor reserves and maintaining a high rate of investment. The subsequent pursuit of multiple objectives, however, led to imbalances in the economy composed of sectors with disparate levels of efficiency: a highly modern sector producing for armament and space exploration; comparatively backward sectors manufacturing consumer goods and producer durables, several of which have required the infusion of Western technology; and an inefficient agricultural sector that has increasingly necessitated food imports to provide for the needs of the population. At the same time, there continue to be shortages of various consumer goods, the available industrial products are of rather low quality, and they are limited in variety.[1]

Following the absorption of labor reserves, except for those of agriculture that could not be mobilized under the incentives applied, the low rate of technological change led to increases in incremental capital-output ratios in the Soviet Union. In the absence of a rise in investment shares, there resulted a decline in rates of economic growth.

Several attempts were made to reform the system of centralized physical planning, in the Soviet Union and elsewhere. Piecemeal reforms were unsuccessful, however, and they may have even brought a deterioration of the situation by combining the negative features of centralized and decentralized systems. These adverse consequences, leading to the subsequent abandonment of the reforms, reflected a failure to recognize the interrelationships of decentralized decision-making, the use of prices as signals for resource allocation, incentives at the production level, and competition among producing units.

Thus, in the absence of scarcity prices, delegating decision-making power to regional authorities and introducing profit critera for firms *à la* Liberman did not bring the desired results in the Soviet Union. In turn, barring the improbable case of solving an all-encompassing economic model on a giant computer, one cannot establish appropriate scarcity prices for individual commodities unless decision-making is decentralized, supply and demand are equated, and competition is ensured. Nor would the shadow prices derived in the model ensure conforming behavior on the part of producing units if appropriate incentives are not provided.

Comprehensive reforms were introduced in Yugoslavia in 1949 and in Hungary in 1968. The reforms aimed at replacing central directives by market relations among producing units; liberalizing prices; linking the prices of exports and imports to world market prices at realistic exchange rates; using interest rates as a cost element and as a criterion of investment choice in partially decentralized decision-making on investment; and relying on profit criteria for decision-making on the level of the producing units.

In Yugoslavia, the reforms represented a response to the situation that was created as the Soviet Union and its allies, accounting for three-fourths of its exports and imports, suddenly ceased all trading relationships with Yugoslavia. In Hungary, the reform was motivated by the increased sophistication of the economy and the salient importance of foreign trade in national income that puts into focus the shortcomings of centralized physical planning. And, in both cases, economists were able to convince a forward-looking leadership of the need for reforms that was not the case in, for example, Poland. The reform efforts were successful in the two countries, despite resistance on the part of vested interests in the bureaucracy, although practical difficulties of implementation were encountered because of the limitations of competition in small national markets.[2]

China does not yet have a highly sophisticated economic structure and foreign trade represents a small share of national income. However, it has some industrially advanced regions and, in its large territory, the multiple objectives of modernizing the economy and providing for the growing and increasingly diversified needs of the population may not be efficiently pursued through central decision-making. In particular, reforms are needed to increase the productivity of investment that has declined over time. According to official figures, the incremental capital-output ratio increased from 1.68 in 1953–7 to 3.76 in 1971–5.[3] Yet, the incremental capital-output ratio is underestimated in China because of the overstatement of rates of economic growth owing to the overpricing of industrial goods.

And, while the reduction in the average number of people supported by each income earner from 2.60 in 1952 to 2.08 in 1978 and, again, to 1.77 in 1981 contributed to economic growth in the past, this ratio may well increase in the future as the share of old people in the population rises. The reduced share of investment in national income, and the decrease in the share of productive investment in total investment, also point to the need for improving investment efficiency.[4] At the same time, a few industries apart, competition may be ensured in China, so that the market mechanism could operate even if import competition is limited at the present stage of its economic development. In turn, postponing the reform would lead to the establishment of an inefficient production structure that may be difficult to subsequently modify.

Readjustment and reform

In recent years, much has been said about the alleged conflict between readjustment and reform in China, when readjustment has been defined in terms of remedying macroeconomic disequilibria that have generated inflationary pressures. Yet, readjustment and reform are not necessarily in conflict and may even complement each other. This has been the case in Hungary, where investments were substantially reduced to redress macroeconomic imbalances in 1980–1 and, simultaneously, additional reform measures were taken to improve the rationality of prices and to further the decentralization of decision-making at the firm level.

Inflationary pressures in China, with the official cost-of-living index rising by 9.3 percent between 1978 and 1980, may be largely explained by the macroeconomic policies followed, or the lack thereof. Such pressures were generated as capital construction expenditures (fixed investment) financed from extra-budgetary funds rose at a rapid rate while, despite a cutback of capital construction financed from the state budget, a large budget deficit was incurred.

Capital construction expenditures financed from extra-budgetary funds increased from 8.4 billion yuan in 1978 to 25.8 billion in 1980, reflecting reduced transfers to the central government, increased levies by local governments, and the institution of investment loans from the People's Bank of China. At the same time, notwithstanding the decline in budget-financed capital construction in state-owned units from 39.6 billion yuan in 1978 to 28.1 billion yuan in 1980, with lower revenues and increased subsidies to urban consumers, the small budget surplus of earlier years turned into a deficit of 17.1 billion yuan in 1979 that was followed by a deficit of 12.7 billion yuan in 1980, equivalent for 3.0 percent of national income in that year. In 1979, one-half of the deficit in the state budget was financed by money creation, and the remainder by running down the accumulated reserves of the Treasury with the People's Bank of China;[5] in 1980, the share of money creation was about two-thirds – 8.0 billion yuan – with the compulsory purchase of long-term treasury bonds by localities and enterprises in early 1981 accounting for the remainder.

China succeeded in limiting inflationary pressures in 1981, with the official cost-of-living index rising by 2.4 percent. This was accomplished by lowering expenditures on capital construction in state-owned units by 21 percent, reducing the budget deficit to 2.5 billion yuan and asking local authorities to lend 7 billion yuan to the central authorities in 1981.

The decline in capital construction was more than offset by increases in the production of domestic consumer goods and by eliminating the deficit of 2.8 billion yuan in the balance of trade of the previous year.

As a result of these changes, the combined value of agricultural and industrial output rose by 4.5 percent over the 1980 level while the increase in national income was 3.0 percent.

It is especially noteworthy that agricultural output increased by 5.7 percent in 1981, although floods and drought reduced the harvest in several areas of the country. This result, and the 5.6 percent average annual rate of increase of agricultural output in the preceding two years that included the year 1980 characterized by natural calamities, reflect the impact of the incentive measures applied and contrast with slow agricultural growth in the previous two decades.

Industrial production increased by 4.1 percent in 1981. Although the production of heavy industry fell by 4.7 percent, this was the result of deliberate efforts to limit output at lower investment levels. In turn, with the reform measures providing inducement to the expansion of production, the output of light industry rose by 14.1 percent and there was a considerable increase in the provision of simple consumer goods by collective (i.e. co-operative) and by individual enterprises.

The reform measures applied thus contributed to the satisfaction of the needs of the population and, in increasing supply, reduced inflationary pressures. At the same time, certain adverse changes occurred owing to the fact that, in the absence of scarcity prices and the lack of competition in a number of industries, the interests of producing units and those of the national economy do no necessarily coincide. The measures taken, and their effects, will be briefly considered in Section III below.

The need for a comprehensive reform

Any adverse consequences the reform measures may have had should not however lead to limiting reform efforts or undoing the measures taken. Rather, such consequences may be eliminated, and the favorable effects of the reform enhanced, by adopting a comprehensive approach. This would require taking measures simultaneously to decentralize decision-making, rationalize prices, provide appropriate incentives to producing units, and encourage competition. In the following, recommendations will be made for a reform package that combines these elements and also provides a macroeconomic framework in which the reform measures can bring fruit.

As regards the macroeconomic framework, Section II will examine the requirements of a suitable credit and interest rate policy as well as budgetary policy in China. This will be followed by a consideration of appropriate balance-of-payments policies pertaining to the inflow of foreign capital, exchange rate, tariffs, and subsidies. A consideration of exchange rates, tariffs and subsidies leads to the issue of domestic price formation. Section III will analyze the pricing of exports and imports and of goods produced for the domestic market, together with possible reforms of the decision-making process in industry. Policies aimed at increasing agricultural value added and the potential role of private initiative will also be discussed in this section.

II THE MACROECONOMIC FRAMEWORK

Credit and interest rate policy

As noted above, financing the government budget deficit in 1980 involved money creation of 8 billion yuan. This amount represented, however, only one-fifth of total money creation. Currency and deposits increased by 40 billion yuan between the end of 1979 and the end of 1980, corresponding to an increase of 25 percent. This compares with annual increases averaging 8 percent in the 1955–79 period, and while the figures need to be adjusted for inflation that reportedly averaged 6 percent in 1980, increases in the real value of the money supply were still 18 percent.

Various considerations explain the acceleration of the growth of the money supply in 1980. Apart from the direct effects of the government budget deficit, reduced budgetary appropriations for working capital led to increased demands for credit. Also, the People's Bank of China began providing investment loans in substantial amounts, totalling 5.6 billion yuan in 1980. At the same time, in the application of government priorities, there were large increases in loans to rural communes and production brigades (3.6 billion yuan) and to urban collective and individual enterprises (2.1 billion yuan). Finally, negative real interest rates, with the rate on loans for circulating capital remaining at 5.2 percent a year for industry and commerce and 4.4 percent a year for agriculture (compounded monthly interest rates), notwithstanding inflation rates of 6 percent following the price stability of the earlier period, may have encouraged the accumulation of inventories.

In accordance with its traditional mode of operations, the People's Bank of China continued to grant loans virtually automatically on the presentation of documents concerning the purchase of materials. At the same time, the decentralization of credit management, which stimulated the local branches of the PBC to attract deposits and to make loans, has added to money creation through the operation of the money multiplier.[6]

Improvements were registered in 1981. The rate of increase in outstanding loans granted by the PBC declined to 14.5 percent from 18.4 percent the year earlier while the rate of increase of the money supply fell from 25.2 percent to 21.2 percent. These results were attained, despite the fact that increased private activity required additional liquidity and time deposits rose to a considerable extent.

Notwithstanding these improvements, there is need to reform the financial system in China, both to carry out an active monetary policy and to conform to the requirements of its changing economic structure. To begin with, rather than continuing to take a passive stance in providing loans for the purchase of materials, it would be desirable that the PBC followed an active monetary policy. This may involve relying on interest rates and/or credit ceilings.

Interest rates on circulating capital to industry were increased to 7.4 percent in April 1982, practically eliminating the 'negative financial transformation' that existed after April 1980 when interest rates on time deposits were substantially raised.[7] Increases in time deposit rates, in turn, contributed to the rise in urban and rural savings. Total time deposits increased from 21.1 billion yuan at the end of 1978 to 39.9 billion yuan at the end of 1980, followed by an increase to 52.3 billion yuan in the next year.

Individuals will receive an interest rate of 8 percent on long-term treasury bonds issued in 1982, of which they are expected to take about one-half. While this rate slightly exceeds the 7.1 percent interest rate on five-year time deposits, the differential is warranted given that the repayment of treasury bonds begins only in the sixth year after issue and it is undertaken in five annual instalments. At the same time, following the decline in inflation rates, the present interest rate structure on demand and time deposits seems appropriate.

It would be desirable, however, to further increase interest rates on circulating capital, so as to limit credit demand for purposes of holding inventories. Interest rates on loans for capital construction would also need to be raised. The PBC presently charges interest rates of 5.2 to 6.6 percent, depending on maturity, while budget-financed loans by the People's Construction Bank of China carry an annual interest rate of 3.0 percent.

But it cannot be expected that, under the present system of economic incentives, interest rates could be increased sufficiently to equilibrate the demand for, and the supply of, credit. Correspondingly, one may employ a combination of higher interest rates and credit ceilings to the branches of the PBC. These branches could eventually become regional banks managed on commercial principles and be subject to reserve requirements. This would permit establishing a separate central bank, to be responsible for overall monetary policy.

Budgetary policy

The compulsory purchase of treasury bonds by local governments and by state-owned and collective enterprises, and borrowing from the local authorities, partly compensated for the reduced transfers to the central government. Such financial transactions can provide only a temporary remedy, however, since they create a repayment obligation for the future. At the same time, notwithstanding these transactions, capital construction expenditures financed from the state budget fell by 7.3 billion yuan in 1981 while the decrease in capital construction financed from extra-budgetary funds was only 3.8 billion yuan, raising the share of the latter from 47.8 percent in 1980 to 51.4 percent in 1981.[8]

In fact, there is evidence that local authorities have utilized the increased availability of extra-budgetary funds to undertake investments that were not warranted by economic considerations. These investments have reinforced autarchical tendencies and have led to the local small-scale processing of materials that would have been better utilized in efficient, large-scale establishments. In Sichuan province, such has reportedly been the case in regard to silk and tobacco, for example.

More generally, local authorities do not have an overview of alternative investment possibilities and they are inclined to pursue regional rather than national interests. At the same time, rapid economic development in China requires substantial investments in infrastructure, in particular in transportation and energy. Also, increased funds would need to be provided to state-owned enterprises for investment purposes. This may be done through the People's Construction Bank of China, with the interest rate increasingly used as an allocative device.

The above considerations point to the need for reducing the share of the local authorities in government revenues and limiting their power of taxation. Central revenues would be further increased through the institution of capital charges on a uniform basis and through higher depreciation allowances as suggested below.

Balance-of-payments policy

Foreign sources of investment in China comprise borrowing abroad as well as foreign direct investment. China attempts to attract increasing amounts of capital in the form of equity and contractual joint ventures, when the former but not the latter involves a capital expenditure by the domestic partner. Furthermore, compensation agreements involving the repayment of foreign loans in kind have assumed importance.

In evaluating the desirability of foreign borrowing, it is customary to introduce liquidity as well as profitability considerations. The former played a role in the cutback of borrowing for major investment projects but, at this point of time, the debt-service ratio is relatively low in China. Correspondingly, attention may be focused on profitability considerations, an appropriate objective being that the investment has a rate of return at world market prices at least as high as the rate of interest on the loan. In this way, it can be avoided that the cost of the domestic production of capital-intensive industrial materials financed from foreign loans, such as steel and petrochemicals, exceed the cost of importing them.

At the same time, the continued encouragement of joint ventures is desirable since, in addition to capital, they bring technological know-how and marketing expertise and involve a sharing of profits rather than a fixed interest charge. Such ventures could be further encouraged by clarifying some of the provisions of China's 1979 foreign investment law and by negotiating investment treaties with additional foreign countries. Joint ventures designed for production for domestic markets, such as automobiles, trucks, and diesel engines, should be evaluated at world market prices, lest high-cost industries be established behind protection and profit transfers made from high prices paid by domestic users. Such is not the case for export-oriented investments and, in particular, for investments in the special economic zones where in addition to wages, China earns foreign exchange from taxes and other fees imposed on foreign operations.

But, one should not give excessive emphasis to the special economic zones that are largely isolated from the domestic economy, and hence multiplier effects are foregone. Rather, it would be desirable to create similar conditions for exports throughout China, so that exporting firms increasingly use domestic materials and also produce for domestic markets. Finally, 'straight' borrowing and sales will often be superior to compensation agreements that may involve getting unduly low prices for exported products.

Making estimates on the rate of return at world market prices would necessitate using a realistic exchange rate in the calculations. Increasing the accounting rate from 1.5 yuan to 2.8 yuan to the US dollar in January 1981 was an important step in this direction. However, notwithstanding the substantial appreciation of the US dollar vis-à-vis other currencies in the following eighteen months, the accounting exchange rate has not been subsequently changed. In a market economy, the exchange rate should equilibrate the balance of payments, with allowance made for the desired inflow of foreign capital. While the exchange rate cannot be called upon to perform this role in China under the present system of import restrictions, a further step in this direction may be taken, and exports encouraged, if a more flexible procedure is applied in setting the accounting exchange rate.

It would appear that foreign exchange retention schemes for exporting firms and the provision of foreign exchange to firms producing inputs for export production have encouraged the expansion of exports in China. There is no particular rationale, however, for the retention of foreign exchange by local authorities that do not engage in productive pursuits.

In increasing the profitability of domestic sales, the high protection of domestic markets through import restrictions and tariffs tends to discourage exports. Also, China's tariff structure has developed in a rather haphazard way, and it unduly raises costs to some industries and provides too little protection to others. There is need, therefore, to rationalize the system of protection by reducing disparities in tariff rates. At the same time, *pari passu* with the establishment of a realistic accounting exchange rate, average tariffs may be lowered.

The expansion of exports would further permit easing the foreign exchange bottleneck and accelerating economic growth through the increased imports of industrial materials and capital goods embodying sophisticated technology. For exchange rates to have appropriate effects, however, they should enter into domestic price formation and decisions on production and exports would need to be decentralized, with producing units aiming at higher profits. These conditions will be considered in Section III in the context of economic reforms in China for manufacturing industry as well as for agriculture, with further attention given to the role of collective and individual enterprises.

III REFORMING THE OPERATION OF THE PRODUCTIVE SECTORS

Reform efforts in manufacturing industry

Manufacturing industry in China made considerable strides during the period following the Second World War. However, it suffered from the usual shortcomings of centralized physical planning, including low-quality production, the accumulation of stocks of material inputs, an excess supply of goods that did not correspond to user needs, as well as shortages of various commodities for which there was demand. Largely as a result of the accumulation of stocks of material inputs, circulating capital per 100 yuan of output increased from 17 yuan in 1956 to 31 yuan in 1979. There were also growing inventories of finished goods. In 1980, inventories of steel products and machinery and equipment reportedly exceeded one year's production. In the same year, stockpiles of unsold goods for export accounted for more than one-third of annual exports.[9]

Various reforms were introduced on an experimental basis to improve the operation of industrial enterprises in China. They included profit retention schemes; the use of retained profits for reinvestment, for social and cultural purposes, for the payment of bonuses, and for reserves; the right to sell above-plan output directly at negotiated prices up to 15 percent higher or lower than plan prices; and greater freedom in labor relations. While the reforms originally applied to a few firms, in 1981 they were extended to 6000 enterprises accounting for about 60 percent of industrial output. Since 1982, investment decisions again require permission by the supervising authorities and, in practice, little change has occurred in labor relations. However, *de facto*, if not *de jure*, the remaining reforms have been extended to practically all industrial firms.

In the Shanghai area, an average of 8 percent of profits was retained in 1980, with workers receiving annual bonuses averaging two months' wages. The profit retention ratio was higher – often by a substantial margin – in other areas where profits tend to be lower;[10] it reportedly varied between 10 and 20 percent in Sichuan province. In the same province, 40 percent of retained profits were to be used for investments, 30 percent for social and cultural purposes, 20 percent for bonuses and awards, and 10 percent for reserves in the 417 firms that participated in the decentralization experiment in 1980.

The introduction of the profit retention and bonus schemes led to the expansion of industrial production while the increased practice of negotiated sales contributed to the satisfaction of the users' needs. In 1980, the 417 firms applying these schemes in Sichuan province experienced production increases one-half larger than the other firms of the province. Profits also increased more rapidly in the former group of firms than in the latter. However, profits on the firm level do not necessarily conform to the national interest, because of the existence of price distortions. This is of particular importance in China where prices were set at the time of the introduction of particular products and seldom changed afterwards. Prices were not raised in response of increases in costs, so as to avoid inflation;[11] nor were prices reduced in cases when productivity increased, in order to provide revenue for the state budget.

Thus, some firms changed their product composition, with little consideration given to their saleability. They could do so, even though inventories accumulated, since profits are measured on the basis of production value rather than sales. There were further cases when the firm raised prices by replacing existing products with new ones that had a higher price. Finally, there were instances of lowering product quality.[12]

These adverse consequences may be limited if profits are based on actual sales rather than on production value. Also, as suggested above, inventory accumulation may be discouraged by raising interest rates on circulating capital, a measure that has been successfully used in Hungary. At the same time, in order to avoid distortions owing to interfirm differences in the cost of circulating capital financed from budgetary appropriations and from bank loans, the same interest rate should be applied to both.[13]

For the same reason, the treatment of funds provided directly from the budget and in the form of loans for capital construction would need to be equalized. Every firm should pay a charge for the use of its fixed capital, over and above depreciation, equal to the rate of interest on investment loans, which would also have to be raised from existing levels. In addition, depreciation charges would need to be increased from their present low level of 4–5 percent a year, in order to account for the obsolescence of equipment.

Under the described procedures, the cost of capital would enter into the calculations of the firm, thus allowing differences in capital intensity among firms and among industries to bear on the cost of production.

At the same time, in view of the high profits noted above, capital charges would not impose an undue burden on most industrial enterprises.

It would further be desirable to limit the present proliferation of profit retention rates. While the purpose has been to differentiate among firms having different production conditions, these cannot be measured even in an approximate way. Nor is there a rationale for varying profit retention rates, and income tax rates, according to the absolute size of profits when there are interfirm differences in the capital stock.

A possible solution is to replace profit retention schemes by profit taxes, with progressivity in the tax rates based on the rate of profit on fixed and circulating capital. These rates would be applied to base level profits, and lower taxes paid on subsequent increases in profits. In this way, one could avoid the arbitrariness involved in setting different profit retention rates for different industries, and for firms within each industry, while appropriating the 'rent' element in profits without affecting incentives to improve operations.

It would further be desirable to modify the present system of bonuses. While bonuses had been designed to reward work performance, they have often become a supplement to wages provided without distinction to all workers in the firm. Also, under the existing schemes, bonuses tend to be higher in firms that earn higher profits. Correspondingly, bonuses have frequently become divorced from individual performance while adding to inflationary pressures as well as to income differentials. Average real wages in state-owned enterprises increased by 5 percent between 1979 and 1981, while industrial labor productivity stagnated. At the same time, in industrial enterprises making losses as well as many non-industrial enterprises bonuses were not provided.

In his report to the Fifth National People's Congress on 30 November and 1 December 1981, Premier Zhao Ziyang demanded that 'the present practice of handing out bonuses indiscriminately should be strictly checked',[14] and subsequently called for limiting bonuses payable in 1982 to the 1981 level. Further steps would include integrating bonuses into an extended piece-wages system; providing bonuses independently of profits; and including bonus payments in production costs.

At the same time, on the example of Hungary, it would be desirable to provide profit-based bonuses to management that directly contributes to the profitability of the firm's operations. Hungary further rejected the Yugoslav system of labor management on the grounds that it tends to be conservative, both in discouraging new investments and in limiting increases in the firm's labor force, and it reduces labor discipline.

It has been reported that in China 'democratic election of factory directors began last year on an experimental basis in a number of provinces, autonomous regions, and municipalities, including Beijing. This is an effective move towards democratic management, ensuring the exercise of democratic rights by the workers.'[15] The experience of Yugoslavia and Hungary raises doubts about the desirability of having workers elect managers, however. A more appropriate alternative would seem to be to entrust the task of hiring – and firing – managers to a board of supervisors, consisting of the representatives of governmental authorities, the banks, management, labor, as well as independent experts, when utilizing experienced cadres on the board of supervisors would also permit making room for the young and the middle-aged in government administration.

A related issue is to provide greater authority to managers to fire undisciplined workers. This possibility has been officially admitted but it involves a rather complicated process. This fact may explain that few workers have been fired, and only for gross indiscipline, such as being absent without leave for several months.

A more difficult question is the need to reduce the labor force of the firm that encounters difficulties and, in extreme cases, closing down the firm itself. Premier Zhao stated that 'factories and enterprises that fail to meet [established] requirements within a certain time limit must either suspend operations pending consolidation or close down.'[16] In fact, a number of plants have closed down; for example, the number of small iron plants run by prefectures and counties has been cut from 466 to 276, representing a reversal of the policy of 'backyard iron furnaces' of some time ago. An extension of this policy would involve closing down high-cost units of particular enterprises.

The pricing of industrial products

The described measures would contribute to improving the performance of Chinese industry. Their effects would, however, be limited as long as prices are not reformed. Establishing rational prices that reflect resource scarcities, in turn, requires the decentralization of decision-making to the firm level as well as effective competition. In this connection, comparisons with Hungary may be of interest.

Its small market size limits the extent of domestic competition in

Hungary. By contrast, China has a number of producing units in practically all industries, thereby providing possibilities for competition. There has in fact been competition following reductions in plan targets for firms manufacturing steel products and machinery as these firms have attempted to increase the extent of capacity utilization.

In turn, given its large market size and relatively low level of industrial development, it would not be appropriate for China to follow the example of Hungary in adopting world market price relations for its domestic sales, as a general principle.[17] At the same time, continuing with the separation of domestic and world market prices for China's exports and imports would not permit exploiting its possibilities in international trade to best advantage. In the following, recommendations will be made for a mixed system of pricing, to be applied in conjunction with decentralized decision-making and profit incentives.

For manufactured exports, the appropriate goal is to equate prices paid to domestic producers to the f.o.b. export price less domestic transportation costs. In conjunction with an appropriate exchange rate policy, this would contribute to the expansion of exports that are profitable from the point of view of the national economy and encourage investment in such activities by ploughing back profits.

Exceptions would need to be made, however, in cases when exports are limited by foreign restrictions (e.g. textiles) or by the extent of foreign demand (tungsten). In such instances, an export quota system may be employed to avoid price-cutting through competition among Chinese exporters. At the same time, it is doubtful that this would be the case for many of the 173 export commodities, for which unified export management was established in May 1982. Extending the export quota scheme to products that are not subject to limitations abroad may have adverse effects by stifling initiative to seek out new markets and to introduce new product varieties.

Rather, it would be desirable to increase the number of industries and products where firms can establish direct market relations abroad. This would permit firms to adjust to world market conditions and to seek out profitable market outlets. With domestic prices linked to export prices, firms would also have a direct interest in obtaining better prices abroad.

It would further be desirable to equate the domestic prices of imported industrial materials to the CIF import price plus tariffs and domestic transportation and distribution costs, so as to induce firms to economize with these products. In the case of materials subject to considerable price fluctuations, however, a price compensation scheme may need to be employed.

Investment projects for the replacement of imported industrial materials should also be evaluated at world market prices. As noted above, this is of particular importance in cases where domestic production is undertaken by utilizing borrowed funds. The importation of capital and that of products, then, become alternatives and the choice between them will require careful economic evaluation. More generally, for industrial materials imports provide an alternative to domestic production, and hence world market prices may appropriately serve as a basis for domestic price formation. At the same time, the application of this procedure is facilitated by the fact that the products in question are homogeneous, so that differences in quality and in specifications do not affect the price comparisons.

Different conclusions apply to differentiated products that account for the vast bulk of manufactured goods, in particular consumer goods, machinery and equipment. For these products, the varieties manufactured in China generally differ in quality and in specifications from those available in the world market. As a practical matter, then, it would not be possible to utilize world market prices in domestic pricing. At any rate, given its large market and relatively low level of industrial development, it would seem appropriate for China to have domestic prices reflect domestic scarcities rather than world market price relationships for these products.

Two alternative procedures for setting the domestic producer prices of differentiated products in the manufacturing sector have been suggested in discussions among Chinese economists. One of these would entail the use of a large input-output table to indicate the inter-industry relationships of costs and prices. The other alternative would involve extending the scope of negotiated prices to eventually encompass all sales of differentiated products.

While the first alternative may appear attractive in theory, it would encounter practical difficulties because of the great variety of industrial products manufactured in China and the importance of quality differences for product prices. Thus, a central authority could not set appropriate prices for all conceivable product specifications and there is the danger that firms would lower quality in the pursuit of profits.

Nor would the central determination of prices by the use of an input-output table ensure that demand and supply for individual products are equated, which is a precondition for establishing rational, or scarcity, prices. This purpose can be served by placing reliance on market relationships that would also permit avoiding reductions in quality.

Negotiated sales among industrial firms are expressions of market relations in China. These relationships have assumed importance in heavy industry, where reductions in plan targets have led firms to seek out market outlets. In so doing, firms have changed their product composition to suit the users' needs and genuine competition has emerged among suppliers.[18]

The scope of negotiated sales in heavy industry could be extended further by reducing plan targets, with a view to their eventual elimination. In this industry, competition could be relied upon to limit price increases, when the first step to liberalize prices would entail enlarging the margins around the prices determined centrally.

The described procedure could be applied in heavy industry because of the existence of excess capacity. This is not generally the case in light industry where, despite the increase of production by one-half between 1978 and 1981, there is unsatisfied demand for a number of products. In such instances, production would need to be increased before negotiated prices could come into general use.

The output of light industry could be increased, first of all, by raising the extent of capacity utilization. While firms in Shanghai reportedly work in three shifts, one-shift operations predominate in some other parts of China. A case in point is a shirt factory in Beijing, which utilizes expensive modern Japanese machinery in only one shift.

In order to increase the extent of capacity utilization, incentives for multi-shift operations would need to be provided. Increasing the cost of capital to the firm, suggested above, would provide such incentives. Furthermore, firms may be allowed to establish a double deduction for part of the cost of overtime in calculating their profit tax.

Investment in light industry would also need to be increased. While the share of light industry in manufacturing output rose from 42.7 percent in 1978 to 51.4 percent in 1981, with a commensurate decline in the share of heavy industry, investment in light industry was only one-quarter of that in heavy industry in 1981. Although this represents an increase compared to an investment share of one-sixth in 1978, further increases are necessary for light industry to fully meet demand by urban dwellers and, in particular, by the rural population.

While the need for increasing the service orientation of heavy industry vis-à-vis light industry and agriculture has been well recognized in China, there is further need for establishing a dynamic equilibrium between light industry and agriculture. This would take the form of expanding the production of light industry to provide consumer goods for the rural population who, in turn, would increase the output of food for the urban dwellers.

In order to ensure that such an equilibrium is attained, appropriate incentives would need to be provided. As far as light industry is concerned, this would entail increasing the scope of negotiated sales *pari passu* with the elimination of excess demand in regard to particular products. It would further be necessary to ensure competition among producing units.

In this connection, reference may be made to recent tendencies for concentration in Chinese industries. Although improvements in productivity could be achieved by reducing the number of the nearly 400 000 state-owned enterprises in China, one should avoid excessive concentration that would reduce competition. Also, while the transformation of certain ministries into corporations will increase their flexibility,[19] the enterprises within the corporations should be encouraged to compete with each other.

Also, as noted above, industrial enterprises should be free to invest by using their own funds as well as funds borrowed at appropriate interest rates. At the same time, the central government would have to make investment decisions in regard to basic industries and utilize economic project evaluation in making these decisions.

Particular importance attaches to improving transportation facilities and increasing the supply of energy. And while this will take time to accomplish, the establishment of highly energy-intensive plants producing industrial materials, which often have also considerable transportation requirements, would need to be postponed further for the sake of providing for the energy needs of consumer goods industries.[20]

Agriculture

Since 1979, a number of important measures have been taken in China to reform agriculture. The measures in question include the introduction of the 'responsibility' system, with remuneration based on output; reductions in compulsory procurement, with higher prices applying to above-procurement sales; increases in absolute prices and changes in relative prices for procurement; and the encouragement of sideline activities.

The responsibility system has replaced the earlier system, denoted in popular parlance as 'eating from the same big public pot', under which work was apportioned by the leader of the production team and remuneration based on hours worked. It now applies to over 90 percent of production teams. The principal variants of the responsibility system include providing remuneration on the basis of the production tasks performed in the framework of the production team and the family responsibility system, *bao gan dao hu*, under which each household retains everything it has produced on the land assigned to it after paying taxes and contributing its share to the accumulation and public welfare funds of the commune. In some instances, households have organized themselves into 'integrated units', made up of three to five households, with specialization according to tasks within each unit.

Furthermore, the area available for household plots has been increased from 7 percent to 15 percent of the total; under the Cultural Revolution, household plots were not officially allowed. Finally, the draft of the revised Constitution calls for separating local government administration from commune management, with a view to avoiding the use of compulsory methods.

The family responsibility system has assumed increased importance, covering 60 percent of the land area of the communes in Sichuan province, with family groups accounting for another 7 percent. In the same province, production on private plots, occupying 13.5 percent of the land area, and sideline activities carried out by the family, reportedly accounted for 47 percent of agricultural income in 1981. A slightly lower proportion, 42 percent, applies to a sample of 18 529 peasant households throughout China, for which data were collected by the State Statistical Bureau; the corresponding figure was 29 percent in 1978.[21]

The establishment of the responsibility system has been accompanied by some easing of acreage limitations and reductions in procurement targets. According to one estimate, private sales in rural areas nearly doubled between 1978 and 1980, approaching one-third of state purchases in that year.[22] Prices for such sales exceeded the procurement price of wheat, that was first permitted to be sold in private markets in 1979, by 70 percent in 1981. Approximately the same price applied to the so-called negotiated sales to the state, accounting for one-sixth of procurement sales, while above-quota sales to the state, in approximately the same volume, were made at a 50 percent premium. Similar price differences were observed in regard to oilseeds, a 30 percent premium applied to above-quota sales of cotton, while the differences were smaller for other crops.

Also, procurement prices were raised and relative prices adjusted for some major crops, thereby reducing differences vis-à-vis world market prices. Increases in the price of cotton have led to higher output and lower imports, more than offsetting increased wheat imports. Nevertheless, the effects of price changes on output have been limited by acreage controls and by continued restrictions on the inter-provincial marketing of grains.[23]

In 1978, the ban on the ownership of small factories by production teams was lifted and limitations on the time allocation of production teams to sideline activities were also abolished. There resulted a considerable expansion of sideline activities in producing simple farm implements, consumer goods, as well as industrial materials. In 1981, such production rose by 9.3 percent compared to a 5.7 percent increase in agricultural output, accounting for 27 percent of the increment in output.

Although the expansion of sideline activities raised fears that the production of agricultural staples would be neglected, no action has been taken to limit their expansion. And while emphasis has again been given to the control of acreage, with the objective of avoiding further shifts from grains to rapeseed and tobacco, the continued development of the responsibility system has been repeatedly endorsed.[24]

Acreage limitations and the continued maintenance of government procurement, however, conflict with the peasants' interest to increase their incomes by changing the product composition of output. This interest could be harnessed to pursue national economic objectives by increasing reliance on prices to guide production decisions while reducing the scope of acreage limitations and government procurement.

In fact, under present-day conditions, the principal gains in agricultural productivity are likely to come through increased specialization within the commune, within individual provinces, and among provinces in China. Increased specialization within the commune would permit limiting the disadvantages of the cultivation of small land areas under the family responsibility system. The extension of the contractual system, applied experimentally in several provinces, would serve this objective as it determines the obligations of the family towards the commune in money terms rather than in kind.

Intra-provincial and, in particular, inter-provincial specialization would further contribute to the better utilization of China's natural resources. At the same time, for the time being, specialization among individual provinces is constrained by the inadequacies of transportation facilities.

Specialization in response to price incentives may, however, further widen income inequalities in rural areas that have increased in recent years. And while income disparities owing to differences in effort are considered desirable, such disparities also result from differences in the quality of land as it is often not possible to produce on poor land more than the amount required under procurement. To eliminate this source of inequality, and to simultaneously provide incentives to increase output, it would be desirable to place increased reliance on land taxes while raising agricultural prices.

Land taxes should be fixed in amount but vary according to the quality of land, so as to absorb a considerable part of the rent element in agricultural incomes. Although China has long had a land tax under the name of agricultural tax, its importance has declined over time; it now accounts for only 3 percent of the value of agricultural output in Sichuan province, for example. While the determination of the land tax encounters administrative difficulties, basing it on past output levels is still preferable to the progressive taxation of agricultural incomes that would reduce income differences at the expense of discouraging effort.

It would further be desirable to review the subsidization of foodstuffs that benefits the recipients of rations in urban areas. These subsidies reportedly increased fourfold between 1979 and 1981, reaching about 6 percent of national income but benefiting only 13 percent of the population.

Finally, a review of agricultural prices would provide an opportunity to align these prices more closely with world market prices. The domestic price of wheat is higher than that of rice in China whereas the opposite is the case in the world market. Also, despite recent changes, cotton is cheaper relative to wheat in China than in the world market. Greater alignment with world market price relations would permit exploiting China's advantages in international trade in agricultural products. While the narrowness of the world rice market and the sensitivity of wheat prices to increased demand in world markets demand caution, steps taken in this direction would increase agricultural – and national – income in China.

Collective and individual enterprises

Following earlier prohibitions, since 1978 individual enterprises can be established in China, and newly-created collective and individual enterpises may receive tax benefits and preferential credits. Provisions have further been made for the establishment of new forms of enterprises. These new forms include joint ventures between state-owned and collective enterprises; between state-owned enterprises and individuals; and between collective enterprises and individuals; as well as enterprises established using funds pooled by individuals, with shareholders receiving part of the profits in the form of dividends.

The purpose of the new regulations has been to create employment and to contribute to the satisfaction of the needs of the population. The results have been quite impressive. In 1980, 810 000 individuals started their own businesses. In 1981, state-owned enterprises provided jobs for only 29 percent of the 6 million newly-employed urban workers while collective enterprises accounted for 49 percent and individual enterprises for 5 percent of the total, with the remaining 17 percent being temporary workers. Collective and the individual enterprises have engaged in a variety of activities, including tailoring, shoemaking, arts and crafts, the manufacture of toys, rubber products, the selling of their own products, as well as personal services, such as restaurants and hairdressers.

Further expansion of individual enterprises is expected following the October 1981 Decision on Solving Urban Unemployment Problems by the Central Committee of the Chinese Communist Party and the State Council. Having reviewed the rise of employment in collective and individual enterprises, the Decision states:

> Nonetheless, a number of problems remain unsolved. This refers mainly to the fact that some places put undue emphasis on arranging jobs in already overstaffed state-owned enterprises and undertakings which is detrimental to the improvement of management. . . . In the future, emphasis should be placed on creating jobs in the collective and in individual sectors of the economy.[25]

This purpose is to be served by permitting individuals to hire two helpers and five apprentices. Furthermore, workers in collective and individual enterprises have been given the same rights and privileges as workers in state-owned enterprises. At the same time, collective and individual enterprises bear sole responsibility for their profits and losses, and they cannot expect that the authorities would help them out in case of financial difficulties.

Given their profit-seeking character, collective and individual enterprises create productive employment in adding to the supply of goods and services. At the same time, these enterprises have considerable flexibility to respond to changes in demand, thus easing shortages in individual commodities. Through their activities, then, the collective and individual enterprises reduce the scope for illicit actions, which tend to proliferate in the absence of market relationships.[26]

The practical application of the October 1981 Decision will, however, require avoiding interference on the part of state and local authorities, which has limited the scope of individual enterprises in several cases where they competed with state-owned units.[27] The danger of interference on the part of the authorities has been recognized in the Decision that took pains to identify the rights and privileges of the co-operative and individual enterprises.

> The ownership of property, regular business activities and incomes of the collective enterprises and individual laborers should be protected by the law and no department or unit is allowed without authorization to interfere in their affairs, transfer their property and resources or swallow them up. They are required to pay taxes and other fees according to state law and the rules and regulations of the various provinces, municipalities and autonomous regions. No department or unit is allowed to change them under any other pretext.[28]

Potentially, collective and individual enterprises can also play an important role in commerce by improving the distribution of goods. Under recent regulations, no organizations, army units, schools, industrial or mining enterprises are allowed to engage in commercial activities, except for the sale of their own products. While these regulations aim at limiting the proliferation of trading activities, provisions would need to be made for providing alternative forms of trading. This may be done by extending the licensing of private traders outside country fairs and urban markets. Furthermore, it would be desirable to remove existing limitations on the sale of goods produced by others and on the transportation of goods for sale by collective and private enterprises.

CONCLUSIONS

This essay has briefly reviewed the experience of centrally planned economies with reforms and the relevance of their experience to China. Attempts made at the decentralization of decision-making in China have further been considered, and recommendations have been put forward for continued reform efforts.

In the discussion, emphasis has been given to the interdependence of decentralized decision-making, the use of prices as signals for resource allocation, incentives at the production level, and competition among producing units. In manufacturing industry, recommendations have been made for the increased decentralization of decision-making to producing units and the application of bonus schemes for management aimed at improving operations, together with the reform of the price system and an effort to ensure competition, so that decisions taken by state enterprises conform to the national interest.

As regards industrial prices, the application has been proposed of a mixed system that would rely on world market prices in regard to exports, as well as for industrial materials, and would extend the scope of negotiated prices to the bulk of industry. Negotiated prices also provide the appropriate norm for collective and individual enterprises that are called upon to play an increased role in China in creating employment and in contributing to the satisfaction of the needs of the population.

The easing of existing constraints on decision-making and the rationalization of prices would also be desirable in agriculture, involving reductions in differences between relative domestic and world market prices. It would further be desirable to make increased use of land taxes that would permit appropriating a greater part of the rent element in agricultural incomes without adversely affecting effort.

As regards both industry and agriculture, increased reliance would need to be placed on interest rates as a device for allocating investment funds and for limiting credit demands for purposes of inventory holdings. Interest rates, together with credit ceilings, should also be used to pursue an appropriate monetary policy that would eventually necessitate establishing a separate central bank. In conjunction with a balance-of-payments policy pertaining to the inflow of foreign capital, tariffs, and subsidies, then a macroeconomic framework would be provided for the decentralization of decision making in the productive sectors of the economy.

Objections may be raised, however, to the regional decentralization of investment decisions as the local authorities are not profit-making units and do not have an overview of alternative investment possibilities. Correspondingly, it would be desirable to partially recentralize state revenues. These revenues could be used for increasing lending to productive units as well as for investments in basic industries, in particular infrastructure, where use needs to be made of economic project evaluation.

Investments in infrastructure are necessary for the expansion of manufacturing industry as well as agriculture and for obtaining gains through increased regional specialization. At the same time, the measures proposed for industry and agriculture are interdependent, inasmuch as the two sectors provide consumer goods as well as inputs for each other. Political and administrative constraints will, however, affect the pace at which progress can be made and there may be differences in this regard between the two sectors.

NOTES

1. For a detailed description, see B. Balassa, *The Hungarian Experience in Economic Planning* (New Haven, Conn.: Yale University Press, 1959).
2. On the Yugoslav reform, see B. Horvat, *The Yugoslav Economic System* (New York: M. E. Sharpe, 1976); a description of the development of the Hungarian reform and an evaluation of recent changes, respectively, are provided in the author's 'The Hungarian Economic Reform, 1968–81', and 'Reforming the New Economic Mechanism in Hungary', Essay 12 and 13 in this volume. All subsequent references to Hungary derive from these sources.
3. Sources for all the figures cited in respect to China are available from the author.
4. Between 1978 and 1981, the share of investment in national income (net material product) was reduced from 36.5 percent to below 30 percent and that of productive investment in the total fell from 82.6 percent to 58.9 percent, with commensurate increases in the share of housing, cultural, educational, and health-related investments that are classified as unproductive.
5. It is conceivable, however, that these reserves were not considered to be part of the money supply.
6. See W. Byrd, *China's Financial System: The Changing Role of Banks* (Boulder, Col.: Westview Press, 1983) pp. 71–5.
7. Interest rates on six-month deposits were increased from 3.7 to 4.4 percent, on one-year deposits from 4.1 to 5.6 percent, on three-year deposits from 4.6 to 6.3 percent, and on five-year deposits from 5.1 to 7.1 percent. Prior to April 1979, interest rates on all time deposits were 2.2 percent. In turn, interest rates on demand deposits were raised to 3.0 percent in April 1980 from 2.3 percent in the preceding two decades.
8. According to an official report, 'the investment not covered by the national budget exceeded the plan to a fairly large extent, and blind and duplicate construction was not eliminated'. 'Communiqué on Fulfilment of China's 1981 National Economic Plan for 1981', *Beijing Review*, 19 May 1982, p. 19.
9. Byrd, pp. 46–7.
10. Byrd (p. 77) reports that, in 1979, profit rates on total assets averaged 24.2 percent in Chinese industry and 47.1 percent in Shanghai alone.

11. A case in point is silk brocade where a collective enterprise in Sichuan could not increase its price despite the rise in the price of silk paid to farmers, leading to a decline in profit margins.

12. The official report on plan fulfilment in 1981 writes: 'Owing to the blind pursuit by some enterprises of output value and speed in disregard of quality of products and market demand, the output of some products that should be limited under the plan also increased blindly, so that there is warehouse overstocking. ... In addition, some enterprises sold shoddy goods for quality goods, decreased quantities at original prices or otherwise raised prices in disguised forms' ('Communiqué', pp. 18, 21).

13. This is being done today on an experimental basis. Such exceptions aside, however, firms do not pay interest on circulating capital provided from the budget. This is also generally the case for budgetary appropriations for capital construction, except for the loans provided through the People's Construction Bank of China in recent years.

14. *Beijing Review*, 21 December 1981, p. 28.

15. 'Election of Directors', *Beijing Review*, 29 December 1981, p. 6.

16. *Beijing Review*, 21 December 1981, p. 21.

17. In fact, the Hungarian price system is much more complicated than this statement would indicate. Also, the adoption of world market price relations necessitates import competition that would not be practicable under present conditions in China. For a detailed discussion of the Hungarian experience, the reader is referred to the papers by the author cited earlier.

18. In Chengtu, for example, a machinery-producing enterprise was given a plan for 1980 that would have permitted utilizing only 28 percent of its capacity; in finding new markets through negotiated sales, the extent of capacity utilization was raised to 61 percent. Also, Shanghai machine-building factories created new kinds of machinery for light industry and agriculture and embarked on the production of durable consumer goods while a steel plant developed 80 new products for use in light industry.

19. The first case is shipbuilding, to be followed by automobiles.

20. In this connection, note may be taken of a statement made in an article in the official Party daily. 'There is an acute shortage of energy supplies such as fuel, oil, and electric power, and communication and transportation facilities are insufficient. However, many of the current projects under construction consume a large quantity of energy resources and materials which need to be transported from far away places.' ('How Are We to Grasp this Year's Economic Work Well', *Renmin Ribao*, 9 March 1981, p. 22 as quoted in *Foreign Broadcast Service*, 11 March 1981, p. L12).

21. In interpreting this figure, it should be noted that household plots are characterized by intensive cultivation and the product can be freely sold at negotiated prices without any tax obligation or payment to the commune.

22. N. R. Lardy, 'Agricultural Price in China', World Bank Staff Working Papers, 606 (1983) p. 20.

23. Lardy, p. 53.

24. Liu Hujia, the Minister of Agriculture, stressed the need to 'further improve the various forms of responsibility system in farm production with remuneration based on output, since they are welcomed by the peasants.

While upholding the principle of collectivization, the system of responsibility in production will not be changed for a long time to come'. (*Beijing Review*, 23 November 1981, p. 5).

25. *Beijing Review*, 8 February 1982, p. 22 – This means that the state does not any more take responsibility to provide jobs to all those who enter working age. In fact, it has not been able to discharge this responsibility in recent years.

26. While in the Chinese press it has been alleged that the introduction of market activities is responsible for illicit actions, such actions would not occur if market activities were given full scope.

27. In Beijing, for example, there is still only one small private restaurant.

28. *Beijing Review*, 3 February 1982, pp. 22–3.

Part V
Economic Policies in a
Developed Country: France

Essay 15   Economic Policies in France: Retrospect and Prospects

INTRODUCTION

The fifteen-year period following entry into the European Common Market was one of rapid economic expansion in France. In particular, policies promoting industrial concentration and investment contributed to the modernization of French industry in the framework of an open economy.[1] The distruptions caused by the May 1968 events were soon overcome, and France experienced the highest rate of economic growth among the Common Market countries. In particular, the income gap between Germany and France declined to a considerable extent. According to estimates made by using purchasing power parities, the ratio of French to German *per capita* incomes increased from 0.73 in 1958 to 0.97 in 1973.[2]

Along with other industrial countries, in 1973–4 France suffered the effects of the quadrupling of oil prices that represented a 'tax' of about 3 percent on its national income. After a brief review of the policies applied in the following three years (Section I), this essay will examine the economic program of the Barre government (Section II) and the practical implementation of this program (Section III). The situation confronting the French government after the doubling of oil prices in 1979 will further be analyzed, with consideration given to alternative policy choices (Section IV).

I DEVELOPMENTS IN THE 1974–6 PERIOD

The quadrupling of oil prices evoked few immediate policy reactions in France and expansionist tendencies continued until after the Presidential elections of May 1974. The lack of reaction may be explained in part by the illness and the death of President Pompidou and by the disinclination of government officials to take restrictive measures during the Presidential campaign. However, there also appears to have been a tendency to favor a *fuite en avant* in the hope that the increased petroleum bill would be financed by a rise in exports.

These expectations were disappointed. Increases in exports fell behind the rise in imports that responded to the rapid growth of GDP in France (4.1 percent between the third quarters of 1973 and 1974) in contrast with the slowdown of economic activity in the other industrial countries, where restrictive policy measures were adopted. Thus, the ratio of merchandise exports to imports, the so-called *taux de couverture*, fell from 103 percent in the third quarter of 1973 to 91 percent in the third quarter of 1974. With the rising balance-of-payments deficit, the effective exchange rate for the French franc, calculated by the International Monetary Fund by the use of trade weights, depreciated by 7.4 percent.

At the same time, the rate of inflation accelerated; the consumer price index increased by 14.5 percent between the third quarters of 1973 and 1974 as against a rise of 7.6 percent in the preceding twelve month period. Increases in consumer prices were fueled by the 20.1 percent rise in hourly wage rates while energy prices were not fully adjusted to reflect the quadrupling of the world market price of petroleum. Correspondingly, despite reductions in working hours, real weekly earnings increased by 3.1 percent.

The application of an anti-inflationary policy was announced in the summer of 1974. It involved higher taxes, credit restrictions, and a slowdown in the growth of public expenditures. The stated objective of the plan was 'to regain a rate of inflation of 1 percent per month in six months and to reach 0.5 percent a month within a year'. Furthermore, the trade deficit was to be eliminated during the course of 1975.

In fact, the rise in consumer prices decelerated, with increases of 10.9 percent between the third quarters of 1974 and 1975 and only 0.7 percent a month in the third quarter of 1975. In the same quarter, the *taux de couverture* of imports reached 102 and the effective exchange rate appreciated by 9.7 percent compared to its year-earlier level. But these results were attained at the cost of a fall in industrial production by 12.7 percent and a decline in GDP of 4.5 percent between the third quarters of 1974 and 1975.

Notwithstanding the decline in GDP, consumption continued to rise in line with increases in real weekly earnings of 2.1 percent during this period. The brunt of the contraction was borne by investments that fell precipitously, following decreases in profit margins. Gross profits as a percentage of value added, excluding production taxes, in non-financial enterprises declined from 28.9 percent in 1974 to 26.8 percent in 1975, following a decrease from 30.4 percent in 1973.

The expansionary measures taken in September 1975 responded to the fall in industrial production and GDP; they were also motivated by the forthcoming municipal elections. The measures included increases in funds available for private consumption; an expansion of public investment; tax benefits for private investment; and postponement of the payment of taxes on business incomes. The measures applied contributed to the rise of industrial production by 13.8 percent, and that of GDP by 5.9 percent, between the third quarters of 1975 and 1976.

But the growth of production brought with it a deterioration of the balance of payments, with the *taux de couverture* of imports falling to 90 percent and the effective exchange rate depreciating by 10.4 percent between the third quarters of 1975 and 1976. And while the rate of inflation (9.6 percent) was somewhat lower than in the preceding year, price increases accelerated towards the end of the period, reaching 1 percent a month. Also, increases in real weekly earnings (4.7 percent between the third quarters of 1975 and 1976) further compressed profit margins, with the share of profits in the value added of non-financial enterprises falling to 26.4 percent in 1976.

II THE PROGRAM OF THE BARRE GOVERNMENT

The years 1974–6 represent the application of 'stop-and-go' policies in France. These policies involved the use of Keynesian measures of demand management that were, in each phase, stronger than the measures employed by partner countries. This is evidenced by variations in the *taux de couverture* of imports as well as in effective exchange rates.

While the policies applied permitted reaching a rate of economic growth somewhat higher than in the other EEC countries (2.5 percent a year between 1973 and 1976 as compared to 1.7 percent for the

Common Market as a whole), this divergence was not sustainable. It entailed a substantial deficit in the current account of the balance of payments, inclusive of private and official transfers ($5.9 billion in 1976 as against an approximate balance in 1973), as well as increases in labor costs, with the rise in real weekly earnings (10.2 percent between the third quarters of 1973 and 1976) exceeding the growth of labor productivity (6.8 percent) by a considerable margin.

The increase in labor costs aggravated the adverse effects on domestic inflation of the balance-of-payments deficit that raised the cost of imported materials through the depreciation of the franc. It further led to a decline in the share of profits in value added in non-financial enterprises from 30.4 percent in 1973 to 26.4 percent in 1976. Parallel declines were experienced in the volume of investment in the industrial sector.

According to the first declaration of the newly-appointed Barre government on overall economic policies on 26 August 1976, 'the principal objective of the new government will be to combat inflation and to maintain the stability of our currency'. As Prime Minister Raymond Barre stated in an interview given to Rhône-Alpes on 5 July 1978, these objectives were to be served by 'reducing the rate of increase of the money supply; limiting the budget deficit to an amount that can be financed without new money creation; moderating the increase in remunerations while assuring the maintenance of the purchasing power of wages; and defending the franc so as to avoid the depreciation of the currency leading to increases in the prices of imported products, and hence in the general price level'.[3]

The stability of the franc, in turn, requires equilibrating the balance of payments that represents 'the external constraint which no country participating ... in international trade can escape'.[4] Correspondingly, 'it is not the pursuit of maximal growth that should predominate in France in the next few months, and even in the next few years, but that of a growth rate which is compatible with the progressive reduction of our external deficit and the stability of our currency ...'[5]

At the same time, Barre excluded 'a return to protectionism that would lead in our country to a decline of economic activity and the standard of living'.[6] Rather, in his view, the balance-of-payments constraint on economic growth could be alleviated over time by 'increasing productivity, avoiding the *déréglements* that lead to internal inflation, external deficit, and the depreciation of the currency, economizing on imported energy, and developing the production of nuclear energy'.[7]

Increasing productivity, in turn, was said to necessitate improving the competitiveness of French industry. This objective was to be pursued by promoting productive investment and structural change. The measures envisaged for the promotion of investment included increasing the rate of self-financing by slowing-down wage increases and liberalizing industrial prices; providing tax incentives to productive investment; and improving the operation of financial markets. Price liberalization was also said to contribute to structural change by remedying distortions in relative prices. The objective of structural change was further to be served by providing benefits to research and development and reducing the scope of government aids and interventions.

The policy stance adopted by the Barre government reflects the desire to increase reliance on market forces and on general policy measures as against specific interventions. General policy measures in the form of increases in the prices of gasoline, fuel oil, and public utilities were also to be used to economize with energy. But, the increased use of nuclear energy was to be brought about by government investment.

All in all, the program of the Barre government gave emphasis to long-term objectives. And while it is customary to view price stability as a short-term objective, Barre regarded reducing the rate of inflation and stabilizing the franc as preconditions for favorable long-term performance. At the same time, in the case of conflicts, the long-term objectives have taken precedence over short-term changes in the price index. Thus, in an interview given to *Le Point* on 5 June 1978 immediately following the liberalization of industrial prices, Barre stated: 'The price indices will go up in the coming months. These increases are adjustments and not inflationary price rises ... Let us not get into a nervous state over prices. Let us try to understand what is happening and understand that our policy is to build a sounder economy.'

At the same time, Barre rejected Keynesian remedies for unemployment on the grounds that these would ultimately have unfavorable long-term effects because of the resulting deterioration of the balance of payments and increases in prices. Rather, he expressed the view that 'there will not be a real and durable improvement in employment without a basic change in the economic situation [without] return to the basic equilibria of the national economy, on which depends the resumption of a sustained and durable growth ...'[8]

III POLICIES AND PERFORMANCE

This essay will examine the policies applied and the results obtained under the Barre government. The discussion will concern fiscal and monetary policy; wage and price policy; exchange rate policy and foreign trade; profits and investment incentives; policies relating to employment and social policies; industrial policy; and energy policy. It will cover the three-year period between the third quarters of 1976 and 1979, thus excluding the effects of the doubling of oil prices of 1979, which will be taken up in conjunction with the future perspectives of the French economy.

Fiscal and monetary policy

Reducing the deficit in the governmental budget was one of the principal measures proposed by the Barre government to combat inflation. In fact, the deficit was reduced slightly from 30.3 billion francs in the twelve-month period between the third quarters of 1975 and 1976 to 27.8 billion francs in the following year. In turn, with actual deficits exceeding the budgeted figure by a substantial margin, an increase to 39.5 billion francs occurred in the period between the third quarters of 1977 and 1978, with a decline to 29.2 billion francs a year later.[9]

While stating that 'he would feel profound anxiety if the deficit reached 25 billion francs in 1978', in an interview given to *L'Expansion* on 28 August 1978, Barre noted that 'even under this hypothesis, we would conserve one of the healthiest budgetary situations among the industrial countries'. In the event, the deficit attained 31 billion francs but, expressed as a proportion of GDP, it remained smaller in France than in the other major industrial countries.[10]

Barre further suggested that 'as long as the growth of the money supply is controlled and the sources of money creation are appropriately regulated, one can accept a budget deficit for the sake of counter-cyclical objectives'.[11] In fact, the government relied largely on borrowing to finance its deficit, except for the last twelve-month period when the financing of slightly one-half of the deficit involved monetary operations that have their counterpart in changes in the money supply, defined to include also quasi-money.

As a result, the rate of increase of the money supply thus defined (M2) declined whereas it had been rising in the preceding years.

Between the third quarters of two consecutive years, the increase was 13.4 percent in 1972–3, 15.3 percent in 1973–4, 16.6 percent in 1974–5, 17.3 percent in 1975–6, 12.0 percent in 1976–7, 13.7 percent in 1977–8, and 13.0 percent in 1978–9. Correspondingly, after rising from 46.2 percent in 1973 to 48.7 percent in 1976, the ratio of the money supply to the gross domestic product stabilized at this level.

The budget deficit was in part financed by the sale of Treasury bills, an increasing proportion of which was purchased by the Caisse des Dépôts. The financing of the deficit further involved the sale of government bonds that reduced the availability of the bond market for private financing. On the other hand, as noted below, the implementation of the *Loi Monory* increased the availability of funds for share issues.

Wage and price policy

Apart from monetary and fiscal policy, moderation in increases in wages and prices was to be one of the pillars of the anti-inflationary policy of the Barre government. According to a statement made by Prime Minister Raymond Barre to the Association of Economic and Financial Journalists on 20 December 1977, 'the objective to be attained in the next few years should be to bring down the rise of prices and remunerations to a rate similar to that of our principal partner countries, i.e., well under 10 percent'.

While a wages policy in the British style was not practised, the government's recommendations that, apart from low income recipients, the rise of remunerations should not exceed the rate of increase of consumer prices, influenced wage setting in the public sector and, indirectly, the private sector.[12] In fact, the rate of increase of real wages decelerated, with increases in real weekly earnings between the third quarters of consecutive years of 4.5 percent in 1972–3, 3.1 percent in 1973–4, 2.1 percent in 1975–6, 1.5 percent in 1976–7, 1.6 percent in 1977–8, and approximately 1 percent in 1978–9.[13]

These changes occurred as increases in wage rates averaged 12.6 percent a year between the third quarters of 1976 and 1979, working hours declined at an average annual rate of 0.6 percent while increases in consumer prices were between 9 and 10 percent in the first two years and exceeded 10 percent in the third. At the same time, comparisons of rates of increase of consumer prices show practically no change vis-à-vis Germany. But, inflation slowed down to a greater extent in Italy and the United Kingdom that had experienced very rapid price increases in the years immediately following the oil crisis. Correspondingly, the average rate of inflation in the European Common Market fell below that in France while it had been higher in the years before 1977. However, France maintained earlier price relationships with the OECD, taken as a whole, with an inflation differential of approximately 1 percent in favor of the OECD.

Increases in the prices of manufactured goods between the third quarter of consecutive years were 6.2 percent in 1976–7, 9.2 percent in 1977–8, and 10.9 percent in 1978–9. The 6.2 percent figure in the first year is much below historical trends, in part because of the temporary price freeze introduced by the Barre government in September 1976 and in part because of reductions in turnover taxes undertaken in January 1977.[14] In turn, the 12.1 percent rise in the prices of imported industrial materials between the third quarters of 1978 and 1979, following approximate stability in the previous two years, contributed to the acceleration of price increases.

Exchange rate policy and foreign trade

Exchange rate stability and improvements in the balance of payments were among the principal objectives of the Barre government. While the effective exchange rate for the franc depreciated by 5.2 percent between the third quarter of 1976 and the first quarter of 1978 – a period of political uncertainty prior to the March elections – it appreciated subsequently, reaching 98.7 percent of the 1976 third quarter level in the third quarter of 1979. And, the real effective exchange rate for the franc regained its three-year earlier level, irrespective of whether this is calculated by adjusting effective exchange rates for changes in wholesale prices, export unit values, or unit labor costs.[15]

At the same time, aided by favorable developments in France's major markets and by improvements in the commodity composition of exports, the French trade position improved to a considerable extent. The *taux de couverture* of foreign trade reached 95 percent in the third quarter of 1979 as compared to 90 percent in the third quarter of 1976. With favorable changes in service items, improvements in the current account of the balance of payments were even larger, contributing to the rise of France's foreign exchange reserves from a low point of $5.3 billion in September 1976 to $15.8 billion three years later.

Profits and investment incentives

The slowdown of wage increases, together with increases in producer prices and the rise of labor productivity, led to a reversal of the tendency to lower profit shares. The share of profits in the value added of non-financial enterprises, net of production taxes, increased from 26.4 percent in 1976 to 27.0 percent in 1977 and, again, to 27.5 percent in 1978. And while the preliminary estimate shows a decline to 27.1 percent in 1979, profit margins in the manufacturing sector increased further.

Increases in profit margins permitted raising the share of self-financing in private enterprises. The financing of new investment was further aided by the *Loi Monory* of July 1978 that provided for the de-taxation of incomes invested in common stocks up to a maximum of 7000 francs per year for a family with three children.

Also, a variety of investment incentives were introduced. They include reductions in the fiscal cost of increases in capital, the creation of new financing instruments for private enterprises in the framework of the *Loi Monory*, and measures aimed at encouraging the establishment of small- and medium-size enterprises. Furthermore, an investment tax allowance equal to 10 percent of the net growth of investment and an increase in the amortizable base of capital acquired through the aid of existing incentives were made available for investments undertaken in 1979 and in 1980.

The question arises as to what extent these measures contributed to investment activity. According to national accounts data, the fall in the volume of business investment in 1974 and in 1975 was followed by increases in subsequent years, except for the year 1977 that preceded the elections for the National Assembly. In 1979, the increase was 4 percent, with public firms showing a larger rise (9 percent) than private firms (2 percent). In turn, orders for equipment – expressed in current prices – that hardly exceeded the 1973 level in 1976, increased by 11 percent in 1977, by 15 percent in 1978, and by 16 percent in 1979, while equipment prices rose by about 9 percent a year.

Employment and social policies

The OECD estimates that between 1976 and 1979 total employment grew by 0.3 percent in France, 0.6 percent in Germany, and 1.3 percent in the United Kingdom. In turn, between the third quarters of 1976 and 1979, the rate of unemployment rose from 4.6 percent to 6.1 percent in France as compared to a decline from 3.5 percent to 3.0 percent in Germany and from 7.0 percent to 5.6 percent in the United Kingdom.[16]

Differential trends in employment and in unemployment largely reflect demographical differences. In the 1975–80 period, the working age population increased at an average annual rate of 0.8 percent in France as compared to 0.4 percent in Germany and in the United Kingdom.[17] Also, France experienced a rise in labor participation rates as a growing number of women entered the labor force. Correspondingly, it had yearly additions of 250 000 to its labor force, contributing to an increase in the total number of unemployed from 870 000 in the third quarter of 1976 to 1 330 000 in the third quarter of 1979.

Special measures were taken however to increase the employment of the young in the form of the *Pacte national pour l'emploi des jeunes*, legislated in July 1977 and renewed in July 1978 and in July 1979, providing fiscal benefits to firms that hire young workers and provide for their training. While the training measures bring long-term benefits, the employment effects of the two pacts remained relatively limited. According to an estimate made by INSEE, the first pact reduced unemployment by 90 000 at the end of 1977 but by only 30 000 in the spring of 1978, while the decrease of unemployment under the second pact was estimated at 30 000 for the end of 1978. In turn, the third pact was supposed to create more employment than the second but less than the first.[18]

At the same time, unemployment compensation was provided up to 90 percent of the preceding year's wages for one year and, in the case of continued education, for two years. In March 1979, these rates were lowered in order to reduce their perverse incentive effects while the unemployment compensation of low-income workers was increased.

Also, in advocating that wages and salaries should not be increased in excess of the rise in the consumer price index, the Barre government made exceptions for people with low incomes. In particular, Prime Minister Raymond Barre proposed to increase the purchasing power of the minimum wage, of family allowances, and of the minimum pension.[19] Available data shows that between 1976 and 1978 the purchasing power of the minimum wage rose by 6.8 percent while comparable figures are 4.9 percent for hourly wage rates, 4.5 percent for weekly earnings, 2.9 percent for technicians and foremen, and 2.4 for managers and administrators. In the same period, the purchasing power of basic family benefits increased by 5.8 percent and that of minimum old-age pensions by 16.1 percent.[20]

All in all, social benefits including health care, family allowances, maternity benefits, old-age pensions, and unemployment compensation increased more rapidly than wages and salaries. Between 1976 and 1979, wages and salaries increased by 39 percent while social benefits rose by 59 percent. In the same period, social charges increased by 61 percent, representing a rise from 14.7 percent to 16.4 percent of GDP.

Industrial policy

The Barre government repeatedly expressed its intention to promote structural change in order to increase the competitiveness of French industry. As noted earlier, apart from incentives to investment, structural change was to be promoted by increasing benefits to research and development and by reducing the scope of government aids and interventions.

Measures taken in favor of research and development included grants to firms creating or developing scientific and technical research departments, and accelerated depreciation equivalent in the first year to 50 percent of the cost of investment in research by companies employing no more than 2,000 workers. But it was the liberalization measures that attracted most attention, in France as well as abroad.[21]

In announcing the 'progressive and irreversible liberalization of industrial prices' in a speech in Blois on 7 January 1978, Barre emphasized that this action finds its inspiration in the needs of a modern competitive industry. As far as government aids and interventions are concerned, in an interview given to *L'Expansion* in April 1978, Barre stated: 'One should not hesitate to let the dead wood fall; i.e. those sectors where we are not well-placed. The future of France does not depend on the number of ships it builds at a loss or on the production of steel it cannot sell. What is more profitable? To have a genuine commercial shipping fleet (equipped, if it is more profitable with ships constructed abroad) or to exhaust ourselves in subsidizing shipbuilding? Also, there is no divine decree that France must produce thirty million tons of steel per year when, in concentrating on basic production (possibly twenty thousand million tons) and buying the rest from abroad, it may develop its mechanical industries under more favorable conditions.'

Government aids have traditionally played an important role in

French industry. Data published in the so-called Hannoun report show that these aids benefited a relatively small number of large industrial concerns, with nine of them receiving 56 percent of the total in 1976. Hannoun is further said to have concluded that state assistance became part of the companies' profit structure.[22]

By reason of the lack of information, it is difficult to ascertain what changes have taken place since 1976 in the size and allocation of government subsidies. It has been reported however that state aid is becoming increasingly tied to the amount of productive investments undertaken. Also, there is a greater willingness on the part of the government to accept 'adjustment by bankruptcy' in cases when future prospects are unfavorable.

However, the government came to the rescue of the major steel producing firms, taking a majority position in these firms with a view to modernizing the industry, involving reductions in capacity by one-quarter and in the number of workers by 30 percent. Following adverse reactions in the affected regions, agreement was reached on a social pact that accomplishes the job-cutting program by a combination of early retirement, bonuses for voluntary departure and guarantees of alternative jobs. The continuation of subsidies to shipbuilding may also be explained by regional considerations, although the five largest shipbuilders are supposed to restructure their operations.

In turn, while the influence of planning on firm decision-making declined practically to vanishing point, the Ministry for Industry appears to have increased its interventions. These interventions do not include prestige projects, such as the Concorde, that cost France dearly in earlier years. Nonetheless, questions arise about the ability of the government to make appropriate choices among sectors and, within individual sectors, among firms.[23] And, although interventions are supposed to be concentrated in new fields such as oceanography and *télématique* – a combination of data processing and communications – development contracts will also be offered in food processing. Yet, in this industry, concentration may offer greater benefits than would assistance to small- and medium-size firms.

Energy policy

As noted earlier, energy policy in France comprises price measures as well as investment policy, in particular in nuclear energy. The price of industrial fuel nearly doubled immediately following the quadrupling of the world market prices of petroleum in 1973–4. However, increases were smaller in energy prices charged to consumers (42 percent between the third quarters of 1973 and 1974) and, in particular, in the price of gasoline (29 percent).[24] Moreover, in the next two years, the price of energy to consumers increased by less than the overall consumer price index.

Price policy was modified by the Barre government, which raised energy prices for the consumer more than the average rise in consumer prices. As a result, France regained first place in terms of increases in energy prices relative to the consumer price index. On a 1973 basis, this ratio was 121 in France in 1978 as compared to 115 in the United States, 110 in Germany, 110 in the United Kingdom, and 98 in Japan.[25] And, between 1976 and 1979, the real price of gasoline rose by 23 percent in France as against an increase of 4 percent in Germany and a fall of 8 percent in the United Kingdom.[26]

Increases in energy prices contributed to the decline of the consumption of primary energy per unit of GDP in France. Expressed in terms of oil equivalents per thousand 1970 dollars, this ratio declined by 12 percent between 1973 and 1977 as against 10 percent in Japan, 8 percent in Germany, 8 percent in the United Kingdom, and 5 percent in the United States.[27]

At the same time, France increased the production of hydroelectricity and of nuclear energy, raising their shares in energy consumption from 5.7 percent to 8.3 percent and from 1.4 percent to 4.5 percent, respectively, between 1973 and 1979. As a result, despite the decline in domestic coal production, France reduced its dependence on external energy sources, from 76 percent in 1973 to 74 percent in 1979. With increased imports of coal and natural gas, the volume of 1979 oil imports was 7 percent below the 1973 level, accounting for 56 percent of energy consumption as compared to 66 percent six years earlier. It is planned to reduce this share to 30 percent by 1990, when nuclear energy should provide the same share of energy consumption.[28]

IV FUTURE PERSPECTIVES FOR THE FRENCH ECONOMY

The following section will present a balance sheet of the economic policies followed by the Barre government. Official government views, as well as the views of the Gaullist party (the RPR) and of the Socialist party, on economic policy issues in the period following the doubling of oil prices in 1979 will further be described. Finally, economic and social objectives, as well as possible measures for pursuing these objectives, will be considered.

The 1976–9 period: a balance sheet

It has been noted that, in the years immediately following the oil crisis, an acceleration of economic growth in France was accompanied by large balance-of-payment deficits. In turn, in the 1976–9 period, France maintained a respectable growth rate of GDP – 3.2 percent as compared to 2.5 percent in the preceding three years – while improving its balance of payments, as evidenced by the tripling of foreign exchange reserves. In the same period, the rate of economic growth averaged 2.9 percent in the European Common Market. And, although Germany had a slightly higher growth rate (3.5 percent), its current account surplus of $3.5 billion in 1976 gave place to a deficit of $4.9 billion in 1979.[29]

Furthermore, in contradistinction to the stop-and-go policies followed in the preceding three years, the Barre government maintained a policy of 'even keel' in reducing the rate of money creation and limiting budgetary changes over time. Correspondingly, there were little year-to-year variations in the rate of growth of GDP.

Economic growth in France was supported by increases in exports and in investment. Exports were favorably affected by the growth of the national economies of France's major trading partners, in particular Germany, as well as by improvements in product composition, leading to increases in France's market shares. According to a recent study, France occupies second place after Japan, and ahead of Germany, in regard to the rate of transformation of the export structure towards products for which world demand is rising rapidly. Nevertheless, the share of modern exports is still higher in Germany than in France.[30]

In turn, investments received fiscal incentives and benefited from increases in profit margins that resulted from the rise of productivity, the liberalization of industrial prices, and the slow-down of wage increases. And while until mid-1979 public firms accounted for much of the expansion of investment, investments by private firms subsequently assumed increasing importance.

Output per man-hour in manufacturing industry increased at an average annual rate of 3.7 percent between 1976 and 1979 as compared to a rise of 2.1 percent a year between 1973 and 1976. This increase was brought about in part by reductions in the work force that were made easier under the Barre government. With the rise in the working age population and higher labor participation rates by women, the rate of unemployment in France surpassed 6 percent towards the end of 1979.

In face of the slow-down of wage increases, low income recipients improved their relative position. The minimum wage was raised more than the average, and social benefits – in particular family allowances and the minimum pension – increased more rapidly than wages. This, however, necessarily involved an increased cost for the community at large.

The liberalization of prices permitted firms to vary their prices in response to demand; i.e. they can offset price reductions for products that face strong competition by increasing the prices of items which are highly demanded. At the same time, the rate of growth of producer prices reported by manufacturers increased from 0.6–0.7 percent a month in 1978 to 0.9 percent, 1.0 percent, and 1.1 percent in the first, second, and third quarters of 1979, respectively. Following a decline to 0.9 percent, the increase was 1.75 percent between January and March 1980.

It is as yet too early to evaluate the results of the policy of structural transformation pursued by the Barre government. While the scope of intervention by the planners continues to decline, the Ministry of Industry engages in specific interventions, the desirability of which is open to question. At the same time, the government apparently eschewed large prestige projects that had proved to be costly in the past and there is a greater willingness to accept 'adjustment through bankruptcy' in uncompetitive firms, except in cases when regional considerations are of importance. Furthermore, the freedom of action of French firms to pursue associations with foreign films has increased, as evidenced by recent attempts on the part of Compagnie Générale d'Electricité, St. Gobain-Ponta-Mousson, and Thomson-Brandt to form partnerships with foreign interests.

Finally, increases in energy prices contributed to the decline of energy consumption per unit of output in France. At the same time, the production of hydroelectricity and nuclear energy increased. With higher imports of coal and natural gas, petroleum imports declined in absolute terms.

Policy alternatives for the eighties

The policy of 'even keel' and the continued modernization of industry put France in a better position to weather the doubling of oil prices in 1979 than was the case in 1974. At the same time, the Barre government wished to avoid a repetition of the situation in the 1974–6 period, when the burden of the quadrupling of oil prices fell on profits, with adverse effects on business investment. Rather, Barre suggested that 'in 1980 more than ever, the principle, according to which we should have a moderate increase in remunerations, applies'.[31] He added that monetary and fiscal policy will not become more expansionist; in fact, more recently, selective credit restrictions were applied and some publicly financed programmes postponed.

The Gaullist party, in turn, favors an expansionist policy, involving a substantial rise in investment. However, as noted by *Le Monde*, it is not at all ensured – to say the least – that a vigorous expansion through increased investment activity would not bring with it, at least in part, the inconveniences of the Autumn 1975 Giscard-Chirac expansion, particularly in regard to the balance of payments and inflation. This plan, one remembers, stimulated imports at the same time as domestic consumption, thus leading to a deterioration of the trade balance and of prices.[32]

The Socialist party too calls for rapid economic expansion. Mitterrand's economic proposals of June 1979 envisaged a rate of growth of GDP of about 5.5 percent for the eighties while the January 1980 programme of the Socialist party called for rapid economic growth without citing a particular figure.[33] As noted by *Le Monde*, questions arise concerning the implications of this programme for inflation, for energy use, and for the balance of payments in general.[34]

Private as well as public consumption would be encouraged under the Socialist program, with increases in the wages of low-income recipients and in social benefits fueling the former and an ambitious programme of collective equipments spearheading the latter.[35] But, in contradistinction to the earlier Common Program of the Socialist and the Communist parties, a rapid expansion of investment is also envisaged. Investments would be undertaken to a large extent in the public sector, augmented by nationalizations, while private investments would be carried out in the framework of a national plan.

Apart from the immediate inflationary effects of the expansionary policies proposed by the Socialist party, these would be expected to lead to a deterioration of the balance of payments through rapid increases in the imports of energy, raw materials, and industrial products. The Socialist program, however, recommends 'disassociating economic growth and the consumption of energy'.[36] But the suggested energy-saving measures are not likely to reduce appreciably the income elasticity of demand for energy, and projections for new domestic energy sources appear to be overly optimistic. Also, while the Socialist program does not repeat earlier statements opposing nuclear energy, the future of nuclear development would seem to be in doubt under the program.

In turn, although expressing opposition to 'indiscriminate protectionism',[37] the program of the Socialist party represents a further step towards a more protectionist stance. The declared aim is to reduce the share of imports of GDP from 22 percent in 1978 to below 20 percent in 1990.[38] Moreover, the view is expressed that 'it is the responsibility [of the state] to take the necessary measures to ensure that the expansion of demand be satisfied by domestic production without risking inflation'.[39] The underlying philosophy is that 'a country which makes the effort of necessary expansion does not cause prejudice to others but just the opposite, if it accepts to maintain the volume of imports and is even willing to let them increase to the extent it considers useful'.[40]

Le Monde raises the question 'whether it could be envisaged to reduce the share of imports if economic growth accelerates. There is no precedent; it is, therefore, an entirely new policy one has to imagine since, until now, purchases abroad rose 1.5 and 2 times as fast as the rate of economic growth'.[41] At the same time, protectionist measures taken by France are likely to meet with retaliation and the existence of the Common Market may ultimately be jeopardized.

Economic and social objectives

Rapid economic growth is considered by the Socialists as a means of returning to full employment. Earlier, Prime Minister Raymond Barre stated that 'the development of the economy should not be sought as an objective by itself. It is, first of all, a means to assure full employment'.[42] However, in presenting the principal options of the VIIIth Plan, Barre reiterated his opposition to 'forcing growth for the sake of creating artificial full employment' when 'the consequence of forcing growth will soon be an increase in prices, external disequilibrium and, as a result, a restrictive policy that brings a slowdown in economic activity and unemployment'. Rather, in his view, 'increasing employment – [necessitates] improving the competitiveness of our productive system' and, further 'for France, the problem of unemployment is a medium-term problem. ... This is why the medium-term strategy proposed in the VIIIth Plan is fundamentally, entirely, oriented towards employ-ment'.[43]

Employment is given less emphasis in a subsequent statement at the Forum of *L'Expansion* on 10 January 1980, made after the recent doubling of oil prices, where 'greater price stability, healthy and durable employment for the French, and the pursuit of social progress' are listed as the principal economic and social objectives for the nineteen-eighties.[44] This change is emphasis, and the use of the expres-sion 'healthy and durable employment' rather than 'full employment', may be explained by the fact that the doubling of oil prices makes it more difficult to increase employment without aggravating inflation and balance-of-payments difficulties. At the same time, rapid increases in the labor force until 1985, with some slowdown in the following five years, are bound to exacerbate the unemployment problem.

According to an INSEE study, the population of working age in France will increase by 912 thousand between 1980 and 1985 and by 612 thousand between 1985 and 1990, with higher labor force partici-pation rates for women raising the number of entrants in the labor market to 1149 thousand in the first case and 665 thousand in the second.[45] At the same time, estimates made by the use of a macroecono-mic model suggest a decline in employment by 334 thousand between 1978 and 1985.[46] While the estimates were affected by the assumed deterioration of the competitiveness of French industry, leading to losses in export market shares, *L'Expansion* also predicts substantial increases in unemployment, with the potential labor force at 25.2 million and employment at 22.1 million in 1990.[47]

Increases in unemployment in recent years have not had the explo-sive social consequences that had been predicted. This is in part because of the importance among the unemployed of new entrants, women and the young, and the existence of transitional unemployment,[48] and in part because the labor unions have been more concerned with the standard of living of their working members than with the unemployed, the bulk of whom are not union members. One may go so far as to speak of a 'social consensus' that the transfer of part of the cost of the quadrupling of oil prices from entrepreneurs to workers has taken the form of increased unemployment rather than lower real wages for those employed.

However, the heads of families have increasingly entered the ranks of the unemployed and the length of unemployment has increased. Thus, between 1976 and 1979, the unemployment rate for men above 40 years increased twice as fast, and the number of unemployed for over one year three times as fast, as the average. If unemployment were to increase at rates even approaching those projected, these tendencies would continue further. It is difficult to escape the conclusion, then, that the continued rise of unemployment will increase social tensions. It is also bound to have adverse long-term consequences for individual behavior and the social fabric.[49]

Among proposed solutions, adding jobs in the public sector and reducing working hours are open to objections. As Barre noted, in a speech to the General Conference of the International Labor Office on 15 June 1980, the former would entail a higher budget deficit or higher taxes, with adverse effects on the economy and, ultimately, on employment. In turn, the experience of recent years indicates that small reductions in working hours would have little effect on employment whereas a substantial decrease would raise production costs unless accompanied by commensurate reductions in weekly wages.[50]

Rather, employment may be increased by raising levels of investment in the productive branches of the economy. Apart from its short-term effects during the period of construction, productive investment will have favorable long-term consequences for employment through the improved competitiveness of French industry as it facilitates the process of structural change.

By increasing the production of internationally traded goods for export and for import replacement, the improved competitiveness of French industry would also alleviate the balance-of-payments constraint on economic growth. A high rate of growth, in turn, is accompanied by increased demand for services, thus further adding to employment.

Until production comes on stream, however, increased investment would have adverse consequences for the balance of payments. In order to avoid reserve losses during this period, it would be desirable to encourage the inflow of foreign captial. This inflow may take the form of public and private firms borrowing in the Euro-bond market and from foreign commercial banks, where loans can be obtained at a real rate of interest much below the productivity of capital in France.

Foreign borrowing would also reduce pressure on domestic credit markets. It would nonetheless be desirable to increase credit facilities to industrial firms by reducing the preferences presently provided to savings for, and investment in, residential construction and, more generally, by limiting the amount of preferential lending that has assumed increasing proportions in France. Also, the competitiveness of the banking system would need to be increased.

It would further be desirable to broaden the existing system of tax benefits to investment and research and development by making some of the temporary measures permanent and introducing others, such as accelerated depreciation. At the same time, promoting the establishment of new industries in adversely affected regions, in particular in the North and the Northeast,[51] would tend to improve the interregional allocation of industrial production and employment. Finally, the tax system would need to be modernized by permitting corporations to offset losses against gains among subsidiaries and by improving the fiscal treatment of savings.

Shifting part of the burden of financing social benefits from the firm to the general budget, too, would contribute to investment and provide incentives to labor-intensive activities by reducing the cost of labor to the firm. However, in order to avoid increases in the budget deficit, taxes on consumption would need to be raised and the share of social security expenditures in the gross domestic product stabilized.[52]

Promoting investment at the expence of consumption would need to be accompanied by measures aimed at reducing income inequalities. While Peter Wiles has convincingly argued that income inequalities have been overestimated in France,[53] the existence of inequalities is undeniable. The situation may be improved by continuing what Lionel Stoleru has called 'la longue marche vers l'impôt négatif' through a greater differentiation of the system of social benefits aimed at helping the poor and by raising the effective rate of taxation of high-income recipients.

CONCLUSIONS

This essay recommended increasing the rate of investment in France for the sake of increasing employment and alleviating the balance-of-payments constraint on economic growth. A higher rate of investment would also permit financing a greater proportion of the transfer implicit in the doubling of oil prices through increases in production.

It has further been suggested to finance investment in part by foreign borrowing and in part by improving the tax treatment of investment and saving at the expense of consumption, while limiting the growth of expenditures in the social security system. At the same time, changes in the orientation of the social security system as well as in the tax system would need to be used to reduce income inequalities in France without, however, sacrificing incentives to work and risk taking.

One would further need to take measures to reverse the recent acceleration of inflation in France, due in large part to increases in the consumer prices of manufactured goods. Excluding energy products, these prices rose at an average annual rate of 15.2 percent in the fourth quarter of 1979 and 18.0 percent in the first quarter of 1980, after increases of 10–11 percent in the preceding quarters. With the nominal exchange rate being approximately maintained vis-à-vis the other Common Market currencies and appreciating vis-à-vis the US dollar and the Japanese yen, the real effective exchange rate for the French franc rose by about 5 percent between the third quarter of 1979 and the first quarter of 1980, contributing to the deterioration of the trade balance in manufactured goods.

However, the devaluation of the franc to fully offset the deterioration of the competitive position of French industry might be interpreted by private industry as a sign that the government accommodates price increases, thereby giving rise to an inflation-devaluation spiral. It may be appropriate, then, to limit changes in the value of the franc vis-à-vis the mark, the currency of France's principal trading partner, to differential changes in unit labor costs.

NOTES

1. For a detailed discussion see B. Balassa, 'The French Economy under the Fifth Republic, 1958–1978', in W. G. Andrews and S. Hoffmann, (eds), *The Fifth Republic at Twenty* (Albany, NY: State University of New York Press, 1981) pp. 204–25.
2. R. Marris and K. Peters, 'Real Domestic Product, Purchasing-Power Exchange Rates, and Related Data, for One Hundred Countries, 1950–1978' (Washington, DC; World Bank, 1980), mimeo.
3. Unless otherwise noted, all further citations in this and in the following sections of the essay are from a collection of statements by Prime Minister Raymond Barre.
4. Speech before the National Assembly, 12 October 1977.
5. Speech before the National Assembly, 12 October 1977.
6. Speech before the National Assembly, 5 October 1976.
7. Statement to the Association of Economic and Financial Journalists, 20 December 1977.
8. Speech before the General Conference of the International Labor Office, Geneva, 15 June 1978.
9. For the year 1978, the initially budgeted deficit was 8.4 billion francs and the actual figure 31.1 billion francs; for 1979, a deficit of 15.1 billion francs was initially budgeted and the actual deficit was estimated at 34.7 billion francs in December 1979 (Le Monde, *Bilan Economique et Social 1979*, Paris, 1980) p. 47.

10. In 1978, the relevant figure was 1.5 percent in France as compared to 2.0 percent in Germany, 15.4 percent in Italy, 6.5 percent in Japan, 5.2 percent in the United Kingdom, and 2.1 percent in the United States (International Monetary Fund, *International Financial Statistics*, April 1980).

11. Speech to the Association of Economic and Financial Journalists, 20 December 1977.

12. In a statement to the Convention of Enterprises on 14 December 1978, Barre cited a leading industrialist to have said in reference to wage increases: 'Mr Prime Minister, every time when you are firm, we will be even more firm. Every time you are not firm, we will yield.' It has also been reported that moderation in wage increases was a condition for private firms to receive government aids and public contracts.

13. The data do not include, however, increases in social security taxes in January and August 1979 that offset the rise in real wages in that year.

14. The 9.9 percent increase in consumer prices during the period were largely due to the 14.7 percent rise in the price of food caused by unfavorable weather conditions.

15. The estimates derived by using trade weights are reported in IMF, *International Financial Statistics*. For 1976, they pertain to the entire year rather than to the third quarter alone.

16. *OECD Economic Outlook*, July 1978 and December 1979.

17. United Nations Economic Commission for Europe, *Economic Bulletin for Europe*, XXXI (1974).

18. C. Fontaine, 'La situation sociale en 1978', *Revue d'Economie Politique*, LXXXIX (1979) pp. 859–76.

19. *Télévision Française 1*, 28 June 1978.

20. Centre d'Etude des Revenues et des Coûts, *Deuxième rapport sur les revenus des Français*, (Paris: La Documentation Française, 1979) pp. 75–83.

21. On reactions in the US press, see M. Bródy, 'Adieu to Controls', *Barron's*, 11 September 1978 and J. O. Goldsborough, 'Giscard's New French Revolution: Capitalism', *Fortune*, 9 April 1979.

22. 'How the State Slices its Cake', *World Business Weekly*, 3 March 1980.

23. For such a proposal see C. Stoffaes, *La grande menace industrielle*, (Paris: Calmann-Levy, 1978) Part III, Ch. III – For a critical appraisal, see Balassa.

24. In making comparisons with world market prices, it should be recognized that the domestic prices of energy in France include a large component of indirect taxes.

25. *OECD Economic Outlook*, July 1979.

26. *International Herald Tribune*, 14 May 1980.

27. Commission of the European Communities, *Europe*, January/February 1980.

28. *Le Monde*, 3 April 1980.

29. IMF, *International Financial Statistics*, June 1980 and *OECD Economic Outlook*, December 1978.

30. G. Lafay *et al.* 'Specialisation and adaptation face à la crise', *Economie Prospective Internationale*, Centre d'Etudes Prospectives et d'Informationes Internationales, No. 1, (1980).

31. Statement at the Forum of *L'Expansion*, 10 January, 1980.
32. *Bilan Economique et Social, 1979*, p. 61.
33. 'Le projet socialiste', Texte présenté a la discussion et au vote des militants, 12/13 January 1980, *Le Poing et la Rose*, Organe du Parti Socialiste, November/December 1979, p. 52.
34. *Bilan Economique et Social, 1979*, p. 61.
35. 'Le projet socialiste', pp. 49–50.
36. 'Le projet socialiste', pp. 56.
37. 'Le projet socialiste', pp. 62.
38. 'Le projet socialiste', pp. 51.
39. 'Le projet socialiste', pp. 62.
40. 'Le projet socialiste', pp. 62.
41. *Bilan Economique et Social, 1979*, p. 61.
42. Declaration to the National Assembly on general policies, 5 October 1976.
43. Speech to the Economic and Social Council, 2 May 1979, pp. 11, 18, 9.
44. Statement at the Forum of *L'Expansion*, 10 January 1980.
45. F. Eymard-Duvernay, 'Combien d'actifs d'ici l'an 2000?' in Dossier Horizon 1985, *Economie et Statistique*, No. 115, (1979), pp. 33–46.
46. Darmon, *et al.* 'Une projection détaillée en 36 branches a l'horizon 1985', (Paris: INSEE, 1980), mimeo.
47. *L'Expansion*, 11/24 January 1980.
48. According to one author, 'in our economy, if every year 10 percent of the workers change jobs and they take three months to find new employment, for this reason of workers' mobility alone the number of job seekers would be 500 000 to 600 000 to which we have to add those who enter the labor market (the young and women) and who encounter a 'normal' delay in finding work' (B. Durieux, 'Propos sur la politique de l'emploi', *Revue Economique*, XXIX (1978) p. 148).
49. As Raymond Barre eloquently expressed, 'work ... is the principal means of integration in the life of the society. In this way, it responds to the desire of each and everyone to measure himself against others and to gain, through his participation in the life of society, the esteem of others. Work, for a man or a woman, is certainly a means to provide for his needs and for those of his family, but it is first of all a privileged means to affirm his dignity' (Speech to General Conference of the International Labor Office, 15 June 1978).
50. The propositions made in the Giraudet report in April 1980 would effectively add a fifth week of vacation, while reducing the work week from 40 to 39 hours for those in physically onerous occupations, in exchange for increased flexibility in working hours for the sake of greater efficiency and machinery utilization. The implementation of these propositions would probably not add to employment but would increase labor costs to the extent that the loss in working hours would not be offset by higher productivity.
51. P. Mormiche, 'Chômage et qualification dans les regions', *Economie et Statistique*, No. 119 (1980) pp. 23–34.
52. For a percentive analysis of the measures that may be used to attain this objective, see B. Majnoni d'Intignano, 'La Sécurité sociale, une nouvelle Penelope?', *Commentaire*, No. 10, Summer 1980, pp. 254–59.

53. P. Wiles, 'An Internationally Comparable Distribution of Disposable Income for Households in France, 1970 – an Imaginative Reconstruction – is France More Equal than She Thinks?' (Paris: Fondation des Sciences Politiques, Service d'Etude de l'Activité Economique) August 1977.

Essay 16 The First Year of Socialist Government in France

INTRODUCTION

With the election of François Mitterrand to the Presidency on May 10, 1981, and the subsequent election of an overwhelming Socialist majority in the National Assembly, the French electorate not only turned its back on twenty-three years of government by the center-right but it brought to power a party that clearly distinguished itself from the old Socialist party, the Section Française de l'Internationale Ouvrière (SFIO), which had led several governments during the Fourth Republic. In his speeches and writings between 1977 and 1981, Mitterrand repeatedly expressed the view that the social democracy, represented by the SFIO, 'has not gone far enough in the reforms and, in particular, it has not appropriated the means to create a radical break with capitalism, by taking away its most decisive weapons'.[1] One also finds frequent references to the division of French society into two camps and to the transposition of this division into the political arena:

> It is his profound conviction, and he has expressed it on a number of occasions, that society is divided into two camps. This division corresponds to the most traditional division of our political future, between the right and the left, which is linked to a second division that finds its origin in the antagonism of the propertied classes and the wage-earners. These two distinctions are interrelated and become a single one with the left representing the exploited classes and the right the domination of the capital. In this scheme of things, the political forces are only the expression of social forces.[2]

The juxtaposition of two camps of society found expression in Mitterrand's statement, made at the National Congress of the Socialist party on 26 November 1978, that the Socialists are engaged in class warfare. Since the election of a Socialist majority, references to 'class warfare' have repeatedly been made in parliamentary debates. Thus, Mrs. Chislaine Toutain, deputy from Paris, speaks of 'the same kind of confrontation of the classes in the National Assembly as the one found in the enterprises'[3] and Jean-Yves Lhomeau in *Le Monde* concludes that 'the elected Socialist deputies represent a "class front", a notion in which the Socialist party has based its strategy'.[4]

The expressions 'break with the capitalism' and 'class warfare' have not, however, appeared in official government pronouncements. Rather, it has been repeatedly stated that the Socialist government aims at reaching its objectives in the framework of what Mitterrand has called 'the community of a mixed economy'.[5]

In presenting the interim plan for the years 1982 and 1983 to the National Assembly on 12 December 1981, Michel Rocard, minister of planning, spoke of a 'triad of reforms: the decentralization, the extension of the public sector, and planning.'[6] The main component of planning is industrial policy, which, in turn, has implications for the policy of protection. Also, the Socialist party set out to improve the lot of the working class and to accelerate rates of economic growth.

This essay will analyze the nationalizations (Section I), decentralization, planning, and industrial policy (Section II), the policies of protection (Section III) and social policy (Section IV), and macroeconomic policies and performance (Section V) during the first year under the Socialist government. The concluding section will further consider the situation created by the 12 June 1982 devaluation of the franc, and will briefly examine the perspectives for economic policy-making in France.

I THE NATIONALIZATIONS

In a wide-ranging speech at his 24 September 1981 press conference, President Mitterrand gave the following reasons for the nationalizations of large industrial groups and banks: to eliminate monopoly and quasi-monopoly positions that provide a basis for political influence and to safeguard national sovereignty while supplying the tools for industrial development in the future. He added: 'We made a choice of efficiency to reconstruct our industry'.[7] The last point was subsequently elaborated by Mitterrand's close advisors, Jacques Attali and Jean-Pierre Chevènement, according to whom the nationalizations would provide the basis for the rapid technological development of French industry.

Five industrial groups, Péchinery-Ugine-Kuhlmann, Saint-Gobain, Compagnie Général d'Electricité, Thomson-Brandt, and Rhône-Poulenc have been nationalized; the state has become the majority owner of Dassault, Matra, and CII-Honeywell-Bull; and it will take a majority position in ITT France. As a result, nationalized enterprises constitute one-third of industrial value added in France. More important, the state has assumed a dominant position in basic industries and a significant position in technologically advanced industries. Among basic industries, the share of the public sector has risen from zero to 71 percent in iron ore, from 1 to 79 percent in iron and steel, from 16 to 66 percent in other metals, from 16 to 52 percent in basic chemicals, and from zero to 75 percent in synthetic fibers. Among technologically advanced industries, the share of the public sector has increased from 58 to 74 percent in armament, from zero to 42 percent in consumer and industrial electronics, and from zero to 34 percent in office, computing, and accounting machinery. Also, the remaining large banks still in private hands at the time of Mitterrand's election have been nationalized.[8]

Mitterrand refers to the nationalizations as 'a choice of efficiency,' adding that 'in France, the nationalizations do work'.[9] Renault has often been cited as an example of a successful state-owned firm. It should be recognized, however, that in the period 1976–9, for which comparable data are available, pretax profits amounted to 5.0 percent of sales at Peugeot compared to 1.5 percent at Renault. Furthermore, while Peugeot had a loss and Renault made profits in 1980, Renault's performance again deteriorated, and that of Peugeot improved, in 1981.

It may be added that Renault was practically free to decide on its investment, production, prices, wages, and employment policy under the preceding governments. The question is, however, whether the freedom of action of nationalized firms will be maintained in the future. On 17 February 1982, in announcing the appointment of the new managers, Mitterrand stated that 'they should have total freedom of decision and action. The necessary controls will be made *a posteriori*'. He added, however, 'I expect that these firms develop new forms of social relations and become an important source of progress for the formation and condition of the workers.'[10]

In fact, state-owned firms are under pressure to sign so-called contracts of solidarity with the unions, resulting in increases in their labor costs, even though part of the cost is borne by the social security system. Renault agreed to give early retirement to 3500 employees aged 55 or older and to replace them by an equal number of new employees. Also, Renault – and other state-owned firms – are apparently less able to resist increases in wages than before.[11] Finally, Renault is reportedly under increased pressure to maintain employment and to absorb some high-cost firms.

Further questions arise concerning the multiannual contracts that the nationalized enterprises will sign with the government authorities. According to the draft bill approved by the Council of Ministers on 25 November 1981,

> The firms in the enlarged public sector ... will have complete freedom of action in the framework of revisable multiannual contracts they will negotiate with the supervising ministries. These contracts will determine the objectives of industrial and social development for the firm, as well as the reciprocal commitment of the firm and the state; their contents and their coherence with the general orientation of the plan will be examined by an interministerial committee.[12]

These contracts, then, provide an opportunity for the government to effect the longer-term orientation of the state-owned industrial enterprises. The government also plans to undertake the restructuring of the newly-nationalized firms and to influence their product composition.[13] This would involve the establishment of 'filières', that is vertical relationships among suppliers and users, as well as increased product specialization among firms.

The practical application of the filière concept, first introduced by Alain Boublil, an advisor to President Mitterrand, may limit the internationalization of the newly nationalized firms that contributed to their competitiveness in recent years.[14] Assigning the manufacture of particular products to a single firm will also reduce the extent of domestic competition.

Further questions arise concerning the financing of the nationalized enterprises. On 12 May 1982, it was announced that the deficit of three major newly nationalized firms (Péchiney-Ugine-Kuhlmann, Rhône-Poulenc, and CII-Honeywell-Bull), in the amount of 3 billion francs, will be financed from the budget. Furthermore, the nationalized banks will have to provide 6 billion francs, one-half in capital contributions and one-half in loans, to the state-owned industrial enterprises in 1982.

While the budgetary financing of nationalized enterprises has macroeconomic implications, government instructions to the nationalized banks to provide additional financing limits their freedom of action and appears to reflect the views of those who regard the satisfaction of the perceived needs of nationalized industry rather than profitability as the principal criterion of lending by the banks. At the same time, the increased use of directed credits, together with stricter credit controls, reduces the availability of funds to private industry.

II DECENTRALIZATION, PLANNING, AND INDUSTRIAL POLICY

While the nationalizations have increased the government's power of economic decision-making, the law on regionalization transfers some of its powers to the 95 mainland departments and to the 25 administrative regions, into which the departments have been combined. The general councils of the departments have traditionally been elected; in the future, regional assemblies will also be elected by popular vote.

The draft bill on planning reform, adopted by the Council of Ministers on 21 April 1982, calls for decentralizing the planning process, with the Planning Commission ensuring the consistency of regional and national objectives. The budgetary financing of local projects would take the form of negotiated contracts.

Although the modalities of regionalization are still to be worked out, it potentially represents an important break with three centuries of centralization. Decentralization is not, however, without its dangers. Apart from the difficulties involved in ensuring consistency between the national and the regional plans, the budgetary demands of the local authorities, and their access to debt financing, may accentuate macroeconomic disequilibria.

According to Christian Goux and Xavier Greffe, president and spokesman for the Commission for Planning Reform, respectively, 'after the nationalization and the decentralization, the reform of planning represents the third pillar [of structural changes in France]'.[15] The planning reform represents a step towards the preparation of the five year plan for 1984–8, which was preceded by the interim plan for the years 1982 and 1983.

The principal objective of the interim two-year plan was to create

400 000 to 500 000 new jobs. This could not be accomplished, however, without new investment taking the place of the rise in consumption which resulted from the measures applied following the establishment of a Socialist government. This idea was expressed by Michel Rocard, in terms not very different from those employed by former Prime Minister Raymond Barre,[16] when he presented the two-year interim plan to the National Assembly:

> Economic growth cannot lastingly be based but on the renewed expansion of industrial investment that not only guarantees the modernization of our industry but is also the best long-term guarantee of employment. Such a policy, that is at the heart of our two-year plan, implies the need to re-establish the necessary profit margins for the resumption of investment which, in the near future, must take the place of the resumption of consumption growth.[17]

The interim plan also called for an across-the-board effort to develop French industry. Thus, according to the draft bill on the approval of the interim plan, 'there are no condemned sectors, only outdated technologies. The development of new technologies would not only permit us to reinforce producer goods industries but also to revive our traditional consumer goods and intermediate goods industries'.[18]

Among industries producing intermediate products, a major financial effort is being made to finance the deficit of Péchiney-Ugine-Kuhlmann and Rhône-Poulenc. In turn, the steel industry will get much of the funds provided by the banks to the nationalized firms within a total commitment of 26 billion francs over four years that includes 6 milliard francs of equity infusion from the budget. Also, in the application of M. Mitterrand's pledge to aid the declining industries of the Lorraine, subsidies to coal production have been increased by one-third to 5.2 billion frances in 1982, accounting for one-half of the budget of the Ministry of Industry. These subsidies will not, however, be sufficient to finance the expected deficit of Charbonnages de France, although the cost of coal to Electricité de France exceeds that of competing fuels. Finally, as discussed later in this essay, the government has established programs to strengthen traditional consumer goods industries, involving the participation of producers at various levels of production as well as wholesalers, in the form of the filières of wood, leather, textiles, machine-tools and toys.

At the same time, under the plan prepared in May 1982, budgetary expenditures on research and development would increase in real terms by 15 percent in 1982 and by 18 percent in 1983, 1984 and 1985. As a result, the share of R&D spending in the gross domestic product would rise from 1.8 percent in 1981 to 2.5 percent in 1985.

The report on the electronics industry, presented by Jean-Pierre Chevènement in March 1982, recommends raising the research effort in this industry by two-thirds between 1980 and 1986.[19] In refusing the application of a policy of selected development, the report also calls for the parallel expansion of all major branches of the industry, with its output rising by 150 percent by 1990. This would involve further developing the industry's strong points, telecommunications-télématique and professional electronic equipment, and attempting to reduce the lag of the French electronics industry in information technology, office systems, automation and components. Fourteen projects have been identified, ranging from large main-frame computers to speech synthesis and recognition modules.

In addition to the report on the electronics industry, a report on the chemical industry was prepared. Once again a comprehensive approach was taken in proposing to maintain and to develop all major branches of the industry while an effort at restructuring would be undertaken.

The projected effort at rapidly increasing spending on research and development will bring beneficial results, provided these expenditures are appropriately used to increase the competitiveness of French industry. This would, however, require a reversal of past tendencies, when original research was emphasized at the expense of commercial applications. According to one observer, indications that 'advanced and esoteric applications' will be studied at the new World Center for Micro-computers and Human Resources, which far exceeds funding in any comparable laboratory in the United States.[20]

Questions arise also about the desirability of the government's guiding production decisions in areas which are subject to rapid change, such as consumer electronics, where private firms would also have to abide by the government guidelines. While reference has often been made to Japan as an example to emulate, it should be recognized that the Ministry of International Trade and Industry (MITI) does not attempt to influence production decisions. Rather than selecting 'national champions', MITI provides general support, with several firms competing in the market.

Furthermore, one may doubt the ability of the French electronics industry to progress in a parallel fashion in all areas. More generally, it should be recognized that an across-the-board effort at industrial development will necessarily encounter limits. There are limits on the amount of budgetary and credit financing; in particular, the absorption of considerable amounts of financial resources by nationalized enterprises will lessen the amount available to private enterprise. Nor can one provide incentives to all industrial sectors without reducing the value of these incentives to each of them. At the same time, conflicts arise as different industries are pressing their case.[21]

There is further a conflict between the employment and the modernization objectives. Efforts made to save firms from bankruptcy will maintain employment but discourage modernization.[22] Also, the recent reduction of social charges in the clothing industry will save employment by reducing labor costs but will not contribute to technological change. Such measures lead to similar demands by other industries; thus, the shoe industry promised to create 6000 jobs and to increase prices by less than the planned 15–20 percent, if its social charges are reduced by eight to nine percentage points.[23]

The policy of aiding small and medium-size enterprises may also encourage high-cost production. This danger is increased by the possibility that local authorities may provide aid, as they consider employment, not competitiveness, to be the principal goal. Thus, national and regional objectives may come into conflict.

Conflicts may further arise among the various ministries responsible for industrial policy. These responsibilities overlap to a considerable extent, and ideological and policy differences among certain ministers make the resolution of conflicts difficult.[24]

The final issue is the policy of protection. The across-the-board approach to industrial policy leads to demands for protecting weak industries against foreign competition – the subject of the following section.

III POLICIES OF PROTECTION

In the course of his press conference of 24 September 1982, President Mitterrand stated that 'we have to set out to regain our domestic market', adding that this is 'an essential objective of my Presidency'. This objective is to be served by agreements on the industries of wood, leather, textiles, machine-tools and toys, with firms accepting the obligation to manufacture certain products; wholesalers to increase the share of domestic products in their purchases, and the government to provide financial assistance and, if necessary, protection.[25]

The reported objectives are to reduce the share of imports in domestic sales from 60 percent to 30 percent for machine tools, from 20 percent to 15 percent for furniture, and from 25 percent to 10 percent for shoes and leather products.[26] The government intends to eliminate a trade deficit in leather and shoes of 1.3 billion francs over a three-year period. To pursue this objective, shoe manufacturers will reportedly be given import licenses in proportion to their success in reaching certain export targets, while distributors will have to buy a certain quota of domestic merchandise before being allowed to import.[27]

It has also been reported that the government has imposed licensing requirements on machine tool imports and has made increased use of the time-honored device of delaying customs clearance.[28] Furthermore, Michel Jobert, Minister of Foreign Trade, announced plans to set up a new unit to monitor imports into France and to establish a commission to hear industry's complaints against unfair practices from abroad. Furthermore, his ministry reportedly plans to contain the growth of imports through stronger controls against dumping, against financial aid and subsidies provided to foreign producers, and against abuse of EEC markets by importing from third countries through the member countries.[29]

There have been few signs so far, however, that wholesalers would limit imports. Also, the government has provided assurances to the Common Market Commission that it does not intend to restrict imports from the Community. Thus, EEC officials are said to be worried less about import restrictions than about the extent and variety of financial aids.[30]

In fact, the government is providing considerable financial assistance under the agreements with individual industries. It has been reported, for example, that the machine tool plan calls for loans and grants of 4.0 billion francs during the years 1982 to 1984. For the same period, the government is offering loans and grants of 1.7 billion francs to the textile industry that would further benefit from reductions in social security contributions, estimated to be worth 2.7 billion francs a year, the stated objective being zero growth of imports.[31]

While the protectionist measures actually taken do not go far, the threat of their future imposition has intensified, and some people speak of a change in atmosphere as regards protection.[32] Thus, according to *Le Matin*, 'the "international division of labor," considered as an established fact by the governments of Valéry Giscard d'Estaing, is thrown to the wolves. In the name of this principle, explain the economic advisors of the present government, entire sectors of the economy were abandoned, thereby adding to the number of unemployed'.[33] The article gives a long list of industries 'to regain', including 'iron and steel, pharmaceuticals, building materials, telephone, electronics, chemicals, shipbuilding, agricultural machinery, printing, and jewelry'.

High-technology industries are amenable to the application of protectionist measures, in view of the important role played by government contracts. Although contracts worth more than 150 000 SDRs (slightly over 1 million francs) require the opening of competitive bidding to foreign firms, ministers have reportedly demanded that such contracts be divided into smaller packages, and all foreign contracts worth more than 200 000 francs now require the approval of the Treasury.[34]

While increased reliance on domestic procurement in high-technology industries has been rationalized on grounds that these are infant industries, competitive pressures will be reduced thereby. The conclusion also applies to traditional industries, where the infant-industry argument has no relevance. At the same time, the measures taken in these industries affect to a large extent imports from developing countries.

Such is particularly the case for textiles and clothing where, along with the United Kingdom, France took the most protectionist attitude within the European Community. France succeeded in influencing its EEC partners, and ultimately, the other industrial countries to strengthen import limitations in the course of the 1981 renewal of the Multifiber Arrangement. France also plans to rigorously enforce the implementation of the new agreement. Thus, according to Dreyfus 'it does to suffice to sign the Multifiber Arrangement for our industries to be protected. We have to supervise its application'.[35]

The protectionist attitude taken vis-à-vis products of export interest to the developing countries appears to conflict with the Third World stance of the Socialist government. A change in this regard would occur if the proposals made by the group of experts appointed by Jean-Pierre Cot, Minister of Co-operation and Development, were to be followed. According to the experts, 'one should ensure the coherence of the policy of co-operation for development with commercial policy. In this perspective, a general attitude of opening vis-à-vis the products of the Third World is necessary and it is in the well-considered interest of France'.[36] In presenting the report, Cot noted that one should 'thrust aside the tentation of protectionism' although adding that 'this does not mean that "negotiated organizational measures" of trade would not be absolutely necessary in the sectors where the situation is "particularly critical"'.[37] These remarks point to the existence of a policy conflict that would need resolution.

IV SOCIAL POLICY

A variety of social measures were taken during the first year of the Socialist government, pertaining to wages and salaries; working hours; paid holidays and retirement, as well as employment creation and social services. Some of these measures had a budgetary cost while others increased the cost of labor to industry.

Although the quarterly rate of increase of the hourly wage rate fell continuously from a peak of 4.2 percent in the second quarter of 1980 to 2.8 percent in the first quarter of 1981, it rose afterwards and reached 4.7 percent (a compounded annual rate of increase of 20 percent) a year later. This result reflects a variety of influences, including the raising of the minimum wage by 25 percent between May 1981 and May 1982, the lack of a deliberate effort on the part of the government to contain the rise of remunerations in the months following the Presidential elections,[38] the lack of success of the government subsequently to negotiate wage restraints with the unions,[39] and, last but not least, reductions in working hours.

On 15 September 1981, Prime Minister Pierre Mauroy announced the government's decision to reduce the workweek from 40 to 35 hours by 1985, with a view to encouraging 'the sharing of work and revenues'. The first reduction, to 39 hours, was scheduled for February 1982, with the modalities to be worked out between the firms and the unions in the framework of 'contracts of solidarity'.

Agreements were reached in a number of firms, leading to a decline in the average workweek from 40.68 hours in the first quarter to 40.35 hours in the last quarter of 1981, with hourly wage rates raised to compensate for this decline in some cases and maintained in others. Lack of agreement elsewhere, however led to strikes.[40] Overruling Mauroy, President Mitterrand declared on 12 February 1982 that the reduction of the workweek from 40 to 39 hours be effected without a cut in weekly pay.[41] This decision was taken, notwithstanding the endorsement of a proportionate reduction in hourly wage rates by the CFTD, the major union favorable to the Socialist party, whose secretary general, Edmond Maire, termed Mitterrand's action as 'un faux pas sérieux' on the grounds that priority should be given to reducing unemployment.

Apart from the reduction of the workweek, the addition of a fifth week of paid vacation, to be applied to all industries by the end of 1982 or in early 1983, raises the cost of labor to the firm. And while labor productivity per hour may rise somewhat as the length of the workweek is reduced, longer vacations are not likely to have such an effect.

Labor costs increased further as a result of early retirement at 55 or 57 years, agreed upon in the framework of contracts of solidarity, but this cost is partly shared by the social security system. In turn, reducing the age of retirement from 65 to 60 years as of 1 April 1983, decided upon in January 1982, would cost 11 billion francs to the social security system and 6.5 billion francs to the complementary retirement schemes managed by the employers and the unions, though a substantial part of the total would be covered through the elimination of the existing 'guarantee of resources' scheme for early retirement.[42]

By April 1982, contracts of solidarity on early retirement, accounting for 95 percent of all such contracts, created 29 000 new jobs while those for reductions in working hours, accounting for 7 percent of the total, created 3000 jobs. Also, 55 000 new jobs were created in public administration in 1981, with 70 000 additional jobs budgeted for 1982.

Nevertheless, unemployment continued to increase, reaching 2 million in April 1982, compared to 1.7 million a year earlier. While the increase was smaller than increases in the other EEC countries, the average length of unemployment rose from 174 to 187 days, the share of those aged 25–49 years in the total number of unemployed increased from 39.4 to 40.0 percent, and that of men rose from 47.8 to 49.9 percent.

As regards social services, the minimum old age pension was raised by 20 percent on 1 July 1981 and by 18 percent on 1 January 1982; rent allocations were increased in two instalments by altogether 50 percent altogether; and family allocations were raised by 25 percent on 1 July 1981, with a further increase of 25 percent for families with two children in February 1982. Additional measures were taken in the framework of the 'family plan', in April 1982, to be applied from 1 September 1982, with an annual cost of 7.2 billion francs and a cost of 4 billion francs in the remainder of 1982. Finally, foregoing the application of the measures introduced by the preceding government to limit the rise of medical expenses, the annual rate of growth of these expenses increased from 15 to 20 percent within a few months following the Presidential elections.

In order to provide financing for increased social expenditures, employer and employee contributions to social security were raised in

November 1981, resulting in additional annual revenues of 15.6 billion francs and 16.8 billion francs, respectively. Nevertheless, the deficit of the social security system continued to rise; it was estimated to reach 18 billion francs in 1982, to which an estimated deficit of 24 billion francs for UNEDIC (the unemployment compensation scheme) should be added. According to a study prepared at Institut National de la Statistique et des Etudes Economiques (INSEE), if present tendencies continue, the deficit of the social security system (including unemployment compensation) would be between 66 and 120 billion francs in 1986, representing 4 to 9 percent of wages and salaries.[43]

In the light of the increased burden of the social security system, recommendations were made – both inside and outside the government – to contain the growth of social spending.[44] These recommendations reflect a desire to limit increases in the social charges of the enterprises as well as increases in deficit of the government budget.

In April 1982, the government assumed the obligation of maintaining social charges for the enterprises at present levels until July 1983, and it postponed reductions in statutory working hours below 39 hours a week until 1984, leaving it to the 'social partners' (business and labor) to negotiate any such reductions in the interim.[45] As a counterpart to earlier increases in social charges, the government also reduced the so-called professional tax on the enterprises. This reduction, however, evaluated at 5 billion francs in 1982 and 6 billion francs in 1983, constitutes only a partial offset to increases in the charges for the enterprises that were estimated at 40 billion francs by Delors and 93 billion francs by the Patronat (the employers' federation).[46] The higher labor costs not only reduced profit margins but also discouraged industrial employment.

V MACROECONOMIC POLICIES AND PERFORMANCE

The reduction of the professional tax and the subsidy to public enterprises, referred to above, will be fully financed by increasing the rate of the value added tax and by measures bearing on the banks and on agricultural credit. With increases in social spending, the rise in public employment, and increases in public investment, the deficit in the state budget rose from 30 billion francs in 1980 (1.1 percent of GDP) to 81 billion francs in 1981 (2.6 percent of GDP), compared to an estimate of 48 billion francs (1.6 percent of GDP) in May 1981. Even larger changes are shown in the consolidated budget of the central and the local governments, from a surplus equivalent to 0.4 percent of GDP in 1980 to a deficit of 2.0 percent of GDP in 1981.

A substantial part of the increased budget deficit was financed through money creation, with the obligations of the Treasury rising from 130 billion francs at the end of 1980 to 165 billion francs at the end of 1981, after having declined by 5 billion francs in the preceding twelve months. In the same period, M1 rose by 15.2 percent, following an increase of 6.8 percent in the previous year. There was less of an acceleration in the growth of M2, from 9.7 to 11.6 percent, largely because the limitations imposed on interest rates on savings deposits led to a displacement of savings towards financial instruments that are not part of M2. Finally, under both definitions, the growth of the money supply was mitigated by the shift in transactions with foreign countries from a surplus of 54 billion francs in 1980 to a deficit of 26 billion francs in 1981.[47]

While, in response to the first motion of censure of the opposition on 16 September 1981, Prime Minister Mauroy declared that, 'instead of having a "recessionary deficit", we will have an "expansionary deficit", the increased budget deficit was not translated into a higher rate of economic growth. Private consumption, lubricated by increased wages and government transfers, rose more rapidly in the second half of 1981 than in the first, but this was offset by the decline in the contribution of the balance of trade to GDP.[48]

Thus, the 6.7 percent rise in the volume of exports of goods and services between the fourth quarter of 1980 and the second quarter of 1981 was followed by a 0.3 percent decline in the next two quarters, whereas a decline of 0.6 percent in the imports of goods and services gave place to an increase of 5.3 percent. Correspondingly, after having declined from 1.3 percent in the fourth quarter of 1980 to 0.3 percent in the second quarter of 1981, the ratio of the current account deficit to GDP reached 2.2 percent in the fourth quarter. (In the same period in Germany, a deficit of 2.5 percent of GDP gave rise to a current account surplus amounting to 0.8 percent of GDP.)

It would appear, then, that the rise in the budget deficit after May 1981 was translated into an increase in the deficit of the trade balance in France. The situation in France thus seems to correspond to that assumed by the Cambridge School, according to which budget deficits are directly translated into trade deficits without contributing to the growth of GDP.

Furthermore, the expansionary measures taken, and increases in wages and salaries, contributed to the acceleration of inflation in

France which contrasts with the decline of inflation rates in all other major industrial countries. As a result, the twelve-month inflation differential between France and its major trading partners – measured by INSEE by weighting the consumer price indices of individual countries by their export shares in the rest of the OECD – rose from 3.0 percentage points in the last quarter of 1980 to 4.6 percentage points in the last quarter of 1981.

These tendencies continued in the first four months of 1982, when the state budget deficit on permanent operations reached 76 billion francs, compared to 51 billion francs in the corresponding period of the previous year.[49] The budget deficit was in large part financed by Treasury bills to which the banks subscribed, with the total outstanding amount rising from 34.5 billion francs on 31 March 1981 to 91.1 billion francs a year later.[50] The increase in the issue of Treasury bills contributed to the growth of the money supply, with M2 rising by 13.0 percent between March 1981 and March 1982, though its expansion continued to be restrained by the loss of foreign exchange reserves.

The expansionary policies followed failed, however, to generate an increase of industrial production, with the three-months' moving average of its 1970-based index declining from 131 in September–November, 1981 to 128 in February–April 1982; it was 129 a year earlier. In turn, the deficit in the balance of merchandise trade reached 27 billion francs in the first four months of the year, compared with 15 billion francs in the corresponding period of 1981, while the German trade surplus nearly tripled. Michel Jobert indicated that, for the year as a whole, the French merchandise trade deficit may reach 100 billion francs, double the 1981 figure.

Furthermore, inflation accelerated, with the consumer price index rising by 13.9 percent in the April 1981–April 1982 period. While this increase appears modest compared to predictions of inflation rates of 25 percent by some representatives of the former majority before the elections, the results were favorably affected by the deceleration of the rise in the price of petroleum and by price limitations imposed on certain services and public utilities.[51]

With the acceleration of inflation and the deterioration of the balance of payments, interest rates also rose in France. Annual rates for overnight transactions in the money markets averaged 16.8 percent in April 1982, compared to 12.2 percent a year earlier. While it has become customary to attribute high interest rates to US policies,[52] the short-term interest rate differential increased by 5.5 percentage points vis-à-vis the United States and by 6.4 percentage points vis-à-vis

Germany during this period. In turn, differences in long-term interest rates, which move in a narrower range, increased by 1.6 percentage points vis-à-vis the United States and by 2.6 percentage points vis-à-vis Germany.

CONCLUSION

With increases in the inflation differential and the deterioration of the balance of trade, confidence in the franc declined as President Mitterrand's first year came to a close. While French citizens were subjected to strict exchange controls, foreigners considerably reduced their holdings of francs, thereby adding to the loss of reserves. The foreign exchange holdings of the Bank of France decreased from 42 billion francs on 8 May 1981 to 19 billion francs on 10 June 1982. Taking into account the decline in French balances with the European institutions, the total intervention by the Bank of France may have exceeded 60 billion francs during this period.[53] As these losses in reserves could not be sustained, changes in parities were agreed upon in the framework of the European Monetary System on 12 June, entailing a 10 percent devaluation of the French franc vis-à-vis the German mark.

The devaluation was accompanied by a four month price and wage freeze. On the price side, exceptions have been made for agricultural, steel and energy prices. Commercial establishments, however, have been instructed to maintain in absolute terms their profit margins on imported goods that increased in price as a result of the devaluation, and they have to absorb the rise in the value-added tax on non-food commodities from 17.6 to 18.6 percent that occurred on 1 July 1982. On the wage side, the minimum wage has been exempted from controls and a 3.2 percent increase was put into effect on 1 July 1982.

While negotiated increases in prices and wages are planned once the freeze ends, inflationary pressures will continue as long as macroeconomic policies remain expansionary. In fact, the lack of success of the October 1981 devaluation is largely explained by the failure to apply the promised anti-inflationary policies. Thus, the freeze on public investment decided upon at the time had little practical effort as new investment plans for the nationalized enterprises were announced; the 'pause' on new public programs proposed by Jacques Delors last December 1981 was rejected; and various social benefits were increased. The reduction of working hours from 40 to 39 a week, with compensating increases in hourly wages, further added to labor costs thereby squeezing profit margins.

The adverse effects of the decline in profit margins, and hence in the rate of self-financing, have been aggravated by the impact of increased borrowing by the public sector. The danger of 'crowding out' the private sector is especially apparent in regard to non-preferential loans, given the increasingly confining credit controls and the proliferation of selective lending.

The government thus faces the unpalatable choice of increasing the rate of money creation beyond the target of 12.5 to 13.5 percent or reducing the availability of credit to the private sector, with adverse implications for investment. In order to escape this dilemma, public sector expenditures would need to be reduced substantially more than is presently envisaged and measures would need to be taken to lower the cost of labor and to rebuild the profit margins of the enterprises. Undertaking such action would contribute to the success of the June 1982 devaluation and may permit that 1983 – if not 1982 as proposed by Prime Minister Mauroy – to become 'the year of investment'.[54]

NOTES

1. R. Rémond, '"Politique 2" de François Mitterrand', *Le Monde*, 21 January 1982.
2. Rémond.
3. J. Y. Lhomeau, 'La lutte des classes à l'Assemblée nationale', *Le Monde*, 4 February 1982. Yet there are only six workers and four employees among the 284 Socialist deputies, including the radicals of the left.
4. Lhomeau.
5. The relevant issues are well stated in a review of the first year of Mitterrand's presidency by Jean-Marie Columbani in *Le Monde*: 'President of the Republic, Mr Mitterrand, has represented himself as a socialist president in accordance with the wishes of a majority of his fellow citizens. But "the people of the left" are not the entire French population. There lies a contradiction that is difficult to resolve. Mitterrand wishes to preserve the trust of the popular [leftist] electorate but, every time he speaks, he wishes to make it understood that, in order to emerge from the crisis, everyone should be mobilized' (5 May 1982).
6. *Le Monde*, 13/14 December 1981.
7. *Le Monde*, 25 September 1981.
8. Banque de Paris et des Pays Bas, *Conjoncture*, October 1981, p. 1142.
9. *Le Monde*, 25 September 1981.
10. *Le Monde*, 18 February 1982.
11. It has been reported, for example, that when Prime Minister Mauroy came

to sign the so-called 'contrat de solidarité', Renault accepted the wage demands of internal transport workers whose strike would have disrupted the ceremonies. Subsequently, Renault had to accept similar demands on the part of several other groups of workers.

12. *Le Monde*, 27 November 1981.
13. It has been reported, for example, that Saint-Gobain would have to return to its traditional orientation in glass and building materials at the expense of its recent diversification into electronics.
14. This appears to be the case in the electronics industry. To begin with, the reduction of Honeywell's share in CII-Honeywell-Bull from 47 percent to 20 percent will necessitate increased French efforts for the development of computer technology, with attendant cost. Thus, *Le Monde* speaks of 'the price of independence in the information technology industries' (22 April 1982). Also, there has been a break in technical co-operation between Saint-Gobain and Olivetti on information processing. Finally, the government vetoed Thomson's proposal to join forces with an American mini-computer company, Systems Engineering Laboratory, and made it agree to start manufacturing hi-fi equipment in France that has so far been imported from Japan and sold under the Thomson label.
15. *Le Monde*, 17 March 1982.
16. On the policies of the Barre government, see B. Balassa, 'Economic Policies in France: Retrospect and Prospects', Essay 15 in this volume.
17. *Le Monde*, 13–14 December 1981.
18. *Le Monde*, 27 November 1981.
19. Chevènement, Minister to Research and Technology, in June 1982 was also given the portfolio of Minister of Industry.
20. J. Diebold, 'The Information Technology Industries: A Case Study of High Technology Trade', in W. R. Cline (ed.), *Trade Policy in the 1980s* (Washington, DC: Institute for International Economics, 1983) p. 651.
21. According to Michel Rocard, 'the great disease of the next months may well be the disease of the filières, with everyone wishing to favor its own. If we will act this way, we will fail' (interview given to *Le Point*, 31 May 1982).
22. The importance accorded to saving firms from bankruptcy was indicated by Mitterrand in his press conference 24 September 1982: 'I asked the Prime Minister, who has begun to do it the last few days, that there be created in his office a sort of working and control unit, so that there should not be a single firm in France which would close without this unit being informed and alerted, and in each department all possible measures be taken'.
23. *Le Monde*, 3 May 1982.
24. In an article in *Le Monde* on 18 February 1982, Pierre Drouin cited Pierre-Yves Cossé, an adviser to Jacques Delors, the Minister for the Economy and Finance, that 'there is need to redistribute the roles among the different public actors of industrial policy. The parallelism of the bureaus of the Treasury, the Ministry of Industry, of the Datar [the agency for regionalization], the Plan, and the various specialized committees are not well adapted to carry out the appointed tasks'.
25. In the first such agreement, it was concluded that the French furniture

industry should produce chairs to replace imports and the wholesalers accepted the obligation to reduce their imports of furniture in favor of domestic merchandise. Also, regarding the wood and leather industries, *Le Monde* states: 'The success of this type of action presupposes that all actors be disposed to play the game: the industrials in agreeing to make an effort to innovate and to limit their prices; the traders and distributors in accepting to play the national card more often, even at the risk of having their profit margins somewhat reduced; and finally the state in assuming the role of organizer and in inducing more to produce than to import' (2 December 1981).

26. *Financial Times*, 21 April 1982.
27. *Financial Times*, 3 December 1982.
28. *Business Week*, 28 December 1981.
29. *Financial Times*, 2 April 1981.
30. *Financial Times*, 3 March 1982.
31. *Business Week*, 28 December 1981.
32. An article in *Le Monde*, reporting on remarks made by Pierre Dreyfus, then the Minister of Industry, bears the title 'the domestic market will be protected if necessary, Mr Dreyfus assures the manufacturers of leather and men's wear' (6/7 September 1981).
33. *Le Matin*, 12 January 1982.
34. *Economist*, 3 April 1982.
35. *Le Matin*, 12 January 1982.
36. *Le Monde*, 13 May 1982.
37. *Le Monde*, 12 May 1982.
38. Among leftist economists, such an effort was urged by Serge-Christophe Kolm, who attributed the failure of Socialist experiences elsewhere to the inability of elected Socialist governments to avoid an acceleration of wage increases ('Quelle relance possible?', *Le Monde*, 8 April 1981).
39. The so-called Delors plan, setting wage increases on the basis of the expected rate of inflation, with subsequent catching-up if actual inflation exceeded this level, was negotiated only for the civil service without, however, the agreement of the major unions.
40. It has been estimated that the number of workdays lost because of strikes reached 527 000 in the last quarter of 1981 compared with 216 000 a year earlier; further increases occurred in early 1982, with the total reaching 579 000 in the first two months of the year.
41. INSEE estimates that 1.2 percentage points of the rise in hourly wages in the first quarter is explained by the increases designed to compensate for the decline in working hours.
42. *Le Monde*, 6 February 1982. The agreement of the employers and the unions would be necessary, however, to provide pensions in excess of 50 percent of salary. The corresponding proportion reaches 80 percent under the guarantee of resources scheme that has had only partial application.
43. M. Féroldi, E. Raoul, and H. Dyniak, 'Sécurité sociale et évolution macro-économique', *Economie et Statistique*, No. 143 (1982) pp. 59–78. It should, however, be added that a tendency toward increased social security expenditures was observable already during the tenure of the preceding

government. Thus, the share of budget-financed social benefits in GDP rose from 17.1 percent in 1973 to 20.0 percent, occurred in 1981.

44. Michel Rocard expressed the view, for example, that 'France has a rate of social guarantees beyond its capacity' (interview given to *Le Point*, 31 May 1982). By contrast, according to Nicole Questiaux, the Minister of National Solidarity, 'France does not provide social guarantees beyond its capacity, it is rather below its capacity' (interview given to *Le Monde*, 9 June 1982).

45. These negotiations created tension and engendered strikes, however, given the intransigent attitude taken by the CGT, the Communist-dominated union, in regard to reductions in working hours. Demands for further wage increases also led to strikes, among others, at Renault, Citroen, and Talbot, with a decline in output resulting in lower exports and higher imports.

46. *Le Monde*, 17 April 1982. A further offset is provided by the subsidy element of preferential credit to industry that would total 28.5 billion francs in 1982.

47. Banque de France, *Compte Rendu, Exercise 1981* (Paris, 1982).

48. For 1981, taken as a whole, the increase in GDP was 0.2 percent compared with the 0.5 percent growth rate estimated in April 1981, when INSEE concluded that 'the phase of a deep recession seems to be ending'. Private consumption rose by 1.7 percent, whereas gross fixed investment by non-financial enterprises declined by 4.4 percent following increases by 2.4 percent in 1978, 2.7 percent in 1979, and 3.7 percent in 1980.

49. The data are not seasonally adjusted, and the first four months of the year account for a more than proportionate part of the deficit; the deficit on permanent operations was 61 billion francs in the whole of 1981, with the deficit on temporary operations accounting for a further 20 billion francs.

50. In early September 1981, when this total reached 50 billion francs, Paul Fabra complained about the large and frequent issues of the Treasury bills, adding that 'what goes on today in the monetary market in Paris has never been seen in the memory of the professionals' (*Le Monde*, 8 September 1981).

51. Calculated in francs, the import price of petroleum rose by 12 percent between March 1981 and March 1982, compared with an increase of 45 percent in the preceding year. Furthermore, the prices of a variety of services had been frozen in late 1981, and, subsequently, contractual arrangements limited increases in these prices to 10–11 percent a year whereas increases in the price of public utilities other than electricity and gas were kept at 10 percent a year. As a result, service prices rose less than the average, which is contrary to long-term trends. Jacques Delors had little success, however, with his 'price cease-fire', under which he requested commercial establishments to freeze prices on 30 percent of their sales between January and April 1982.

52. Thus, André Lajoinie, president of the Communist group in the National Assembly, proposed in an interview given to Radio Europe 1 on 27 June 1982, that 'one should disconnect the interest rates in effect in France from those in effect internationally by the fault, especially, of the United States'.

53. The numbers do not include foreign borrowing by the nationalized firms that increased considerably after May 1981. According to *Le Monde*, 'The French policy of borrowing everywhere continues' (4/5 July 1982).
54. Before the June measures, INSEE estimated that industrial investment would decline by 7 percent in 1982, after having fallen by 11.5 percent in 1981.

Essay 17 French Economic Policies under the Socialist Government: Year III

INTRODUCTION

In 'The First Year of Socialist Government in France'[1] the author described the structural changes that followed the victory of the left in the French Presidential and parliamentary elections. He further examined the macroeconomic imbalances created by an expansionary policy, which involved increases in wages, social benefits and public expenditures.

The first devaluation of the French franc, in October 1981, was not accompanied by significant macroeconomic measures; the devaluation of June 1982 was followed by a temporary price and wage freeze and the government expressed its intention to limit the budget deficit; however, only in conjunction with the devaluation of March 1983 did it institute an austerity policy intended to re-establish macroeconomic equilibrium.

The new policy aimed at reducing by one-half the trade deficit, which exceeded 100 billion francs according to the balance-of-payments statistics, and at limiting the rate of inflation to 8 percent in 1983. In order to pursue these objectives, the government proposed to slow increases in wages, to limit the budget deficit to 3 percent of GDP, and to pursue a restrictive monetary policy by setting a 9 percent target rate of growth for the money supply. At the same time, it was suggested that a slowdown of economic activity ought not to be followed by a significant increase in unemployment.

The present essay will examine the extent to which these objectives have been attained (Section I). It will further evaluate the effects of the macroeconomic and social policies followed since May 1981 on the external debt (Section II) and on business profit (Section III) in France. Finally, the structural policies pursued by the socialist government will be analyzed.

I FIRST RESULTS OF THE AUSTERITY POLICY

The French government won its wager on the reduction by one-half of the trade deficit in 1983, a result which surpassed the expectations of most observers. The decline of imports, which fell by 10 percent in volume compared to their trend during the first nine months of 1983, was in large part responsible for the improvement in the balance of trade. During the same period, the volume of exports increased by 3 percent, without however fully attaining the level reached two years earlier. Finally, France's terms of trade improved by 1.2 percent during the first nine months of 1983 over the corresponding period of 1982.

On the side of exports, several factors contributed to these results: the direct and indirect effects of the American economic expansion: French deliveries on major contracts signed with socialist and with developing countries; and the successive devaluations of the franc, which more than compensated for the difference between the rate of inflation in France and in other countries. The devaluations also affected imports, thus reinforcing the effects of the decline in the consumption of industrial goods, the fall in investments, and the reduction in the inventories of petroleum products, which in itself represented 10 to 12 billion francs in 1983.[2]

In 1984, the difference between rates of economic activity will favor the French balance of trade even more than in 1983. According to OECD estimates, the French gross domestic product would not change in 1984 while GDP would increase at an average rate of 2.1 percent in the major industrial countries; the estimates for 1983 are 0.5 percent for France and 0.8 percent for other countries.[3] On the other hand, inventory reduction in petroleum products has come to an end; and, despite the recent agreement with Saudi Arabia on arms shipments, major contracts with socialist and with developing countries are on the decline.[4]

Finally, the competitiveness of French industry is deteriorating once again. Thus, the gap between the rise in the prices of consumer goods in France and in her principal trading partners has increased from 3.8 percent in 1981 to 4.4 percent in 1982 and, again, to 5.8 percent between October 1982 and October 1983.[5] Furthermore, the French consumer price index rose by 9.3 percent between December 1982 and December 1983, representing only a slight improvement compared to the figure of 9.7 percent for the preceding year.

At the same time, the French consumer price index underestimates inflationary tendencies for several reasons. Binding price guidelines exist for two-thirds of industrial products; most services are subject to strict price control; the prices of public utilities, in particular electricity and gas, were not sufficiently increased in 1983; the prices of petroleum products were calculated at an exchange rate of 8.00 francs to the dollar in December 1983, although the exchange rate had in fact surpassed 8.30 francs; and, in accordance with the Quilliot law, rents are indexed at 80 percent of the increase in construction costs, which rose less than the general price index because of unfavorable conditions in the building industry.

In 1983, wages increased, on average, at the same rate as prices. At the same time, social transfer payments rose by 12 percent. Nevertheless, given a decrease in employment and the rise in taxes and social charges, the disposable income of households declined by 0.5 percent in real terms.

Until October 1983, the government succeeded in avoiding an increase in the number of unemployed workers, which remained at about 2 million. This result was obtained in the first instance by what Mr Mauroy called 'the social treatment of unemployment': the training of young people, pre-retirement and retirement at sixty. Employment-training contracts involved 78 000 young people between June 1982 and June 1983 compared to 72 000 in the previous twelve-month period; the number of workers taking pre-retirement benefits increased from 39 000 to 86 000 between July 1982 and July 1983[6] and the number of applications for retirement at sixty during the first ten months of 1983 totalled 552 000, or 190 000 more than in 1982.[7]

It has also been suggested that there has been a 'statistical treatment of unemployment'. Thus, the rules change by the National Employment Agency, which went into effect in October 1982, may have discouraged a large number of unemployed persons from registering on official lists of employment-seekers. Further contributing to this situation, according to an INSEE study, were the review of individual cases of long-term unemployment, which led to the elimination of several thousands of employment-seekers from the rolls; restrictions on the maximum duration of unemployment benefits to job-seekers, which terminated the indemnization of 150 000 persons; and the adoption of monthly rather than bi-monthly check-ins, with stricter rules on elimination from the rolls in case of absence or delay.[8]

Another indication of the situation on the job market is provided by the relationship between unfilled demands for jobs and unfilled offers of jobs.[9] With a one-half reduction in the number of unfilled vacancies between February 1983 and February 1984, this ratio rose from 18 to 41. At the same time, the number of unemployed surpassed 2.2. million.

According to official estimates, the government kept the budget deficit within the limits fixed by the initial law of finance for 1983 (118.7 billion francs), or 3 percent of GDP. However, the budgetary outcome was improved by the carry-over to 1984 of 2 to 3 billion francs of financial aid to the steel industry and by the transfer of 3 billion francs from the Caisse de consolidation et de mobilisation à moyen terme to the budget.[10]

The official projections assume that the budget deficit would remain at 3 percent of GDP in 1984. Still, the deficit would be higher than in preceding years; it averaged 1.5 percent of GDP between 1975 and 1980; it rose to 2.6 percent of GDP in 1981 and to 2.8 percent in 1982. According to calculations by the OECD, the budget deficit would absorb 21 percent of gross savings and 53 percent of net savings in the private sector.[11]

At the same time, this comparison does not take account of the 'debudgétisation' being carried out, which involves the transfer of several categories of current expenditures from the budget, including the financing of the electronics industry's development program by the PTT (3.4 billion francs), the excess cost of Algerian gas being assumed by Gaz de France (1.3 billion francs), and the shiftover to the Caisse des Dépôts of housing subsidies (7.0 billion francs) in 1984. In addition, the service of the public debt is estimated at 70 billion francs in the budget, assuming a reduction of 1.5 percent to 2 percent in the rate of interest; as in previous years, this hypothesis appears to be overly optimistic. Finally, the limitation of increases in public utility prices to 5 percent in 1984 will bring about deficits in the public utility sector.[12]

The declared objective of a 9 percent growth in the money supply (M2) in 1983, as compared to a growth of 12 percent in 1982, was attained. This result is largely explained by the weakening of demand for bank credits on the part of private industry that reduced its investments, as well as by the loss of reserves owing to the deficit in the balance of payments. In contrast, according to INSEE, credit to the Treasury increased by 29 percent between December 1982 and December 1983; this represents the monetization of more than one-half of the budget deficit.

For 1984, the money supply objective has been reduced to 5.5–6.5 percent. Given the increase in the budget deficit and the re-equilibration of the balance of payments, this has necessitated reducing credit ceilings for the banks, with exception made for the financing of exports, housing, and foreign exchange advances. The lower ceilings, in turn, limit the availability of credit to private industry.

II THE EXTERNAL DEBT OF FRANCE

The budgetary, monetary and social policies of the new socialist government aimed at economic expansion through increases in wages, social benefits, and public expenditures. This policy brought about only a modest increase in production while resulting in a substantial rise in the external deficit. As noted above, the trade deficit was over 100 billion francs in 1982. In the same year, the current account deficit was 80 billion francs, or 2.6 percent of GDP; it has been 26 billion francs in 1981. The current account deficit reached 35 billion francs, or 2.1 percent of GDP, during the first half of 1983; balance was approximately restored during the second half of that year.

The successive deficits in the current account balance made recourse to foreign borrowing necessary. Borrowing needs increased further owing to the credits granted to developing and to socialist countries for the financing of their imports from France. At the same time, the repayment of some of these credits is subject to doubt.

According to official estimates, the gross external indebtedness of France increased from $29.5 billion in May 1981 to $53.7 billion at the end of 1983.[13] According to Jacques Delors, in 1984 the surplus in current account transactions other than interest payments should make it possible to finance interest charges on the debt. Increases in foreign export credits and in net direct investments abroad would nevertheless require a further rise in the amount of gross indebtedness by approximately 50 billion francs,[14] thus adding to the external debt estimated at 442 billion francs at the rate of exchange in effect at the end of 1983.

In order to avoid a further rise in the external debt – the reduction of which was declared to be a policy objective by Delors at the Forum of

L'Expansion – while assuring the financing of interest charges of 50 billion francs and of increases in foreign export credits and net direct investment abroad, it would be necessary for France to attain a surplus of 100 billion francs in current transactions other than interest payments in 1985.[15] This would necessitate an improvement in the balance of these transactions by an amount equal to 4.1 percent of the gross domestic product compared to 1982, when interest payments were 15 billion francs, and an improvement of 2.3 percent compared to 1983, when the deficit in the current account balance was entirely due to interest payments. Without an increase in domestic production, this change would entail a decline in the resources available for consumption and for investment. At the same time, the increase in the budget deficit would augment further the burden of adjustment falling on the private sector.

Experience indicates that economic growth through increases in consumption brings about a rapid rise of imports into France. Thus, an acceleration of economic growth should be sought through the development of exports. This, in turn, would require the maintenance of a realistic exchange rate as well as new investments. Investments would also be necessary in order to limit the rise in unemployment. The possibilities of 'social treatment' and of 'statistical treatment' of unemployment being largely exhausted, INSEE expects an increase in unemployment by 200 000 in 1984 and by 600 000 by 1988.

III BUSINESS SAVINGS

Investment is dependent on business savings. Table 17.1 shows the evolution of the share of business savings in the value added of corporations and quasi-corporations since 1970. It is observed that, after a decrease following the first oil shock, this ratio partly recovered its former level, but this was not the case after the second oil shock. On the contrary, the share of business savings in value added decreased further, falling from 11.5 percent in 1980 to 9.6 percent in 1981 and, again, to 9.0 percent in 1982. In turn, preliminary figures for 1983 seem to underestimate the interest payments of business firms, thus overestimating their savings. This is equally the case for 1984, for which projections are very uncertain.

The decline in the ratio of business savings to value added is largely explained by increases in social charges, and in interest payments. The first of these items rose steadily throughout the entire period; it is responsible for the greater part of the increase in labor costs. As for the second factor, differences are observed between the periods that followed the two oil shocks.

The share of interest payments in value added increased from 7.2 percent in 1973 to 8.7 percent in 1974, but it decreased to 7.9 percent in the following year and to 7.4 percent by 1979. Such a recovery did not occur after the second oil shock, and the share of interest payments in value added reached 10.2 percent in 1982.

This last result is explained by the fact that the compression of profit margins after 1980, due in large part to increases in social charges, forced business firms to borrow. Reductions in profit margins also led to a decline in the self-financing ratio, which fell from 61.6 percent in 1980 to 53.7 percent in 1981 and to 53.4 percent in 1982. At the same time, the possibilities of recovery for this ratio remain uncertain.

The figures of Table 17.1 exclude several factors which influence the profitability of business firms, such as their distributed earnings and depreciation allowances. These factors are taken into account by Edmond Malinvaud, who presents estimates on the amortization of physical assets, revalued each year, and on the decrease in the real value of the debt through inflation. Net profits are then expressed as a percentage of net capital.

The calculations reported in Table 17.2 indicate that, after having fluctuated between 6 percent and 7 percent during the 1960s, the net rate of profit of non-financial enterprises stabilized at slightly above 7 percent at the beginning of the 1970s. This rate decreased to 6.2 percent in 1974 and 1975 and to 4.4 percent in 1976 and 1977; it rose to 5.2 percent in 1978 and to 5.3 percent in 1979; and it fell again to 4.2 percent in 1980. The decline accelerated in the following years; the net rate of profit was 3.5 percent in 1981 and 1.3 percent in 1982.

Malinvaud suggests that, in order to obtain an indicator of profitability, the real rate of interest must be subtracted from the net rate of profit. The results of these calculations for the periods following the two oil shocks are again very different. With the exception of the year 1975, when it rose above 6 percent, the rate of profitability remained between 3 percent and 4 percent from 1974 to 1979 – i.e. at the 1960–73 level, on an average. In turn, the gap between the rate of net profit and the rate of real interest fell to 0.4 percent in 1980, and it became negative in 1981 and 1982.

The figures of Table 17.2 also show a divergence between the two periods in regard to net business savings (gross savings minus depreciation allowances). Net business savings became negative in 1975,

TABLE 17.1 Characteristic ratios for enterprises: all corporations and quasi-corporations

	1970	1971	1972	1973	1974	1975	1976	1977	1978	1979	1980	1981	1982	1983	1984
Shares in value added:															
– Remuneration of employees of which social charges paid by employers[1]	64.5	65.1	65.0	65.2	67.2	69.3	69.9	69.7	69.4	68.9	69.8	71.2	71.1	70.6	69.0
	10.9	11.1	11.0	11.1	11.7	12.9	13.3	13.6	13.7	13.9	14.3	14.5	14.6	15.1	15.0
– gross profit (margins)	29.8	29.3	29.4	28.5	27.3	25.3	25.2	25.3	25.3	25.3	23.4	23.4	23.5	23.7	24.0
– interest effectively paid	6.6	6.9	6.7	7.2	8.7	7.9	7.9	8.1	7.6	7.4	8.6	9.8	10.2	9.9	9.0
– taxes on revenue and wealth	3.5	3.3	3.4	3.7	4.4	3.1	3.8	3.8	3.2	3.4	3.4	3.5	3.4	3.2	3.0
– corporate savings	16.1	15.4	15.4	13.8	11.1	10.9	11.4	11.5	12.5	12.9	11.52	9.6	9.0	9.5	11.0
Rate of investment	21.6	21.4	21.1	20.3	20.1	19.1	19.7	19.0	18.6	18.3	19.3	18.6	18.4	17.7	17.0
Rate of self-financing[2]	76.1	73.1	74.3	69.9	57.0	59.6	64.2	63.4	69.9	72.3	61.6	53.7	53.4	56.2	64.0

[1] All corporations and unincorporated enterprises.
[2] Self-financing: net profits + dividends + investment subsidies.

SOURCE: Projet de loi de finances pour 1984. Comptes prévisionnels de le Nation pour 1983 et principales hypothèses économiques pour 1984 (Paris, 1983) pp. 60–1.

TABE 17.2 Profitability of non-financial corporations and quasi-corporations (excluding state-owned firms)

Year	Gross Profit (billion francs)	Dividends (billion francs)	Amortization (billion francs)	Decline in the Real Value of Corporate Debt (billion francs)	Net Profits (billion francs)	Net Capital (billion francs)	Net Profit Rate (percent)	Interest Rate (percent)	Rate of Profitability (percent)
1962	22.5	7.4	14.5	2.9	18.3	270	6.8	2.0	4.8
1963	24.5	7.8	16.5	5.7	21.5	310	6.9	1.1	5.8
1964	28.6	8.4	18.3	2.4	21.1	350	6.0	1.8	4.2
1965	30.9	8.9	20.1	2.8	22.5	390	5.8	3.0	2.8
1966	34.9	9.9	22.1	3.4	26.2	430	6.1	3.6	2.5
1967	38.3	10.9	24.4	3.0	27.8	460	6.0	4.6	1.4
1968	42.7	11.5	25.4	7.4	36.2	500	7.2	3.6	3.6
1969	46.7	13.5	28.5	8.7	40.4	510	7.9	4.0	3.9
1970	50.9	14.3	33.0	10.4	42.6	580	7.3	4.9	2.4
1971	55.9	15.8	37.3	12.7	47.1	660	7.1	3.1	4.0
1972	64.6	18.2	42.4	14.4	54.8	742	7.4	2.6	4.8
1973	66.4	22.3	48.7	28.7	68.7	890	7.7	1.4	6.3
1974	62.6	26.3	61.5	34.1	61.5	1000	6.2	2.3	3.9
1975	69.8	28.5	73.7	49.4	74.0	1200	6.2	0.1	6.1
1976	82.7	29.2	96.4	44.9	60.4	1370	4.4	0.4	4.0
1977	92.9	32.4	99.5	43.5	69.3	1552	4.4	1.4	3.0
1978	114.5	35.8	113.2	56.7	93.8	1800	5.2	1.4	3.8
1979	134.9	44.2	127.3	60.4	112.2	2100	5.3	1.3	4.0
1980	132.1	48.3	147.0	69.3	102.7	2472	4.2	3.8	0.4
1981	122.2	51.0	171.6	93.7	95.3	2700	3.5	4.8	−1.3
1982	132.4	53.4	193.0	76.5	69.3	3000	2.3	5.7	−3.4

SOURCE: E. Malinvaud, *Essais sur la Théorie du Chômage* (Paris: Calmann-Levy, 1983) p. 218.

but turned positive again in 1978 and in 1979. In contrast, negative net business savings, which amounted to 14.9 billion francs in 1980, increased to 49.9 billion francs in 1981 and to 60.0 billion francs in 1982.

The divergence between the two periods is largely explained by the special character of the May 1981–March 1983 expansion. The driving force behind this expansion was the increase in wages and social transfer payments, which brought about a reduction in the profit margins of business firms.[16] This is the opposite of what occurs in the course of 'normal' expansions, such as the present American economic expansion, which lead to higher profit margins. At the same time, increases in production costs, with an upward shift of the marginal cost curve after May 1981, discouraged the expansion of production in French industry and contributed to the rapid rise in imports.

According to Malinvaud, the minimum rate of profitability to assure the productive investment necessary for economic growth is about 4 percent in France; he adds that this figure is highly approximate, and that the rate in question concerns an aggregate which applies to a given economic structure. Malinvaud also emphasizes the fact that borrowing cannot permanently substitute for profits in the financing of business firms without compromising their solvency.[17]

Thus, an increase in profit margins is required in order to encourage productive investment, which is a necessary condition for economic growth based on a rapid increase in exports and for reducing unemployment. To this end, the restoration of the freedom of industrial price setting is a first priority. The pursuit of this objective would further necessitate a decline in the share of wages and salaries in value added, which would also lower the share of private consumption in GDP. Finally, taxes and social charges on business, which have increased much more rapidly and are much higher than in other large industrial countries, would need to be reduced.

According to the calculations of the OECD, the share of taxes and social charges in the gross domestic product rose from 36 percent in 1973 to 42 percent in 1980 and to 44 percent in 1982 in France; this rate varied from 27 percent in Japan to 37 percent in the Federal Republic of Germany in the year 1980, with only slight changes compared to previous years, except for countries at the bottom end of the scale. Furthermore, the share of social charges in French GDP increased from 14 percent in 1973 to 18 percent in 1980 and to 20 percent in 1982 while this share varied little in the other major industrial countries, ranging between 4 percent in Canada and 13 percent in the Federal

Republic in 1980.[18] Following previous increases, the share of taxes and social charges in the GDP of France is expected to surpass 45 percent in 1984, when the share of social charges in GDP would reach 22 percent.

In order to effect a significant reduction of social charges for business firms, there would be need to lower social expenditures and to make increased use of other modes of financing these expenditures. A decrease in the budget deficit would permit the assumption of a larger part of social expenditures by the government and one may also envisage increasing employees' contributions to the social security system.

A reduction in the so-called professional tax would also contribute to business savings. Finally, fiscal measures could be used to encourage investments more directly. Accelerated depreciation provisions or tax exemptions on reinvested profits may prove useful to this end. In addition, the introduction of a 'carry-back' provision would permit business firms in difficulties to recover taxes paid on profits in previous years.

IV STRUCTURAL POLICIES

In presenting the interim plan for the years 1982 and 1983 to the National Assembly on December 12, 1981, Michel Rocard, the then Minister of Planning, spoke of a 'triad of reforms: decentralization, extension of the public sector, and planning.' This section of the essay provides a provisional evaluation of this 'triad' of structural policies in France.

According to a critique of the report on the implementation of the interim plan, entitled 'L'art et la manière d'accommoder les restes,' by Francois Simon, 'hastily conceived, the document expressed the very unrealistic optimism which characterized the parliamentary majority at the end of 1981. Everything was then based on the mirage of growth, which was projected to average 3 percent over the two years covered by the Plan.'[19] In actual fact, GDP increased by only 0.7 percent between the fourth quarter of 1981 and the fourth quarter of 1983.

Furthermore, despite the rise in public employment,[20] overall employment decreased slightly in contrast to the interim plan objective for the creation of 400 000 to 500 000 jobs. And, industrial investment, which Rocard had described as the motor of economic growth and the generator of employment in presenting the interim plan to the National Assembly, continued to decline while consumption increased. Thus, one cannot accept the claim made in the implementation report on the interim plan that 'the fundamental objectives which it set for itself have essentially been attained, notably in comparison with other countries.'

The projections of economic growth of the IXth Plan (1984–8) ought also be revised downward. According to the statement annexed to the legislation on the IXth Plan, adopted by the National Assembly on 16 June 1983, 'the objective is to arrive by the end of the period at a rate of growth higher by one percentage point than the weighted average growth rate of our partners in the OECD.'[21] By contrast, according to INSEE projections, the rate of growth of the French economy will be 1.9 percent during the period 1984–88 – inferior to the average 2.6 percent growth rate of the partner countries.[22] This is consistent with the fact that, given the interest charges on its external debt, France cannot hope to have a rate of economic growth equal to that of other member countries unless she makes major efforts to develop her exports as suggested above.

The development of exports is one of the major objectives of the IXth Plan, but the means to be used for reaching this goal are not indicated in the Plan. In turn, as suggested in *Le Monde*, 'the more stringent enforcement of industrial norms [recommended in the planning document] seems to be a barely-disguised protectionist measure.'[23]

In more general terms, the Plan gives few indications of the means by which the major macroeconomic equilibria are to be restored. At the same time, as Pierre Drouin has observed, 'The austerity plan casts a shadow over the IXth Plan.'[24] Drouin goes even further in suggesting that 'these great machines, the plans, have seen their form embellished in passing from one to the next, but, little by little, they have been drained of their power.' In fact, as this author predicted some twenty years ago,[25] the plan has lost its importance as uncertainties have multiplied in conjunction with the opening of the French economy, and the Socialists' ascension to power has not reversed this tendency.

The IXth Plan introduces contracts with the regions and with the nationalized enterprises. In the establishment of contracts with the regions, the General Commission on the Plan shares responsibility with DATAR, the regional development agency. However, it is the Ministry of Industry and Research which establishes the contracts with the nationalized enterprises, and the inclusion of these contracts in the plan becomes a formality. The contracts with the regions include pluri-annual commitments on the part of the government. Nevertheless, the resources available to the regions have not been increased, and investments by regional and local authorities have even declined. This outcome may be largely explained by budgetary constraints as well as by the losses suffered by the left in the local elections. In fact, with the exception of Corsica, the election of regional assemblies has been postponed to a future date.

It is too early to evaluate the practical value of contracts with the enterprises. At the same time, one observes that the public authorities have exerted pressure to avoid lay-offs in these enterprises, which has impaired the rationalization of their operations and has contributed to the increase of their losses.

The question needs further be raised as to whether the specialization of the activities of nationalized enterprises, mandated by the Ministry of Industry and Research, is in the national interest. Instead of a policy of 'national champions,' Japan – which is often considered a model for France in this area – has encouraged competition among Japanese firms in both national and international markets. In turn, sales to the government and foreign sales financed by government credits reinforce the monopolistic position of specialized public enterprises in France.

Finally, questions arise concerning the freedom of action of the managers of nationalized enterprises. It would appear that the replacement of Jean-Pierre Chevènement by Laurent Fabius as Minister of Industry and Research has reduced interventions by the Ministry. But the expiration of the three-year contracts of the managers of nationalized enterprises increases their dependence on the Ministry. The managers are also dependent on the labor unions, whose representatives sit on their Boards of Directors in accordance with the law on the democratization of the public sector.

At any rate, since the nationalized enterprises are in principle protected from bankruptcy, the behavior of their managers will not be the same as that of the managers of private enterprises. Thus, the danger of bureaucratization exists and bureaucratization may slow technical progress instead of accelerating it, as was asserted at the time of nationalization. At the same time, it appears that the government has increased its long-established interventions in the banking sector. In the recent case of Creusot-Loire, government authorities practically dictated the terms of rescue operations to the nationalized banks. These banks have also been requested to increase their aid to nationalized firms.

CONCLUSIONS

This essay has examined the effects of the measures applied in France since the installation of the Socialist government and policy perspectives for the future. It appears that, despite the positive results of the austerity policy, the French economy will feel the negative effects of the policies followed between May 1981 and March 1983 for years to come.

First of all, interest on the external debt rose from 10 billion francs in 1980 to 37 billion in 1983; it has been estimated that it will reach 50 billion francs in 1985. In order to avoid further increases in of the debt, the current account balance, excluding interest payments, would have to improve by an amount equal to 4.1 percent of GDP in comparison to 1982, and 2.3 percent of GDP in comparison to 1983.

In 1983, improvements in the current account balance were accomplished at the expense of investments while consumption continued to increase. This prolonged the effects of the policies applied after May 1981, which engendered a rise in consumption and a decrease in investments. Thus, instead of creating new productive capacities, foreign borrowing sustained the growth of consumption in France.

The rise in consumption and the decrease in investments also reflect changes in the distribution of income in favor of wage-earners at the expense of business firms. In 1982, the share of savings and that of self-financing in the value added of non-financial enterprises reached their lowest level for the entire post-war period. A recovery of profit margins is necessary to permit the resumption of business investment that has become increasingly negative since 1980, after adjustment is made for amortization. At the same time, only an increase in productive investments can guarantee balanced economic growth, based on rapid increases in exports, and avoid a further rise in unemployment.

Freedom in setting prices, decreases in the share of wages and salaries in value added, and reductions in social charges on business firms would contribute to this objective. In order to finance business investment, it would further be desirable to lessen the recourse of the government to financial markets by means of a reduction in the budget deficit.

Finally, private and public enterprises should be allowed to rationalize their operations; this would require a more liberal layoff policy. In fact, the example of the United States indicates that such a policy contributes to employment growth within a short period by giving firms greater flexibility and improving their competitiveness.[26]

NOTES

1. Essay 16 in this volume.
2. According to (Institut National de la Statistique et des Etudes Eco-

nomiques) INSEE purchases of industrial goods by households declined by 2.5 percent in 1983, while investments decreased by 2.9 percent.

3. The average rate of growth of these countries (Federal Republic of Germany, Italy, Belgium, United States, Japan and Canada) was obtained by weighting with their exports to France 1980 (OECD, *Economic Outlook*, December 1983). According to *L'Expansion*, the rate of growth of GDP would be 0.3 percent in France for 1983 and 1984 (6/19 January 1984).

4. The amount of major contracts declined by 40 percent in 1983 (from 94 billion francs in 1982 to 56 billion francs in 1983), involving a shortfall of 12 billion francs in terms of deliveries in 1984 (*Le Monde*, 3 February 1984).

5. INSEE's calculations based on the national price indices weighted by the countries' export shares to the rest of the OECD during the 1976–8 period.

6. *Le Matin*, 2 September 1983.

7. *Le Monde*, 9 December 1983.

8. O. Marchand and C. Thelot, 'Le nombre des chômeurs', *Economie et Statistique*, No. 160 (1983) pp. 29–45. The former Secretary of State for Labor under the Barre government attributes the difference of 425 000 between the total employment statistics and the number of job-seekers, which occurred between 1 October 1982 and 1 October 1983, in equal measure to the 'social treatment of unemployment' and to the 'statistical treatment of unemployment'. (*Temps Forts de l'Aries*, Numéro spécial, 1983.)

9. This ratio is utilized by Edmond Malinvaud in his *Essais sur la Théorie du Chômage* (Paris, Calmann-Levy, 1983) p. 200.

10. *Le Monde*, 3 December 1983.

11. According to the definitions used by the OECD (*OECD Economic Outlook*, December 1983), the budget deficit would be 1.9 percent of GDP in 1981, 1.6 percent in 1982, 3.4 percent in 1983 and 3.8 percent in 1984. This represents a more rapid increase than that given in the official figures. Another approach would be to evaluate variations in the public debt, which is estimated by the OECD at 17.7 percent of GDP in 1981, 20.8 percent in 1982, 24.2 percent in 1983, and 28.3 percent in 1984. According to these figures, the public debt would increase by 188 billion in 1982, 204 billion in 1983, and 244 billion in 1984, equivalent to 5.2 percent of GDP in 1982, 5.2 percent in 1983, and 5.8 percent in 1984. One should add, however, that these magnitudes are expressed in gross terms as net figures are not available.

12. *Le Monde*, 23 September 1983.

13. The official figures do not include the short-term debt that also rose to a considerable extent as the nationalized banks increased their exposure abroad. According to the estimates of *Le Monde*, the gross external debt rose from $37 billion to $68 billion during this period while French financial claims abroad declined from $62 billion to $55 billion (27 December 1983). The Ministry of Finance puts the value of outstanding medium-term and long-term French credit abroad at $29.8 billion.

14. *L'Expansion*, 6/19 January 1984.

15. In a speech he gave at the Academy of Social and Political Sciences on 'The External Aspects of French Monetary Policy', Mr Renaud la Génière, the

Governor of the Bank of France, also emphasized the need to reduce the French external debt, attributing its recent rise largely to the increased financing needs of the governmental administrations (*Le Monde*, 28 January 1984).

16. Having increased after 1973, the share of wages and salaries in value added declined between 1976 and 1979; in contrast, this ratio continued to rise after 1980, exceeding 71 percent of value added in 1981 and 1982.

17. Malinvaud, pp. 225–28.

18. P. Mantz, A. Ramond, M. Tabouillet and M. Ungemuth, 'Le poids des prélèvements obligatoires: portée et limites de la mesure', *Economie et Statistique* No. 157 (1983) pp. 47–60.

19. *Le Monde*, 10 December 1983.

20. Employment in public administration increased by 81 000 in 1981, 122 500 in 1982, and 21 000 in 1983 (*L'Express*, 21–27 October 1983).

21. This objective is again taken up in the report annexed to the second planning law, which projects a difference in growth rates of 0.7 percent to 1.0 percent near the end of the period covered by the IXth Plan (*Les moyens d'exécution du 9e Plan*, Paris: 1983, p. 172).

22. Equipe DMS, 'Quels efforts pour quel avenir? Une projection de l'économie française à l'horizon 1988,' *Economie et Statistique*, No. 161 (1983) pp. 51–77. At the Forum of Expansion on 5 January 1984, Mr Delors also underlined the fact that 'it is in the interest of France, it is even indispensable, that its economic cycle be retarded, compared to that of other countries'.

23. *Le Monde*, 18 June 1983.

24. *Le Monde*, 9 June 1983.

25. Bela Balassa, 'Whither French Planning?', *Quarterly Journal of Economics*, LXXIX (1965) pp. 537–54.

26. According to the OECD, between the second semester and the corresponding period of 1984, the unemployment rate fell from 10.3 percent to 9.0 percent in the United States while it increased from 8.1 percent to 8.5 percent in France; during the first half of 1985, the respective rates are estimated at 7.75 percent in the US and 10.0 percent in France.

Part VI
Trade Between Developed and Developing Countries: Policies and Prospects

Essay 18 Trends in International Trade in Manufactured Goods and Structural Change in the Industrial Countries

INTRODUCTION

This essay will examine recent trends in trade in manufactured goods between the industrial and the developing countries and indicate the implications of these trends for structural change in the industrial countries. The essay will cover the 1973–81 period, with consideration given to changes during the 1973–8 and 1978–81 subperiods, each of which began with an oil shock, followed by a world recession.[1]

Section I of the essay will provide information on changes over time in the current dollar value of trade in manufactured goods between the industrial and the developing countries. It will further analyze trends in the volume of trade in manufactured goods, and its relationship with economic activity, in the two groups of countries. Finally, the relative importance of trade with the developing countries for the manufacturing sector of the industrial nations, and changes thereof, will be indicated.

The commodity composition of trade in manufactured goods between the industrial and the developing countries will be the subject of Section II of the essay. It will examine the changing importance of trade with the developing countries for the manufacturing sector of the industrial nations in a seven commodity-group breakdown. The discussion will also cover the employment effects of trade in manufactured

403

goods as well as its conformity to the comparative advantage of the two groups of countries. The essay will conclude with policy recommendations that aim at promoting international trade and structural change.

For purposes of the statistical analysis, industrial countries have been defined to include the United States, Canada, the European Common Market (EC),[2] the European Free Trade Association (EFTA)[3] and Japan; among developing countries, distinction has been made between OPEC[4] and non-OPEC countries. The two groupings exclude Southern Europe other than Greece and Portugal; Australia, New Zealand, and South Africa; and the centrally planned economies.

I TRADE IN MANUFACTURED GOODS BETWEEN THE INDUSTRIAL AND THE DEVELOPING COUNTRIES

Changes in export and import flows, 1973–81

The period beginning with the first oil shock saw considerable increases in the surplus of the industrial countries in their trade in manufactured goods[5] with the developing countries. In terms of current dollars, the surplus grew from $36 billion in 1973 to $114 billion in 1978 and, again, to $172 billion in 1981.

In 1981, over one-half of the surplus in this trade was with the OPEC countries. In that year, OPEC provided markets for two-fifths of the manufactured exports of the industrial nations to the developing countries, but supplied a negligible proportion of their imports of these commodities. The export share of the OPEC countries rose from one-quarter in 1973 to two-fifths in 1978, and stabilized afterwards.

In 1973, the industrial nations covered 43 percent of their oil imports from OPEC by the exports of manufactured goods. This ratio rose to 62 percent in 1978, but declined to 48 percent in 1981. The increased coverage of oil imports by manufactured exports between 1973 and 1978 reflects the rise in the spending of oil revenues by OPEC while the subsequent decline indicates delays in using increases in these revenues following the 1979–80 oil price rise.[6]

The extent of coverage of oil imports by the exports of manufactured goods, and changes in this coverage over time, vary to a considerable extent among the industrial countries. Between 1973 and 1981, the ratio increased from 41 to 61 percent in the European Common Market and from 19 to 33 percent in Canada; it remained practically unchanged in the European Free Trade Association (68 and 69 percent) and in Japan

(43 and 42 percent); and it declined from 52 and 33 percent in the United States.

The results for the European Common Market were not, however, due to rapid increases of manufactured exports to OPEC; together with the United States, the EC was at the lower end of the range as far as the growth of these exports is concerned. But, while the current dollar value of oil imports from OPEC rose more than tenfold in the United States, oil imports into the EC increased less than five times. In turn, EFTA and Japan expanded their manufactured exports *pari passu* with the approximately eightfold rise in their oil imports from OPEC, and export increases of a similar magnitude were more than sufficient to compensate for the fivefold increase of oil imports into Canada.

In the trade of the industrial countries with the non-OPEC developing countries, changes in the ratio of their manufactured imports to the exports of these commodities are of interest. For the industrial countries, taken together, this ratio rose from 39 percent in 1973 to 45 percent in 1978. Nevertheless, given the small import/export ratio in the initial year, the surplus of the industrial countries in manufactured trade with the non-OPEC developing countries grew from $24 billion in 1973 to $51 billion in 1978. The surplus increased further, to $80 billion in 1981, when the import/export ratio reached 46 percent.

Import/export ratios in trade in manufactured goods with the developing countries increased in all industrial countries and country groups, the exception being Japan. While Japan was only slightly above the industrial country average in terms of the growth of manufactured exports to the non-OPEC developing countries, the increase in its imports of manufactured goods from these countries hardly exceeded one-half of the industrial country average. In turn, US-manufactured exports to the non-OPEC developing countries grew more rapidly than those of Japan, whereas imports into the United States rose at double the Japanese rate. As a result, the US import-export ratio in manufactured trade with the non-OPEC developing countries increased from 71 percent in 1973 to 77 percent in 1981; by contrast, the ratio for Japan fell from 22 to 16 percent.

In the same period, the ratio of the imports of manufactured goods to the exports of these commodities in trade with the non-OPEC developing countries rose from 29 percent to 39 percent in the European Common Market and from 29 percent to 37 percent in the European Free Trade Association, reflecting below-average increases in their exports and roughly average changes in their imports. Finally, Canada had an approximate balance in its trade in manufactured goods with the non-OPEC developing countries throughout the period under consideration.

Trends in the volume of manufactured trade and in the gross domestic product

The above discussion concerned trade in manufactured goods between the industrial and the developing countries in terms of current dollars. Next in this chapter, trade expressed in terms of constant prices will be considered. Table 18.1 provides information on the rate of increase of the gross domestic product in the industrial countries and on their 'apparent' income elasticities of import demand, defined as the ratio of the rate of growth of imports to that of the gross domestic product.[7]

The apparent income elasticity of demand for manufactured imports originating in the developing countries averaged 3.6 in the industrial countries during the 1963–73 period; the volume of imports into these countries rose at an average annual rate of 16.5 percent while their combined GDP grew 4.6 percent a year. The apparent income elasticity increased to 4.1 in 1973–8 as the rate of growth of imports was 10.2 percent and that of GDP 2.5 percent; it increased further to 4.2 percent in 1978–81, when import growth was 8.4 percent and GDP growth 2.0 percent; and it averaged 4.1 for the entire 1973–81 period.

Considerable differences are observed, however, among the industrial countries and country groups. While Japan leads in both periods in terms of GDP growth, it had the lowest import growth rate in 1973–8 and the second lowest (next to the EC) in 1978–81. Correspondingly, Japan had by far the lowest income elasticity of import demand for manufactured goods originating from the developing countries. In fact, between 1973 and 1981, Japan's imports of manufactured goods from these countries increased hardly more than its gross domestic product.

The EC and EFTA had the highest income elasticities of import demand in 1973–8, but relatively low elasticities in 1978–81. In turn, the elasticity rose to a considerable extent in the United States between 1973–8 and 1978–81, approaching the EC average for the entire period. Increases occurred also in Canada, but the average for the entire period was reduced by the low 1973–8 income elasticity of import demand.

Apparent income elasticities have also been calculated in regard to the developing countries' imports of manufactured goods from the industrial countries. In 1973–8, increases in GDP averaged 8.2 percent in the OPEC countries while the volume of imports grew at an average annual rate of 24.2 percent, resulting in an income elasticity of 3.0. The corresponding figures for the non-OPEC developing countries were 4.1 percent and 7.2 percent, with an income elasticity of 1.8.[8]

In 1978–81, however, the gross domestic product of the OPEC countries declined, reflecting in part the political events in Iran and in part the unfavorable economic developments that occurred in several large oil-exporting countries. During this period, the volume of imports of manufactured goods increased at an average annual rate of 6.9 percent. In turn, imports grew 9.5 percent, and GDP increased 4.3 percent, a year in the non-OPEC developing countries, resulting in an apparent income elasticity of demand of 2.2.

A longer time perspective may be taken in regard to the combined manufactured imports of all developing countries from the industrial nations. In the 1963–73 period, the apparent income elasticity of demand for these imports was 1.3, with the gross domestic product and the volume of imports growing at average annual rates of 6.2 and 8.2 percent, respectively.[9] The elasticity rose to 2.4 in 1973–8 and increased again to 3.5 in 1978–81.

A comparison of export and import volume growth rates is of further interest. In their trade in manufactured goods with the developing countries, the volume of the industrial countries' exports and imports rose at average annual rates of 8.2 and 16.5 percent, respectively, between 1963 and 1973. Average increases were 12.5 and 10.2 percent a year in 1973–8, when manufactured exports to OPEC grew particularly rapidly.

The rate of increase of the industrial countries' exports of manufactured goods to the developing countries declined, however, in 1978–81 as the acceleration of the growth of exports to the non-OPEC developing countries did not compensate for the deceleration of export expansion to OPEC. The average volume growth rate of 8.3 percent for the manufactured exports of the industrial nations to the developing countries approximately equalled their import growth rate of 8.4 percent.

The conclusions are modified if value rather than volume data are compared. Thus, the current dollar value of manufactured exports from the industrial to the developing countries rose by 53 percent between 1978 and 1981 while the imports of these commodities from the developing countries increased by 58 percent.

The results reflect an improvement in the terms of trade of the developing countries in manufactured goods. The improvement oc-

TABLE 18.1 Change in the volume of trade in manufactured goods between industrial and developing countries and in the gross domestic product of the industrial countries

| | Exports to | | | Imports | GDP percent | Apparent Income Elasticity percent |
| | OPEC | non-OPEC | All LDCs | from All LDCs | | |
	average annual rate of growth					
1963–73						
Industrial Countries	—	—	8.2	16.5	4.6	3.6
1973–78						
United States	23.7	6.3	10.6	11.1	2.5	4.4
Canada	33.7	8.8	16.5	6.8	3.4	2.0
EC	23.3	6.2	12.5	12.1	2.1	5.8
EFTA	23.8	5.4	10.7	8.4	1.5	5.6
Japan	26.4	9.9	14.2	3.0	3.6	0.8
Industrial Countries	24.2	7.2	12.5	10.2	2.5	4.1
1978–81						
United States	-1.3	10.6	6.9	10.5	1.6	6.6
Canada	2.5	13.9	8.2	13.6	2.0	6.8

EC	7.8	7.9	7.9	5.3	1.4	3.8
EFTA	8.5	6.8	7.5	8.6	2.6	3.3
Japan	10.3	7.9	8.8	6.6	4.1	1.6
Industrial Countries	6.9	9.5	8.3	8.4	2.0	4.2
1973–81						
United States	13.7	7.9	9.2	10.8	2.2	4.9
Canada	21.0	10.7	13.3	9.3	2.9	3.2
EEC	17.2	6.8	10.8	9.5	1.8	5.3
EFTA	17.8	5.9	9.5	8.5	1.9	4.5
Japan	20.1	9.1	12.1	4.3	3.8	1.1
Industrial Countries	17.4	7.1	11.7	9.5	2.3	4.1

NOTE: The apparent income elasticity has been defined as the ratio of the average annual rate of growth of imports to that of the gross domestic product.

SOURCES: 1963–73 and 1973–8; Balassa 'Trade in Manufactured Goods: Patterns of Change', World Development IX 1981.
1978–81: Value of trade – GATT *International Trade*, 1980/81 and 1981/82.
Unit values – Industrial countries: United Nations
Monthly Bulletin of Statistics.
Unit values – Developing Countries: Estimated from the export unit value indices of the principal developing country exporters of manufactured goods, accounting for 72 percent of the total.
Gross domestic product – World Bank economic and social data base.

curred in 1981, when European countries did not raise their export prices in terms of domestic currency to fully offset the appreciation of the dollar whereas developing country exporters, which generally link their currencies to the US dollar, continued to increase their prices in dollar terms.

Changes in the relative importance of trade in manufactured goods between the industrial and the developing countries

In the 1973–8 period, the developing countries assumed increased importance as markets for the manufactured exports of the industrial nations. Thus, their share in the extraregional exports of manufactured goods of the industrial countries rose from 37 percent in 1973 to 47 percent in 1978 and to 49 percent in 1981.[10] And while data on average shares would seem to indicate a deceleration over time, incremental shares remained practically constant – 54 percent in 1973–8 and 53 percent in 1978–81.

The developing countries also assumed increased importance as sources of supply for manufactured goods imported by industrial countries; their share in the industrial countries' extraregional imports of these commodities increased from 20 percent in 1973 to 24 percent in 1978 and to 25 percent in 1981. Again, incremental shares showed little change; they were 29 percent in 1973–8 and 27 percent in 1978–81.

In 1973, the developing countries accounted for the largest share of extraregional manufactured exports in the United States (42 percent), with EFTA (31 percent) at the lower end of the range. In turn, in 1981, these countries had the highest share in the extraregional exports of the EC (54 percent), followed by the United States (51 percent), with Japan falling to last place (42 percent). The results reflect differences in incremental export shares that were especially high in the EC (63 percent) and much below average in Japan (44 percent) during the period.

However, the United States retained first place as far as the relative importance of developing countries in the extraregional imports of manufactured goods is concerned. The US import shares were 23 percent in 1973 and 30 percent in 1981, with an incremental share of 33 percent. In turn, EFTA remained at the last place, the relevant figures being 14, 19, and 21 percent. Finally, the share of the developing countries in Japanese imports of manufactured goods rose between 1973 and 1978, but declined slightly afterwards as incremental import shares in 1978–81 did not exceed the average share at the beginning of the period (23 percent).

International trade in manufactured goods increased more rapidly than manufacturing output in the industrial countries throughout the period under consideration. Correspondingly, the share of exports to the developing countries in the production of manufactured goods in the industrial countries increased even more than their share in the extraregional exports of these countries. The relevant proportions were 2.9 percent in 1973, 5.2 percent in 1978, and 6.4 percent in 1981. The deceleration in the rise of average shares notwithstanding, incremental shares rose from 8.5 percent in 1973–8 and 11.3 percent in 1978–81, averaging 9.5 percent for the entire period (Table 18.2).

Similar trends are observed in regard to the share of imports from the developing countries in the consumption of manufactured goods in the industrial countries. These shares increased from 0.9 percent in 1973 to 1.5 percent in 1978 and to 2.0 percent in 1981, with incremental shares being 2.4 percent and 3.8 percent in 1973–8 and 1978–81, respectively.

Exports to the developing countries had a higher than average share in the production, and lower than average share in the consumption, of manufactured goods in Japan. Developing countries made little headway in entering the Japanese market, with their share in the consumption of manufactured goods rising only from 0.7 percent in 1973 to 1.0 percent in 1981. During this period, their incremental share in consumption was 1.2 in Japan, compared to a range of 3.1 to 3.5 percent in the other industrial countries and country groups, excepting Canada.

As a result of these changes, in 1981 the developing countries had the highest share in the consumption of manufactured goods in the United States and EFTA (2.3 percent), followed by the EC (2.0 percent) and Canada (1.6 percent). In the same year, the developing countries provided markets for 10.0 percent of manufacturing output in EFTA, 8.3 percent in the EC, 7.9 percent in Japan, 4.1 percent in the United States, and 3.0 percent in Canada.

Policy implications of the results

Changes in the manufactured imports of the OPEC countries are largely explained by the effects of the 1973–4 and 1979–80 oil price increases on their foreign exchange revenue and by the speed at which increases in these revenues were translated into higher imports. Following the quadrupling of oil prices, the merchandise trade surplus of the

TABLE 18.2 The relative importance for the industrial nations of trade in manufactured goods[a] with the developing countries[b]

	1973				1978				1981			
	X_{LDC}/X	X_{LDC}/P	M_{LDC}/M	M_{LDC}/C	X_{LDC}/X	X_{LDC}/P	M_{LDC}/M	M_{LDC}/C	X_{LDC}/X	X_{LDC}/P	M_{LDC}/M	M_{LDC}/C
United States	41.6	1.8	22.9	1.1	51.1	3.0	27.4	1.8	50.6	4.1	30.2	2.3
Canada	35.9	1.2	12.5	0.8	50.7	2.4	17.4	1.3	47.7	3.0	20.4	1.6
EC	37.3	3.7	18.1	0.9	49.8	6.8	23.3	1.6	54.4	8.3	24.4	2.0
EFTA	31.0	5.2	14.4	1.2	39.7	8.9	17.8	1.9	43.7	10.0	19.2	2.3
Japan	36.0	3.7	22.6	0.7	42.6	6.3	24.4	0.8	42.1	7.9	23.9	1.0
Industrial Countries	37.4	2.9	19.7	0.9	47.4	5.2	24.4	1.5	49.0	6.4	25.5	2.0

	1973–78				1978–81				1973–81			
	$\Delta X_{LDC}/\Delta X$	$\Delta X_{LDC}/\Delta P$	$\Delta M_{LDC}/\Delta M$	$\Delta M_{LDC}/\Delta C$	$\Delta X_{LDC}/\Delta X$	$\Delta X_{LDC}/\Delta P$	$\Delta M_{LDC}/\Delta M$	$\Delta M_{LDC}/\Delta C$	$\Delta X_{LDC}/\Delta X$	$\Delta X_{LDC}/\Delta P$	$\Delta M_{LDC}/\Delta M$	$\Delta M_{LDC}/\Delta C$
United States	58.7	4.9	30.7	2.9	49.9	7.5	34.8	4.2	53.6	6.0	33.0	3.5
Canada	63.1	4.5	23.9	2.0	44.0	4.7	26.6	2.6	51.6	4.6	25.2	2.3
EC	59.1	11.5	27.2	2.6	70.8	17.2	21.7	4.3	62.9	13.1	26.8	3.1
EFTA	46.2	13.8	23.7	2.9	57.3	13.9	19.3	3.7	50.0	13.9	21.3	3.3
Japan	46.4	9.2	26.8	0.9	41.4	15.1	22.8	2.2	44.1	11.1	24.6	1.2
Industrial Countries	54.4	8.5	28.6	2.4	52.5	11.3	27.2	3.8	53.6	9.5	27.7	2.9

NOTES [a]The definition of manufactured goods used here corresponds to that employed in trade statistics (SITC classes 5 to 8 less 68). For 1981 production figures had to be estimated or the basis of incomplete information.
[b]Explanation of symbols: X = exports, M = imports, P = production, C = consumption ($P + M - X$), LDC = Developing Countries and Δ denotes increment.

SOURCES: GATT, *International Trade*; United Nations, *Yearbook of Industrial Statistics*; OECD, *Indicators of Industrial Activity*, various issues.

OPEC countries increased from $21 billion in 1973 to $84 billion in 1974. It declined to $43 billion by 1978 as manufactured imports were catching up with the higher revenues. The OPEC surplus rose again to $113 billion in 1979 and to $168 billion in 1980, when oil prices increased two-and-a-half times; it declined only to $120 billion in 1981, indicating the time lag involved in adjusting to higher revenues.

Nevertheless, differences are observed within OPEC as the capital-surplus countries continued to accumulate reserves while some other OPEC countries borrowed abroad in order to finance their ambitious development programs. The non-OPEC developing countries also stepped up their foreign borrowing during the period under consideration, so as to finance their rising merchandise trade deficit that grew from $15 billion in 1973 to $37 billion in 1978 and to $78 billion in 1981.

Foreign borrowing made it possible for the non-OPEC developing countries to finance their growing deficit in manufactured trade with the industrial countries, notwithstanding their higher oil bill. This increase, in turn, benefited the industrial countries in a situation of under-utilized capacity. Assuming that the increment in net exports, over and above what would have occurred if the 1973 ratio of net exports to production had remained unchanged, added to manufacturing output in the industrial countries, incremental output between 1973 and 1981 was 4.6 percent larger than it would have been otherwise.[11]

The trade-induced rise in incremental output appears to have been the largest in the EC (7.2 percent), followed by Japan (6.9 percent), EFTA (6.6 percent), with Canada (1.9 percent) and the United States (1.6 percent) at the other end of the scale. At the same time, these figures represent an underestimate inasmuch as they do not allow for multiplier effects and an overestimate inasmuch as they do not take account of alternative uses of the capital overflow from the industrial countries in their own economies.

In turn, the observed rise in the industrial countries' income elasticity of demand for the imports of manufactured goods originating in the developing countries, and the increased developing country share in their consumption of these commodities, do not provide an indication of increased protectionism in the industrial countries.[12] Japan provides an exception, however, as it had by far the lowest income elasticity of demand for manufactured imports from the developing countries, and these countries had by far the lowest share in its domestic consumption of manufactured goods.

These results cannot be explained on the grounds that factor endowments are more similar between the developing countries and Japan than between the developing countries and other industrial countries. Although such might have been the case during the sixties, the situation changed to a considerable extent afterwards. At the same time, with relatively high economic growth rates, Japan's factor endowment changed rapidly, and this should have led to rapid increases in imports from the developing countries if these imports had not been subject to restrictions.

This is not to say that the expansion of the developing countries' manufactured exports could be explained by demand considerations alone. In this regard, a statement made by the author concerning the 1973–8 period continues to apply.

> While access to industrial country markets has provided opportunities for export expansion, the exports of manufactured goods from the developing countries had responded to the policies followed by these countries. A number of developing countries adopted an export-oriented strategy during the 1960s and have continued with this strategy after 1973. Available evidence suggests that countries following an export-oriented strategy were better able to surmount the adverse effects of the quadrupling of oil prices and the 1974–1975 world recession than countries with an import-substitution orientation.[13]

Developing countries following an export-oriented strategy also relied less on foreign borrowing than did import substitution-oriented countries. In turn, with lower indebtedness, they escaped the difficulties the latter group of countries experienced as world interest rates rose.[14] Excessive foreign borrowing under import substitution orientation, then, helped the expansion of manufacturing output in the industrial countries in a situation of under-utilized capacity but subsequently created difficulties for the borrowing countries themselves.

II EFFECTS OF TRADE ON PRODUCTION, EMPLOYMENT, AND RESOURCE ALLOCATION

Recent trends in the trade of individual commodity groups

We have seen that the developing countries assumed increased importance as markets for the industrial nations between 1973 and 1981. The same picture emerges in regard to individual commodity groups, for which comparable production and trade data are available for the entire period. They include iron and steel, chemicals, other semi-manufactures; engineering products, textiles, clothing, and other consumer goods. For all these commodity groups, the share of the developing countries in the extraregional exports, and in the production, of the industrial countries rose between 1973 and 1978 and, again, between 1978 and 1981 (Table 18.3).

In 1973, the developing countries' share of the extraregional exports of the industrial countries varied from 26 percent in the other consumer goods category and 29 percent in clothing to 42 percent in chemicals and 43 percent in textiles. The differences narrowed to a considerable extent between 1973 and 1981. Other consumer goods and clothing (46 percent) remained at the lower end of the range; semi-manufactures joined textiles (53 percent) at the upper end; and the developing countries came to account for 49 percent of the industrial countries' extraregional exports of engineering products.

The share of exports to developing country markets in production in the industrial countries, too, increased in every commodity group. At the lower end of the range, this share rose from 0.9 to 2.6 percent in the case of clothing, from 1.1 to 3.0 percent for other semi-manufactures, and from 1.2 to 3.3 percent for the other consumer goods category; at the upper end, the relevant shares were 3.4 and 4.9 percent for chemicals, 3.5 and 6.5 percent for iron and steel, and 3.7 and 8.7 percent for engineering products. In the latter category, increases in exports to the developing countries provided 12.8 percent of incremental output in the industrial countries between 1973 and 1981. Incremental shares varied from 4.9 percent (other consumer goods) to 10.0 percent (steel) in the other commodity groups.

The developing countries also increased their share in the extraregional imports of the industrial countries in every commodity group between 1973 and 1981. While this share remained relatively low in engineering products (9.9 percent in 1973 and 16.2 percent in 1981), iron and steel (10.7 and 16.1 percent), and chemicals (11.2 and 13.7 percent), it increased from 39.8 to 45.2 percent in textiles, from 63.3 to 73.8 percent in clothing, and from 27.7 to 44.4 percent in the other consumer goods category.

Imports from the developing countries, expressed as a percentage of consumption in the industrial countries, too, rose in all commodity groups. Varying between 0.4 and 0.5 percent in 1973, these imports reached 1.0 percent of consumption in the case of iron and steel, 0.7

TABLE 18.3 The relative importance for the industrial nations of trade in individual commodity groups with the developing countries[a]

	1973				1978				1981			
	X_{LDC}/X	X_{LDC}/P	M_{LDC}/M	M_{LDC}/C	X_{LDC}/X	X_{LDC}/P	M_{LDC}/M	M_{LDC}/C	X_{LDC}/X	X_{LDC}/P	M_{LDC}/M	M_{LDC}/C
Iron and Steel	41.0	3.5	10.7	0.4	44.8	5.0	11.6	0.5	49.7	6.5	16.1	1.0
Chemicals	42.2	3.4	11.2	0.4	45.5	4.6	12.1	0.6	47.5	4.9	13.7	0.7
Other Semi Manufactures	36.7	1.1	34.0	1.0	50.7	2.5	38.1	1.6	53.0	3.0	34.8	1.5
Engineering Products	36.6	3.7	9.9	0.5	48.2	7.0	15.1	1.0	48.9	8.7	16.2	1.5
Textiles	43.0	2.8	39.8	1.3	49.3	3.6	45.8	2.7	52.6	5.0	45.2	3.0
Clothing	28.7	0.9	63.3	6.0	40.8	1.7	69.1	10.9	46.5	2.6	73.8	14.4
Other Consumer Goods	26.2	1.2	27.7	1.4	41.2	2.3	37.0	2.4	46.2	3.3	44.4	3.3
Total Manufacturing	37.4	2.9	19.7	0.9	47.4	5.2	24.4	1.5	49.0	6.4	25.5	2.0

	1973–78				1978–1981				1973–1981			
	$\Delta X_{LDC}/\Delta X$	$\Delta X_{LDC}/\Delta P$	$\Delta M_{LDC}/\Delta M$	$\Delta M_{LDC}/\Delta C$	$\Delta X_{LDC}/\Delta X$	$\Delta X_{LDC}/\Delta P$	$\Delta M_{LDC}/\Delta M$	$\Delta M_{LDC}/\Delta C$	$\Delta X_{LDC}/\Delta X$	$\Delta X_{LDC}/\Delta P$	$\Delta M_{LDC}/\Delta M$	$\Delta M_{LDC}/\Delta C$
Iron and Steel	47.6	7.3	11.5	0.7	64.8	17.5	25.4	4.8	54.3	10.0	18.9	1.8
Chemicals	47.8	5.9	12.7	0.7	51.9	5.8	15.8	1.0	49.7	5.8	14.3	.9
Other Semi Manufactures	61.5	6.5	42.3	3.4	58.0	5.2	22.0	1.1	60.0	5.9	35.3	2.3
Engineering Products	55.7	11.2	19.0	1.6	50.4	15.9	18.0	3.8	53.4	12.8	18.5	2.3
Textiles	59.5	5.6	49.1	6.1	61.7	17.2	45.0	6.3	60.7	8.7	48.0	6.1
Clothing	50.0	3.2	73.1	19.6	56.3	12.2	84.5	41.5	53.1	5.2	77.8	25.5
Other Consumer Goods	53.2	3.6	43.4	3.5	54.9	7.8	63.6	7.5	54.1	4.9	51.9	4.7
Total Manufacturing	54.4	8.5	28.6	2.4	52.5	11.3	27.2	3.8	53.6	9.5	27.7	2.9

NOTES: [a]The classification system used corresponds to that applied in GATT, *International Trade*. For explanation of symbols, see Table 18.2.

SOURCES: See Table 18.2.

percent for chemicals, and 1.5 percent for engineering products in 1981. At the other end of the scale, the share of imports rose from 6.0 percent to 14.4 percent in the case of clothing, followed by textiles (1.3 and 3.0 percent) and other consumer goods (1.4 and 3.3 percent).

Clothing also leads in terms of incremental consumption shares (25.5 percent between 1973 and 1981), followed by textiles (6.1 percent) and other consumer goods (4.7 percent). These results occurred, notwithstanding the continued operation of the Multifiber Arrangement and the restrictions imposed on some of the other consumer goods originating in the developing countries. Moreover, incremental shares doubled between 1973–8 and 1978–81 in the case of clothing and other consumer goods, exceeding the increases shown for total manufacturing, while they remained constant for textiles.

The next question concerns the extent to which changes in net exports in trade with the developing countries affected manufacturing output in the industrial countries. Under the assumptions made earlier, the average 4.6 percent increase in output between 1973 and 1981, associated with increases in the ratio of net exports to production, covers considerable differences among commodity groups. The resulting rise in incremental output appears to be the largest for engineering products (7.3 percent) and iron and steel (5.1 percent), followed by chemicals (2.9 percent), other semi-manufactures (2.5 percent), and textiles (1.1 percent). In turn, no changes occurred in other consumer goods while trade in clothing with the developing countries appears to have reduced incremental output by 15.2 percent.

Employment effects

Trade in manufactures also affects employment in the industrial nations. Table 18.4 shows that, during the period under consideration, average labor input coefficients were two-fifths higher in the industrial countries' imports than in their exports of manufactured goods in trade with the developing countries. The ratios exhibited considerable stability over time, and differences among industrial countries and country groups were relatively small. The exception is Canada where labor input coefficients were lower for exports, and higher for imports, than the industrial country average.

The results reflect inter-industry differences in labor input coefficients, calculated from the 1975 US Census of Manufacturing in an eleven commodity group breakdown by subdividing the engineering product group into five categories (machinery for specialized industry, office and telecommunication equipment, road motor vehicles, other machinery and transport equipment and household appliances). Labor input coefficients, expressed in man years per million dollars of output, are lower than the manufacturing average for engineering products (18.6), with a range from 6.9 for motor vehicles to 21.0 for household appliances; other semi-manufactures (18.0); iron and steel (15.9); and chemicals (13.2). By contrast, labor input coefficients exceed the manufacturing average in the case of clothing (40.6), other consumer goods (28.9), and textiles (26.7).[15]

The observed differences in average labor input coefficients for the industrial countries' manufactured exports and imports in trade with the developing countries were more than offset by their surplus in this trade, resulting in a net gain in employment.[16] The estimated gain was 701 000 jobs in 1973, 1 439 000 jobs in 1978, and 1 474 000 jobs in 1981; the slowdown after 1978 is explained by the decline in export-import ratios in trade with the developing countries.

Among the industrial countries and country groups, employment gains decreased after 1978 in the EC and EFTA, they underwent little change in Canada, while continued increases were shown in Japan and, in particular, in the United States. Nevertheless, in 1981, net employment gains were by far the largest in the European Common Market (710 000) and Japan (523 000), followed by the United States (142 000), and the European Free Trade Association (98 000), with Canada showing an approximate balance. The relatively low US net employment gain, compared to its trade balance in manufactures with the developing countries, is explained by its low export/import ratio. The same considerations account for the lack of a net employment gain in Canada.

Among individual commodity groups, iron and steel, chemicals, other semi-manufactures, all categories of engineering products, and textiles exhibited net employment gains in the industrial countries. These gains increased between 1973 and 1978 and showed little change afterwards, the exception being the other semi-manufactures category that experienced large increases in net employment gains as the trade surplus of the industrial countries increased to a considerable extent.

In 1981, net losses in employment were shown in only one commodity group – clothing – with practically no net effect for the other consumer goods category. In the case of clothing, net employment losses for the industrial countries, resulting from their trade with the developing countries, were estimated at 163 000 in 1973, 279 000 in 1978, and 283 000 in 1981.

To put these figures into perspective, they should be compared with actual employment statistics. The results show that, in 1981, net employment losses due to trade with the developing countries did not reach 3 percent of employment in the textiles, clothing, and leather products sector of the industrial countries.[17] The ratio was the highest for the United States, but it did not exceed 6 percent in this case either.

Alternatively, one may compare changes in trade-induced employment losses with changes in employment. Between 1973 and 1980, employment in the textiles, clothing, and leather products sector of the industrial countries declined by 1.7 million, compared to an increase of 0.1 million in net employment losses due to trade with the developing countries. In none of the industrial countries and country groups did the increase in the trade-induced loss in employment reach 15 percent of the decline in employment in this sector.

Comparative advantage in trade in manufactured goods

We have considered the effects of trade in manufactured goods between the industrial and the developing countries on employment in the former group of countries. Next, the factor intensity of this trade will be examined, with separate consideration given to physical and human capital.

Physical capital/labor and human capital/labor ratios have been derived from US data with calculations made in 'stock' and in 'flow' terms. The former have been defined as the value of fixed capital per worker (physical capital) and the discounted value of the difference between the average wage and the unskilled wage (human capital), and the latter as nonwage value added per worker (physical capital) and the average wage (human capital).

Table 18.4 provides information on average capital/labor ratios for the exports and imports of manufactured goods in trade between the industrial and the developing countries. As is apparent from the table, capital/labor ratios are substantially higher for the exports than for the imports of the industrial countries. In 1973, the ratio for exports exceeded that for imports by 29 percent for physical and by 19 percent for human capital, utilizing the stock measure, and by 33 percent for

TABLE 18.4 *Employment and capital/labor coefficients in the trade of the industrial countries with the developing countries in manufactured goods*

| | Stocks | | | | | | | | Flows | | | | | |
| | E/O | | PK/E | | HK/E | | TK/E | | PK/E | | HK/E | | TK/E | |
	X	M	X	M	X	M	X	M	X	M	X	M	X	M
USA														
1973	18.4	25.5	12.8	9.8	28.1	25.0	40.9	34.8	9.0	6.7	9.4	8.0	18.4	14.7
1978	18.2	25.8	12.5	9.3	28.1	25.4	40.6	34.7	9.1	6.7	9.4	8.1	18.5	14.8
1981	18.5	25.3	12.5	9.3	28.1	25.9	40.6	35.2	9.0	5.8	9.4	8.2	18.4	15.0
Canada														
1973	17.0	28.0	14.0	8.8	27.9	22.0	41.9	30.8	9.0	5.8	9.4	7.3	18.4	13.1
1978	15.5	27.4	13.8	8.6	27.5	22.7	41.3	31.3	9.7	6.3	9.8	7.4	19.5	13.7
1981	15.4	26.7	13.0	9.0	26.7	24.0	39.7	33.0	9.4	6.4	9.4	7.7	18.8	14.1

EC														
1973	18.0	25.6	13.7	11.4	27.3	21.8	41.0	33.2	9.2	6.6	9.3	7.5	18.5	14.1
1978	18.4	25.7	12.8	10.5	27.5	22.8	40.4	33.3	8.6	6.6	9.3	7.7	17.9	14.3
1981	18.1	25.9	12.9	9.8	27.2	23.3	40.1	33.1	8.7	6.7	9.2	7.7	17.9	14.4
EFTA														
1973	18.7	23.9	13.2	11.1	28.5	19.6	41.7	30.7	9.0	7.1	9.2	6.9	18.2	14.0
1978	18.8	26.6	13.1	9.9	28.4	22.1	41.5	32.0	8.7	6.8	9.2	7.4	17.9	14.2
1981	18.7	26.4	13.0	9.9	28.0	22.5	41.0	32.4	8.8	6.9	9.2	7.5	18.0	14.4
Japan														
1973	18.5	25.4	14.9	11.7	27.5	21.2	42.4	32.9	8.0	6.4	9.3	7.4	17.3	13.8
1978	17.8	25.6	13.8	11.7	28.3	23.0	42.1	34.7	8.3	7.2	9.5	7.8	17.8	15.0
1981	17.7	23.9	13.7	12.4	28.4	23.8	42.1	36.2	8.4	7.4	9.5	8.0	17.9	15.4
Industrial Countries														
1973	18.2	25.6	13.7	10.6	27.6	23.2	41.3	33.8	8.8	6.6	9.3	7.7	18.1	14.3
1978	18.2	25.8	13.1	9.9	27.9	24.0	41.0	33.9	8.7	6.7	9.4	7.8	18.1	14.5
1981	18.2	25.5	13.1	9.8	28.0	24.7	41.1	34.5	8.8	6.8	9.4	8.0	18.2	14.8

SOURCES: B. Balassa, 'The Changing International Division of Labor in Manufactured Goods', *Banca Nazionale del Lavoro, Quarterly Review*, pp. 243–85 and 'A Stages' Approach to Comparative Advantage', in I. Adelman (ed.), *Economic Growth and Resources Volume 4: National and International Issues* (London: Macmillan) pp. 121–56.

NOTE: E/O = employment/output ratio; PK/E = physical capital/labor ratio; HK/E = human capital/labor ratio; TK/E = (aggregate) capital/labor ratio.

physical and 21 percent for human capital, utilizing the flow measure.

Between 1973 and 1981, the aggregate ratios (physical and human capital combined) changed little for exports, and increased slightly for imports. The results were practically the same under the stock and the flow measures, with a 3 to 4 percentage points reduction in the difference in capital/labor ratios between exports and imports.

It appears, then, that trade in manufactured goods between the industrial and the developing countries conformed to their comparative advantage. While textiles may appear to be an aberrant case, it should be recognized that the industrial countries and, in particular, the United States export high-quality textiles and import low quality textile products from the developing countries.[18]

By-and-large similar results are obtained for the trade of individual countries and country groups with the developing countries; exceptions are Canada whose exports tend to be relatively more capital-intensive compared to its imports from the developing countries, and EFTA where the opposite is the case. In Canada, the high export share of the capital-intensive, natural resource-based other intermediate products category contributed to this result, while the EFTA countries are the most liberal among industrial countries in admitting labor-intensive manufactures from the developing countries.

The results changed little between 1973 and 1981. An exception is engineering products where the developing countries increased their exports to a considerable extent. This change also conformed to the comparative advantage of the two groups of countries, with the developing countries gaining in the exports of labor-intensive radios and television sets as well as in exporting labor-intensive parts, components, and accessories in the framework of the international division of the production process.

Policy implications of the results

The data show that the industrial countries tend to exchange manufactured goods intensive in physical and in human capital for products intensive in unskilled labor. Such an exchange apparently occurs through inter-industry as well as through intra-industry specialization.

The large differences observed in capital/labor ratios among commodity groups are indicative of the mutual gains the industrial and the developing countries can obtain through specialization according to comparative advantage. This result is strengthened if account is taken of differences in capital/labor ratios within individual commodity groups. It receives further support if consideration is given to the high research intensity of the manufactured exports of the industrial countries.

Apart from traditional gains owing to differences in factor proportions, the industrial countries derive benefits from trade in manufactured goods with the developing countries through the exploitation of economies of scale. This source of gain has assumed increased importance as the share of the developing countries in the domestic production of manufactured goods in the industrial countries has risen. Apart from economies of scale in production, gains are obtained through economies of scale in research inasmuch as a larger sales volume permits reducing unit expenditures on research and development.

Further gains can be obtained through intra-industry trade in the form of horizontal or product specialization, such as the exchange of capital-intensive for labor-intensive textiles, and vertical specialization in the framework of the international division of the production process, involving the importation of labor-intensive parts, components, and accessories from the developing countries. Horizontal specialization permits reducing costs by concentrating on fewer commodities while vertical specialization lower costs through the purchase of lower-priced inputs. Finally, increased competition from developing countries provides inducements for technological improvements as it has been the case in the textile industry.

The developing countries, too, enjoy gains from improved resource allocation, the exploitation of economies of scale, and competition through inter-industry and intra-industry trade in manufactured goods with the industrial countries. They enjoy the futher benefit of procuring sophisticated machinery and equipment in a world of rapidly changing technology.

International specialization in manufactured goods also affects employment. While at the actual level of trade the industrial countries have a net employment gain, a balance expansion of exports and imports would have negative employment effects for them. This is because labor input coefficients are, on the average, two-fifths higher for the imports than for the exports of the industrial countries in their trade in manufactured goods with the developing countries.

Nevertheless, projections made earlier by the author indicate that the net employment effects of the expansion of trade in manufactured goods are likely to be negligible.

Also, the expansion of trade in manufactured goods would involve the upgrading of the labor force, with increases in the number of professional, technical, and highly skilled workers and a decline in unskilled and semiskilled workers in the industrial countries. The upgrading of the labor force, in turn, would contribute to the increases in the productivity and higher rates of economic growth.[19]

CONCLUSIONS

This essay has examined the increased importance of the developing countries as markets for the manufactured goods produced in the industrial nations. In the 1973–81 period, developing countries accounted for one-half of the increment in the extraregional exports of manufactured goods by the industrial countries and provided markets for one-tenth of the increment in their manufacturing output. These shares were higher than the average for engineering products, where economies of scale are of special importance.

In turn, the industrial countries increased their imports of manufactured goods from the developing countries at rates exceeding four times the rate of growth of their GDP. In the 1973–81 period, the developing countries provided over one-quarter of the increment in the extraregional imports, and three percent of the increment in manufacturing consumption, of the industrial countries. Their share was the highest in clothing, accounting for over three-quarters of the increase in extraregional imports and for one-quarter of the rise in consumption.

It further appears that increases in the industrial countries' net exports of manufactured goods in trade with the developing countries had multiplier effects on their economies in a situation of under-utilized capacity. In turn, the rapid rise of their manufactured exports to the industrial countries had favorable effects on the process of economic growth in the developing countries.

NOTES

1. The essay updates and extends earlier papers by the author, including 'The Changing International Division of Labor in Manufactured Goods', *Banca Nazionale del Lavoro, Quarterly Review* (1979), pp. 243–85; 'Prospects for Trade in Manufactured Goods between Industrial and Developing Countries, 1978–1990', *Journal of Policy Modeling*, II (1980)

pp. 437–53; and 'Trade in Manufactured Goods: Patterns of Change', *World Development*, IX (1981) pp. 263–75.

2. Belgium-Luxembourg, Denmark, Germany, France, Greece, Ireland, Italy, the Netherlands and the United Kingdom – Data for 1981–3 include Greece; this causes little distortion in the results as Greece accounts for less than 1 percent of EC trade in manufactured goods.

3. Austria, Finland, Iceland, Norway, Portugal, Sweden and Switzerland.

4. Algeria, Ecuador, Gabon, Indonesia, Iran, Iraq, Kuwait, Libyan Arab Jamahiriya, Nigeria, Qatar, Saudi Arabia, United Arab Emirates and Venezuela.

5. Manufactured goods have been defined as commodity classes 5 to 8 in the UN Standard International Trade Classification less nonferrous metals (68). The same definition is used throughout in the paper.

6. Data on oil imports are provided in GATT, *International Trade*, Geneva, various issues.

7. The expression 'apparent' income elasticity is used to refer to the fact that this measure neglects the effects of changes in relative prices on the volume of imports. Nor does the measure consider the interactions of changes in demand and in supply.

8. Estimates based on United Nations, *Monthly Bulletin of Statistics*, various issues and World Bank economic and social data base.

9. Estimated by regression analysis from data published in United Nations, *Monthly Bulletin of Statistics* and *Yearbook of National Accounts Statistics*.

10. Extraregional trade has been defined to exclude trade in manufactured goods between the United States and Canada, one-third of which is exempt from duty under the US–Canadian Automotive Agreement while a substantial part of the remainder represents intra-company transactions, as well as trade within the European free trade area that encompasses the EC and EFTA.

11. The calculations have been made by relating the differences between the incremental ratio of net exports to output in the 1973–81 period and the average ratio in 1973 to the increment in output between 1973 and 1981. Needless to say, the results are subject to qualifications due to the use of current price data.

12. For supporting evidence, see B. Balassa, 'The Tokyo Round and the Developing Countries', *Journal of World Trade Law*, XIV (1980) pp. 243–85.

13. Balassa, 'Trade in Manufactured Goods: Patterns of Change'.

14. B. Balassa, 'The Problem of the Debt in Developing Countries', Essay 6 in this volume.

15. The calculations reflect the assumption that the same coefficients apply to the other industrial countries and that they are invariant within a particular category, irrespective of whether the products are exported or replace imports. Employment gains and losses have been calculated by adjusting the coefficients for changes in industrial prices.

16. The calculation assumes constant labor input coefficients and disregards the loss in employment associated with the outflow of capital.

17. Employment data pertain to 1980 and originate in OECD, *Labor Force*

Statistics, 1961–1980. While data on the employment effects of trade are not available for leather products this represents a relatively small fraction of the total.

18. B. Balassa, 'Industrial Prospects and Policies in Developed Countries', in F. Machlup, G. Fels, and H. Muller-Groeling (eds), *Reflections on a Troubled World Economy* (London: Trade Policy Research Center, 1983) pp. 257–78.

19. Balassa, 'The Changing International Division of Labor in Manufactured Goods'.

Essay 19 Industrial Protection in the Developed Countries

INTRODUCTION

Much has been said in recent years about growing industrial protectionism in the developed countries, but little effort has been made to assess quantitatively the increases in protection that have actually occurred. This essay will provide estimates for the major developed countries (the United States, the European Common Market, and Japan) on changes in their tariff and non-tariff barriers on manufactured imports in general and on imports from the developing countries in particular. The protection of agricultural products is, however, excluded from the preview of the essay.

Section I will examine tariff reductions undertaken in the framework of the Tokyo Round of negotiations, with attention paid to the implications of these reductions for the developing countries. In Section II, the imposition of non-tariff barriers to trade in the United States, the European Common Market, and Japan will be described and alternative indicators will be used to gauge the scope of these measures. Finally, in Section III, import penetration ratios and data on changes in import/GDP ratios will be utilized to indicate the restrictiveness of the measures applied, with separate consideration given to imports from the developing countries.

I TARIFF REDUCTIONS IN THE TOKYO ROUND

In the framework of the Kennedy Round of multilateral negotiations, tariff rates were lowered by 50 percent across-the-board, with exceptions made for so-called sensitive items, such as steel, textiles, clothing, and footwear. As a result of these changes, average tariffs on the total imports of manufactured products declined by 41 percent in the United States, 40 percent in the European Common Market (EC), and 42 percent in Japan. With reductions being smaller on several products of interest to the developing countries, the average tariff on manufactured products imported from these countries decreased to a lesser extent – by 31 percent in the United States, 36 percent in the EC, and 35 percent in Japan.[1]

Following these reductions, average tariffs on manufactured products, weighted by total imports, were 7.0 percent in the United States, 8.3 percent in the European Common Market, and 10.0 percent in Japan.[2] However, tariff averages were generally higher on industrial products imported from the developing countries, on which smaller reductions were undertaken in the Kennedy Round as well as in the course of the earlier tariff negotiations.

In the Tokyo Round of multilateral negotiations, the United States proposed an across-the-board tariff cut of 60 percent whereas the European Common Market put forward a harmonization formula aimed at reducing high tariffs to a greater extent than low tariffs. The position taken by the EC reflected the desire for an evening-out of the tariff structure in the United States that earlier occurred in the EC, where the common external tariff was set as the average of tariffs in the individual member countries.

In the event, a compromise Swiss formula was adopted, involving tariff reductions calculated as the ratio of the pre-Tokyo Round tariff to itself plus 14 percent. Under the formula, a 20 percent duty was to be reduced by 59 percent, a 10 percent duty by 42 percent, and a 5 percent duty by 26 percent. However, exceptions have again been made for sensitive items, such as textiles, clothing, and footwear.

Tariff reductions agreed-upon in the Tokyo Round of negotiations will be fully implemented in the second half of the eighties, although advance reductions have been made by the EC and Japan. Once the reductions are completed, tariff averages weighted by the total imports of manufactured products will decline by 30 percent in the United States, 28 percent in the European Common Market, and 46 percent in Japan (Table 19.1). In the case of Japan, additional tariff reductions on machinery and transport equipment will have contributed to the results, but the extent of the decrease in tariffs is considerably smaller if comparisons are made with the duties actually applied rather than with legal tariffs.[3]

TABLE 19.1 Pre- and post-Tokyo Round tariff averages and percentage changes in tariffs for major developed countries

| | Tariffs on Total Imports | | | | | | | | | | | | Tariffs on Imports from LDCs | | |
| | Raw Materials | | | Semi-Manufactures | | | Finished Manufactures | | | Semi- and Finished Manufactures | | | Semi- and Finished Manufactures | | |
	Pre	Post	Percent Change	Pre	Post	Percent Change	Pre	Post	Percent Change	Pre	Post	Percent Change	Pre	Post	Percent Change
United States															
Weighted	0.9	0.2	77	4.5	3.0	33	8.0	5.7	29	7.0	4.9	30	11.4	8.7	24
Simple	3.3	1.8	45	10.0	6.1	39	13.0	7.0	46	11.6	6.6	43	12.0	6.7	44
European Common Market															
Weighted	0.2	0.2	15	5.8	4.2	27	9.7	6.9	29	8.3	6.0	28	8.9	6.7	25
Simple	1.9	1.6	16	8.9	6.2	30	9.9	7.0	29	9.4	6.6	30	8.5	5.8	32
Japan															
Weighted	1.5	0.5	67	6.6	4.6	30	12.5	6.0	52	10.0	5.4	46	10.0	6.8	32
Simple	2.5	1.4	45	9.8	6.3	36	11.6	6.4	45	10.8	6.4	41	11.0	6.7	39

SOURCE: General Agreement on Tariffs and Trade, The Tokyo Round of Multilateral Trade Negotiations, II-Supplementary Report (Geneva) 1980, pp. 33–37.

As in the Kennedy Round, tariff reductions have been smaller than the average on imports from the developing countries, which supply a high proportion of the so-called sensitive items. Reductions in m.f.n. tariffs weighted by the imports of manufactured products from developing countries will be 24 percent in the case of the United States, 25 percent in the European Common Market, and 32 percent in Japan.[4]

Following these reductions, tariffs on manufactured products, weighted by total imports, will average 4.9 percent in the United States, 6.0 percent in the European Common Market, and 5.4 percent in Japan.[5] The corresponding averages, weighted by imports from the developing countries, will be higher – 8.7 percent in the US, 6.7 percent in the EC, and 6.8 percent in Japan.

Jeffrey Nugent has shown that, for a given tariff average, the protective effect of tariffs is the higher, the greater is their dispersion.[6] The dispersion of tariffs has been reduced to a considerable extent in the Tokyo Round, especially in Japan, although in the latter case the change is again much smaller if comparisons are made with the tariffs actually applied before the Tokyo Round. The dispersion of post-Tokyo Round tariffs remains the most pronounced in the United States, thereby increasing the protective effect of the US tariff compared to that of the other major developed countries.

As is well-known, averaging tariffs by import value introduces a downward bias in the calculations, because high tariffs are given small weight and low tariffs large weight. An alternative is to calculate a simple average of tariffs; these averages show larger tariff reductions for the US and the EC, and smaller reductions for Japan, than the weighted averages; at the same time, the simple (unweighted) averages are uniformly higher than the weighted averages (Table 19.1). While the unweighted averages do not involve a downward bias, they are subject to the shortcoming of giving equal weight to all tariff items, irrespective of their relative importance, when the number of items varies to a considerable extent among product categories, with textiles and clothing accounting for nearly one-third of the total. Also, comparisons of unweighted tariff averages for total imports and for imports from the developing countries, published by GATT, have little economic meaning.[7]

Irrespective of the averaging procedure employed, it is apparent that tariffs have a tendency to escalate from lower to higher degrees of fabrication, thereby raising the effective rate of protection (of value added). In the major developed countries, post-Tokyo Round weighted averages of tariff rates are 0.5 percent or less on raw materials, 3 to 5 percent for semi-manufactures, and 5 to 7 percent for finished manufactures (Table 19.1). Tariff escalation does not extend, however, to machinery and transport equipment. Tariffs on these products, exported chiefly by developed countries, are lower than tariff averages for all finished manufactures and, to an even greater extent, tariffs on products of interest to the developing countries, such as clothing, footwear, and travel goods.

Thus, as shown in Table 19.2, there is a considerable degree of tariff escalation for individual product categories. And while quantitative limitations in the framework of the Multifiber Arrangement represent the binding constraint in the case of textiles and clothing, tariff escalation tends to discriminate against finished goods within this category. More generally, the escalation of tariffs discriminates against the imports of processed goods from the developing countries.

At the same time, the finished manufactures of interest to the developing countries are subject to higher tariffs than other finished products. And although these countries receive preferential treatment under the General Scheme of Preferences,[8] the imports of textiles, clothing, and shoes are not covered by the scheme and products that came to be imported in larger quantities are also excluded. However, the developing countries have benefited from m.f.n. type tariff reductions that have been unilaterally extended to them.

All in all, in the Tokyo Round of negotiations, tariffs on manufactured goods have been lowered to a considerable extent, thereby extending the tariff reductions that had begun on an item-by-item basis in the period following the Second World War and continued with across-the-board reductions (with some exceptions) under the Dillon (1960–1) and the Kennedy (1963–7) Rounds. In fact, while tariff reductions in the postwar period were originally aimed at reversing increases in protection during the depression of the nineteen-thirties, tariffs fell below these levels at the end of the nineteen-fifties and declined to a considerable extent afterwards.[9]

But, from the mid-sixties, the United States and the European Economic Community imposed quantitative limitations on the imports of textiles and clothing, first from Japan and subsequently from the developing countries. Furthermore, non-tariff barriers were applied to the imports of certain manufactured goods from Japan in the second half of the sixties and such barriers came into greater use after 1973.

In Section II of the essay, non-tariff barriers on manufactured products in effect at the end of 1980 and the barriers imposed (or removed) in 1981, 1982, and 1983 will be briefly described. Also,

TABLE 19.2 *Pre- and post-Tokyo Round sectoral tariff averages for developed countries, combined*

Products	Import weighted averages			Simple averages		
	Pre-	Post-	Percent change	Pre-	Post-	Percent Change
Textiles and Clothing						
Raw materials	1.1	0.8	25	3.7	2.9	21
Semi-manufactures	14.7	11.5	22	13.7	9.6	30
Finished manufactures	20.6	16.7	19	17.6	11.8	33
Leather, footwear, rubber, travel goods						
Raw materials	0.2	0.0	80	2.0	1.0	50
Semi-manufactures	6.8	4.4	35	6.9	4.5	35
Finished manufactures	11.5	10.2	11	14.4	10.2	29
Wood, pulp, paper and furniture						
Raw materials	0.4	0.2	54	1.3	0.7	46

433

Semi-manufactures	3.1	1.9	38	6.3	3.7	41
Finished manufactures	7.1	4.2	41	8.6	5.1	41
Base metals						
Raw materials	0.3	0.0	82	0.5	0.2	61
Semi-manufactures	4.3	3.2	26	7.0	4.6	34
Finished manufactures	9.4	5.9	37	10.2	6.1	40
Chemicals						
Semi-manufactures	7.8	5.0	36	10.2	6.2	39
Finished manufactures	10.5	6.0	43	11.1	6.2	44
Non-electrical machinery						
Finished manufactures	7.7	4.1	47	8.1	4.4	46
Electrical machinery						
Finished manufactures	9.2	6.1	34	13.2	5.0	42
Transport equipment						
Finished manufactures	7.8	5.0	36	10.0	6.5	35

SOURCE: See Table 19.1.

alternative measures will be used to indicate the scope of these measures in the United States, the European Common Market, and Japan. Finally, in Section III, an attempt will be made to evaluate the restrictive effects of non-tariff barriers in these countries.

II NON-TARIFF BARRIERS TO TRADE

The non-tariff barriers considered in this essay include global and bilateral quotas, import licensing, orderly marketing arrangements, so-called voluntary export restraints, safeguard measures, and the restrictive application of standards. The discussion will not cover production and export subsidies or anti-dumping and countervailing measures. The trade implications of subsidies are difficult to gauge while anti-dumping and countervailing actions have been assumed to offset distortions introduced by exporters.

Non-tariff barriers may pertain to all imports or to imports from particular sources of supply. The United States and the European Common Market limit the imports of textiles and clothing originating in developing countries in the framework of the Multifiber Arrangement; in several other cases, restrictions are targeted against particular suppliers.

Apart from the MFA, non-tariff restrictions in effect at the end of 1980 in the United States included an orderly marketing agreement with Korea and Taiwan on the importation of non-rubber footwear, safeguard measures limiting the imports of color television sets from these two countries, and safeguard measures on CB radios, porcelain-on-steel cookware, high carbon ferro-chromium, industrial fasteners (nuts, bolts, and screws), and clothespins applying to all sources of supply.[10]

In the European Common Market, non-tariff barriers employed on the Community level in 1980 included the Multifiber Arrangement, as well as orderly marketing arrangements on jute products and iron and steel applying to major suppliers. There were also a number of non-tariff measures imposed by EC member countries, usually pertaining to suppliers that made inroads in the domestic markets of the individual countries. Restrictions were imposed by France, Italy, and the United Kingdom on the imports of passenger automobiles from Japan as well as on the imports of radios, TV sets, and communication equipment from Japan, Korea, and Taiwan; by Germany and the United Kingdom on the imports of flatware from Japan; and by France and Italy on the imports of various consumer goods, mainly from Korea and Taiwan.

In turn, Japan made use of discretionary licensing to limit the imports of leather footwear, telecommunications equipment, and pharmaceuticals and applied standards to protective effect on automobiles. But Japan also employs informal restrictions on imports that, for reasons noted below, are not considered in this essay.

In 1981, the United States negotiated voluntary export restraints on passenger automobiles imported from Japan. In the following year, voluntary export restraints were negotiated on carbon steel products with the European Common Market and, in 1983, the United States implemented safeguard measures in the form of tariff increases on motorcycles and tariff increases as well as a quota on speciality steels. However, restrictions on the importation of non-rubber footwear from Korea and Taiwan were eliminated in 1981, and restrictions on the importation of color television sets from the same countries were lifted in 1982.

In 1981, the European Common Market extended import restrictions on steel to Korea; Belgium and Germany introduced limitations on the imports of automobiles from Japan; and the United Kingdom imposed restrictions on the importation of video tape recorders from Japan. In the following year, France introduced restrictions on the importation of motorcycles and video tape recorders from Japan. Finally, in March 1983, the EC reached an agreement with Japan on export restraints for video recorders and large color television tubes as well as on the 'surveillance' of the imports of hi-fi equipment, quartz watches, forklift trucks, light vans, and motorcycles. In the same year, France and Britain imposed restrictions on the imports of tableware from Korea.

In re-negotiating the Multifiber Arrangement in 1981, the United States and the European Common Market limited the possibilities of quota transfer from one category to another as well as from one year to the next. Additional limitations were imposed on the growth of the imports of particular items in the United States in December 1983.

Japan did not introduce new restrictive measures between 1980 and 1983 and liberalized its administrative system on imports. At the same time, it is difficult to evaluate the informal barriers to imports that remain in effect in Japan.

In this connection, it should be emphasized that the non-tariff barriers considered in this paper are of the 'visible' kind; for lack of information, it has not been attempted to identify administrative measures that may impinge on imports. Such measures are of particular importance in Japan, followed by France, while the United States relies on visible procedures of import restraint. As the following calculations refer only to visible measures, a bias is introduced in the comparisons.

The GATT Secretariat has used the ratio of restricted imports to total imports (for short, the import ratio) to indicate the extent of the application of restrictive measures. The same ratio has been employed for this purpose by William Cline[11] and, in the framework of a programming model, by Deardorff and Stern.[12] In all these cases, the import ratio has been calculated as an *ex post* measure, that is, the import figures utilized in the calculations already reflect the restrictive effects of non-tariff barriers that have been introduced over the years.

At the same time, the extent to which imports are affected by non-tariff barriers varies from country to country. A country whose restrictive actions are more stringent will import less of the restricted commodities than a country whose actions are more liberal. Such is the situation, for instance, in regard to automobiles. France limits imports from Japan to 3 percent of domestic sales while Japanese exports of automobiles are limited to about 25 percent of sales in the US market. A more liberal policy towards automobile imports, then, involves a higher ratio of restricted imports to total imports in the United States than in France.

In this essay, the import ratio has been calculated for the non-tariff measures in effect at the end of 1980 as well as for the measures introduced in the years 1981, 1982, and 1983 (Table 19.3). In all cases, the estimates refer to the 1980 dollar values of imports, exclusive of trade among the member countries of the European Common Market. The above objections thus apply to the 1980 estimates but not to the estimates for subsequent years. The latter provide an *ex ante* measure of import restrictions, since the restrictions introduced subsequently could not have influenced trade flows in 1980.

But, both the *ex ante* and the *ex post* measures are affected by the availability of natural resources. Thus, in a country poor in natural resources, such as Japan, simple intermediate products (paper, chemicals, etc.) that are rarely subject to non-tariff barriers will account for a large share of imports, thereby reducing the share of restricted imports.

To escape this shortcoming, the ratio of the imports of restricted items to the total consumption of manufactured products (for short, the import/consumption ratio) has also been calculated. It should be

TABLE 19.3 *Measures of import restrictions for manufactured goods in developed countries*

		United States	European Common Market	Japan
I. Restricted imports as a share of total manufactured imports	1980	6.20	10.80	7.20
	1981	5.53	1.38	—
	1982	0.69	0.18	—
	1983	0.30	2.50	—
	1981–83	6.52	4.08	—
II. Restricted imports as a share of total consumption of manufactured goods	1980	0.56	1.30	0.33
	1981	0.49	0.16	—
	1982	0.06	0.02	—
	1983	0.03	0.25	—
	1981–83	0.58	0.43	—
III. Consumption of restricted manufactured goods as a share of total consumption of manufactured goods	1980	20.3	23.7	15.7
	1981	12.4	2.3	—
	1982	2.1	0.3	—
	1983	0.2	2.1	—
	1981–83	14.7	4.7	—

SOURCE: Data files of the Office of the United States Trade Representative Executive Office of the President, and of the World Bank.

recognized, however, that in its *ex post* form this ratio is subject to the same objections as the commonly used import ratio.

A third measure relates the consumption of restricted items to the total consumption of manufactured products (for short, the consumption ratio).[13] This measure is not subject to the bias introduced in the *ex post* case and it is not influenced by inter-country differences in the availability of natural resources. Nevertheless, consumption may have been affected by the imposition of import restrictions. Also, the use of the consumption ratio does not permit separating restricted from unrestricted imports within a particular commodity group. Thus, in making calculations, the entire group has been included in the restricted category whenever some of the products are subject to non-tariff barriers.

The latter considerations explain that, in 1980, the ratio of the consumption of restricted products to the total consumption of manufactured goods was relatively high, between 15 and 25 percent, in the major developed countries. The EC ratio was at the upper end of the scale, followed by the United States and by Japan. The United States improves its position if the other two ratios are considered; its import ratio was in fact lower than that of Japan in 1980. By comparison, Cline has found both of the ratios he calculated to be higher in the United States than in the Common Market countries, with Japan at the end of the line. There are several major differences in the procedures applied, which appear to account for the differences in the results.

First, Cline includes processed food in his calculations without, however, allowing for the effects of the Common Agricultural Policy in the EC. This has led to the overestimation of the share of restricted imports in the United States, where Cline lists meat, dairy products, sugar and confectionary among restricted items, while in the EC he includes only meat and canned fish in France and canned fish in Italy.

The inclusion of processed food also raises the share of restricted imports in Japan, where the items in question comprise meat, dairy products, canned fruits and vegetables, canned fish, and cereals. However, Cline does not include in his calculations Japanese restrictions on automobiles, telecommunications equipment, and pharmaceuticals, thereby lowering the reported Japanese share.

A further difference in the estimates pertains to the treatment of restricted imports. While in the present study only imports from countries subject to restrictions have been included in calculating the import ratio, Cline's figures comprise imports from all sources even if only some of the suppliers are subject to restrictions.

Finally, Cline's calculations include restrictions on US imports of color TV sets from Japan and footwear from Korea and Taiwan that were abolished in 1980 and 1981, respectively, as well as US restrictions on automobile imports from Japan that were introduced in 1981. At the same time, Cline has considered the trigger price mechanism on steel used in lieu of anti-dumping action as a restriction while in the present essay steel is included for 1982 when the Voluntary Export Restraint agreement with the EC came into effect.

As shown in Table 19.3, restrictions on automobiles imported from Japan entailed substantial increases in all three ratios in the United States between 1980 and 1983. Increases were smaller in European Common Market, although a number of restrictions were introduced on imports from Japan in 1983. Finally, Japan did not add new restrictions in the 1981–3 period.

A different picture emerges if restrictions applied to imports from developing countries are considered. Putting aside the stricter implementation of the MFA, the United States actually liberalized imports from these countries between 1980 and 1983 by lifting restrictions on footwear and on color TV sets imported from Korea and Taiwan; there were few instances where EC countries introduced import restrictions on products originating in developing countries; and no such case has been reported in Japan. It appears, then, that the protectionist measures applied by the major developed countries after 1980 have been chiefly oriented against each other's exports, with imports from developing countries largely escaping the effects of the new measures.

III THE RESTRICTIVE EFFECTS OF TRADE BARRIERS

In the previous section, alternative measures have been employed to gauge the scope of non-tariff barriers in the major developed countries. It should be emphasized that none of the three measures can be used to assess the restrictive effects of these barriers. While they show the proportion of imports or consumption subject to non-tariff barriers, they do not provide an indication of the extent to which imports have been reduced as a result of their imposition. Nor does any of the three measures provide an indication of changes in the restrictiveness of import barriers over time that has occurred, for example, in the application of the Multifiber Arrangement.

Two attempts have been made recently to measure the effects of quantitative restrictions in the United States, leading to very different conclusions. According to Morici and Megna, these restrictions provided average protection to US manufacturing industries equivalent to a 0.57 percent tariff in 1982.[14] Under the assumptions made by these authors regarding import demand elasticities, the cost of protection was estimated at $5 million.[15] In turn, according to Munger, the cost of quantitative import restrictions to US consumers was $11.5 billion in 1980.[16] The reasons for these differences can be found in the methodologies of the two studies, which are open to criticism in both cases.

Morici and Megna underestimate the effects of the two most important restrictions imposed on manufactured goods in the United States: the Multifiber Arrangement and the limitations on Japanese exports of automobiles. As to the first, 'it is assumed that if the MFA were removed, foreign suppliers would only be able to recapture three years of lost import growth in any single typical year'.[17] But, the losses have been estimated by taking 1973 as the base year, disregarding the fact that the imports of cotton textiles had been restricted for some years beforehand. Furthermore, the protective effects of quantitative restrictions should be calculated by relating actual imports to imports without restrictions in long-term equilibrium rather than to imports that may be attained one year after the removal of the restrictions. Nor can the protective effects of limitations on automobile imports from Japan be estimated by reference to 'the depressed state of the automobile market during the first year of the agreement'.[18]

The estimates reported by Munger include coffee, meat, and sugar, accounting for one-third of[19] the total, while excluding automobiles that become subject to restrictions in 1981. At the same time, Munger equates the cost to consumers to the cost of protectionism, although one has to deduct increases in producer surplus and in government revenues in estimating the latter.[20] In fact, considering that imports accounted for only about one-tenth the consumption of manufactured goods estimated at $1.4 trillion in 1980, the cost of protection will be but a small fraction of the cost to consumers estimated by Munger.

To improve on these estimates, information would be needed on the tariff equivalents of quantitative restrictions and on the underlying domestic demand and supply elasticities. Reliable data are not available for the United States and even less for the European Common Market and Japan. Correspondingly, in the present essay, the restrictive effects of imports have been indicated in an indirect way.[21]

Two measures have been used to gauge the impact of non-tariff barriers on imports. The import penetration ratio, defined as the percentage share of imports in domestic consumption, will be employed to indicate the restrictive effects of non-tariff barriers at a particular point of time. In turn, for lack of production figures on a disaggregated basis, changes in the ratio of imports to the gross domestic product will be used to show changes in the restrictiveness of these barriers over time.

The two sets of ratios have been calculated for the total imports of (a) iron and steel, (b) passenger automobiles, and (c) telecommunications equipment, as well as for the imports of (d) textiles, (e) clothing and (f) other consumer goods, including footwear, travel goods, sports goods, and toys, from the developing countries. The results are shown in Table 19.4; in the case of the EC, the data refer to the four largest countries, France, Germany, Italy, and the United Kingdom, that account for 85 percent of the gross domestic product of the Common Market countries.

A high (low) import penetration ratio has been interpreted to reflect the ease (restrictiveness) of non-tariff barriers. It has further been

TABLE 19.4 *1978 Import penetration ratios and changes in the ratio of imports and GDP, 1978–91*

	United States		European Common Market		Japan	
	Import penetration ratio, 1978	*Percent change in import/ GDP ratio*	*Import penetration ratio, 1978*	*Percent change in import/ GDP ratio*	*Import penetration ratio, 1978*	*Percent change in import/ GDP ratio*
Total imports						
Iron and steel	8.7	25	6.0	−16	0.9	94
Passenger vehicles	8.8	19	7.4	23	1.1	−33
Telecommunications equipment	14.7	31	13.6	32	3.5	23
Imports from developing countries						
Textiles	1.6	13	3.7	−10	2.3	−32
Clothing	11.3	17	11.4	23	7.4	−4
Other consumer products	3.7	40	1.6	36	1.1	3

SOURCE: GATT, *International Trade, 1981–82.* United Nations, *Industrial Statistics* and *Monthly Bulletin of Statistics*, various issues.

assumed that changes in the import/GDP ratio for products subject to nontariff barriers will provide an indication of changes in the restrictiveness of the measures applied over time.

The obvious drawback of these measures is that they cannot distinguish between the impact of restrictive measures and the effects of other factors that may bear on the importation of a particular product or product group. Thus, the import penetration ratio for a particular commodity group will also reflect the country's comparative advantage and the extent of over- or under-valuation of its currency in a particular year while changes in the real exchange rate (the nominal exchange, adjusted for changes in relative prices) will affect changes in the ratio of imports to GDP over time.

The first-mentioned factor is of relevance for Japanese imports of passenger automobiles from the other developed countries, as Japan appears to possess a comparative advantage in regard to automobiles that will reduce the amount imported, even though imports would be higher in the absence of the discriminatory application of standards. (Note further that Japan does not restrict the importation of steel which is included for completeness in Table 19.4.)

Such considerations will not, however, affect US and EC imports of the commodities in question. Also, all developed countries are at a comparative disadvantage vis-à-vis developing countries as far as textiles, clothing, and other consumer goods are concerned, so that import penetration ratios for these product groups will appropriately indicate the restrictiveness of the measures applied against imports from the developing countries.[22]

The US dollar appreciated in real terms vis-à-vis other major currencies between 1978 and 1981. However, the extent of appreciation was small and the changes took place towards the end of the period, so that trade flows might not have been much affected until 1982. A much larger appreciation occurred in the years 1982 and 1983, which have been excluded from the analysis.

At the same time, it should be emphasized that considerations of comparative advantage and currency over-(under-) valuation will not be relevant in cases when import restraints are binding. This is because the binding restrictions limit the amount imported in absolute terms and thus determine the import penetration ratio. Such will generally be the case whenever quotas, orderly marketing agreements, or voluntary export restraints are utilized. In turn, import licensing may or may not be binding depending on the circumstances of the case.[23]

These considerations indicate the usefulness of the import penetration measure for indicating the restrictiveness of nontariff barriers, the exception being Japanese imports of automobiles. It should be added that this measure has the advantage of capturing not only the effects of visible but also of invisible barriers to imports. At the same time, import penetration ratios are usefully complemented by data on increases in the import/GDP ratio.

The data reported in Table 19.4 exclude trade among the EC countries and trade between the United States and Canada that are regarded as internal trade. This adjustment gives rise to a downward bias in the US results since only about one-third of United States trade in manufactured goods with Canada is exempted from tariffs in the framework of the US-Canadian automotive agreement.

Nevertheless, in all three industries for which import penetration ratios for total imports have been calculated, these ratios were higher in 1978 in the United States than in the European Common Market. The differences increased further between 1978 and 1981 as far as iron and steel are concerned while the import/GDP ratio increased slightly more in the Common Market than in the United States in automobiles and equiproportionate changes occurred in telecommunications equipment.

The import penetration ratio on telecommunications equipment was much lower in Japan than in the other major developed countries in 1978. Restrictions on imports, in particular of telephone equipment, appear to have kept this ratio low, and subsequent increases fell short of those in the other major developed countries. And while Japan's comparative advantage in automobiles contributed to the low import penetration ratio in 1978, the subsequent decline may be interpreted to reflect the continuation of regulations that have a protective effect.

As far as imports from the developing countries are concerned, the United States had a relatively low import penetration ratio for textiles in 1978, followed by Japan and the European Common Market. However, US imports of textiles from the developing countries rose to a considerable extent after 1978 while imports declined in absolute terms in the EC and, in particular, in Japan. As a result, by 1981, the United States reached the Japanese import penetration ratio while differences remained vis-à-vis the European Common Market.

Import penetration ratios for clothing were approximately equal in the United States and the European Common Market in 1978, with a slightly smaller increase occurring in the latter than in the former between 1978 and 1981. In turn, Japan had much lower import penetration ratios in 1978 and a decline took place over the next three years.

Import penetration ratios for other consumer goods, too, were the lowest in Japan in 1978 that also occupies last place as far as increases in these imports are concerned. At the same time, the import penetration ratio for these products was much higher in the United States than in the European Common Market in 1978 and the changes that occurred between 1978 and 1981 did not modify this relationship.

With other consumer goods being the mirror image of textiles as far as import penetration ratios in the United States and the European Common Market are concerned, and the two economies having similar import penetration ratios in clothing, the restrictiveness of their barriers to imports from developing countries appear to have been similar in 1978. However, between 1978 and 1981, textile imports increased rapidly in the United States while declining in the European Common Market and differences in other product groups were small.

Finally, 1978 import penetration ratios were generally the lowest, and increases in imports from developing countries between 1978 and 1981 the smallest, in Japan. Yet, with Japan moving up on the scale among developed countries, one would have expected its imports from the developing countries to increase rapidly over time.

CONCLUSIONS

This essay has reviewed recent changes in trade barriers in the major developed countries: the United States, the European Common Market, and Japan. The investigation has covered tariff and non-tariff barriers affecting the imports of manufactured products from all sources of supply and from the developing countries.

Tariff reductions undertaken during the postwar period have been continued in the framework of the Tokyo Round of multilateral negotiations, lowering tariffs to levels not seen during this century. While the reductions have been extended to the developing countries under the most-favored-nation clause, tariffs have been lowered less than the average on products of interest to these countries. Also, notwithstanding the changes that have occurred, the escalation of tariffs continues to discriminate against the imports of processed goods from the developing countries.

Tariff reductions under the Tokyo Round, to be completed in the second half of the eighties, contrast with the increased use made of non-tariff barriers. At the same time, in recent years, the imposition of new barriers has been directed largely against imports from other developed countries rather than against the products of the developing countries.

The ratio of restricted imports to total imports and to total consumption and the ratio of the consumption of restricted items to total consumption have been used to gauge the scope of import restrictions. But these measures cannot provide an indication of the extent to which imports have been reduced as a result of the imposition of non-tariff barriers, or of changes in the restrictiveness of such barriers over time.

For these purposes, use has been made of import penetration ratios and changes in import/GDP ratios. While, in the absence of binding restrictions, these ratios are affected by the structure of comparative advantage, the over- or under-valuation of national currencies, and changes thereof, they will appropriately indicate the impact of restrictions that effectively limit imports.

The measures applied show the United States to be somewhat less restrictive than the European Common Market, with Japan being the most restrictive. Yet, given its smaller domestic market, one would have expected import penetration ratios to be higher in Japan than in the US or the EC. At the same time, the results point to the effects of informal barriers that are of especial importance for Japan but could not be included in the survey of restrictive measures for lack of information.

The restrictive effects of the measures taken is even more pronounced as far as Japan's imports from the developing countries are concerned. And while, with Japan moving up on the scale among developed countries, one would have expected its manufactured imports from the developing countries to have increased rapidly, such has not been the case.

At the same time, the United States and the European Common Market share the responsibility for having rendered the Multifiber Arrangement more stringent and having created new barriers against the imports of several commodities from Japan. It is in the self-interest of the developed countries to eliminate these barriers, so as to benefit from the reallocation of resources in accordance with their comparative advantage. More generally, it would be desirable to limit reliance on quantitative import restrictions through the adoption of a safeguard code while ensuring multilateral surveillance in the application of this code. Finally, there would be need to reduce tariffs on products of interest to the developing countries that are subject to tariff escalation and above-average tariffs.

The proposed liberalization of trade could not be accomplished without a new round of multilateral trade negotiations. In fact, in the absence of such negotiations, there is danger of backsliding. At the same time, involving the developing countries in the negotiations would not only allow the more industrialized of these countries to adopt more rational trade policies but would strengthen the argument for trade liberalization in the developed countries and permit giving attention to products of interest to developing countries in the course of the negotiations.

NOTES

1. B. Balassa, 'The Structure of Protection in Industrial Countries and Its Effects on the Exports of Processed Goods from Developing Countries', *The Kennedy Round: Estimated Effects on Tariff Barriers* (New York, United Nations, 1968).
2. The data refer to m.f.n. tariffs and do not take account of tariff preferences under the General System of Preferences. They differ somewhat from the results reported in the study cited in note 1, because of differences in coverage. While the earlier study defined manufactured products as SITC classes 5 to 8 less 68 (nonferrous metals), the cited figures pertain to semi-manufactures and finished manufactures as defined by GATT.
3. For raw materials, semi-manufactures, and finished manufactures, taken together, actual tariff reductions were estimated to have been only slightly more than one-half, on the average, than reductions in legal tariffs in Japan. Cf. *Twenty-Fourth Annual Report of the President of the United States in the Trade Agreement Program* (Washington, DC: Superintendent of Documents, 1979) p. 59.
4. Estimates of the effects of Tokyo Round tariff reductions on trade and employment are provided in A. V. Deardorff and R. M. Stern, 'A Disaggregated Model of World Production and Trade: An Estimate of the Impact of the Tokyo Round', *Journal of Policy Modeling*, III (1981), pp. 127–53. For a critique of the methodology utilized, see B. Balassa, 'Comment' on A. V. Deardorff and R. M. Stern, 'The Economic Effects of Complete Elimination of Post-Tokyo Round Tariffs', in W. R. Cline (ed.), *Trade Policy in the 1980s* (Washington, DC: Institute for International Economics, 1983) pp. 711–22.
5. Alternative estimates for industrial products, inclusive of raw materials, are reported in the *Twenty-Fourth Annual Report of the President of the United States on the Trade Agreements Program*, pp. 53–62 and, inclusive of process food, in W. R. Cline, *Exports of Manufactures from Developing*

Countries: Performance and Market Access (Washington, DC: Brookings Institution, 1984).

6. J. Nugent, *Economic Integration in Central America: Empirical Investigations* (Baltimore, MD: Johns Hopkins University Press, 1974) Ch. 2.

7. A more appropriate weighting scheme involving the use of production values for this purpose, and has not been utilized here because of the lack of comparable data.

8. Excluding duty-free items, two-thirds of industrial imports from the developing countries, inclusive of raw materials, were classified as GSP items, and one-third of the total was not subject to ceilings or other limitations, although ceilings will be imposed if certain limits are exceeded. Cf. General Agreement on Tariffs and Trade, *The Tokyo Round of Multilateral Trade Negotiations*, II Supplementary Report (Geneva: 1980) p. 40.

9. Cf. B. Balassa, 'The "New Protectionism" and the International Economy', *Journal of World Trade Law*, XII (1978) pp. 409–36. Reprinted as Essay 4 in B. Balassa, *The Newly Industrializing Countries in the World Economy* (New York: Pergamon Press, 1981) pp. 109–26.

10. Restrictions applied earlier to speciality steels and to color television sets imported from Japan were lifted in the course of 1980.

11. Cline.

12. Deardorff and Stern.

13. This measure has also been used by Cline.

14. P. Morici and L. L. Megna, *US Economic Policies Affecting Industrial Trade: A Quantitative Assessment* (Washington, DC: National Planning Association, 1983) p. 47.

15. US manufactured imports in 1982 were $146 billion. Under the assumption of an average import demand elasticity of 2.14 made by the authors (p. 106), quantitative import restrictions with a tariff equivalent of 0.57 percent would have reduced imports by 1.8 billion. Assuming linear demand and supply curves, the cost of protection approximately equals one-half of the tariff equivalent of quantitative restrictions (0.29 percent) times the change in imports resulting from the imposition of these restrictions ($1.8 billion), or $5 million.

16. M. C. Munger, 'The Costs of Protectionism', *Challenge* (1984) p. 56.

17. Morici and Megna, p. 23.

18. Morici and Megna, p. 27.

19. Munger, p. 56.

20. H. G. Johnson, 'The Cost of Protection and the Scientific Tariff', *Journal of Political Economy*, LXVIII (1960) pp. 327–45.

21. The procedures applied do not however permit estimating the welfare costs of the restrictions applied.

22. It should be added, however, that technological changes have improved the competitive position, in particular in the United States, in recent years.

23. If non-tariff barriers are not binding, imports will also be affected by tariffs.

Essay 20   Trade and Trade Relations between Developed and Developing Countries in the Decade Ahead

INTRODUCTION

Trade between developed and developing countries, and the trade policies of the two groups of countries, are matters of considerable interest. It has been suggested, for example, that this trade should have a central role in any 'new round' of GATT negotiations. Yet, it is difficult to find a comprehensive statement of what the interests of developed and developing countries in trade liberalization actually are.

This essay aims to define the interests of the developed and developing countries in the liberalization of their mutual trade. Possible approaches to harnessing these interests for promoting North-South trade in the decade ahead will also be analyzed. The context for the discussion is the trade policies of developed and developing countries in the postwar period.

Section I of the essay will describe the policies applied by the two groups of countries in the postwar period and analyze their increasing interdependence through trade in manufactured goods. Section II will evaluate trade liberalization by *developing* countries from the perspective of the *developed* countries, and trade liberalization by *developed* countries from the perspective of the *developing* countries. Finally, Section III will examine the possible ways and means of a North-South round of trade negotiations, with consideration given to the problem of adjustment to increased imports in developed and in developing countries.

I TRADE POLICIES AND INTERDEPENDENCE THROUGH TRADE IN MANUFACTURED GOODS

Trade policies by developed countries

In the years following the Second World War, the developed countries reduced their tariffs in the framework of successive rounds of trade negotiations on an item-by-item basis. The negotiations involved a compromise between the principles of reciprocity and of non-discrimination. With the developing countries offering few tariff concessions, the developed countries exchanged such concessions on products of interest to them.

The developing countries nevertheless benefited from the tariff reductions that were made under the most-favored-nation clause. By the early sixties, tariffs on manufactured goods imported from the developing countries had declined to a considerable extent, although remaining higher than the developed countries' overall tariff average on manufactured goods. At the same time, these tariffs showed a tendency towards escalation from lower to higher levels of fabrication, thereby discriminating against processing activities in the developing countries.[1]

In the framework of the Kennedy and the Tokyo Rounds of negotiations, tariffs have been reduced substantially across the board, with exceptions made for sensitive items that have included products of interest to developed (steel) as well as to developing countries (textiles). As tariff reductions have again been smaller on manufactured goods imported from the developing countries, post-Tokyo Round tariffs on such goods remain somewhat higher than the overall average. The relevant figures are 9 and 7 percent in the United States, 7 and 6 percent in the European Common Market, and 7 and 5 percent in Japan.[2]

There is also a greater frequency of relatively high tariffs on the developed countries' imports from the developing countries than on their overall manufactured imports. Thus, in the United States, the share of imports subject to tariffs of 10 percent or higher is 20 percent in the first case and 9 percent in the second while comparable figures are 12 and 6 percent for the EC and 18 and 13 percent for Japan.[3]

Furthermore, although the extent of tariff escalation has been reduced, processing activities in the developing countries continue to suffer discrimination, as tariffs are generally nil on unprocessed goods but rise with the degree of fabrication on processed goods. Since the effective rate of tariff on the output whenever the latter is higher than the tariff on the inputs, relatively low output tariffs may give rise to high effective rates of protection on the processing activity.

Much has been said in recent years about the proliferation of import restrictions that represent non-tariff barriers to trade in the developed countries. The long recession of the years 1980–2 has in fact led to the imposition of some protectionist measures in the United States and in the European Common Market. However, the pervasive restrictions and the international cartels of the nineteen-thirties have not been repeated.

Also, the ire of protectionists has been largely directed against other developed countries and, apart from some tightening of the Multifiber Arrangement, few measures have been taken against developing countries during the recession. At the same time, in the United States, quantitative restrictions on footwear originating in developing countries have been abolished.[4]

Thus, the deceleration of the growth of manufactured imports from the developing countries can be attributed to the decline in GDP growth rates in the developed countries rather than to increased protection. In fact, the apparent income elasticity of demand for manufactured goods imported from the developing countries (the ratio of the rate of growth of these imports to that of GDP) continued to increase (Table 20.1).[5] Similar conclusions are reached if one considers the share of imports from the developing countries in the apparent consumption of manufactured goods (production plus imports minus exports) in the developed countries. This ratio increased from 0.9 percent in 1973 to 1.5 percent in 1978, and again to 2.0 percent in 1981, with incremental shares (the ratio of increases in imports to increases in apparent consumption) rising from 2.4 percent in 1973–8 to 3.8 percent in 1978–81. (Table 18.3.)

Notwithstanding some tightening of the Multifiber Arrangement, the developing countries also succeeded in raising their share in the markets for textiles and clothing in the developed countries. This result indicates the success of the developing countries in circumventing the restrictions imposed by the developed countries on textiles and clothing. This has occurred through upgrading as well as through the shift of exports to products, and the shift of the place of production to countries, which are not subject to restrictions.

More generally, while the expansion of exports has been constrained

TABLE 20.1 *Changes in the volume of trade in manufactured goods between developed and developing countries, related to changes in GDP*

	Imports	GDP	Apparent income elasticity[a]
	(average annual rate of growth)		
Industrial countries			
1963–73	16.5	4.6	3.6
1973–78	10.2	2.5	4.1
1978–81	8.4	2.0	4.2
1973–81	9.5	2.3	4.1
Developing countries			
1963–73	8.2	6.2	1.3
1973–78	12.5	5.3	2.4
1978–81	8.3	2.4	3.5
1973–81	11.7	4.2	2.8
Oil-importing developing countries			
1973–78	7.2	4.1	1.8
1978–81	9.5	4.3	2.2
1973–81	8.1	4.2	1.9
Oil-exporting developing countries			
1973–78	24.2	8.2	3.0
1978–81	6.9	−1.6	−4.3
1973–81	17.4	4.4	4.0

NOTE: [a] The ratio of the average annual rate of growth of imports to that of the gross domestic product.

SOURCE: Balassa, 'Trends in International Trade in Manufactured Goods and Structural Change in the Industrial Countries', Essay 18 and sources cited therein.

by existing import restrictions as well as by the threat of the imposition of restrictions, the process of diversification in the developing countries has permitted them to increase their shares in developed country markets for manufactured goods in an unfavorable world environment. At the same time, the success of the developing countries in exploiting the possibilities available in developed country markets has been determined to a great extent by the policies applied by the developing countries themselves.

The policies followed by the developing countries have also affected their ability to export primary commodities. But developed country policies have also had important effects. Foods produced in developing countries and competing with domestic production in the developed countries encounter barriers in these countries and often have to compete with their subsidized exports. The Common Agricultural Policy of the EC as well as Japanese restrictions affect, in particular, sugar, cereals, vegetable oils and oilseed, beef and veal, wine, and tobacco while the United States limit the importation of sugar and, to a lesser extent, oilseeds.

It has been estimated that a 50 percent reduction in the trade barriers of the developed countries on food would lead to a 11 percent increase in the exports of these commodities from the developing countries.[6] This figure understates, however, the impact of the developed countries' agricultural policies on developing countries' food exports by excluding the effects of export subsidies. Yet, subsidies to food exports have increased over time, in particular in the European Common Market, contributing to a decline in the world market shares of the developing countries.

Thus, the policies applied by the developed countries have retarded the growth of food exports from the developing countries, which did not surpass the 1973 level in 1981. In the same period a slight decline is shown in the exports of raw materials as the recession in the developed countries affected developing country exporters of these products more than proportionately.[7]

But, the policies applied in many developing countries have also discriminated against their exports of primary products. While an increasing number of developing countries have come to provide incentives to manufactured exports, such measures have rarely been used in favor of primary commodities.

Trade policies by developing countries

In the early postwar period, the dominant development strategy pursued by the developing countries involved import substitution in the manufacturing sector behind high protective barriers. This strategy favored manufacturing activities producing for domestic markets and discriminated against manufactured as well as primary exports and against primary production in general.

In the first half of the sixties, Korea, Singapore, and Taiwan joined Hong Kong in pursuing an outward-oriented development strategy. Under this strategy, similar incentives are provided to exports and to import substitution as well as to primary and to manufacturing activities.

As the possibilities for import replacement in the narrow markets of developing countries were increasingly exhausted, and the high economic cost of continued import substitution came to be recognized, several large Latin American countries, including Argentina, Brazil, and Mexico, began to promote manufactured exports. Nevertheless, discrimination against primary activities was generally maintained and import substitution continued to be favored, albeit to a lesser extent than beforehand, in the countries in question. Furthermore, several other countries, such as India, Chile, and Uruguay, continued to pursue an inward-oriented development strategy.

Available information for the decade prior to the quadrupling of oil prices in 1973–4 indicates the effects of alternative development strategies on exports and on economic performance in the countries under consideration. The first group of Far Eastern countries exhibited rapid growth in the exports of both primary and manufactured goods. Export expansion, together with low incremental capital-output ratios (ICORs) associated with efficient resource allocation, further led to rapid economic growth in these countries.

The second group of Latin American countries improved their export performance in manufactured, but generally not in primary, products; they were successful in reducing their ICORs, although these ratios remained above the levels observed in Far Eastern countries; and they accelerated their economic growth without, however, attaining the growth rates observed in the Far East. Finally, countries which continued to pursue import substitution oriented policies exhibited low export growth rates, low investment efficiency, and poor economic performance in general.[8]

The adverse effects of external shocks, in the form of the quadrupling of oil prices of 1973–4 and the world recession of 1974–5, were especially pronounced in the Far Eastern newly-industrializing countries that had higher than average export and import shares in national income. These countries nevertheless continued with the application of outward-oriented policies and were able to surmount the effects of external shocks within a relatively short time. Thus, they increased their export market shares and reached economic growth rates even higher than in the period prior to 1973. The outward-oriented NICs also limited reliance on external borrowing, thereby avoiding excessive foreign indebtedness.

In an effort to maintain past economic growth rates, most other newly-industrializing countries relied greatly on external borrowing after 1973 while increasing the protection of their domestic industries. With higher protection leading to losses in export market shares and to a deterioration in the efficiency of investment, the borrowed funds were generally not used productively. Correspondingly, these inward-oriented NICs experienced a decline in GNP growth rates while their debt burden increased to a considerable extent.

Similar conclusions apply to the oil-importing less developed countries. On the whole, countries following relatively outward-oriented development strategies relied to a lesser extent on foreign borrowing; put the borrowed funds to better use, and reached higher rates of export and GNP growth than did countries pursuing an inward-oriented development strategy.[9]

Preliminary results indicate that outward-oriented economies have also been better able to surmount the second oil shock of 1979-80 and the ensuing world recession than inward-oriented economies. The former group of countries has again gained export market shares and has succeeded in limiting the decline in rates of economic growth. The latter group has however further lost market shares, experienced low economic growth rates, and suffered the effects of higher interest rates on their large external indebtedness.[10]

Trade in manufactured goods between developed and developing countries

Data on trade in manufactured goods between developed and developing countries provide an indication of growing interdependence between these groups of countries over the past two decades. Parallel with the increases in the imports of manufactured goods by developed countries from the developing countries, the developing countries expanded their imports of these products from the developed countries (Table 20.1). Increases in developing country imports were financed through higher export earnings, in particular through the growth of manufactured exports to the developed countries, as well as through foreign borrowing. In 1981, however, a slowdown occurred as several large oil-importing developing countries experienced growing difficulties in obtaining foreign loans. Following rapid increases in earlier years the rate of growth of manufactured imports by the oil-exporting developing countries also declined, reflecting a slowdown in the growth of their export earnings.

Nevertheless, the share of the developed countries in the apparent consumption of manufactured goods in the developing countries, taken together, continued to increase throughout the period under consideration. According to rough estimates made by the author that represent only general orders of magnitude, this ratio rose from 21.3 percent in

1973 to 29.6 percent in 1978 and to 33.3 percent in 1981, with incremental shares increasing from 36.5 percent in 1973–8 to 44.0 percent in 1978–81 (Table 20.2). Not surprisingly, import shares are the highest for engineering products; in 1981, the developed countries provided slightly over one-half of the apparent consumption of the developing countries in these products.

With rapid increases in their imports, the developing countries assumed growing importance as markets for the manufacturing industries of the developed countries. Thus, the share of exports to the developing countries in the developed countries' production of manufactured goods increased from 2.9 percent in 1973 to 5.2 percent in 1978 and, again, to 6.4 percent in 1981. Incremental shares were even higher, 8.5 percent in 1973–8 and 11.3 percent in 1978–81 (Table 18.3).

Despite the increases that occurred, the ratio of manufacturing production in the developing countries to that in the developed countries remained relatively low: 13.9 percent in 1973, 15.0 percent in 1978, and 15.6 percent in 1981.[11] Correspondingly, notwithstanding the continued imbalance of trade in manufactured goods between the two groups of countries, export-production ratios continued to be substantially higher in the developing than in the developed countries.

According to the author's rough estimates, the share of exports to developed countries in the production of manufactured goods in the developing countries increased from 7.3 percent in 1973 to 10.4 percent in 1978 and to 12.5 percent in 1981, with incremental shares of 13.3 percent in 1973–8 and 19.5 percent in 1978–81 (Table 20.2). In 1981, export shares were the highest in clothing, followed by the group of other consumer goods. Export shares were higher than the average also for engineering products, reflecting in part the success of the developing countries in exporting labor-intensive engineering products, such as radios and television sets, and in part increased intra-industry specialization, with the developing countries exporting labor-intensive, and importing capital-intensive, parts, components, and accessories.

II MULTILATERAL TRADE LIBERALIZATION AND THE INTERESTS OF DEVELOPED AND DEVELOPING COUNTRIES

Trade liberalization in developing countries and developed country interests

In gauging the interests of the developed countries in trade liberaliza-

TABLE 20.2 The relative importance for the developing countries of trade in individual commodity groups with the industrial nations

	X_{DC}/P	M_{DC}/C	X_{DC}/P	M_{DC}/C	X_{DC}/P	M_{DC}/C	$\Delta X_{DC}/\Delta C$	$\Delta M_{DC}/\Delta C$	$\Delta X_{DC}/\Delta P$	$\Delta M_{DC}/\Delta C$
Developing countries										
Iron and steel	3.6	24.6	3.3	25.2	5.1	27.0	3.1	25.7	10.0	31.8
Chemicals	3.3	21.5	4.0	25.8	4.9	27.1	4.7	29.5	6.9	29.9
Other semi-manufactures	7.4	8.0	10.3	15.1	8.0	14.9	15.5	26.4	3.1	14.6
Engineering products	6.1	34.7	8.6	43.0	13.7	51.1	10.4	47.9	46.1	80.9
Textiles	4.0	8.7	7.1	9.6	7.3	11.9	11.7	11.0	8.1	22.2
Clothing	36.8	7.4	55.9	14.6	58.3	17.6	78.0	32.2	63.5	24.6
Other consumer goods	12.1	10.1	17.9	16.9	20.1	19.7	22.8	22.6	24.6	25.4
Total manufacturing	7.3	21.3	10.4	29.6	12.5	33.3	13.3	36.5	19.5	44.0

Explanation of Symbols: X = exports, M = imports, P = production, C = consumption, DC = developed countries, LDC = developing countries.

NOTE: The production estimates for the developing countries are subject to considerable error possibilities. Also, the estimates for 1973 have been obtained through interpolation of the reported figures for 1970 and 1978 while the 1981 estimates have been derived through extrapolation by the use of production indices.

SOURCE: UNIDO, *Handbook of Industrial Statistics* (New York: United Nations, 1982).

tion by the developing countries, the question needs to be answered as to how the volume and the pattern of developed country exports would be affected thereby. This question will be considered in regard to trade with the newly-industralizing countries (NICs) that account for the overwhelming share of the developed countries' manufactured imports from the developing countries, provide the largest markets for their manufacturing industries, and have been exhorted by the developed countries to liberalize their trade.

The NICs protect their manufacturing industries by the use of tariffs and quantitative import restrictions. Quantitative restrictions came into greater use after 1973 in conjunction with the increased inward orientation of a number of the NICs and, again, after 1979 in attempting to cope with their increased debt burden. Import restrictions are applied even in outward-oriented NICs, with the exception of Hong Kong and Singapore, although these have much more limited scope and are administered in a more liberal fashion than in inward-oriented NICs.

Several years ago, an OECD report expressed the fear that a newly-industrializing country 'may find itself moving into surplus on current account when in fact the availability of external capital and the possibilities for its profitable use would have permitted higher levels of domestic activity and consumption'.[12] This fear has not been realized and so a newly-industrializing country has accumulated excessive foreign exchange reserves. These countries have few opportunities, therefore, to draw on their foreign exchange reserves while, under present conditions, most NICs may not increase their foreign debt.

It follows that reductions in trade barriers by the NICs could not give rise to higher imports unless their exports are simultaneously increased. Excluding such a possibility for the time being, the relevant issue is how the composition of imports would be affected. This will be considered first for manufactured goods alone.

The NICs use import restrictions to save foreign exchange as well as to protect their domestic industry. They limit the imports of non-durable consumer goods that have been produced in those countries, but demand for variety and for luxury goods creates demand for imports. The NICs also protect their incipient industries producing intermediate goods (iron and steel, chemicals, and other semi-manufactures) and relatively simple engineering products (electrical and non-electrical machinery and transport equipment).

As a result of the application of protectionist measures, the share of consumer goods and intermediate products in the imports of the developing countries from the developed countries declined in recent years whereas the share of machinery and machine tools used in their manufacture, which dominate the engineering goods category, increased to a considerable extent. Correspondingly, the liberalization of trade by the NICs would lead to increases in the imports of non-durable consumer goods, intermediate products, and simple engineering goods and to a decline in the imports of sophisticated machinery and machine tools necessary for their domestic production.

This conclusion needs to be qualified by reference to cases where NICs have made a push into technologically advanced products. Examples are personal aircraft and simple computers in Brazil. It is such instances that have evoked the ire of US exporters who have seen markets closing to them, but the vociferous complaints should not mask the fact that these commodities are few in number, so that their existence does not introduce a major modification in the argument.

One needs to consider, however, possible changes in the importation of primary commodities. Since these commodities are rarely protected by the NICs, their imports would decline, and the importation of manufactured goods – largely from the developed countries – correspondingly increase, following reductions in protection.

Reductions in primary product imports by the NICs would adversely affect the developed countries as well as the less developed countries (LDCs), since some of these commodities are exported by developed countries and others by LDCs. But, in the latter case, too, there would be a decline in the export earnings of the developed countries, owing to reduced purchases of their products by the adversely-affected LDCs. Thus, ultimately, any increases in the manufactured exports of the developed countries to the NICs would be offset by reductions elsewhere, so long as the export receipts of the NICs remained unchanged.

Next, consider the case when the NICs expand their exports, so as to obtain foreign exchange for increasing their imports upon the liberalization of trade. This is indeed the expected consequence of trade liberalization that reduces the bias of the system of incentives against exports. For one thing, the cost of domestically-produced inputs will decline; for another, the exchange rate will tend to depreciate in order to equilibrate the balance of payments following the liberalization of imports.

Part of the increase in the exports of a particular newly industrializing country would find markets in other NICs as they liberalize their own trade. This will not improve, however, the net foreign exchange position of the developing countries, taken together. At the same time, increased imports from the developed countries will have to be paid for by higher exports to them.

Thus, while trade liberalization will change the pattern of the NICs' imports from the developed countries, increases in these imports would necessitate a corresponding rise in exports. The same result may be achieved if the developed countries liberalize their imports, since the NICs – and developing countries in general – use their increased foreign exchange earnings to buy goods from the developed countries.

It follows that many of the economic benefits the developed countries may derive from trade liberalization by the NICs can also be obtained if the developed countries liberalize their own trade. The question arises, then, why the developed countries demand that the NICs liberalize their imports.

Part of the answer lies in the desire for stability – the wish to avoid sudden interruptions in exports due to the unanticipated imposition of restrictions by the NICs. Similar considerations explain opposition on the part of developed countries to the provision of export subsidies by the NICs, which lead to encroachment on developed country markets and disturb existing trade patterns in third countries.

A more general consideration is the national power of decision-making. The developed countries wish to influence the composition of their manufactured imports, rather than being subject to decisions taken by the NICs. A related issue is the popular belief that reductions in foreign trade barriers represent a 'benefit' and reductions in the country's own trade barriers a 'cost' to the country concerned. Finally, there is the equally popular 'fairness' argument, according to which benefits should not be provided unilaterally to countries that are able to 'carry their own weight'.

These considerations indicate the importance of domestic political factors in motivating demands in the developed countries for trade liberalization by the NICs. In this connection, it has been claimed that the NICs could obtain better conditions of market access in the developed countries if they liberalized their own trade. But, this argument should not be carried too far, since it would imply that Hong Kong, with its free trade policies, would receive the most favorable treatment among developing countries. In fact, Hong Kong's exports suffer more discrimination than possibly those of any other NIC.[13] Nor does Singapore receive special treatment by reason of its liberal trade policy.

It may be suggested, however, that it is the interest of the developed countries that the NICs participate in the GATT process and operate within the GATT rules of conduct. This would, however, require some reconsideration of present GATT procedures as suggested below.

An additional consideration is that trade liberalization by the NICs is in the interest of the LDCs. This is the case because the LDCs are evolving a comparative advantage in simple non-durable consumer goods, such as clothing and shoes, and should be able to increasingly enter the markets of NICs, just as the NICs have earlier done in the markets of Japan.

Trade liberalization by the NICs would thus contribute to the industrialization of the LDCs, in line with the stages approach to comparative advantage.[14] This is indeed a desirable objective, although it should not be forgotten that the markets for non-durable consumer goods are many times larger in the developed countries than in the NICs. Thus, 'second tier' exporters would derive considerable benefit from trade liberalization by the developed countries.

But the principal argument for reductions in trade barriers by the NICs lies in their own self-interest. This is because, as we have seen, the adoption of an outward-oriented development strategy leads to improvements in the efficiency of resource allocation and rapid economic growth. Economic growth, in turn, will eventually make the NICs full-fledged partners of the developed countries. At the same time, providing secure access to developed country markets will increase incentives, and reduce domestic opposition, to liberalizing trade in the NICs.

The discussion has centered on the newly-industrializing countries, in regard to which demands for trade liberalization and 'graduation' have been made. This is not to say that the less developed countries would not benefit from liberalizing their own trade. In fact, as noted above, outward-oriented less developed countries showed a much better performance than inward-oriented LDCs during the 1973–8 period of external shocks. Still, infant industry arguments provide more of a rationale for protection in the LDCs than in the NICs.

Trade liberalization in developed countries and developing country interests

At the GATT Ministerial meeting in November 1982, proposals were made for a North–South round of trade negotiations, under which developed countries would make tariff concessions to the developing countries on a preferential basis in exchange for the developing countries liberalizing their imports on a m.f.n. basis. The emphasis was on trade liberalization by the NICs, which would, however, enjoy only temporary preferences that would cease upon 'graduation'.

The proposal evoked little interest on the part of the NICs and understandably so. In the language of trade negotiations, these countries were asked to offer concessions to reduce their tariff and non-tariff barriers in exchange for temporary tariff preferences, losing their GSP status in the process, while the developed countries liberalized their own non-tariff barriers. In order to discern the elements of an equitable bargain between the two groups of countries, the interests of the NICs in the liberalization of trade by the developed countries need to be examined.

Tariff reductions by the developed countries would bring benefits to the LDCs, which are major producers of food and raw materials which they could increasingly export in a processed form once the escalation of tariffs is removed. The benefits would be smaller for the NICs that tend to export the products of footloose industries (e.g. relatively simple engineering products), and products made of imported materials (e.g. textiles and clothing), so that they suffer little discrimination due to the escalation of tariffs.

For the NICs, existing and potential non-tariff barriers in the developed countries represent the most important obstacles to trade. Notwithstanding the efforts made by the NICs to evade the MFA, the expansion of their textiles and clothing exports is constrained by the provisions of the 1981 Agreement, and they are subject to the limitations introduced subsequently on the importation of these products in the United States. Also, the NICs are adversely affected by restrictions on steel imports imposed by the EC, with US limitations on steel imports applying to Brazil.

At the same time, the danger of the imposition of restrictions, whether in the form of quantitative import restrictions, export limitations, and countervailing or anti-dumping duties of a protective intent, creates a risk for the NICs and discourages investment in their export industries. In fact, in the United States, demands for the imposition of restrictions have reportedly been made in large part for their nuisance value, that is, to discourage developing countries from exporting.

It may be added that the developed countries would also derive benefits from the liberalization of their own trade. Such benefits stem from the upgrading of the labor force, the exchange of high-skill for low-skill products in trade with the developing countries, the spreading of research and development expenditures over a larger output, and the anti-inflationary effects of imports.

Trade negotiations between the developed countries and the newly-industrializing developing countries

The above discussion concerning the interests of the developed countries and the NICs in trade liberalization leads to a possible policy package that would combine the perceived objectives of the two groups of countries. Such a package would include lowering tariffs, reducing export subsidies, dismantling quantitative import restrictions, establishing an effective safeguard code, reforming the GATT review mechanisms and, more generally, giving a greater role to the developing countries in the GATT.

The last point underlies the importance of GATT, which provides the only appropriate venue for negotiating the liberalization of trade. Negotiations would need to be carried out on a multilateral basis as bilateral approaches would be counterproductive by leading to charges of *divide et impera*. Nor would it be appropriate to provide special privileges, as it has been suggested, to countries with high indebtedness.

There is a further argument for multilateral negotiations that transcends North–South relationships. This is the need to avoid backsliding that is likely to occur in the absence of a new round of multilateral negotiations. As first stated sixteen years ago:

> It would . . . appear that if no efforts are made to liberalize trade, the alternative is likely to be increased protectionism rather than the maintenance of the status quo. For lack of a better expression, we may speak of an 'instability effect', according to which economic and political relationships are hardly ever in a position of stable equilibrium but have the tendency to move in one direction or another. Thus, in the absence of pressures for the liberalization of trade, protectionist counter-pressures may gain force in the United States as well as abroad.[15]

In fact, backsliding has occurred in recent years, in particular as far as trade among the developed countries is concerned. Thus, these countries would derive additional benefits from a new round of multilateral trade negotiations. Nevertheless, the negotiations may appropriately focus on North–South relationships. This would represent a change of the past pattern, when the developed countries negotiated among themselves and the developing countries were the passive observers.

The principal participants in the negotiation would be the OECD countries and the NICs. Using *per capita* incomes and the share of industry in national income as classification criteria, the NICs may be defined to include Argentina, Brazil, Mexico, Uruguay, Israel, Yugoslavia, Hong Kong, Korea, Singapore, and Taiwan. Issues related to negotiations with Mexico and Taiwan, who are not members of GATT, will be taken up below.

The question arises, however, as to how the negotiations are to be prepared. For reasons mentioned above, a bilateral approach would not be appropriate for this purpose. Developing countries would also object to the use of the OECD framework, since the impression may be created that the OECD countries are colluding in their dealings with the NICs.

A possible alternative would be to use the Development Committee for this purpose. In this Committee, the developed countries as well as the NICs are represented, and using it as a framework for preparing North–South trade negotiations would permit associating Mexico, although not Taiwan. But, parallel discussions could proceed with Taiwan on an informal basis.

The use of the Development Committee framework would also permit involving the World Bank and the IMF in the preparation of the negotiations. This would be desirable, so as to increase collaboration between the World Bank, the IMF, and GATT as well as to help the NICs to make the necessary adjustment to trade liberalization. In particular, one may envisage the developed countries providing additional financial resources through these two multilateral institutions to help the adjustment process in the NICs.

III MODALITIES FOR NORTH–SOUTH TRADE NEGOTIATIONS

Steps towards a North–South round of trade negotiations

Trade liberalization would create adjustment problems in the NICs as well as in the developed countries, but the time involved in the negotiations would ease the process of adjustment. Experience indicates that multilateral trade negotiations take several years following the completion of the preparatory phase. Also, the implementation of the agreement customarily involves a period of four or five years.

Nor should the difficulties which several of the NICs presently experience in servicing their external debt be used as arguments against undertaking the negotiations. Considering the length of the preparatory period, it can be safely said that, by the time the liberalization of trade begins not only will these problems be overcome but the NICs would proceed to higher levels of economic development.

According to estimates published by the World Bank, the gross domestic product of the middle-income oil importing countries would rise at an average annual rate of 4.5 percent between 1982 and 1985 and by 4.4 to 6.9 percent between 1985 and 1995, with a central value of 5.7 percent. The corresponding *per capita* income growth rates can be derived by adjusting for expected population growth rates of 2.2 percent.[16]

However, during the sixties and the seventies, most of the NICs were growing at rates much in excess of the average for the middle-income oil importing developing countries. For these countries, 1990 *per capita* incomes have been estimated by assuming that, after stagnation in 1982–3, they would regain their past growth rates. In turn, it has been assumed that the NICs which had below-average growth rates in the 1960–81 period (Argentina, 1.9 percent; Chile 0.7 percent; Israel, 3.6 percent; and Uruguay 1.6 percent)[17] would reach the central variant growth rate projected for the middle-income oil importing countries.

Under the stated assumptions, by the year 1990, the Latin American newly industrializing countries, Korea, and Yugoslavia would approximately reach Italy's 1960 and Japan's 1963 *per capita* incomes. In the same year, Hong Kong, Israel, and Singapore would surpass Italy's 1980 and Japan's 1975 incomes per head.

Two observations may be made in regard to these estimates. First, the *per capita* income levels the NICs are expected to reach towards the end of the decade would impose certain obligations on them in regard to their trade policy vis-à-vis developed as well as less developed countries. Second, and more important, these countries could accelerate their economic growth if they reformed their trade policies.

The content of the negotiations

As far as the obligations to be taken in the course of the negotiations are concerned, it would be desirable, first of all, that the developed countries reduce their overall tariff level and lessen the extent of tariff discrimination against the processing of primary commodities by the developing countries. In turn, the NICs should lower the level, and rationalize the structure, of their tariffs.

There is further need to reduce export subsidies. In the developed countries, subsidies are provided mainly to agricultural exports while in the NICs industrial exporters are the main beneficiaries. In inward-oriented NICs, export subsidies are designed to reduce the bias against exports associated with industrial protection. With reform of the system of protection, this rationale would largely disappear.

More important than tariff reductions is the liberalization of quantitative import restrictions. It would be desirable that the developed countries gradually phase out the MFA as well as their restrictions on steel imports. Also, agricultural policies would need to be reformed, involving reductions in the protections afforded to agriculture. In turn, the NICs would accept the obligation to phase out their own import restrictions. As a result of these changes, the developed countries as well as the NICs would place exclusive reliance on tariffs as measures of protection.

The proposed reforms would need to be accompanied by the establishment of an effective system of safeguards. The principal requirement for such a system is the assurance that safeguards are of a temporary character. This would necessitate setting time limits for the unilateral application of safeguards, with any further extension requiring the consent of a multilateral forum associated with the GATT. Extensions would be countenanced only in exceptional circumstances and made dependent on a plan for domestic adjustment.

An important part of the proposed safeguard mechanism would be the role assigned to the multilateral review process. More generally, the dispute settlement mechanism in the GATT would need to be strengthened and rendered more effective. The developed countries have special responsibility both to initiate cases before the GATT, when they consider that they have been injured by actions taken abroad, and to accept the conclusions of the review process, when their actions are found to have caused injury elsewhere.

In the review process, a greater role would need to be given to the NICs and to the developing countries in general. But this will depend to a considerable extent on the developing countries themselves; in particular, subscription to the codes established in the framework of the Tokyo Round negotiations is a precondition for participation in the dispute settlement mechanism in regard to these codes.[18]

Giving a greater role to the developing countries in the GATT, too, presupposes their willingness to participate in GATT affairs. The NICs could also caucus together, with a view to developing common positions in the GATT, in general, and for a North–South round of negotiations in particular.

The adjustment problem

It has been noted that the time involved for the preparation of the negotiations; the negotiations themselves, and the gradual liberalization of trade barriers would provide considerable opportunity for adjustment. But, for adjustment to be successful, it would be desirable for the countries involved to begin taking appropriate measures in advance of the negotiations.

In the developed countries, the adjustment measures should be part of a long-term policy towards declining industries, in particular agriculture, clothing, shoes, and steel, the purpose being to encourage the movement of resources from these industries to modern sectors. Thus, adjustment assistance to workers should focus on retraining and relocation while compensation for income losses would be made under regular social security provisions. In turn, firms that reduce their productive capacity in the industries in question might receive credits for purposes of establishment in other industries.

In some highly protected NICs, the adjustment effort could be greater than in the developed countries. But the character of adjustment will not necessarily be the same. Thus, firms might receive assistance to improve their technology, to increasingly specialize, and to adopt large-scale production methods while remaining in the same industry.

The World Bank and the IMF might play a role in promoting adjustment in the newly-industrializing countries. This is done to a certain extent today and could be stepped up in the future. The IMF, and the World Bank in its program lending, also often include import liberalization as a loan condition. Again, a further extension of this practice would be desirable, so that the process of liberalization begins prior to the North–South negotiating round.

CONCLUSIONS

Having reviewed changes over time in international trade between developed and developing countries, this paper has considered the interests of the two groups of countries in the liberalization of their mutual trade. Proposals have further been put forward for a strategy that may be followed in regard to the modalities and the content of trade negotiations. No attempt has been made, however, to provide detailed recommendations on the conduct of the negotiations or to examine the impact of trade liberalization on individual countries within the two groups.

While the paper has concentrated on the gains which both developed and developing countries may derive from reciprocal trade liberalization, one should emphasize the interests of the developed countries and of the newly industrializing countries in liberalizing their own imports. In fact, the governments of these countries could utilize the opportunity provided by the proposes North–South trade negotiations to overcome domestic protectionist pressures. This is analogous to the situation wherein reformers in developing countries rely on the World Bank and the IMF to demand the implementation of policies they favor.

At the same time, the existence of an assymetry between the developed and the developing countries should be noted. As the developing countries spend all of their foreign exchange earnings on goods imported from the developed countries, trade liberalization by the latter group of countries would not adversely affect their balance of payments. In turn, in liberalizing their trade, the developing countries would have to find markets for their exports so as to pay for the increased imports.

Correspondingly, while their national interest, as well as the interests of the world economy, demand that the NICs reduce their trade barriers, they would have to be provided with security of market access in the developed countries. This fact, then, puts a particular responsibility on the developed countries to take adjustment measures that would permit liberalizing their trade.

NOTES

1. B. Balassa, 'The Structure of Protection in Industrial Countries and Its Effects on the Exports of Processed Goods from Developing Countries', in *The Kennedy Round: Estimated Effects on Tariff Barriers* (Geneva: UNCTAD, 1968) Table 2.
2. B. Balassa and C. Balassa, 'Industrial Protection in the Developed Countries', *The World Economy*, VII (1984) (forthcoming) Table 1 – Isaiah Frank suggests however that these figures are misleading as average tariffs

on imports from the developing countries are raised by the large imports of textiles and clothing that are subject to relatively high tariffs but are effectively limited by quantitative restrictions rather than by tariffs.

3. W. R. Cline, *Exports of Manufactures from Developing Countries: Performance and Prospects for Market Access* (Washington, DC: The Brookings Institution, 1984) Table 2.1.

4. See Balassa and Balassa (1984).

5. Manufactured industries are defined according to the convention used in trade statistics, i.e. excluding food, beverages, tobacco, petroleum products, and non-ferrous metals.

6. A. Valdes and J. Zietz, *Agricultural Protection in OECD Countries: Its Cost to Less Developed Countries* (Washington, DC: International Food Policy Research Institute, 1980).

7. The data refer to the volume of exports of the developing countries to the developed countries. They derive from United Nations, *Monthly Bulletin of Statistics*.

8. See B. Balassa, 'Export Incentives and Export Performance in Developing Countries: A Comparative Analysis', *Weltwirtschaftliches Archiv*, CXIV (1978) pp. 24–61.

9. See B. Balassa, 'The Newly-Industrializing Developing Countries after the Oil Crises', *Weltwirtschaftliches Archiv*, CXVII (1981) pp. 142–94. Reprinted in B. Balassa, *The Newly Industrializing Countries in the World Economy* (New York: Pergamon Press, 1981) pp. 29–81.

10. See B. Balassa, 'Adjustment Policies in Developing Countries: A Reassessment', Essay 5 in this volume.

11. The data have been adjusted according to the definition of the manufacturing sector used here. They originate in UNIDO, *Handbook of Industrial Statistics*.

12. OECD, *The Impact of the Newly-Industrializing Countries on Production and Trade in Manufactures* (Paris: OECD, 1979) p. 57.

13. In an article entitled 'America Needles Hong Kong', *The Economist* (17 December 1983) reports that the United States issued fourteen suspensions against Hong Kong goods under the MFA in 1983.

14. See B. Balassa, 'The "Stages" Approach to Comparative Advantage', in I. Adelman (ed.), *Economic Growth and Resources, vol. 4: National and International Issues* (London: Macmillan, 1977) pp. 121–56. Reprinted in Balassa, *The Newly Industrializing Countries in the World Economy*, pp. 149–67.

15. B. Balassa, *Trade Liberalization among Industrial Countries: Objectives and Alternatives* (New York: McGraw-Hill, 1967) p. 152.

16. World Bank, *World Development Report 1983* (Washington, DC, 1983) p. 27.

17. World Bank, pp. 148–9.

18. For a more detailed discussion, see B. Balassa, 'The Tokyo Round and the Developing Countries', *Journal of World Trade Law*, XIV (1980) pp. 93–119. Reprinted in Balassa, *The Newly Industrializing Countries in the World Economy*, pp. 127–48.

Index of Names

Index of Subjects